THE FOREIGN POLICY
OF PALMERSTON
1830–1841

William Lamb, Viscount Melbourne
from the portrait by John Partridge
in the National Portrait Gallery

THE FOREIGN POLICY
OF PALMERSTON

1830-1841

BRITAIN, THE LIBERAL MOVEMENT AND
THE EASTERN QUESTION

BY

SIR CHARLES WEBSTER
K.C.M.G., Litt.D., F.B.A.

VOLUME II

NEW YORK
HUMANITIES PRESS
1969

PUBLISHED IN GREAT BRITAIN BY
G. BELL & SONS LTD.

TO THE MEMORY OF
HUMPHREY SUMNER

PRINTED IN GREAT BRITAIN

CONTENTS OF VOLUME II

CONTENTS

CHAPTER VII

TSAR AND SULTAN: THE DEVELOPMENT OF THE EASTERN QUESTION
1835–1839

" I have a thousand times said that war is not necessary. I repeat it ; but it is necessary to shew that war is not dreaded through fear but avoided through principle."
PONSONBY, 17 October, 1838.

CHAPTER VII

TSAR AND SULTAN: THE DEVELOPMENT OF THE EASTERN QUESTION, 1835-1839

DURING these four years the situation in the East developed along lines similar to that in the West and was strongly influenced by it. The story is confused by the strange and emotional personalities of Ponsonby, Durham and the Sultan himself, each of them intent on a personal policy and each seeing only a small part of the European picture and imperfectly realising the interests at stake and the forces at work. Palmerston used each of his subordinates in turn, prevented them from doing harm by their extravagances, defended them from their enemies and ultimately brought his curious team into some sort of harmony.

He had also to cope with the extraordinary conduct of the half-mad David Urquhart who, through the patronage of the King and a lapse of judgment on Palmerston's part, was given a position at Constantinople for which he was altogether unfitted. Finally he had to keep along with him his too ardent Monarch, his diffident Prime Minister, and a Cabinet which sometimes seemed to forget the Eastern Question altogether.

His own conviction that British interests could only be maintained by a strong and determined policy, that the mistake of 1833 must never be repeated, that Russia would yield if she realised this, that time was on the Sultan's side if only the crisis could be prevented from arising too soon, that Britain could by the mutual fears and jealousies of her rivals and the strength of the British fleet and British commerce and finance obtain a mastery of the situation, was ultimately triumphantly justified.

Thus he tried with little success to reform the Ottoman Empire, with much more to increase British influence at Constantinople and reduce that of Russia; he more than anyone else kept Mehemet Ali quiet; he shewed a strong face to Russia, doubtful of her ultimate intentions, pretty sure she could not act at once, preparing to resist her when the time came, but ready to compromise on inessentials; finally he attempted to keep the centre of diplomatic action in London and to devise a new European treaty to replace that of Unkiar Skelessi.

In none of these objects did he have complete success in these years. The time had not yet come. His attention had to be devoted mainly to the struggle in the Iberian Peninsula. Only when that had worked itself out with its effect on the Franco-British *entente* could the Eastern Question become once more the central problem of European diplomacy. Meanwhile he more than held his own. Both at Constantinople and at the capitals of the Great Powers the determination and strength of Britain were realised. In every government, Turkish, Russian, French and Austrian, he had strong opponents. But in each he had powerful assistance. In Russia the realism of Nesselrode and Orlov, in Turkey the influence of Vogorides, the Prince of Samos, and, after many experiments and disappointments, the capacity of Reschid Pasha, in France the help of Broglie at the beginning, then of the remnant of the Doctrinaires as well as of the French Ambassador in London. In final analysis also, Metternich aimed at the same ends, though he wanted different methods, and Vienna, not London, as the diplomatic centre.

The story is a complicated one. An attempt has been made, therefore, to describe its different aspects in separate sections, even though this involves occasionally some reconsideration of an incident already discussed.

1. RELATIONS WITH THE SULTAN
AND HIS ADVISERS

In 1834 Ponsonby had made a good beginning to reestablish at Constantinople British prestige and authority, so fatally weakened by the events of 1833. For four years the struggle continued there with every resource of oriental diplomacy. The Sultan's one aim was to recover from his hated rival, Mehemet Ali, the territory yielded in 1833. For this purpose he turned to Britain and Russia. Neither were ready to give him what he wanted, the power to attack, though both were ready to defend him and accepted his authority as Sultan over the whole Ottoman Empire. Each was afraid that the other might use its position as champion of the Sultan to establish its own ascendancy at Constantinople. Each was associated with an ally whose interests and methods were different. Both Austria and France, uneasily consorting with Russia and Britain respectively, wished to control events so as to accommodate their particular interests in the Eastern Question with their necessities in other parts of Europe. The representatives of all these states at Constantinople endeavoured by bribery and by the use of the favourites and indirect methods of approach to get past the official machinery to the source of power and decision, the Sultan himself. All were imperfectly served and Mehemet Ali himself, who used much gold, was better informed of the secrets of the Porte than any of the European Powers. The dragomans and other agents whom they used were constantly revealing these secret discussions to their rivals who, only partially informed, always tended to believe what most suited the policy which they were recommending to their chiefs. The difficulty of translating Turkish language and ideas into Western idioms added to the confusion in everybody's mind.[1]

[1] The methods of Ponsonby are now pretty well completely revealed and much light has been thrown by recent researches on those of the French and of Mehemet Ali himself. But we are still very imperfectly informed of those of Russia and Austria, the correspondence with Constantinople having been only very cursorily surveyed. Campbell told Mehemet Ali "that it was easy for him to foresee what would happen at Constantinople as he was better informed than the Sultan himself of what passed in the Divan there. Mehemet Ali laughed and said perhaps such is the case." From Campbell, 17 July, 1838, *F.O.*

Ponsonby had waited, he told Palmerston later, to see what happened to the Tory Government before he resigned, and in any case he preferred dismissal to resignation. It very nearly came. Wellington told Esterhazy that Ponsonby had been encouraged from London to send alarmist reports from Constantinople to mislead public opinion about Russia. He promised to recall Ponsonby but later said that he could not do so because of the Government's weakness.[1]

Meanwhile Ponsonby had continued on the course which he had mapped out for himself, to destroy the Russian control over the Sultan and to substitute that of Britain in its place. He used his own strange methods throughout these four years and, extravagant in language and action as he often was, he succeeded to a very large extent in intimidating his rivals, who never ceased to complain of him, and in imposing his personality on the Sultan and his advisers.

He was never, partly owing to the foolish parsimony of the Treasury, given an official residence during these years. The house at Pera was not large enough and not sufficiently isolated to save it from the fires of Constantinople. Ponsonby wished, therefore, to build a new one in the country. "Pera", he wrote, "is the most detestable place in Europe." He did in fact live mostly outside Constantinople at Therapia. Palmerston, on the other hand, insisted that he should live at or near Pera so as to be easily accessible to the Sultan's Ministers and to British merchants. Perhaps this is the reason no house was ever obtained. Ponsonby got very tired of his job at times. He asked in 1838 to be transferred to Vienna which he had heard Lamb was leaving. He was also worried because he had not served long enough to get a pension.[2]

In 1835 the three most powerful men at Constantinople were Husrev, the Seraskier or Commander-in-Chief, Pertev, the Kiahay Bey, or Grand Vizir, and Achmet Pasha, the Sultan's reigning favourite. Of these Pertev was the most patriotic and incorrup-

Turkey, 343, Pt. 1. Palmerston himself recognised that Pisani, whose brother was in the Russian service, probably told him most of what he did. To Melbourne, 30 Oct., 1835: *B.P.*

[1] From Ponsonby, 21 April, 1835: *B.P.* Esterhazy to Metternich, 11, 27 March, 1835: *V. St. A.*

[2] From Ponsonby, 7 Dec., 1836. To Ponsonby, 8 Feb., 1837, 22 May, 1838: *B.P.* From Ponsonby, 1 June, 1833: *F.O. Turkey*, 223. "I have fifty people to lodge and feed." He had to keep large stores because of the plague when he could buy nothing.

tible of all the Ministers, though he took money as a matter of course; old Husrev was Mehemet's mortal foe; Achmet was pro-Russian and in their pay. The Reis Effendi, Akif, a weak creature, was also soon bought by the Russians. In these circumstances Ponsonby's real diplomacy, as distinct from formal demands which could be openly avowed, had to be by subterranean methods. He seems early to have made a deep impression on the Sultan who conferred on him in December 1835 a decoration, "the highest in the Empire and were it an order which it *is not*, might be described as the Garter of Turkey." He could, however, only see the Sultan himself at rare intervals and nothing of great importance passed at these interviews. He was never sure of obtaining one and in 1838 thought of trying to establish the right of Ambassadors to see the Sultan on their demand. But close touch was kept through Vogorides and MacGuffog, whose devotion never failed, and was certainly not mainly due to the meagre sums which Ponsonby obtained for them out of Secret Service funds. Ponsonby himself also saw Pertev on occasions. His intercourse with the Reis Effendi was mainly through the Chief Dragoman, Frederick Pisani, whose interviews were recorded in formal notes and reports. Throughout 1835 and the first part of 1836 Ponsonby was able to report a satisfactory position in the Sultan's councils and the jealous despatches of his fellow Ambassadors confirm his claim.[1]

Palmerston had hoped that Urquhart, who became Secretary of Embassy in 1836, would be able by his knowledge of Turkish to assist Ponsonby to establish close confidential relations with the Sultan and his Ministers which might be revealed if left to the

[1] From Ponsonby, 8 April, 1836: *B.P.*; do., 6 Dec., 1835; 15 Feb., 1837 (with minutes by Backhouse and Palmerston), 7 May, 1837, *F.O. Turkey*, 256, 303. Presents were only given on a very limited scale for Palmerston pointed out that his small Secret Service funds could not compete with the unrestricted liberality of the Tsar which Ponsonby constantly reported. No money was available for bribes to the Ministers such as the Russians used. Gifts of horses and a carriage, weapons and scientific instruments, were sent to the Sultan and a few presents of special English products such as sporting rifles and pistols were given to the Turkish Ambassador. Ponsonby secured permission to accept for himself the special honour from the Sultan, but in spite of his entreaties Palmerston peremptorily refused the high order which the Sultan pressed upon him. Vogorides said he only wanted a present of small value just to shew the esteem of the British Government. Ponsonby asked for £1000 for Pertev. Backhouse said it was difficult to give open presents to Turkish Ministers and Palmerston told him to leave the matter alone. The Russians shortly afterwards gave Pertev a snuff box worth £1500, but Husrev, his enemy, admitted that "no bribe would move that old *Tartar*". (7 July, 1837: *B.P.*)

Dragomans. But the insane vanity of Urquhart prevented what in any case could hardly have been allowed by the Ambassador. So far from helping Ponsonby, Urquhart did his best to undermine his position both at Constantinople, in England, and in Palmerston's confidence. Urquhart's own extravagances made these treacherous attempts of little importance, but Ponsonby was more than ever alone, and the quarrel prevented him from taking that leave at the beginning of 1837 which would have renewed his contact with Palmerston and perhaps moderated his extravagance of language.[1]

He had all the more need of it because of the attacks upon him in 1836 when a special effort was made by his enemies to get him recalled over the Churchill affair. This is generally described as a great defeat and humiliation for Ponsonby and it certainly caused him great trouble and anxiety. But he got out of it eventually with considerable success, and in the long run his instinct was probably right and the attitude that he took increased his prestige with the Sultan's Ministers while the dislike of his colleagues could hardly be made greater than it was already.[2]

Churchill, a journalist, who represented the *Morning Herald*, accidentally injured a boy while shooting on 5 May and was put into gaol and beaten in a specially humiliating manner. He was of course entitled to the substantial compensation which he loudly demanded. Achmet, the favourite, a Russian partisan, and Akif, the Reis Effendi, a creature of his, were thought by Ponsonby to be thwarting justice as they probably were. It was necessary "for the Sultan's own good to break down the insolent pretensions of the Pashas" and Achmet was more to blame than Akif. Ponsonby regarded the affair as a contest between himself and Russia for the control of the Divan, refused any intercourse with Akif, and suggested to the Sultan the dismissal of both Ministers. He indicated to Palmerston in a private letter that he would resign rather than give way. "I hope", he wrote, "that you will take what I am about to say, in the sense I intend it to have, and not as an offensive expression of sentiments. I mean that if His Majesty's

---

[1] See my article "Ponsonby, Urquhart and Palmerston", *Eng. Hist. Rev.*, July 1947, 327–351.
[2] Professor Puryear gives an interesting account of the Churchill incident (*International Economics*, etc., 45–49) but he relies largely on Roussin's reports which were very biassed and does not seem to have followed the later developments of the controversy.

Government disapprove of what I have done in the matter they should send out somebody to perform such orders as they may give in contradiction of it. His M. Govt. ought not to depend on me for executing them." Butenev rallied to the side of his creatures and Stürmer naturally supported him. But there was less reason for Roussin to take such an uncompromising position. His colleagues apparently persuaded him that Ponsonby had threatened to join Russia in a partition of the Ottoman Empire if his demands were refused. What Ponsonby did say was that Britain could hardly be expected to support a state whose Ministers refused such just claims as had been made in the Churchill case.[1]

Both Roussin and Stürmer wrote a series of alarming reports to their Governments which in due course were sent to London in order that representations might be made to Palmerston. Pozzo di Borgo and Hummelauer were delighted with so congenial a task and they got Nourri Pasha, the Turkish envoy at London, to join with them. Sébastiani shewed himself more cooperative on this than on any other question and at the orders of Thiers supported them in a private letter. Metternich told Fox that Ponsonby was 'mad', and Thiers Granville that Ponsonby was endangering the peace of Europe.[2]

Palmerston was the last man to accept foreign complaints against an Ambassador in such a case. He gave short shrift to them. He realised at once the issues at stake, refused to believe the accounts sent home by Stürmer and Roussin of Ponsonby's conduct, and, though he was afraid Ponsonby had gone too far, sent strong letters to Granville and Lamb. "All the other Ministers and Ambassadors at Constantinople", he wrote at the outset to Granville, "think they have now got Ponsonby into a hobble and even Roussin, who is jealous of him, has, it seems, joined. Metternich has sent me quires about the matter. I tell everybody that as yet I have only half the story. . . . They would all, and their Courts too, exult at getting rid of Ponsonby; he has been too active and successful to be forgiven by any one of them. I hope that in this instance he has not gone too far, though I half fear he

[1] From Ponsonby, 15 May, 10, 28 June, 14, 22 July, 20 Aug., 7, 22 Sept., 18 Nov., 1836: *F.O. Turkey*, 273–278. do., 7, 16 May, 11, 17, 20 June, 21 July, 1836: *B.P.* The number shows how much the question occupied Ponsonby's attention and there are others on smaller points.

[2] From Granville, 27 June, 1836: *F.O. France*, 523. From Fox, 23 June, 1836: *B.P.* Sébastiani to Thiers, 28 June, 29 July, 1836: *A.A.E.*

has." To King Leopold, who had ventured to convey Louis
Philippe's 'grief' to Palmerston and thought that Ponsonby was
playing into the hands of Russia, Palmerston sent an impassioned
defence of his Ambassador who "has like many other English
Ambassadors and Ministers at home and abroad been grossly
calumniated by the Tory Party in Europe."

After he had received Ponsonby's reports he wrote even more
strongly to Paris and Vienna, both officially and in private letters:
"Ponsonby has acted, I think, with much skill and judgment. . . .
All the others have been caballing against him from personal or
political jealousy. We shall have a difficult job to determine what
to do. The outrage was atrocious." And he added scathing
comments on Roussin's conduct in cooperating with the three
Eastern Powers before ascertaining what he had to protest against.
To Lamb he admitted that the conduct of the representatives of
the three Eastern Powers was not so bad as that of Roussin:
"However we have triumphed and it is an important victory.
It is now an English victory. They might have made it an
European one." These letters produced an immediate effect at
Paris. Thiers at first defended Roussin, but Desages admitted
to Aston that the Ambassador was wrong, and under his influence
Thiers lowered his tone. Metternich, of course, never admitted
anything. The Russian Court kept outside the whole affair, and
Durham attributed the comparative reticence of Butenev to his
own influence at St. Petersburg.[1]

Palmerston himself was, indeed, perturbed when he first heard
of the incident. "We should only be playing the game of Russia",
he told Ponsonby in a hasty note, "if we were to break unnecessarily
with the Sultan upon a separate quarrel of our own." He even
consulted Backhouse as to the policy to be adopted, almost the
only time such a course is recorded. The Under-Secretary, who

---

[1] To Granville, 5, 14 July, 1836; F.O. France, 517, do., 28 June, 5 July,
1836: B.P. To Aston, 19 July, 1836: F.O. France, 517, do., 18 July, 1836:
Aston P. From Aston, 22, 25 July, 1836: F.O. France, 523; do., 25, 27 July,
1836: Aston P. Desages to Bourqueney, 27 June, 1836. "Le traitement
infligé a Churchill est une abomination'" He had told Thiers he had gone too
far in his strictures, though Ponsonby should not have demanded the resignation
of the Reis Effendi but made 'un tapage infernal' until he got satisfaction.
Bour. P. To Lamb, 18 July, 1836: B.P. From Lamb, 5 Aug., 1836: F.O. Austria,
257; do., 26 July, 5 Aug., 1836: B.P. From Durham, 14 July, 1836: F.O. Russia,
225. From Leopold, 30 June, 1836; To Leopold, 5 July, 1836: B.P. Metternich
was impressed by the dismissal of Akif, and Tatischev thought Ponsonby had
been far from 'mad'. Lamb wrote that this time Stürmer had over-reached
himself in writing pro-Russian reports against Ponsonby.

had his own information, did not consider Ponsonby's demands justified. The Prime Minister, as always critical of Ponsonby, took the same view. But when Ponsonby's full account of all he had done reached him, Palmerston took up his cause with great vigour. "Ponsonby has really done us a valuable and important service and has acted with courage, firmness and ability," he told Melbourne. In spite of the opposition of all his colleagues the Ambassador had achieved a 'signal triumph', whose good effects would be felt beyond the incident itself. Palmerston wanted, therefore, the Government to approve the action taken and to mark that approval to the whole world by giving Ponsonby a step in the Peerage. He added that Lord John Russell agreed with him. The King was also violently on Ponsonby's side and the news of the dismissal of Akif announced in the *Morning Chronicle* was looked upon by public opinion as a triumph over Russia to such an extent that Palmerston had to damp the feeling down by the insertion of a leader next day. But the battle in the Cabinet was lost and it was decided that Ponsonby's demand for the dismissal of Achmet could not be supported. How long this took to settle is not known, but the final instructions were not sent till the beginning of November. Palmerston explained that he had delayed them to give Ponsonby a chance to carry out his own policy first. "It is very possible you may be right", he wrote, "in wishing us to demand the dismissal of Achmet, but we are not up to so vigorous a measure, and we do not think the occasion requires it. We should not have insisted on the dismissal of the Reis Effendi; and the accomplishment of that was your merit." And he went on to explain the difficulties of enforcing such a demand and the resulting loss of prestige if it were made and not enforced.[1]

Meanwhile Ponsonby was waiting for instructions. The dismissal of the Reis Effendi, which even Metternich admitted to be a 'great triumph', did not satisfy him. Moreover, owing to the pressure put on the Porte by the other Ambassadors, it was given

[1] To Ponsonby, 5, 11 Nov., 1836. *F.O. Turkey*, 272; do., 23 June, 11 Nov., 1836; Minutes, Palmerston and Backhouse, 5 July, 1836; To Melbourne, 19 July, 1836 *Appendix* p. 847; From do., 24 June, 1836: *B.P.* Hummelauer to Metternich, 17 July, 1836: *V. St. A.* From Will. IV, 22 June, 4, 7 July, 1836: *B.P.* It is hard to account for the long silence in spite of Ponsonby's urgent requests for a decision. The course adopted seems peculiarly cruel at such a time. Ponsonby who had asked for an Earldom some time before, did not of course know at this time that Palmerston had tried to make him a Viscount as he succeeded in doing in 1839.

out that the dismissal was due to other causes and other officials connected with the case were promoted. No compensation was paid to Churchill who had demanded a very large sum. Finally, Husrev, Achmet's rival, was dismissed from the position of Seraskier. Ponsonby, therefore, persisted in his demand for the dismissal of Achmet himself and was sure that with Palmerston's support he could obtain it. But this never came and the uncertainty was painful. Ponsonby had to report the triumph of his enemies and the substitution of Russian for British influence in the councils of the Sultan. Husrev's dismissal, he said, might cause him to promote a revolution at Constantinople to regain it and thus bring the Russians to the Bosphorus. He recognised that Butenev was entitled to do all he could to destroy his influence but that Stürmer, and above all Roussin, should join him was a betrayal of the interests of their Governments.[1]

When the instructions at last reached him, he had, as perhaps Palmerston anticipated, accepted the situation, and at once said that he would carry them out however much he disliked them. Then he made a surprising recovery. For though Achmet was promoted to be Capitan Pasha, he was thus removed from the Sultan's immediate entourage. Pertev, who had overthrown Husrev and succeeded him as the main instrument of power, was a devoted and incorruptible Moslem which meant that he was anti-Russian. Indeed he offered to Ponsonby to do whatever he demanded about Achmet. Faithful to his instructions, Ponsonby refused to embarrass the Sultan or his Minister by asking for more than they would do by themselves. His Government, he said, had delayed in order that the Sultan might act of his own free will. They would not press him to do what his natural inclinations should have suggested. Pertev was much relieved. For some time Ponsonby still failed to get compensation for the insistent Churchill, but eventually through the interposition of Vogorides that also was obtained from the Sultan's private purse. Before the year was out Roussin explained his role in the affair and Ponsonby agreed to bury the past. Reschid Pasha was appointed Reis Effendi in June, Sarim acting as his deputy until he could come back from London [2]

[1] From Ponsonby, 20 Aug., 7, 22 Sept., 18 Nov., 1836, 4 Jan., 1837: *F.O. Turkey*, 276–278, 301; do., 30 Oct., 7, 20 Dec., 1836: *B.P.*
[2] From Ponsonby, 18, 29 Nov., 1836: 4 Jan., 19 Feb., 14 June, 16 Sept., 1837: *F.O. Turkey*, 278, 301–6. Reschid was appointed Under-Secretary for

Palmerston described this handling of a difficult situation as 'perfect'. He took pains to tell Reschid Pasha, who was still at London, that the dismissal of Halil which had led to his own appointment as Reis Effendi, was due to Ponsonby's action and he praised Ponsonby warmly to him.[1]

The incorruptible Pertev only survived the malignant attacks of his enemies a few months before he too was dismissed by the Sultan, who was told he was only a 'puppet' in his Minister's hands. His fall had been partly due to an endeavour to follow British advice to create a militia which the Sultan suspected was aimed at reducing his own power. But by that time Reschid had become Reis Effendi and was gaining steadily in the Sultan's favour. The contest for the control of Mahmud continued and lasted until his death, a fact which was perhaps one of the reasons why the Great Powers at last agreed on a common solution. For, as Mehemet more than once bitterly complained, it was the rivalry between the Great Powers on which the Sultan relied and he was as much afraid of their agreement as of their quarrels.[2]

However that might be, Ponsonby had no option but to fight for the Sultan's confidence and he might claim that, in spite of the treachery of his subordinate, Urquhart, and the refusal of his Government to accept his advice, he had succeeded as well, perhaps better than, any of his rivals. "I do enjoy at least as much influence here as any other Minister," he claimed in July 1837.[3]

Pertev's overthrow made new combinations necessary. Akif Pasha, a more flexible *intrigant*, had the Sultan's ear, while it was Halil Pasha, his nominee, Husrev's ungrateful protégé, who succeeded to Pertev's position, though Husrev was always in the background and often saw the Sultan. Reschid Pasha, now Foreign Minister, was already by reason of his superior qualities of mind playing a considerable part in affairs and it was he who undertook the main burden of the commercial negotiation which was just

Foreign Affairs in November, 1836. This was a new post. From Ponsonby, 7, 20 Dec., 1836: *B.P.*

[1] To Ponsonby, 11 Nov., 1836, 17 Jan., 1837: *B.P.*

[2] From Ponsonby, 16 Sept., 13 Nov., 1837: 31 Jan., 6 June, 25 July, 1838: *F.O. Turkey*, 305, 329B, 331–332. It was the failure to save Pertev that made Ponsonby desire at this time to secure the right of Ambassadors to an audience with the Sultan. But Roussin would not support him and with Palmerston's approval he dropped the idea. (To Ponsonby, 6 June, 25 July, 1838: *F.O. Turkey*, 329A.)

[3] From Ponsonby, 7 July, 1837: *B.P.*

about to begin. Ponsonby found him rather timid and afraid of Russia, but with "somewhat more belief in the *will* and ability of England to resist Russia than some of his colleagues". It was, perhaps, only natural that Reschid felt he would be safer away from Constantinople and he made a deal with Akif Pasha to be appointed Ambassador at Paris. He would, however, be able to influence policy from there, he told Ponsonby, whose opinion of him gradually grew very favourable. "He has pleased the Sultan. There is no other man I know of capable of conducting at all to the taste of the Sultan a large part of the affairs of the Government." Meanwhile Reschid was to negotiate the commercial convention and since it was dangerous for him to see Ponsonby often, the latter established relations with the clique of Rayahs, some of whom had been with Reschid in Paris and London, who were now advising him. The Prince of Samos also acted as intermediary. Thus Ponsonby could report, at the beginning of 1838, "our influence here when considered in one point of view is very great—that is to say, the Sultan and his Ministers believe what I say to them and I doubt if they believe one word that is said by any other Minister." But he added the next month: "The Porte will not trust you until you shall have committed yourselves by some act that will prove you to be in earnest in your declaration of the *intention* to support the independence of Turkey."[1]

In March Halil and Akif were deposed by the joint efforts of the Sultan's favourite, Riza Bey, Husrev and Reschid, the latter delighted to avenge the murder of his friend Pertev. The Sultan, indeed, reorganised the whole system of Government and the Grand Vizir's office was reduced to a nullity. But Husrev now had a commanding influence in the three Camarillas that took its place. Achmet Pasha, the Capitan Pasha, had now lost all influence and Riza Bey, the favourite, was Husrev's man. Reschid was growing in influence and remained at the Foreign Office until the commercial convention was finally approved in August. Ponsonby had still some doubts about him but believed that he did not take money and was anti-Russian.[2]

[1] From Ponsonby, 5 Jan., 5 Feb., 1838: *B.P.* A more coherent description than usual of the position of the Sultan's Ministers and an interesting appreciation of Reschid. Among Reschid's advisers was M. Cor, a Frenchman, whom Palmerston described as a remarkably intelligent man (13 Sept., 1838: *B.P.*) He later acted as French Dragoman.

[2] From Ponsonby, 15, 26 March, 19 April, 1838: *F.O. Turkey*, 330; do., 21 April, 1838: *B.P.*

Bulwer came out in the spring of 1838 as Secretary of Embassy. He was by now an experienced official and Ponsonby liked him. Though Bulwer criticised his chief's policy to Palmerston, he recognised his good qualities, remained loyal to him and was of great assistance in getting the right contacts with the Sultan's officials. This was all the more necessary as the Seraglio were intriguing against Reschid and Husrev's loyalty to him was doubtful.[1]

The success of the commercial convention, and the joint cruise of the British and Turkish fleets produced an immense impression on the Tsar. Butenev, who had been on leave, was sent back post-haste and did a good deal to retrieve the position. He was helped by the increasing jealousy of Roussin who never quite forgave Ponsonby for his success in negotiating the commercial convention. Butenev began his usual policy of corrupting or influencing the favourite Riza Bey and old Husrev. The Turkish and British fleets were not allowed to go to the coast of Syria. Ponsonby found his position less favourable. Husrev became less dependable with the result that Reschid's position became a dangerous one, and he remembered the fate of Pertev. It was partly for this reason that Ponsonby eagerly supported his immediate despatch to Europe where he was to visit Vienna, Berlin and Paris on his way to London. Meanwhile the Sultan reinsured himself with Russia, and partly for that reason Ponsonby failed to obtain the military and naval cooperation which he had planned. Nevertheless it was to Britain that the Sultan was looking for a solution of his problem. The diamond necklace for the Queen was especially magnificent and the Misham Order was pressed on Palmerston. But Ponsonby was well aware that British influence depended on whether Palmerston could satisfy the demands which Reschid was soon to make on behalf of the Sultan, and, as will be seen, the refusal to overthrow Mehemet Ali almost destroyed Ponsonby's influence completely.[2]

---

[1] From Ponsonby, 21 May, 1838: *B.P.* Bulwer began a private and very free correspondence with Palmerston not shewn to Ponsonby of which only a very discreetly edited version is given in his book. He wrote on 4 Aug., 1838: "I have been uneasy at the thought that anything in the letters which I write . . . should seem from any accidental difference of opinion, if such there be, to impugn in the slightest degree Lord Ponsonby's judgment." *B.P.*

[2] From Ponsonby, 24, 27 Aug., 17 Oct., 7 Nov., 18 Dec., 1838: *B.P.* P. E. Mosely (*Russian Diplomacy, etc.*, Chap. VI) gives an interesting account, based on the Russian Archives, of Russian action in the autumn of 1838 to overthrow Ponsonby's position.

The Sultan and his advisers were always dissatisfied with the representatives of the Great Powers at Constantinople but they had neither the wish nor the men to transact their business in foreign capitals. However, in this period the Sultan began to be more consistently represented abroad. At Vienna Mavrojeni continued his long mission and through his intercourse with Metternich and Frederick Lamb was able to present a point of view different to that of Ponsonby. A succession of envoys went to the Western Powers and particularly to Britain to obtain that support which Ponsonby, for all his ardour in the Turkish cause, was forbidden to promise. Namick Pasha got on so well that he was recalled at the behest of the Russians. His successor, Nourri Pasha, had no French and Palmerston found him an 'oaf' on whom he could make no impression.[1]

It was, perhaps, for this reason that the Sultan in 1836 determined in the greatest secrecy to send a Frenchman, M. Blaque, a lawyer and journalist, the head of the Sultan's Printing Establishment, personally well-known to the Sultan and a friend of the Sultan's reigning favourite. This mission was arranged by Ponsonby and Vogorides. The Reis Effendi himself was not informed. Unfortunately M. Blaque died at Malta on his way to England and the exact object of his mission which Ponsonby announced with the greatest portentousness was never fully stated.[2]

Reschid on his first mission in 1836 (which had included Paris) brought for a short time an entirely new atmosphere to Turkish diplomacy in London. When he was recalled to take the office of Reis Effendi, Sarim Effendi, sent on a special mission on the accession of Queen Victoria, was quite acceptable, but here again Palmerston confessed that "to us who are not used to interpreters it is heavy and desperate work, to do business by these intermedi-

[1] To Ponsonby, 16 July, 1835: *B.P.* "Nourri is a greasy stupid old Turk, without an idea in his head": do., 14 Aug., 1835: *B.P.* "A perfect nullity with whom it is impossible to get on at all. He is like a Turk in a melodrama on the stage: one of Bluebeard's attendants." His interpreter, "young Vogorides", was also quite inadequate. This unfortunate intercourse lent aid to Urquhart's advocacy of Turkish-speaking British officials at Constantinople.

[2] From Ponsonby, 6, 8 Feb., 8 April, 1836: *B.P.* "The object will be to afford to His Majesty's Government official and formal knowledge of the Sultan as it is understood by *himself*: and to explain his wishes and his expectations from his Majesty." (6 Feb.) Later Mme Blaque threatened to publish her husband's papers which might have been inconvenient and Ponsonby got Reschid to stop it by the threat of the loss of her pension. (11 May, 1838.) There is no evidence for Urquhart's assertion that M. Blaque was murdered by the Russians.

aries."[1] Ahmed Fethi Pasha, who came over from Paris for a short time, was better able to talk to British ministers but had no great weight. Not, therefore, until Reschid Pasha came back once more at the end of 1838 was a real negotiation attempted in London. Reschid, as had been seen, was only gradually trusted and recommended by Ponsonby and he had not the Sultan's full confidence, but he was of course a man of quite different measure to the others and was able at the end of 1838 to transfer for a short time the centre of negotiation to London, while Ponsonby was left neglected at Constantinople.

[1] To Ponsonby, 21 March, 1838: *B.P.*

2. THE ATTEMPT TO MODERNISE
THE OTTOMAN EMPIRE

(i) PALMERSTON'S PROGRAMME

The principles of the Liberal Movement could not be applied in the East and Palmerston never thought of so doing. But his conscience would not have been comfortable if he had made use of the Ottoman Empire without attempting to improve it. He hoped also by reforming it to make it more capable of resisting its enemies and able to play its part in the balance of power in Eastern Europe.

He had laid down his programme in a letter to Ponsonby at the end of 1833:

"Our great aim should be to try to place the Porte in a state of internal organization compatible with independence, and to urge the Govt. to recruit their army and their finances, and to put their navy into some order. The latter is the least important of the three because England and France can supply the deficiencies of Turkey in that respect. The army ought to be their first object; and why is it necessary to put their provinces into a state of rebellion as they have done in Albania by forcing men into the ranks? Cannot they obtain recruits by voluntary enrolment? If pure Mussulmen will not enlist, will not their Christian subjects do so? especially if they were to admit officers of the same class into regimental commands." He then suggested employing half-pay British officers as instructors and went on to consider finance. "Is it hopeless to get them to put their finances into better condition? If, instead of granting out monopolies which ruin commerce, they would allow people to trade freely and levy moderate duties on commerce, they would find their revenue greatly improved. If instead of sending Pashas to eat up the provinces they govern, and then be squeezed in their turn by the Sultan, they would *pay* their Govt. officers and not allow them to plunder, the security which such a system would afford to the population would be a wonderful stimulus to industry and production."

He had no illusions, he said, as to the difficulty of all this: "You will ask whether I fancy myself writing to the Prophet or to his earthly Vice-Regent, or how I imagine that a British Ambassador is to accomplish this regeneration of a rotten empire? I imagine no such impossibilities; but I see how active you are, and what influence you have obtained, and what channels of information you have opened for yourself, and I therefore point out to you the great landmarks by which your efforts should be directed."[1]

In answer Ponsonby stressed some of the difficulties. He could not even mention the army to the Sultan or his Ministers—yet. Ponsonby himself at that time believed that the best barrier to Russia was in the "strength vigour and interests" of the Rayah population. But it was at present impossible to arm them: "To enlist Rayahs in a Turkish army, is, I believe, against the law of the Empire, and I doubt if Turkish soldiers could be at present induced to associate in the necessary intimate manner with the Giaours." Nevertheless, possibly under the influence of the Prince of Samos, one of whose main objects was to raise the status of his coreligionists, Ponsonby considered with some hope the possibility of setting up Rayah municipal and provincial governments which might have a militia under their control: "The various Rayah provinces under the administration of coreligionists elected by themselves will I think cheerfully submit to the sovereignty of the Sultan and find their own best interests upon resisting the dominion of Russia." But he had to admit that arming the Rayahs would upset the whole balance of the Empire: "The fact, however, will be that the Rayahs armed will soon obtain entire equality with the Turks, but possibly, being themselves divided into so many nations, and having such diversity of interests, they may be content with equality and not seek for more. I think this even likely provided the Turk shall not attempt to persecute or insult and I also think the Turk will not attempt either [because of the] over ruling necessity derived from his own weakness." Needless to add, he claimed that the best way to obtain all these reforms was to send a fleet into the Dardanelles and relieve the Sultan from his fear of Russia.[2]

Ponsonby was to become even less optimistic as he learnt more about the Ottoman Empire. But Palmerston did not take these

---

[1] To Ponsonby, 6 Dec., 1833: *B.P.* On this subject see a good article by Professor F. S. Rodkey, "Lord Palmerston and the Rejuvenation of Turkey, *1830–1839*," *Journal of Modern History*, Dec., 1929, June, 1930, and F. E. Bailey, *British Policy and the Turkish Reform Movement, 1826–1853.*

[2] From Ponsonby, 17 Jan., 1834: *B.P.*

or later cautions to heart and went on advocating a Rayah army
until the catastrophe of 1839. Neither he nor Ponsonby could of
course do much to improve the central or provincial administration the iniquities of which the Consular reports described. How
strongly Palmerston felt about it is seen by a minute he wrote on
one of these from Trebizond which gave an account of the ill-
treatment of the Kurds: "This is a curious paper and shews what
has been one of the most active causes in converting into desert
wastes those fertile districts which under the vigorous police of the
Roman Empire were full of cities and of fixed inhabitants." All
that Ponsonby could do was to support the Prince of Samos in his
slow and cautious approach to the problem.[1]

Whatever the influence of the Prince of Samos there is little
evidence that the Sultan was working to emancipate the Rayahs
in this period. Akif and Halil caused the Sultan to sanction
Pertev's death by tricking the Minister into advocacy of a militia
instead of the Sultan's regular army. The Sultan, reported
Ponsonby, was moved by motives of self-preservation: "With the
fall of the Janissaries all control over his power fell also, and his
authority was established by a new army recruited from distant
Provinces, having nothing to connect the soldier with the mass of
the people or with the chiefs of the nation and separated into small
divisions placed in barracks at considerable distances one from the
other." A militia would have deprived the Sultan of power
because, like the Janissaries, they would have been armed instruments of the chiefs of the nation.[2]

Nothing could be done, therefore, to effect any real reform in the
Ottoman army which was as badly led and supplied in 1839 as in
1832. As to the fleet, the Turks are not natural sailors. Before
the Greek revolution the working crews were largely Greek.
They supplied the seamanship while their loyalty was secured by
the presence of Turkish soldiers and officers. But, according to
Stratford Canning, in 1832 two-thirds of the crews were landsmen

[1] Minute Palmerston, 25 Dec., 1835, on a memoir of Brant, Consul at
Trebizond: *F.O. Turkey*, 256.
[2] Professor Temperley stated (*Crimea*, 40) "That the improvement of the lot
of the rayas was the supreme and last object of Mahmoud seems clear." But he
produced but little evidence for this judgment. From Ponsonby, 31 Jan.
1838: *F.O. Turkey*, 329. There is no certainty of course about the causes of
Pertev's death. The Seraglio never yielded up its secrets completely and
Ponsonby later thought Mehemet Ali had a hand in the plot. But the judgment
of Ponsonby, who by this time knew the Sultan better than any other Englishman
had ever done, is a valuable one.

and the fleet was quite inefficient. The Turk, however, has always been a good soldier when he has been given a modicum of organisation, supply and leadership. The army had resisted Russia stubbornly in 1828. Its collapse in 1832–1833 was due to incapacity in high places and the same was true in 1839. Palmerston was right in thinking that it could play an important part in the balance of power of the Near East. What he did not realise was that the Sultan only maintained the Ottoman Empire because the Turk monopolised, or nearly so, the use of organised force. Palmerston failed to perceive that if the Rayahs were armed or a local militia created whose allegiance to the central authority was doubtful, the Empire was bound to disintegrate. Nor could the command of Ottoman troops be given to an infidel. Sève Pasha had to become a Mahommedan before he could become Ibrahim's trusted general. When Husrev was urged to employ the Polish general, Chrysanowski, in a similar position, the Seraskier made it a condition that he should make a formal change of religion. It took Palmerston a long time to realise these limitations to his planning.[1]

Still less was it possible to do much about administrative reorganisation. Partly under the influence of Reschid, but also because he distrusted all his servants, the Sultan reduced the status of the Grand Vizir, and the favourites became even more influential: "The Sultan fears the establishment of any Corps in the state, even one of Ministers of his own selection, as has been seen by the degradation of the powers of the Grand Vizier, who is almost a nullity and by the capricious elevation of sometimes one favourite and sometimes another to be the temporary instruments of his Govt, whereby all the Ministers become little more than chief clerks of their respective departments executing a will, itself moved by the intrigues and misrepresentations and falsehoods of the Seraglio."[2]

The Executive was, it is true, reorganised in March 1838 to suit this situation. Three Councils were established; (1) at the Seraskier's palace where military affairs were settled; (2) at the Porte, the old centre, where finance and commerce were discussed and (3) at the Sultan's palace where final decisions were to be taken. Old Husrev presided at the third, but every question was a matter of intrigue in the Seraglio with the Sultan's favourites, as

---

[1] From Stratford Canning, 17 May, 1832: *F.O. Turkey*, 210.
[2] From Ponsonby, 31 Jan., 1838: *F.O. Turkey*, 329.

Ponsonby reported to Palmerston in the autumn in a very intimate letter: "There is no such thing as a Minister here who has either will or influence or courage enough to discuss any point with the Sultan. Everything is done in the Serail by the favourite or in case of great difficulty the Sultan asks Husrev's opinion." No wonder Ponsonby asked for authority to give a handsome present to Riza Bey, the reigning favourite, which, he said, would please the Sultan also.[1]

Nothing could, indeed, be done except by the subterranean methods which Ponsonby had learnt to apply through Vogorides and MacGuffog. One cannot help but admire the persistent and methodical manner in which the Prince of Samos worked towards his ends. Nearly always it was by his intervention that Ponsonby obtained the Sultan's consent to some necessary step. Vogorides had long had a plan to get the system set up at Samos used in other Greek islands and in 1838 he succeeded in obtaining the Sultan's consent to apply it to Cyprus.[2] But for the larger schemes of Palmerston nothing could be done. Yet even late in 1838 after so many disappointments we find Palmerston again urging the same programme that he had put forward in 1834 of reorganising the army, navy and finance so that the Sultan could beat Mehemet by his own means, "that instead of harassing his subjects by a conscription carried on with every species of violence he should try to procure voluntary recruits and should take Christians as well as Turks if they chose to enter, just as we in India enlist Mahommedans and Hindus indiscriminately."[3]

In fact only two of the items on Palmerston's programme were attempted, the despatch of British officers and the negotiation of a new commercial convention. The first was a rather humiliating failure, with some redeeming indirect advantages, the second was a triumphant success.

(ii) The Army and Navy

As regards officers the Sultan passionately desired to strengthen his army and naturally desired expert advice. His first instinct was to seek assistance from the French army which had done so

[1] From Ponsonby, 26 March, 1838: *F.O. Turkey*, 330; do., 17 Oct., 1838: *B.P.*
[2] From Ponsonby, 10 Feb., 1838: *F.O. Turkey*, 329.
[3] To Ponsonby, 13 Sept., 1838: *Bulwer*, II, 281, and *B.P.* The passage quoted is omitted by Bulwer.

much for Mehemet. Reschid Bey had supplied some French officers during his first visit to Paris. Russia protested and played on the religious objections of the Turks. Consequently Nourri was ordered to approach Palmerston for some assistance in equipment and training, though he does not seem to have been authorised to ask for British officers to be sent to Turkey. One of the results of the interest thus awakened was the despatch of the Polish General, Chrysanowski, whom Tsartoriski himself had recommended. He was described by Palmerston as "a remarkably intelligent well informed little fellow" who had served in the Russian army in the war against the Turks in 1828–1829 as a Captain of Artillery. Consequently his appointment was bound to be obnoxious to the Russians and Chrysanowski had no illusions on that head. He suggested that he should be attached unofficially to Reschid Pasha's headquarters and he got his payments arranged from British sources. Ponsonby got Husrev to view the appointment favourably at first and Chrysanowski gave some advice and learnt some of the conditions of the Turkish Army. But then the Russians moved and the little Pole hastened to fly. He was afraid of being handed over to Russia and shot as a deserter.[1]

Palmerston got the Pole to go back by giving him letters of 'denization'. These were only a partial protection against Russia, since Britain recognised the inalienable character of nationality, but Ponsonby gave him the protection of the Embassy. Reschid backed Ponsonby's request that Chrysanowski should be given a command but at the last moment Husrev shewed jealousy and the Pole had to act only in an advisory capacity. In 1838 he moved to Baghdad for a time. But his reports on the Turkish army were the best Palmerston received and throughout the critical years 1839–1840 the advice and information of Chrysanowski were of the greatest value to him.[2]

Nourri had also asked for young Turks to be trained as instructors in British ships of war. Palmerston was only too glad to

[1] From Ponsonby, 29 Dec., 1835: *F.O. Turkey*, 256.

[2] To Ponsonby, 4 Nov., 1835, 7 March, 1836; From Ponsonby, 30 July, 1838: *B.P.* The despatches and private letters abound in references to Chrysanowski who from the first made a most favourable impression on Palmerston. The General treated the Turkish officers with great tact and, unlike the British officers sent out, was content to serve in any capacity. His weakness was that his natural dread of being betrayed to the Russians made him avoid Constantinople. Tsartoriski said there were 100 Poles living quietly there. Professor Rodney (*Journal of Modern History*, Dec., 1929) has collected together many of the references in the despatches.

arrange this, but urged the superior advantages of employing British officers: "The military and naval art is the art of war; and that art can be fully learnt only in war itself. We have a vast number of officers who have so learnt it, and we could send the Sultan now British officers to instruct his army and navy who are much more competent as teachers than these Turkish young gentlemen will be five years hence." As a result, in addition to various stores, Colonel Considine and Captain du Plat with other officers were sent to Constantinople. No doubt they were fairly competent and Captain du Plat performed prodigies of valour in surveying the defences of the Balkan towns in the height of winter. But they wanted a command and Considine was soon dissatisfied with his position and returned to England. Command was, however, just what the Turkish Government could not give and it is surprising that Palmerston did not at once realise the fact. "Unless they have command I do not see that they can be of much use," he wrote at the outset, and he continued to press this view on the Porte. The failure of Considine's mission, he thought, "makes us ridiculous", and with his usual pertinacity he sent him out again. But the Turks, alleging Russian opposition, refused to employ him or pay him and Palmerston had to admit that he could not go on paying for British officers to advise the Turks. Considine was sent to Tunis where he seems to have done little better. He was, indeed, not the sort of man to win the Turks' confidence and all that Palmerston got out of this attempt was a certain amount of military information, and the Turks nothing at all.[1]

The Turks had less need for such inadaptable assistants because they had already secured expert advice from other quarters in Captain Helmuth von Moltke, who du Plat reported had come there disguised as a merchant in 1835. Palmerston thought this was a Russian trick and protested strongly against it. Ponsonby and others suspected that Moltke was to be used to fortify the Dardanelles. Lord William Russell's report of the mediocre quality of the greatest soldier since Napoleon has caused much derision but he obtained the information from the most competent authorities in Berlin. Shortly afterwards he insisted that Moltke was not to be trusted, and Palmerston hastened to inform Pon-

[1] To Ponsonby, 4 Nov., 1835, 7 March, 1836, 17 Jan., 1837, 12 Feb., 1838: *B.P.*

sonby that he was dangerous. But the Prussian Government sent
out other officers whom Russell and even Ponsonby admitted were
good Russian haters. Moreover they made no fuss about their
status. They were also provided with plans made in the Prussian
General Staff for the fortification of the Balkans as well as the
Straits. Russell, who kept bombarding Palmerston with schemes
to preserve the Ottoman Empire, attached great importance to
these. It does not seem, however, that the Prussian officers did
very much to improve the Turkish army though Moltke's eye
detected all the mistakes of strategy in 1839. More important
was the Hanoverian General, Jochmus, whom Palmerston sent
out in 1838, who with the "little Pole" was to be of real service in
1840.[1]

Palmerston did not have much greater success with his renewed
efforts to improve the Turkish fleet which he began after his failure
with the Army—and for the same reason. "If the Sultan would
let us send him some naval officers", he wrote in 1838, "it would
be the making of his fleet and a good fleet would be the salvation
of his Empire. But I do not think any naval officer would go or
could be of any use unless he had command. The Sultan should
man a couple of line-of-battle ships with Greek sailors and give
them English officers and then put a number of young Turkish
naval officers to learn their business on these ships and he would
soon have an efficient navy without bringing religious and national
prejudices into play." This last clause was added because of
what he had gradually learned about the army, but it did not
really meet Turkish prejudices. Ponsonby dutifully did his best
to get the programme carried out. But Captain Walker who was
sent out with other officers was refused command, ostensibly
because of the fear of Russian protest. Not until 1840 was he given
such a position, one of Ponsonby's greatest triumphs. The

[1] To Lord William Russell, 11 May, 1837: *F.O. Prussia*, 209. From Lord
William Russell, 17, 24 May, 1837: *F.O. Prussia*, 210. In a private letter, after
further enquiry, Russell repeated his view of Moltke: "His abilities are only
considered to be of a very second rate nature and the value of his counsels,
however well meant they may be, is much abated [sic]." (13 July, 1837: *B.P.*)
do., 4, 11 Jan., 26 March, 21 Dec., 1837, 3 Jan., 1838; To Ponsonby, 12 Jan.,
1838; To Lamb, 30 April, 1837: *B.P.* Palmerston took no notice of the plans
sent by Russell, who said he acted so because Ponsonby was not a military man.
Some lie in the Broadlands Archives apparently unread. Ponsonby reported
most hostilely at first on the secret and suspicious conduct of Moltke, and the
other officers, but by 1839 he was convinced of their anti-Russian attitude
though, he wrote, they might be inciting the Sultan to war. From Ponsonby,
26 March, 1839: *F.O. Turkey*, 355.

cruise of the Ottoman fleet with the British in the autumn of 1838 no doubt helped to improve its efficiency and morale. But little had been done when the crisis came in 1839 and that little was of no avail since most of the fleet deserted to Mehemet.[1]

This was not much to have effected in four years on so important a question. But it must be remembered that Palmerston had little time to devote to Turkish affairs. His military talents were absorbed in Spain until the end of 1837. When the crisis came in 1840 he was able to apply the lessons of these years with remarkable ability and success.

(iii) THE COMMERCIAL CONVENTION, 1838

There is a very different story to tell about the commercial convention where in the end, after many doubts and hesitations, Palmerston and Ponsonby had a veritable triumph.[2] The origin of this instrument has been vehemently claimed by Urquhart and his claim has been supported by many historians. It is certainly true that after his travels in the East he saw more clearly than anyone else the necessity of change and what its effects might be. The report that he sent home at the beginning of 1834 won Ponsonby's warm approval because it was so hostile to Russia whose exports to Britain, Urquhart claimed, could be supplied by Turkey if the impediments to trade were removed. Thus would be provided a "two edged sword against Russia, Turkey would be strengthened and Russia weakened". But, Ponsonby insisted, Russia knew this fact well enough and would never allow the change to be made if she could prevent it. The Turks had received his first suggestions extremely well, "but all the favor engaged in that quarter is and must be totally unavailing so long as the Russian nightmare lies upon the bosom of Turkey." Nothing could be more true. It took four years before Ponsonby could create the necessary confidence in the Sultan to enable him to get a new treaty sanctioned.

[1] To Ponsonby, 14 April, 1838: *B.P.*

[2] The negotiation of the commercial convention and its later effects have been discussed at length by Professor Puryear in his *International Economics etc.*, chaps. 3 and 4. There are more concise descriptions by F. E. Bailey (*British Policy, etc.*, 122–127) and Professor Temperley (*Crimea*, 31–39) where the political implications are more clearly shown. All that is attempted here is to assign the responsibility for action and to shew the immediate political effects. The economic results belong to a later period.

Meanwhile the agitation for a new commercial treaty continued in many quarters. The traders in Constantinople had long been pressing for something to be done. Palmerston himself had begun to urge the abolition of monopolies before Urquhart paid any attention to the subject. The trading connections with nearly every country were being overhauled with a view to finding an outlet for the growing production of Britain. It would have been remarkable if the trade with the Ottoman Empire had been overlooked.[1]

But monopolies were only one aspect of a complicated problem. The relations between the Christian Powers and Turkey were based on the Capitulations made when their subjects first began to trade in a country where the infidel could not be put on an equal footing with the true believer. These had been in the course of time implemented in commercial treaties which laid down the maximum tariffs for exports, imports and goods in transit. The Porte had had to accept special regimes for its land frontiers with Austria and Russian by treaties made after it had been defeated in war. Britain and France had generally been on the Sultan's side and their treaties contained no such stipulations. Nevertheless the tariffs were low, three per cent, and had they really been put into practice they would have allowed a freer exchange of goods than existed between any two European states.

But to the duties at the Porte were added so many other charges that, as Bulwer pointed out, "our imports were taxed, forty, fifty, sixty per cent, and Turkish exports sixty, seventy, a hundred." This result was produced by inland charges (as later in China where the treaties were based on similar Capitulations) and also by monopolies. For the Sultan, needing money, created monopolies in order to sell them and his Pashas did likewise. But while Mehemet Ali managed his own monopolies a far less proportion of the profits of Turkish monopolies went into the Sultan's pocket. Much of them was taken by intermediaries. The regulations were such that only by bribery could trade be carried on at all. There were also financial difficulties, for the expenses of the war had inflated the currency. In addition there were (as in many European countries and especially Austria

---

[1] From Ponsonby, 31 Jan., 1834: *B.P.* To Ponsonby, 6 Dec., 1833, *F.O. Turkey*, 220. In an admirable economic lecture Palmerston shewed to his own satisfaction at any rate that the Sultan would gain financially by the abolition of monopolies.

and Russia) prohibitions against exporting or importing many articles.[1]

The Sultan, deprived of his Greek provinces and saddled with a war indemnity, needed, as everybody admitted, more money. The first move to change the system came indeed from Turkey, and Nourri Effendi was ordered to raise the question in London. As we have seen, Palmerston had no opinion of Nourri who could speak no European language and found the greatest difficulty in carrying out his mission. He sums up his negotiation on this subject as follows: "He is a great hog and not a diplomatist. We have made no advance about commercial matters; he wants me to agree to pay more than 3 per Cent Import Duty; I say, what equivalent advantage can you offer us in exchange? He says, the satisfaction of doing a good and generous action by a friend. I reply commerce knows nothing of philanthropy and romance, and we must have a quid pro quo; but he cannot think of any quid."[2]

Poor Nourri's position was made all the more uncomfortable by the fact that Urquhart, now working on the subject in London, was constantly giving him unnecessary advice, demanding to know what Palmerston had said to him, and warning him not to visit the Russian Ambassador. Nourri could not ascertain that Urquhart had any authority, but was afraid that he would write injurious reports to Constantinople. He was told not to take any notice and to let the Foreign Office know if Urquhart annoyed him again.

This is an excellent example of Urquhart's manners and methods. He was working at the tariff at the orders of the Foreign Office and furnishing the Board of Trade with valuable information, but he had of course no authority to decide a matter on which the Board of Trade and Foreign Secretary had not come to any conclusion. He apparently then left Nourri alone and at the beginning of 1836 was told by Backhouse, at Palmerston's orders, to

[1] The best account of the system is given by Professor Puryear who has seen many of the consular reports of these years. There was, indeed, naturally a constant stream of complaint. Professor Temperley well illustrated the difficulties by shewing that twelve different processes were necessary to secure permission to pass through the Bosphorus (*Crimea*, 33). No firman was, however, required for vessels to go up to Constantinople and return into the Mediterranean. (Minute, Backhouse, 1836: *B.P.*)

[2] To Ponsonby, 16 July, 1835: *B.P.* The demand for the revision of the tariff and the intimation of the '*quid pro quo*' had previously been exchanged in writing. To and from Nourri Effendi 11, 13 May, 1835: *F.O. Turkey*, 268.

come to an understanding with Poulett Thomson. The reports and memoranda which he was submitting were no doubt of considerable use in view of his local knowledge, but they were only part, though an important one, of a large documentation and insisted on lower duties than the Turks were likely to accept.[1]

What Urquhart was stressing was the total abolition of the internal duties, a sensible proposal but one which had necessarily to be compensated by a considerable increase in the tariff. He made every effort to get complete control of the negotiations. "I have no hesitation", he wrote, "in saying that I feel perfectly certain of the failure of the proposal with regard to the tariff if the negotiations are undertaken through the machinery of the Dragomans." Urquhart's dislike at being kept in a subordinate position which left the final decisions to those responsible to Parliament is shewn by his next suggestion that a parliamentary inquiry should be made into British trade in the Levant. On this Palmerston wrote a characteristic minute. "I see no practical object to be gained by such an inquiry but I do see a great loss of valuable time that would ensue from it to me and the President of the Board of Trade. It might be very amusing to a number of idle gentlemen about Town to come down and speak pamphlets in the Committee in answer to preconcerted questions and thus to have their works printed at the expense of the public, but I should oppose any such inquiry if moved by others and certainly shall not move it myself."[2]

The result of these discussions was that a draft convention was sent to Constantinople with instructions that the Consul-General,

[1] See my article, "Urquhart, Ponsonby and Palmerston," *English Historical Review*, July, 1947. Memorandum of a conversation which took place between Nourri Effendi, M. Vogorides [the younger] and M. V. Salamé [a Foreign Office representative] at the Levy [Undated] *F.O. Turkey*, 268. From Nourri Effendi, 23 Oct., 1835: *F.O. Turkey*, 268. Backhouse to Urquhart, 11 Feb., 1836: *F.O. Turkey*, 279. Minute by Palmerston, 11 Dec., 1835: *F.O. Turkey*, 266. Mrs. Robinson (*David Urquhart*, 59–60) quotes a correspondent's assertion that it was Urquhart that inspired the Turkish Government to ask for the revision. Urquhart no doubt made the suggestion, but all commercial circles in Constantinople were talking along similar lines. The document quoted in the text shews the Turkish Ambassador's real attitude towards Urquhart and Urquhart himself later alludes to "my rupture with Nourri Effendi". (Urquhart to Backhouse 27 Jan., 1837: *F.O. Turkey*, 309.)

[2] From Urquhart, 4 Feb., 1836: Urquhart to Backhouse, 18 April, 4 May, 1836; Minute, Palmerston: *F.O. Turkey*, 279. Urquhart later reported that the Commercial Bank of Liverpool would set up a bank in Constantinople —but only if the British banking laws were altered so that all property of the stockholders was not answerable for banking debts.

Cartwright, and two merchants were to enter into negotiation with the Porte concerning it. Urquhart had no doubt considerable influence on the terms proposed. He was, however, given no authority by Palmerston, though no doubt the idea that he would be useful in the negotiations was one of the motives which induced Palmerston to insist on his taking up his position as Secretary of Embassy at this time.[1]

But of course Ponsonby had the responsibility for the negotiation as for all else at Constantinople. Once there Urquhart began discussions in which he tried to insist on very low duties. As soon as Ponsonby's quarrel with Urquhart began he ordered the latter to cease negotiating about the commercial convention. It is, therefore, Ponsonby who is responsible for the delay which took place. Bulwer attributed it to his indolence, but this seems hardly fair. There were many other reasons. His plan to go on leave, and the row with Urquhart, rendering it quite impossible for the latter to be allowed to give any assistance, necessarily prevented immediate action. Ponsonby added later the illness of Houloussi, the acting Reis Effendi, and of Pertev, and the plague. But above all it was necessary to create the right political atmosphere in order to obtain so great a change as the abolition of the monopolies and inland duties in which so many powerful vested interests were concerned. Ponsonby could not be expected to concern himself with the details of the complicated negotiation any more than Lamb did at Vienna with the Austrian Treaty. It was the function of the Ambassador merely to exercise a very general supervision and to intervene at the highest level if a deadlock occurred.[2]

Ponsonby was not on very good terms with Cartwright, who in any case was hardly the man to tackle so big a problem. He had already found that the Sultan wished to obtain political advantage from the negotiation. In April 1836 when the Minister of Finance advised the abolition of the export duties on grain the Sultan told Ponsonby he dare not do it because of Russia. It is hardly surprising, therefore, to find Ponsonby refusing to put the plan into operation immediately. Other governments were moving at Constantinople in the question of monopolies, but in 1837 while

[1] To Ponsonby, 28 July, 1836: *F.O. Turkey*, 272.
[2] Urquhart to Backhouse, 27 Jan., 1837: *F.O. Turkey*, 309. As early as 24 Oct., 1836, Urquhart had insinuated in a letter to Ponsonby that the latter did not care about the convention. They then became reconciled again but the final rupture occurred in the early days of January.

Roussin was on leave Ponsonby got on very intimate terms with the French Chargé d'Affaires, D'Eyragues, and decided to act with France alone. This should be remembered in connection with the French protests in 1838. D'Eyragues took up the matter enthusiastically and made some progress with the Sultan and his advisers. But these latter were at this period still determined to raise the tariff without making the concessions concerning the other duties and monopolies. These obstacles were not overcome and the Ambassador even suggested at the end of 1837 that perhaps a new convention was not really necessary. It could only be secured, he said, if England and France threatened to insist that they would claim back the duties levied in defiance of the Capitulations. He clearly did not want to take a step which might play into the hand of his pro-Russian opponents in the Seraglio.[1]

It was the hope that the convention would have political effects that induced the Sultan to shew the necessary energy and decision to overcome the vested interests which were opposing change. However great Mahmud's reforming zeal in his earlier years, by 1838 he was in no mood to carry out so great a departure from established custom. His support of Reschid Pasha, for example, was more due to that Minister's connection with the Western Powers, with its possibility of obtaining help against Mehemet, than any real sympathy with Reschid's reforms. Reschid, indeed, had to leave Constantinople to save his life immediately after the convention was concluded, so powerful were his enemies. But the Sultan as his health declined was all the more eager to settle matters with his rebellious vassal. The convention would serve that purpose in two ways. By aiming a blow at Mehemet's monopolies it would weaken him and might even provoke him to such action as would bring on him the might of Britain. And it would predispose the British Government and British public opinion in the Sultan's favour and make more likely the success of Reschid's mission. This is, of course, a matter of speculation since the Sultan did not reveal his mind even to his nearest subordinates and favourites. But, despite Bulwer's later assertions, Ponsonby's claim that he carried the convention by an appeal to political

---

[1] From Ponsonby, 8, 16 April, 26 Dec., 1836, 15 March, May, 27 Aug., 1837: *F.O. Turkey*, 274, 278, 302–304. D'Eyragues was given a snuff-box by the Sultan for his work as Chargé d'Affaires, about which Ponsonby wrote enthusiastically.

motives is in accordance with all the contemporary evidence available.

Palmerston had not as yet taken any very special interest in this problem. The struggle in Spain was absorbing his attention. But at the beginning of 1838 here, as in Austria, he endeavoured to get action. He then did two important things. He wrote despatches, partly at Ponsonby's suggestion, threatening the Sultan with reprisals if he refused to negotiate but urging that the abolition of monopolies, while not really injuring the Sultan, would strike a blow at Mehemet Ali whose whole financial system depended on them. And he appointed Bulwer Secretary of Embassy, despite Ponsonby's intimation that he did not want one. Clearly someone was needed at Constantinople to do the work which MacGregor was doing at Vienna.[1]

Ponsonby, though he did not welcome the suggestion of a new Secretary, liked Bulwer and at this juncture took up the question of the treaty with far more energy since it might strike a blow at Mehemet. His claim that he obtained the treaty is obviously justified and Bulwer's romantic account written long afterwards is nothing but a fairy tale. The Ambassador immediately pressed Palmerston's argument on the Sultan and in April, before Bulwer arrived, had got the commercial convention brought to his personal notice. The vested interests were, however, working strongly against the abolition of monopolies and Ponsonby urged Palmerston to tell the Turkish Ambassador in London that, if British demands were not accepted, an account of the Turkish disregard of the Capitulations would be demanded. Reschid Pasha was now gaining influence and no doubt the convention could hardly have been secured without his help, which Ponsonby secured by backing him against his enemies, and threatening to leave him to the mercies of Husrev if he refused. Part of the price was the European mission which may have saved Reschid's life. But this, as Ponsonby pointed out, was only the *formal* part of the work: "It is in the Seraglio and with the Sultan himself I have been and still am endeavouring to bring it to a satisfactory conclusion."

In this situation Palmerston's plan for a political treaty described in Section 5 of this chapter, which made a deep impression on the Sultan and his advisers, must have counted for a great deal. It is quite probable that without it the negotiation would not have suc-

[1] To Ponsonby, 6 Feb., 14 April, 6 June, 1838: *F.O. Turkey*, 328, 329.

ceeded. For the convention added to the Sultan's difficulties with Russia and might perhaps finally determine Mehemet to declare his independence. It was the promise of guarantee against Russian threats, and the hope that the step would lead to a treaty countenancing an attack on Mehemet that caused the Sultan to take so momentous a decision against such powerful opposition.[1]

Bulwer, who came at the end of April to put the convention into shape with the Turkish Ministers, seems to have performed his minor, but all-essential, part of working out the detail with efficiency and tact and above all without worrying Ponsonby too much. But he never realised the political conditions of his work since he did not believe Mehemet could be overthrown and indeed did not desire it. Palmerston later pointed out his errors on this subject on which of course Bulwer had no influence. But meanwhile Bulwer with the help of Cartwright conducted well the negotiation as to the exact rates of duty. He eventually, no doubt under pressure from Ponsonby, accepted higher rates than had originally been intended in order to get the treaty through quickly. For Ponsonby saw that it was necessary to take advantage of the political position established by the prospect of armed cooperation against Mehemet. Roussin's suspicions, which Ponsonby turned aside by a denial that a treaty had been made, were justified. But the secret was also kept from Bulwer. The Secretary's assurances to the French and Austrian Ambassadors that no political issue was in question no doubt rang quite truly.

But Ponsonby's claim that he decided the main issue is surely justified: "It was carried", he wrote later, "by acting upon the passions of the Sultan and the fears of his Minister." Palmerston realised this and responded to the appeals to get the ratification through the Board of Trade as quickly as possible and without changes so that no opportunity could be given to Tahir Bey, the Chief of the Customs, and the rest of the opposition, "Armenian or Greek Bankers, of some of the Greek merchants, of many of the Pashas and other functionaries and a crowd of their dependants whose illegitimate gains will be cut off."[2]

[1] From Ponsonby, 12 March, 21 April, 10 May, 19 Aug., 1838: *F.O. Turkey*, 330–332; do., 7 Nov., 1837: *B.P.* He was delighted that Palmerston had arranged for Bulwer to live outside the Embassy.
[2] Bulwer's letters on the treaty were legitimately much cut down for print (*Bulwer*, II, 273, 283), but he also omitted significant sentences about Mehemet, e.g. "Egypt and Syria if regained could not be maintained" on which Palmerston

The treaty was hailed everywhere as a great triumph for Britain. "There has been nothing like it since Canning's speech on sending the troops to Portugal," wrote Lyons from Athens. "Joy and gladness, hope and confidence are revived all over the Levant, the eyes which shrank from the Russian flag with astonishment and dismay now look once more upon the British flag with pride, and all men say England is herself again." Butenev hastened back to his Embassy to repair the shattered Russian influence. Roussin also was furious at Ponsonby's success. He had perhaps some reasonable grounds for thinking that Ponsonby might have given to him the same confidence previously accorded to his Chargé d'Affaires, and he suspected not unjustly that political arrangements were secretly associated with the commercial. But the treaty was in fact to the advantage of all the Western Powers, and, though Molé was only too ready to see in it another excuse to break away from the English alliance, Desages soon admitted as much to Aston. Though Molé tried to get Egypt exempted from the convention he soon gave way. France was, indeed, one of the first states to follow the British example. Roussin himself took steps to deny at Constantinople that the attack by the *Journal des Débats* on the convention in any way represented the opinion of his Government, and asked Ponsonby for a copy of it in order to make one like it.[1]

The Russians on the other hand were much more cautious. They were not sure that the increase of duties would suit them better than their present position. It was on this fact that Urquhart, furious at his dismissal and the success of the negotiations which he had prophesied were bound to fail without his assistance, based his futile opposition to the treaty. But Russia made a new treaty in 1842 and by that time most other trading states had done the same. A great increase of trade resulted especially of that of Britain. Corn from the European provinces of Turkey came to British markets as Urquhart had prophesied. No doubt much of this expansion of trade was inevitable. But the indirect effects

---

wrote "why not?" His reply is in *Bulwer*, II, 286. From Ponsonby, 15 Dec., 1838: *F.O. Turkey*, 333. This interesting and important despatch describes some of the obstacles that had to be overcome.

[1] From Lyons, 7 Dec., 1838: *B.P.* For the Russian reaction see Mosely, *Russian Diplomacy*, etc., 115–118. Butenev was more alarmed about Reschid's mission than the convention and was reassured by Bulwer's assertion that there were no political clauses. From Bulwer, 28 Aug., 1838: *B.P.* From Aston, 10 Sept., 1838: *Aston P.* From Ponsonby, 23, 29 Oct., 1838: *F.O. Turkey*, 332.

on the Ottoman Empire were considerable, part of that gradual westernisation which was ultimately bound to destroy it.[1]

One of Roussin's main objections to the treaty had been that Mehemet would refuse to accept it and the resulting clash with the Sultan would bring the Russians to Constantinople. Mehemet did demur at first but soon gave way. His admirers said that his control over all trade and commerce in Egypt and Syria was such that the treaty would really be a dead letter there. Ponsonby was immediately on the alert with plans to force the submission of the Pasha, whose legal position, he claimed, was most vulnerable. But the question was never really tested, for before the effect of the treaty on Egypt could be seen the attack on Mehemet had begun. The same cause hindered the immediate application of the treaty in Turkey itself but gradually its full operation was ensured, not without some struggle between British representatives and the reactionaries.[2]

---

[1] For the later Russian action see Puryear's detailed description and analysis in *International Diplomacy, etc.*

[2] From Bulwer, 16, 26 Sept., 12 Oct., 1838: *B.P.*; From Campbell, 28 Sept., 1839. *F.O. Turkey*, 343; From Ponsonby, 14 Oct., 1838: *B.P.* "I believe the Pasha possesses no property whatsoever and that he cannot possess any, being considered as the slave of the Sultan. . . . If therefore Mehemet Ali shall pretend to evade the commercial treaty made by his Sovereign under the plea of being himself the sole proprietor in Egypt, it is easy to destroy that plea."

3. THE CONTEST WITH RUSSIA

As we have seen, the Tsar had gradually lost interest in the attack on the Liberal Movement in the West. He carried out the promises which he had made to Metternich, sent funds to Don Carlos and hated Louis Philippe as much as ever, but he put no great zeal into the contest. But in the East he had his own struggle with Britain and at times it looked as if the war which so many expected was bound to come. The manoeuvres for influence extended to all the countries bordering on Russia, and the main lines of her relations with Britain during the next hundred years had been laid down by 1840. It says a good deal for the statesmen who directed these affairs that in 1841 they were on better terms than they had been at any other period since the Napoleonic wars. Palmerston's attitude to Russia has been the theme of many scolding pens. But his actions in these years resulted in a brilliant success and it seems clear that it could not have been obtained by a policy of appeasement, instead of a vigorous assertion of British interests.

The quarrel over Stratford Canning and the Lievens meant that Palmerston had two new Ambassadors to deal with. Orlov, who like all intelligent Russians would have liked to escape from the deadly routine of the Imperial Court, had hoped to succeed Lieven, and had perhaps worked against him for that reason, but the Tsar could not spare him from his side. All the world was surprised, however, when in February 1835 the Tsar transferred Pozzo di Borgo from Paris to London. This was considered partly as a hit at Louis Philippe. It was more likely due to the lack of trained Russian diplomatists and the Tsar's thought that Pozzo di Borgo's appointment would be pleasing to Wellington. Whatever the motive, the change had a disastrous effect on the ageing diplomat who had struck deep roots into Parisian life during his twenty years' residence. Granville wrote that he was 'mystified' and 'indignant' at the transfer, adding sarcastically: "He quite feels for the embarrassment of Apponyi and Werther and other minor members of the Corps Diplomatique bereaved as they now will be of their daily counsellor and guide."[1]

[1] Bligh to Wellington, 10 Jan., 1835. *F.O. Russia*, 217; Granville to Aston, 10 Feb., 1835: *Aston P.*; Esterhazy to Metternich, 31 July, 1835: *V. St. A.*

Pozzo di Borgo might perhaps have recovered from the shock to his pride and habits of life but for the publication of his secret despatches in the *Portfolio*, Urquhart's journal, for which the Poles provided the Russian documents. In a sense they did him credit. "Pozzo need not be ashamed of his," wrote Palmerston, "for they are most ably written." But this revelation of his hostility to both Wellington and Metternich in 1829, two men whom he had in the eighteen thirties assiduously flattered, put him in a most difficult position. Wellington forgave both Pozzo di Borgo and Matuszewic easily enough. He laid the main blame on Princess Lieven. But Metternich, as usual, was vindictive. He confessed his bitter feelings to Hummelauer but told him not to reveal them. Meanwhile he made an attempt to get Pozzo di Borgo removed from his post. It was rumoured, indeed, that Nesselrode would be appointed in his stead. Metternich's move failed. But the Ambassador had lost the confidence of the Tsar, who in 1836 actually spoke slightingly of him to Barante, words which Louis Philippe repeated to the Austrian Ambassador and must have penetrated everywhere in diplomatic circles. Pozzo di Borgo lost all his usual poise and nerve. He tried to court the Whigs and only succeeded in losing the confidence of the Tories. He was quite inadequate to the strain of the controversies of 1838, and the Russian Government consulted Clanricarde as to who should succeed him.

Palmerston failed to treat him with sufficient courtesy, but got on with him well enough. It was convenient to have an Ambassador who was hardly likely to be trusted by Austria or the Tories, and could, therefore, give no trouble. He wrote kind words about him to Durham. Even when he described Pozzo di Borgo as in his 'dotage', he said that suited his convenience. But the Ambassador became quite incapable of serious business and when the crisis of 1839 came a special envoy had to be sent to London.[1]

[1] To William Temple, 14 Jan., 1836: *B.P.* Hummelauer to Metternich, 16 Feb., 27 June, 1836; Metternich to Hummelauer, 13 March, 1836: *V. St. A.* From Lamb, 5 Aug., 1836; To Durham, 9 May, 1836; To Clanricarde, 1 March 1839: *B.P.* Barante, *Mémoires*, V, 243. Apponyi to Metternich, 27 Jan., 1836, *V. St. A., Frankreich*. From Hummelauer, 15 April, 1836: *V. St. A.* He communicated to Wellington and Aberdeen Metternich's despatch to St. Petersburg about the *Portfolio*. Wellington in return communicated a letter to Fitzroy-Somerset to whom Matuszewic had written an exculpatory letter concerning the accusations made against the Duke's character. Matuszewic, the Duke wrote, had got his brief from "a certain lady, not fat, but fair and more than forty, who had a good deal of influence in the Russian Embassy". (Wel-

Meanwhile Palmerston, anxious to avoid another incident, incurred the displeasure of William IV by ascertaining informally that Durham would be acceptable to the Tsar before securing the King's assent. The King at first strongly objected to Durham's appointment and, as Nesselrode interpreted Palmerston's informal and confidential enquiry as a sort of recantation of the course taken over Stratford Canning, the King became very indignant and it took a very tactful and well-reasoned letter from Melbourne to secure his approval. The King naturally distrusted the accounts of Russia sent by his Ambassador who, he wrote, "really appears to forget that His Lordship is the servant of His Britannic Majesty and not of the Emperor of Russia." No doubt he repeated this view to others and Ellice with his usual malice reported it to Durham. The Ambassador's indignation was intense and he wrote bitter letters to Palmerston about it. Palmerston wrote him a friendly warning and got him to write a despatch pointing out the need of special vigilance over Russian activities even if they were not immediately dangerous. This produced some effect and though the King still spoke of Durham's 'delusions' and 'gullibility', he did not question his good faith. Durham was duly grateful, but the King's suspicions mounted again in 1837, because the increased prominence of Princess Victoria caused Durham to be talked about as her adviser. Palmerston, who throughout this Embassy treated Durham with exceptional tact and skill, arranged that the Ambassador should send him a 'private letter', in appearance not intended for royal eyes, which he could shew to the King to justify Durham. This was done, and just before the King's death Palmerston was thus able to get the G.C.B. for Durham and a friendly royal message. Durham was also allowed to accept Nicholas's gift of the Order of St. Andrew, an exception from the strict rule that Ambassadors should not accept foreign Orders which would not have been made under any other circumstances.[1]

lington to Fitzroy-Somerset, 12 Jan., 1836: *V. St. A.*) To Granville, 2 Feb., 1836: "Pozzo lives quiet and gives little trouble, and as it was said of George 4th that he was as good as no King at all, a similar remark may be made upon Pozzo"; do., 29 March, 1836: *B.P.* From Melbourne, 24 Dec., 1838: "No doubt you will agree with me that we should not interfere at all in the choice of an Ambassador." (*B.P.*)

[1] From Melbourne, 29 June, 1835: *B.P.* Lloyd Sanders, *Melbourne Papers*, 333. Palmerston was not supposed to see the King's letter to which this was a reply and there is no copy at Broadlands. To Durham, 2 May, 1837; From Durham, 3 June, 1837; From Will. IV, 28 Feb., 28 March, 23 July, 21 Oct., 1836: *B.P.* S. Reid, *Lord Durham*, II, 124. C. New, *Lord Durham*, 291–292.

Durham's character was already known at St. Petersburg and the Ambassador was again given an exceptional position which produced its full effect. The Tsar found genuine interest in a sort of intimacy with a brilliant and unconventional personality. Durham delightedly recounted the special honours paid to him at which both Court and diplomatic circles were astounded. He had, however, gone with the full intention of endeavouring to reconcile the two countries, a role which suited his vanity if not his political interests. He came, therefore, after no very profound enquiry to conclusions about both the strength and intentions of Russia different to those held by Palmerston. They were both agreed that the danger of war was not immediate. But Durham thought that better relations would be established by moderating public opinion in Britain and making every possible concession to the Tsar. Palmerston thought that Russia could only be checked if the Tsar and his Ministers were fully convinced that the British Government and people were determined to resist Russian aggression. In the circumstances, the two got on extraordinarily well. Durham was throughout most careful to avoid any possible charge of disloyalty to his chief, whose rival he had been thought to be, and Palmerston's differences of opinion were couched in friendly and restrained language.[1]

The Ambassador was convinced that he had the Tsar's confidence. When the Tsar was away on his long tours, of which there were many in 1837, he made little or no effort to get in touch with other diplomatists. Barante, the French Ambassador, was not intimate with him and, partly because of continual illness but also by choice, he saw little of the other members of the diplomatic circle. Their reports about him are pointed with irony—and perhaps with jealousy. Meanwhile by bribery, Cayley, an unpaid Vice-Consul who knew Russian well, obtained copies of secret information from the Finance Office about the military establishments and financial situation of Russia. Palmerston suspected

Palmerston thought Nicholas had given Durham the Order to embarrass him. To Granville, 27 June, 1837: *B.P.* Neither of Durham's biographers knew of Palmerston's last move to justify Durham who wrote (12 April, 1837): "I see in the papers a sharp war going on in which I am made a party respecting the Princess Victoria's establishment. The whole is a lie from beginning to end. . . . The object of all this is no doubt to confirm, if not encrease, the prejudices existing in a certain quarter—and I have little hopes of the measure not being successful." Palmerston cut out the last sentence and sent the rest to the King.

[1] Durham told Palmerston (5 April, 1836: *B.P.*) that he wrote to no one else about his mission. (To Melbourne, 31 Oct., 1835: *B.P.*)

that some of this information had been planted on Durham but
admitted that it was a useful check and later authorised Clanricarde to spend money to continue it.   Durham himself boasted
so much of his exceptional information that it was clear that he had
some special machinery of this kind, and Londonderry after a visit
almost said as much in a book which he presented to Nesselrode!
Durham, however, did thus supply factual information as well as
hasty impressions, and his advocacy of the Russian case on many
subjects may have had some effect on the Cabinet, if not on
Palmerston.

Durham told Esterhazy on his return that he had improved
relations with Russia in the face of the opposition of King,
Cabinet, Parliament and the Press, and the Ambassador admitted
the claim.   Durham added that the Tsar wished him to become
Foreign Minister, but he had refused because of the kind way
Palmerston had treated him personally.   Esterhazy believed,
however, that he was still quite ready to accept the position if he
got the chance to do so.   But it seems pretty certain that Durham's
mission was not really so important as he thought.   Perhaps its
main effect was to keep a little quieter some of his Radical followers in England.   The depth of the Tsar's real feelings for him
may be gauged by the fact that he told Clanricarde in 1839 that he
would like to hang him with his own hands for his conduct in
Canada.[1]

Clanricarde, who got the Embassy by a species of political black-
mail, had been an old enemy of Palmerston, and his wife, Canning's
daughter, though with some of her father's brilliance, was a tartar.
Melbourne who was strongly against the appointment, described
her as "a clever, lively woman thinking and talking of nothing but
politics, a decided enemy of us and our Government, always
having been so, even when Clanricarde was in office".   But
Palmerston, perhaps, thought he had a debt to pay to Canning and
in the result the appointment turned out quite well.   Clanricarde

---

[1] From Durham, 20 May, 1837; To Clanricarde, 20, 28 Nov., 1838, 28 Jan.,
1839; From Clanricarde, 31 Oct., 1838, 7 Jan., 1839: B.P.   Both Durham's
biographers, Mr. Stuart Reid and Professor Chester New, while writing from
Durham's point of view, do justice to Palmerston.   But they exaggerate Durham's
influence on his chief, and accept too easily Durham's own accounts of what he
accomplished during his Embassy which is by no means borne out by other
observers.   Durham's estimate of his own importance may be gauged by his
claim to have reestablished British influence at Constantinople by staying a few
days there en route to Russia! (Reid, Lord Durham, II, 16.)   Esterhazy to
Metternich, 22 July, 1837: V. St. A.

had a point of view almost the same as that of his chief to whom he sent many amusing comments on his predecessor's activities. They got on well together and Clanricarde was a competent representative during his two years' stay. His Secretary of Embassy, Bloomfield, was no more than a functionary.[1]

Before Durham arrived public opinion in Britain was already moving strongly against Russia.[2] This was partly due to Urquhart's propaganda in the *Portfolio*. Palmerston was in no way responsible for that publication, but there can be no doubt but that he welcomed the attacks made on Russia and was glad that the British public had become thoroughly aroused. Edward Ellice, his greatest foe and critic, wrote to Grey from Constantinople whither he had accompanied Durham, urging what was in effect a policy of appeasement towards Russia, silence on her policy and the removal of the British fleet from the Mediterranean. As regards the last suggestion, Palmerston pointed out that it was just the absence of such a fleet that caused the Cabinet to refuse his proposal to assist the Sultan in 1833. He was even more emphatic on the necessity of speaking out about Russian policy. "It is not true", he told Melbourne, "that every tyro understands that policy; on the contrary not one man in a hundred thousand has until very lately been sufficiently aware of it; and Russia has advanced specially because nobody observed, watched and understood what she was doing. Expose her plans, and you half defeat them. Raise public opinion against her and you double her difficulties. I am all for making a clatter against her. Depend upon it, that is the best way to save you from the necessity of making war against her."[3]

The clatter grew to an uproar in the succeeding years. But the attack could not have succeeded had it not been based with all its extravagances on genuine reasons for alarm and suspicion. There was generous indignation at the Tsar's treatment of Poland which was increased by his brutal speech to the Poles at Warsaw in October 1835; there was intense irritation at the policy of commercial prohibition, which Durham, who could not mention

---

[1] From Melbourne, 13 Feb., 1838: *B.P.* The reappointment of Durham was considered at the end of 1839 but Melbourne wrote that there were many reasons against it and it would have been quite impossible.

[2] There is a good account of the growth of public opinion in Britain in Mr. C. W. Crawley's *Anglo-Russian Relations, 1815–1840.* (*Camb. Hist. Journal*, 1929, 47–73.)

[3] To Melbourne, 30, 31 Oct., 1835: *B.P.*

Poland to its tyrant, told the Tsar was the main cause of ill-feeling; there was the resentment at the treaty which the Tsar had made with the Sultan, not only at the treaty itself but at the manner in which it was made; there was a gradual realisation that Russian expansion menaced not only the Ottoman Empire and the over-land route to the East, but Persia and thus indirectly Britain's Indian possessions. But above all, as Palmerston wrote, there was "the apparently threatening naval armaments which are so natur-ally calculated to give umbrage to the people of this country." The Russian fleets were kept in the summer on a war footing both in the Black Sea and the Baltic, a course no other country, and least of all Britain, could adopt because of the expense.[1]

In Palmerston's eyes the fleet was the most important aspect of the situation. Though it may be that Durham and others were right in thinking that it was in no condition to fight Britain, so many Sail of the Line within striking distance could not be ignored. An increase in the British fleet was made in 1833 as a result of Unkiar Skelessi, and another in 1838, after Palmerston had tried in vain to obtain a reduction in the Russian fleet. In 1836 steps were taken to make the striking force of the fleet more efficient, Minto, the new First Lord, having reported that Britain had practically no fleet at all. He explained the situation to Pozzo di Borgo, who was an old friend, and promised that the reorganis-ation should be done as quietly as possible so as not to seem to menace Russia. Palmerston himself later told Pozzo di Borgo that while Russia kept her fleet in summer on a war footing Britain must have more ships on the seas. The Cabinet readily agreed to these increases, Melbourne in 1838 suggesting that though Britain on many occasions had been under the special protection of Providence "no man ought to count upon such interposition of Divine favour". The necessary funds were also obtained without much difficulty from the House of Commons, but everyone grudged the expenditure the Tsar had forced on them.[2]

Palmerston naturally constantly demanded reports about the Russian fleet. Durham was able to supply a good deal of factual

[1] To Durham, 31 May, 1836: *F.O. Russia*, 221.
[2] To Durham, 14 Jan., 1836: *B.P.* do., 12 Feb., 1836: *F.O. Russia*, 221. To Clanricarde, 29 Dec., 1838: *F.O. Russia*, 243. Only informal enquiries were to be made. Palmerston suggested that Russia should equip only one divi-sion of the Baltic fleet and one-third of the Black Sea fleet instead of as usual putting the whole of the two fleets on a war footing. Hobhouse (Broughton, *Recollections*, V, 169) reports Melbourne's attitude with some surprise.

information from his secret sources. He inspected the Baltic
fleet as the Tsar's guest and gave it as his opinion that, shut up as
it was seven months in the year, it was not a formidable fighting
machine. When, in the Spring of 1836, he thought that he had
demonstrated the good will of the Tsar towards Britain he wished
to shew it to the world in some striking form. "A public and
marked alliance", he wrote, would be perfectly compatible with
British relations with France. He even proposed that a British
squadron should be sent to the Baltic to exercise with the Russian
fleet. Such a demonstration would shew, he claimed, that Russia
was under British influence. It would at any rate have served to
advertise Durham's position, but of course Palmerston refused to
agree, and in an unusually sarcastic answer gave in brief his whole
attitude towards the problem: "We should not be disposed to send
our summer exercise squadron into the Baltic to assist at the Water
Kalisch. First of all we think the said 'Naumachia' not over
complimentary to us. We have complained for some years of the
Russian practice of parading a great fleet every summer in time of
peace; our complaints have produced no effect; we have at last
thought it necessary to arm on our side and the main reason
understood by all parties for this increase of force in the discussions
about it in Parliament was the necessity of not leaving our own
shores and commerce entirely unprotected with a fleet of 20 Sail
of the Line swaggering away within a week's sail of us. What does
Russia thereupon? Why she resolves to add 9 Sail of the Line to
her fleet to overtop the 8 which we are adding to ours. Her
proceeding is very offensive, and it would not be fitting for us to
send our ships to witness the bravado—besides our squadron
would play second fiddle as the Prussians did by land [at Kalisch].
Then again, if we are better than them by sea, the less we are with
them the fewer opportunities they will have of profiting by our
example; and, lastly, if our fleet were to go this year into the
Baltic, theirs would return the visit next year in the Channel."[1]
The Tsar, indeed, might have been pleased because he was
anxious to learn as much as possible from British experience, and
Russian officers were inspecting British dockyards and naval
establishments for that purpose. Palmerston claimed the right to

[1] From Durham, 22 March, 1836; To Durham, 19 April, 1836: *B.P.*
Melbourne had commented: "I concur with you that there would be nothing
but evil in the appearance if a more intimate union than in fact exists." (5 April,
1836: *B.P.*)

similar facilities in Russia, and, not considering the response adequate, withdrew the privileges of which the Russians had made such abundant use. The Tsar scoffed at British fears of Russian attack, but when Durham first asked him the reasons for the increase of the fleet, he replied, so it was reported at St. Petersburg, "to prevent questions of that kind", and, after an inspection of Sevastopol and the Black Sea fleet, he said, "Now let the English come if they want their nose made bloody." It would have been a grave lapse of duty if Palmerston had failed to watch closely the construction of so large a navy, and he never ceased to ply Durham's successors with demands for accurate information about it.[1]

Less than six months after his arrival Durham embodied his views in a long and comprehensive report of 3 March, 1836, on which he spent great pains. It is well written and both his biographers compare it to the more famous report on Canada. But it was much inferior to that great document. It was necessarily superficial, as Durham himself confessed, and much of it was based on speculation. It concluded with an eloquent passage on the weakness of Russia in attack: "Abroad her soldiers fall by thousands sullen and dispirited, evincing the passive devotion of fatalism, but neither the brilliant chivalry of the French nor the determined unyielding courage of the English. At home they fight with desperate unconquerable fury, for national and domestic objects, consecrated by religious feeling and patriotic traditions. Such a nation, therefore, cannot be successfully led over her frontiers." This was hardly convincing to those who, like Palmerston, remembered 1813-1814, and it took no account of Russia's Eastern expansion which Durham himself agreed was a most difficult problem. Grey praised it warmly, but there is no evidence that either this or Durham's constant advocacy of the Russian point of view made any impression on Palmerston.[2]

Durham did his best to popularise his views among his own supporters, but was not very effective against the efforts of the refugee Poles and the *Portfolio*. The latter made a prodigious sensation over all Europe. Durham complained bitterly that it was circulated abroad by the Foreign Office and also of the personal

---

[1] To Durham, 8 Nov., 1836: *B.P.* "Fas est hostes doceri," Palmerston wrote, "but not 'docere'." T. Schiemann, *Geschichte Russlands*, III, 284, 328.

[2] There is an excellent summary of the report (*F.O. Russia*, 223) in Stuart Reid, *Lord Durham*, II, chap. XVIII. Melbourne wrote on it: "There is nothing in it that one has not heard fifty times." (27 March, 1836: *B.P.*)

attacks on himself. Tatischev was involved and was summoned back to Russia. Metternich hoped at least that he had got rid of this tiresome check on his conduct. Though he was studying the *Portfolio* carefully and sent a vindication of some of the charges against himself to the Tsar, he told the Archduke Louis and Kolowrat that he had burnt his copy of the first number and they tried to borrow one from Fox. Metternich was much afraid of the effect at St. Petersburg, but in London, though he never ceased to complain of the *Portfolio*, he hoped that the revelation of Austrian opposition to Russia would do good and Hummelauer at the outset wrote enthusiastically of the good effect on public opinion.[1]

The naval question and the commercial negotiations were the only issues between the two countries in which Durham played an important role. The Polish question he avoided as much as possible and recommended Barante to do the same and concentrate on the East where the real danger of war was. "The continual junction of this dead body to living Russia", he wrote, ". . . . is a source of continual and irremediable weakness." He did, of course, by means of appeals to Nesselrode and other officials try to mitigate the lot of the Poles. He claimed to have produced some effect but there is little evidence that he in fact did so. In the Cracow dispute, it is true, the Tsar, in order not to offend Durham, allowed Austria and Prussia to bear nearly all the burden of the British protests and carefully concealed the fact that Russia had been the real author of the occupation and purging that so moved Palmerston.[2]

But the Polish question could not be ignored. The Emperor's speech at Warsaw in 1835 was made with such brutality that it had to be edited for publication. The Emperor himself was conscious that his anger had led him too far. "Be indulgent to me in your reports," he said to Barnett, the British Consul at Warsaw.[3]

[1] From Durham, 18 July, 1836; From Fox, 14 March, 1836; From Lamb, 5 Aug., 1836: *B.P.* Hummelauer to Metternich, 27 Feb., 1836: *V. St. A.* He, however, got less enthusiastic as the numbers came out, suspected that Palmerston was behind it, as he was not attacked, and asserted that the Cabinet could have stopped it if they had not been divided in opinion about it. (do., 15 April, 1836: *V. St. A.*)

[2] From Durham, 27 Jan., 18 June, 1836: *B.P.* The appointment of the mild Kozlowski, he thought, was due to his efforts. Durham believed Nesselrode at once when he indignantly denied that any Polish children were removed from Poland (C. New, *Durham*, 296). Yet we know that this was done. Probably Nesselrode himself did not know the truth.

[3] From Barnett, Warsaw, 23 Oct., 1835: *B.P.* The circulated version omitted the words "Je ne suis plus qu'Empereur de Russie et c'est à ce titre que vous

The debate in the House of Commons was milder than that in the French Chambers where the Tsar was violently attacked. But nevertheless indignation in Britain was immense and Hummelauer reported that the Tsar's speech had entirely reestablished Palmerston's popularity. Palmerston seriously considered whether it was necessary to make an official protest against the Tsar's claim that Poland no longer existed, but Melbourne deprecated taking notice of words of which there was no official report. Palmerston was indeed well aware that he could do no more for the Poles now than in 1832. He protected their refugees so far as he could, for the Tsar's hand reached out towards them wherever he could put pressure on a Government. Nicholas had naturally an intense jealousy of those in the free state of Cracow, though Barnett reported that they were comparatively harmless. But, indeed, that free state was an intolerable challenge to the Autocrat and at the Kalisch Conference in 1835 the Tsar forced Austria and Prussia to sign a secret agreement that it should be abolished. That fate was only deferred because of Prussia's opposition to the incorporation of Cracow in Austria to which the Tsar had agreed. But meanwhile Cracow must be cleaned up and above all no connection allowed with any other Government than those of the three Eastern States.[1]

Palmerston did not know of this document, but Cracow had been established by a treaty to which Britain was a party and its independence, therefore, was a matter with which Britain had a right to concern herself. Thus in 1836 when, after the murder of a Polish spy, the three Courts began their campaign against Cracow by a joint occupation and expulsion of undesirable elements, Palmerston at once decided to protest. He was careful about his facts, took legal advice and surrounded himself with textbooks on international law from which he had always a quotation ready at hand in his interviews with Bülow and Hummelauer. He admitted that action to prevent a hostile attack by refugees was perhaps justifiable. But the occupying Powers rested their claim on the quite insignificant unrest that had occurred. Palmerston then wrote a tremendous indictment. Melbourne at first was hardly

m'appartenez". Metternich strongly condemned the Warsaw speech. Poland's independence could be crushed, he said, but not her nationality (From Fox, 7 Nov., 1835: *B.P.*).

[1] From Melbourne, 14 Dec., 1835: *B.P.*, *Appendix*, p. 849. Hummelauer to Metternich, 17 Nov., 1 Dec., 1835: *V. St. A.* F. Martens, *Recueil*, IV, 472, first printed the correct version of the secret agreement, but the *Portfolio* had got hold of the truth. To Granville, 17 Nov., 1835: *B.P.*

prepared to go so far but eventually agreed that Britain could not keep silent: Geography, however, has left to Britain as to France whatever their rights, "only the faculty of remonstrance and the appeal to moral opinion which you say is so strong. I think that this power should under these circumstances be exercised, but with caution and dignity, because tho' a great deal of what you say is true yet, after all, admonitions which you cannot enforce and complaints of wrongs which you cannot redress do run risk of becoming ridiculous—at least they have a tendency that way." But Palmerston was thinking of Parliament and it does not seem that this advice had much effect. After a well-argued historical review the despatch suggested that this attack on the Treaty of Vienna tended to invalidate other parts of it which the three Powers were concerned to preserve. Lastly Palmerston said he would appoint a British Consul to Cracow to keep in touch with events.[1]

Both the Tsar and Metternich received the despatch with due recognition of its importance. The former, indeed, said so little that he earned Palmerston's thanks while Hummelauer reported with alarm and indignation that Pozzo di Borgo only gave the most perfunctory support to the efforts of Bülow and himself at London. Metternich entered into long explanations of the revolutionary centre at Cracow which he managed to link up with the latest attempt to assassinate Louis Philippe. But Metternich, wrote Palmerston, has behaved like the gentleman he is. It was Ancillon who got into the worst position by refusing to receive the despatch from Lord William Russell. Seeing that he had already told Bülow in London to communicate a Prussian despatch on the same subject, though that wary diplomat had ignored the instruction, his position was quite untenable. Palmerston simply threatened to break off diplomatic relations and though there was a long controversy, in the end Ancillon had to eat his words. He only complicated matters for Metternich whose main aim was to prevent Palmerston making public the refusal to allow a British Consul to be appointed to Cracow.[2]

[1] From Melbourne, 8, 12 April, 1836: B.P. To Lord William Russell, 15 April, 1836: F.O. Prussia, 204. Similar despatches were sent to Vienna and St. Petersburg. From Hummelauer, 27 June, 1836: V. St. A.
[2] To Lord William Russell, 3, 10 May, 1836; To Fox, 10 May, 1836: B.P. Hummelauer to Metternich, 3, 17, 24 June, 1836: V. St. A. Professor Bell (Palmerston, I, 267–271) devotes a surprisingly large space to this incident and gives the main references to the despatches in the F.O. Archives. There is a

The contest with Metternich about the appointment of the Consul continued hotly, much to the alarm of Louis Philippe, who Granville said was "terribly excited". Palmerston threatened him with violent attacks in the House of Commons unless he gave way. But Metternich called his bluff and said that he did not mind such abuse, if Ministers behaved in a restrained way. He insinuated also that Palmerston was trying to stir up discontent among Austrian subjects, an argument which, Granville wrote, "shews how deeply irritated Metternich is against you". He was profuse in historical explanation of how the situation had arisen through Tsartoriski's desire in 1815 to maintain "in however narrow a corner a shadow of Polish independence". This independence, in spite of the agreement he had signed at Toeplitz, he, with even more than his usual duplicity, promised to respect.

Lamb in reporting this urged that it was impossible to preserve real independence anyhow and that it was not a British interest to persist. "Deploring as much as any man the loss of the independence of Poland," he wrote, "I yet feel, that being lost, Europe would stand much better off if the very memory of it were effaced. We have questions yet to be solved which divide the three Powers, but this one unites them, and, if we alarm them in this, we sacrifice the present to the future—that which is full of hope to that which is irreparable." This attitude is a good example of Lamb's limitations and it was of course never accepted by Palmerston, who persisted for a long period in defending the position which he had taken up, though his words in the House were perhaps made more diplomatic by the pains and courtesy with which Metternich had argued his case.[1]

The serious incident of the *Vixen* in 1837 is one of the best examples of Palmerston's good sense and diplomatic skill in handling an awkard position. Public opinion was stirred because the seizure of a British trading ship naturally aroused much

good deal of explanatory material in the private letters. Professor Bell makes much of the fact reported by Barante from St. Petersburg (*Memoirs*, V, 344) that Metternich had informed Paris but not London of the intention. But there was no more than verbal communication and I cannot find evidence to shew that this distinction had any effect on Palmerston. Thiers took little action on this matter, partly because he was at the time applying pressure to Switzerland to get rid of refugees (see above p. 229) and partly to curry favour with Austria.

Louis Philippe thought it might complicate matters just when the Duke of Orleans was to visit the Central Courts. From Granville, 27 May, 1836: *B.P.*

[1] To Lamb, 8 Dec., 1836: From Lamb, 23, 26 Dec., 1836: *B.P.* From Granville, 6 June, 1836: *B.P.*

feeling and the question of the Circassian revolt which Urquhart
had advertised in the *Portfolio* and made popular was connected
with it. Indeed Urquhart had planned or at least encouraged the
whole affair. He and Hudson, who had visited the locality, had
constantly urged support should be given to the tribesmen who
had for so long resisted the attempt of Russia to control the whole
of the Caucasus. Ponsonby suggested some munitions should
be sent to them. The King was interested and Palmerston himself
considered that Russia was establishing a position which would
threaten the flank not only of Turkey but of Persia. But he had
warned Ponsonby in 1834 at the time of Urquhart's visit that he
could do nothing for them. He later tried to use his good offices
to get the war between Russia and the Circassian rebels suspended
on the basis of an assurance not to attack each other. But he was
forced to agree with Melbourne that however sympathetic he
might be to the rebels, he had no power to help them and that, if
he did, whether they were considered to be Russian subjects or an
independent state (as Urquhart claimed they were) Russia would
have grounds for war against Britain. He has no shadow of
responsibility for the *Vixen* and it seems certain, in spite of
Urquhart's charges, that Ponsonby only gave Bell such advice as
he could not as British Ambassador refuse.[1]

The arrest of the *Vixen* had been preceded by that of another
ship, the *Lord Charles Spencer*, taken on the high seas. Nesselrode
admitted the illegality of this action for which he was prepared to
pay compensation, and that question would have been closed but
for the fact that by implication he claimed a position for Russia
in the Black Sea which Palmerston could not accept.

This matter was still under discussion when the *Vixen*, sent

[1] To Ponsonby, 31 Oct., 1836: *F.O. Turkey*, 272; do., 28 Oct., 1834: *B.P.*
From Ponsonby, 1 Sept., 1834: *B.P.* To Durham, 21 Dec., 1836: *F.O. Russia*,
222. From Durham, 14 Aug., 1836: *F.O. Russia*, 225. I have treated this question at some length for though the *Vixen* case has received great attention, the
respective roles of Palmerston and Metternich have been much misunderstood
(e.g. V. J. Puryear, *International Economics etc.*, 52. H. C. F. Bell, *Palmerston*,
I, 283). They are revealed in the public despatches of which a number were laid
before Parliament and can be seen in *B.F.S.P.*, XXVI, 2–60, but the Broadlands
Papers add a good deal of important detail. Professor Chester New (*Durham*,
295) corrects Mr. Stuart Reid's view (*Lord Durham*, II, 67) that it was Durham
and not Palmerston to whom a peaceful settlement was due. From Ponsonby,
28 Oct., 1836: *F.O. Turkey*, 277; do., 30 Oct., 1836: *B.P.* Hudson to Sir
H. Taylor, 8 Feb., 1836: *F.O. Turkey*, 273 (a long letter describing the heroic
struggle of the Circassians). See also on the question of Ponsonby's responsibility my article, "Urquhart, Ponsonby and Palmerston," *Eng. Hist. Rev.*, July
1947.

from Constantinople by a British merchant, George Bell, in November 1836, was captured in the port of Soujouk Kalé, of which the Russians were in occupation. The vessel and its cargo were confiscated and its captain and crew were sent as prisoners to Odessa, but soon released. With the best of intentions a notice was published in the *St. Petersburg Gazette*, exonerating the British Government, but making incidentally claims of full sovereignty over the Caucasus. This was reproduced in the *Morning Chronicle* and caused an immense sensation which Urquhart's journalistic friends increased by all means in their power. Meanwhile Durham reported that Russian public opinion was just as strong on the subject and the Tsar could not give way even if he wanted to, which he did not.

Palmerston was angry at being forced into a position of this kind against his will. He was not going to be made to go to war by Urquhart and Bell. At the same time he was anxious not to recognise Russia's claims on the whole of Circassia, where he hoped some independence might remain, nor in any way to allow her to claim special rights over the navigation of the Black Sea. He approached the subject with great caution. The prestige of both Russia and Britain was at stake. "All Europe", wrote Minto, "has its eyes upon us." "The question is a serious one", Palmerston told Durham informally, "and goes to nothing less than peace and war between the two countries." He, therefore, referred the papers to the King's Advocate and told Pozzo he could make no comment until he had legal advice. Meanwhile he hoped to enlist the sympathies of both France and Austria in favour of the Circassians. From France there was no response. Indeed Granville would not even make the suggestion to Molé who he was sure would refuse all help. But Palmerston received a very different communication from Vienna. Metternich, Lamb reported, wanted Palmerston to stand on his rights. He consented to publish the British case as he had already done the Russian. He agreed that Austria's policy should be to get peace in the Caucasus and this Lamb noted "is more than neutrality, for peace in the Caucasus is independence". Though Metternich was a little vague on the legal aspect of the question and said that he must preserve his position as the advocate of Nicholas, Lamb was certain of his sympathy and cooperation and hoped much from his influence at Berlin as well as at St. Petersburg. Lamb himself strongly urged Palmerston to stand firm. The smaller Courts would be on Britain's side and the Sultan himself, he said, whose mother, seven wives and two sons-in-law came from Circassia, would be deeply impressed. Meanwhile it would only be politic to be a little more cooperative on the question of a free Press in Malta.[1]

For once Palmerston put his trust in Metternich's promise. Melbourne on the other hand said that he was most afraid of Metternich when he was friendly. He was strongly against pressing British claims to trade with the whole of the Black Sea coast. "Recollect", he told Palmerston, "that powerful ministers have in general found themselves unable to incline this nation to vindicate her rights in distant countries." Lord Holland also was against a strong course. Though he promised to warn Pozzo di Borgo that Government, Parliament and people alike would refuse to acknowledge Russian claims on Circassia, he urged Palmerston to say as little as possible. He also distrusted Austria and was doubtful of the case put forward by the lawyers and the British representatives in the Levant. Such arguments in any case it was doubtful wisdom for Britain with her large Colonial possessions to put forward: "Peace in this is my dear delight and she often dwells with silence."[2]

Palmerston seems to have been in agreement with these views from the outset. He had also, as Esterhazy pointed out to Metternich, his hands full in Spain. He, therefore, devised a plan by which neither Britain nor Russia should give up their claims. He would not admit the blockade under which the Russian officer had acted. But he would recognise the sovereignty of Russia over the port of Soujouk Kalé which had been legitimately ceded by Turkey to Russia in the Treaty of Adrianople, and thus the legality of the seizure of a ship which was breaking Russian regulations for that port. If Nesselrode did not put forward his claim to the rest of

[1] From Minto, 18 March, 1837: *B.P.* To Granville, 3 Feb., 1837: *Bulwer*, II, 248; do., 7 Feb., 1837; From Granville, 20 Feb., 1837: *B.P.* Esterhazy to Metternich, 4, 27 Feb., 23 March, 1837: *V. St. A.* To Lamb, 11 Feb., 1837; From Lamb, 3, 7, 25 Feb., 5 March, 1837: *F.O. Austria*, 262, 264, do., 3 Feb., 1837: *B.P.* The British claimed that the cargo was salt and the Russians gunpowder. The matter was never made clear, since it made no difference to the argument.

[2] From Lord Holland, 17 March, 1837; From Melbourne, 4 and 17 March, 1837: *B.P.* Of Metternich he wrote: "He ruined Napoleon, when Napoleon trusted him most. I know not what object he may have in pushing us forward against Russia."

the Circassian coast the matter would be over. As for the future, in case some other *Vixen* appeared, the best solution would be for Russia to abandon her claims on the whole of Circassia which he insisted had been independent in 1829. Nesselrode did not, of course, accede to this last suggestion. But he was glad to accept Palmerston's way out of the immediate difficulty. A series of notes were exchanged on the lines Palmerston had stipulated. A flurry was caused by Pozzo di Borgo mixing up the case of the *Lord Charles Spencer*, where Palmerston had laid down the British doctrine of the open sea, with that of the *Vixen*, but Palmerston was able by June to regard the whole matter as settled. As to the future, he had no power to stop British ships, he told Durham, but would do so if he could. He was aware that such a settlement would not please the Radicals and the Tories. *The Times* and the *Morning Post* had already begun the attack. "I expect to be properly blown up in the House of Commons when I have to state that the *Vixen* affair is arranged and *how*," he confessed to Durham. But by confining the dispute to the occupation of a single port he had made it very difficult for his opponents to raise the whole issue before Parliament.[1]

It was fortunate that Palmerston had taken the safe course and not relied on Metternich's good offices. For on the news that the Tsar was displeased with his attitude and that Tatischev was coming back to Vienna immediately, the Chancellor got into a panic. He reinsured himself with a despatch to Esterhazy which reaffirmed all the objectionable doctrines of blockade. It was accompanied by a more informal one full of hostility to Palmerston whose bluff, he said, had been called. His Ambassador was too sensible to shew the official despatch to Palmerston as Metternich had directed, but Metternich used it to disillusion Lamb. That

---

[1] To Durham, 21 March, 23 April, 2, 22 May, 1837: *B.P.* do., 19 April, 1836 (2 despatches). The second gave the method he wished Nesselrode to pursue, of which Durham had already been apprised in a private letter. Durham did not communicate this, to Pozzo di Borgo's annoyance. He got the method accepted without putting it formally on record; do., 22 April, 1837 (the *Lord Charles Spencer* despatch which Pozzo di Borgo mixed up with the others), *F.O. Russia*, 231. Palmerston claimed that, "It will require as great sagacity [as his own] in those who may want to bring the real question to an issue to see where and how they may do so." (22 May, 1837: *B.P.*) The Foreign editor of the *Morning Post*, Honan, explained to Esterhazy that the attitude of his paper towards the question of the *Vixen* had been dictated to him by the 'Party' which saw in it an opportunity to attack Palmerston. *The Times* was actuated by the same motive. (Esterhazy to Metternich, 23 March, 1837: *V. St. A.*)

Ambassador was very crestfallen. This was the nastiest trick Metternich had played on him since 1833. He could only report in long despatches and letters Metternich's assurances that he would never allow Europe to become Cossack. Metternich would be with Britain on the great issue against Russia, he wrote, but he could not be relied upon for smaller matters. Lamb's opinion of Metternich sank rapidly. He regarded the *Vixen* settlement as a defeat. It had revealed to the world that we were not prepared to fight for our rights in the Black Sea. Meanwhile he could not help admiring the cunning Esterhazy. "What tact Esterhazy has shewn! not the dupe of Metternich's momentary velleité of independence, and then not weak enough to go to you with his silly arguments but treating him like a child and telling him they had done wonders." This was as near a confession of bad judgment as Lamb ever got. But for some time he was very bellicose and talked of war with Russia and the entrance of British ships into the Black Sea quite in Ponsonby's style.[1]

Palmerston took the whole matter much more coolly. "I own that for once Metternich has taken me in," he wrote, "and I believed that, seeing that Austria and England have a common interest as regards the encroachment of Russia, he meant to take a straight line for the moment. I shall be more just to him in future." He put on record for Metternich's edification his view of the Austrian suggestion that a blockade of the Circassian coast should be recognised, and urged Austria to advocate Circassian claims at St. Petersburg. But he had not relied on Metternich and the solution did not seem to him so great a defeat as it did to Lamb. On the contrary, whatever Metternich might say, Russia had accepted the method that Palmerston himself had suggested and made no effort to make Britain admit Russian claims to sovereignty and blockade. The situation remained exactly as it was before the incidents. Palmerston had got out of an awkward fix, at the price, it is true, of hot attacks by Tories and others, which Urquhart, now dismissed for his part in the plot, was on the way home to stimulate. Meanwhile Orlov was sent in July to

---

[1] From Lamb, 21 April, 14 May, 1837: *F.O. Austria*, 265; do., 21, 30 April, 10, 23 May, 1837: *B.P.* Lamb thought that Esterhazy had not even confessed to Metternich that he had not used the despatch of 8 April. But the Ambassador told his Chief that he had suppressed it so as to avoid argument and preserve Austrian influence for the future. Metternich to Esterhazy, 8 April, 1837; Esterhazy to Metternich, 12 May, 1837: *V. St. A.*

congratulate the young Queen on behalf of the Tsar, and Esterhazy saw in this visit a desire to establish better relations with Britain by direct contact. Orlov told him that he had not yet found Palmerston very responsive. There were, indeed, to be other very sharp passages of arms before the two countries could come to an understanding. But Metternich, who had played a humiliating role in the *Vixen* incident, might have taken the point that Russia did not want his interference, but preferred to come to terms with Palmerston by direct negotiation.[1]

Austria had failed lamentably to assist Britain in the Caucasus. But that was far from Vienna. Lamb and Palmerston hoped for better things in enlisting her aid in two threatened localities nearer home, Serbia and the mouth of the Danube.

The first of these episodes shews Palmerston at his worst. Urquhart after his visit home in 1834 had first drawn attention to Serbia's importance, but now that the whole position of the Ottoman Empire was under review it could hardly have escaped notice. It seems to have been the Under-Secretary of State, Fox-Strangeways, who first suggested consular representation at Belgrade on the model of that already established at Bucharest. Ponsonby had long ago pointed out the necessity of attacking in European Turkey Russian influence "which under the novel title of Protector assumes indefinite powers". It was clear that Serbia was coming more and more under such influence with obvious dangers both strategic and economic. But Palmerston began to tackle the problem before he had made any diplomatic preparations to ensure success. "The British Government has two objects in view with respect to Servia," he informed Lamb, "first that Servia should form a barrier against the further encroachments of Russia, secondly that Servia should afford an opening for the extension of the commerce of Great Britain."[2]

---

[1] From Melbourne, 29 April, 1837, *Appendix*, p. 854; To Durham, 2 May, 1837: *B.P.* Esterhazy to Metternich, 22 July, 1837: *V. St. A.* To Lamb, 10 June, 1837: *F.O. Austria*, 262.

[2] To Lamb, 7 Oct., 1837: *F.O. Austria*, 263. From Ponsonby, 15 July, 1836: *F.O. Turkey*, 276: "Servia, Bulgaria as well as Moldavia and Wallachia are more or less under Russian protection (a protection indeed extended to all the Rayah subjects of the Sultan)." Minute, Fox-Strangeways, 26 May, [1836], "a Vice-Consul at Belgrade might be of use in watching the opening of trade in that quarter and in finding sure and regular conveyance of correspondence to Bucharest and Jassy—as well as for superintending the exchange of despatches between Mess[enge]rs and Tatars, fumigation, etc.": *F.O. 96 (Miscellanea)*, 18.

These were reasonable ends but Palmerston refused to estimate with any sense of reality the methods by which he was to achieve them. Obviously the only state that could assist him much was Austria whose interests in checking Russia were clearly the same as those of Britain. Yet he told Lamb he distrusted Austria who would try to prevent Serbia from improving herself and might even make a deal with Russia for the partition of her territory.

But the only way that the problem could be solved, answered Lamb, was to enlist the interests of Austria, already irritated by Russia's control of the Danube mouths, though at present blind to the Russian danger in Serbia: "If we do not instigate and assist Austria to resist her, the chances are all in favor of Russia. Without direct interests with Servia, without a point of contact with her, what assistance can we render her? If she counts upon us in the hour of need, we shall assuredly disappoint her. I defy any Govt. that can exist in England to move the nation to raise a finger in her defence."

And, indeed, Palmerston, much as he disliked it, had to encourage Lamb to obtain Austrian assistance when the situation grew worse owing to the action of his own agent. He had sent out to Belgrade a vigorous representative as Consul, Colonel Hodges, a man who knew nothing of the Balkan peoples and languages but, claimed Palmerston, "firm, resolute, bold in character", and one whose "political principles are according to the most approved standard of the present day". Hodges, like Palmerston himself, could not try to advance British interests without associating them with an attempt to improve the lot of those who were to be used as instruments for that purpose. He obtained the confidence of the Obrenovitch Prince, Milosch, who was uneasily ruling, under the Sultan's suzerainty, a people who were determined not to accept too much government from anybody. Hodges thought, and no doubt rightly, that if the condition of Serbia was to be improved, that could only be done by a vigorous exercise of power from above. He encouraged Milosch, therefore, to assert himself for that purpose against the Serbian leaders. These latter relied on their native customs, which might be termed 'constitutional', and the Russian Consul, in order to undermine Hodges' influence, naturally supported them. The curious result, therefore, was that in Serbia Britain was supporting autocratic rule and Russia, with the active countenance of the Austrian Consul, a sort of constitutionalism.[1]

Lamb saw at once the danger of this method of handling so complicated a problem. "Colonel Hodges", he wrote, "seems to me to be an active politician and I think you had better keep him quiet. It is hardly probable that even in Servia we can agree with Austria upon the mode in which the country ought to be governed. If she will secure us against its falling under Russian influence it is all we want and we must not thwart her in a natural dependency of hers, where our main object is that she should retain her influence and exclude other protectors. If the Colonel meddles even for Milosch's good unless by previous understanding with Austria, be assured he will do mischief and sacrifice great interests to a trifling one." Nevertheless Lamb made every possible effort to get Metternich to help, and remove the obnoxious Austrian Consul. When he found that Metternich would do nothing he worked through the Austrian military and financial authorities, as he began to do more and more at this time. He got fair words and many promises of action from the soldiers who were anxious to keep Russian influence out of Belgrade and the Danube. But without Metternich's active support the cumbrous Austrian machine could produce no results and Lamb had to confess that he was baffled. There was, indeed, much to be said for Metternich's argument that Hodges' activity had simply roused the Russians to greater exertions and the best policy for Britain was to leave Serbia alone.[2]

Melbourne early saw that Britain could do nothing effective. "If, as is certain," he warned Palmerston, "you have little hope of inducing Austria to assist Milosch against Russia, you should take care that he is not induced to go further than he otherwise [would do] relying upon assistance from us which I do not see how we can afford him." But Palmerston would not give in. He thought of inviting the French to nominate a Consul, much to Metternich's alarm, but his relations with France were now such as did not encourage him to rely on her. He told Ponsonby to

[1] To Lamb, 10 Jan., 18 May, 1838: *F.O. Austria*, 270; do., 11 Jan., 1838; To Ponsonby, 17 Jan., 1837; From Lamb, 16 July, 1837: *B.P.* T. Schiemann, *Geschichte Russlands*, III, 295. Metternich suggested that all the three states should withdraw their Consuls, a course which Palmerston indignantly rejected. (18 May.) Hodges was recommended to him by some of his old constituents in South Hampshire.
[2] From Lamb, 3, 26 Jan., 1 April, 23 May, 1838: *F.O. Austria*, 271: do., 22 Sept., 1837, 1 April, 1838, 4 May, 1839: *B.P.*

get the Sultan to support Milosch. Ponsonby had no very great
opinion of Milosch, but he gradually warmed to the contest and
thought that here was a means of striking a great blow at Russia.
The Sultan was, however, by no means inclined to increase the
power of a subordinate over whom he had only a shadowy control,
and on his return to Constantinople, Butenev, who succeeded in
ousting the Prince of Samos from the discussions, found it comparatively easy to get the Turkish Ministers to accept the Russian
point of view. Ponsonby got the Porte to order Milosch to send
a deputation to Constantinople to discuss the new constitution, but
the decision was to decrease not increase the power of the Prince.[1]

The result was what might have been expected. The unrest in
Serbia increased until it became a revolution. Hodges had to
retire into Austria, and to his chagrin Milosch first followed him
and then made a humiliating reconciliation with his opponents
and the Russian Consul. "I fear that Servia, Wallachia and
Moldavia may now be considered to belong wholly to H.I.M. the
Emperor of Russia," wrote Ponsonby. Milosch did not in fact
manage to appease his enemies sufficiently and was later removed
in favour of his son. But by this time Palmerston had abandoned
the struggle. Hodges, after remaining some time near the Serbian
frontier, where he was naturally suspected of intrigue, went to
Vienna and thence departed for the more suitable job of tackling
Mehemet Ali at Alexandria. And Metternich was so far right,
that the Russians were less happy in Belgrade when left to themselves, and the elevation of the Karageorgevitch family in place of
the Obrenovitch brought them many problems. Nor, if the Serbs
were for long deprived of the benefits of modern civilisation and
the trade of Britain was still largely excluded, was the strategic
situation much impaired by the result. The arm of Russia was
not strong enough to control such hardy and freedom-loving
people as the Serbs. She could only produce a negative result.[2]

In the question of the Danube mouths Palmerston had more
success. Even Metternich responded to the suggestion that the
control by Russia over the Sulina Channel, which she had acquired

[1] From Melbourne, 11 April, 1838; To Ponsonby, 12 Feb., 21 March,
22 May, 1838: *B.P.* From Ponsonby, 5 Oct., 1837, 7 March, 18 April, 30 July,
20 Oct., 18 Nov., 8, 16 Dec., 1838: *F.O. Turkey*, 306, 330–338; do., 11 March,
21 May, 18 Nov., 1838: *B.P.*
[2] From Ponsonby, 15, 27 Jan., 1839: *F.O. Turkey*, 354. To Lamb, 17 Aug.,
28 Nov., 1839; From Lamb, 17 Feb., 4, 8 May, 9 June, 31 Aug., 8 Sept., 16
Nov., 1839: *F.O. Austria*, 279–282.

by doubtful means as a result of the Treaty of Adrianople, was a threat to Austrian commerce down the Danube to the Black Sea. Quarantine regulations were applied by the Russians in such a way as to hamper both Austrian trade and that of the Principalities, and other irritating restrictions were resented by the trading classes of both countries. Lamb was at first not optimistic that anything could be done, though he reported the growing realisation that Austrian commercial interests were at stake and the consequent increase of illwill towards Russia. But until Austria revised her commercial system of prohibitions he thought British interest was slight and suggested waiting until the commercial treaty was negotiated.[1]

This negotiation had been begun in 1836 by McGregor as part of the general campaign for the extension of British trade. 'Intolerable delay' was caused by the complications of the Austrian internal system. Kolowrat himself confessed that the question had fallen into 'inextricable confusion', but the Archdukes, who entirely failed to understand the problem, refused to allow the fundamental law of the Empire to be changed. "Against the treaty", wrote Lamb, "are the whole of the bankers of Vienna who make great profit by the present state of things, Eichoff, the Minister of Finance, who is reported to share in these profits, the Archduke Louis, moved by narrowness of understanding, obstinacy, timidity and conscientiousness as to introducing changes in an Empire where he is but a locum tenens, and the real difficulty of combining partial changes with the absurd and embarrassing relations in which they stand to Hungary. In favor of the treaty are Metternich and Kolowrath, weakly, without much knowledge or confidence in themselves upon this subject, and the latter in the hands of Eichoff and opposed by all the subalterns in the offices who are the real rulers of these affairs in this Empire. Notwithstanding this discouraging state of things, I have in the fire all the irons it will hold to stir it to my purposes, but without much hope of success." Fortunately Metternich had the good sense to enlist the aid of Neumann, who had negotiated the commercial treaty of 1829 with Britain, and with his expert assistance the treaty was at length completed. It contained provision for the free navigation of the Danube and everyone saw in it an intention of Austria to

---

[1] From Lamb, 2 Nov., 1836, 30 April, 5 May, 16 July, 1837: *B.P.*; do. 14 May, 1837: *F.O. Austria*, 265.

COMMERCIAL TREATY WITH AUSTRIA 581

trade through the Black Sea to a greater extent than before. Lamb claimed great political results for the treaty as likely to throw Austria into the forefront of resistance to Russian encroachment there. It was, indeed, considered a great blow by the merchants of Odessa, who had done all they could to prevent the Danube mouth from being freely opened, and it enabled the grain of the lower Danube to compete with Russian grain in Western European markets, mainly British. There was much negotiation with Russia concerning the freedom of navigation of the Sulina Channel, but on the whole that Power acceded to all demands with a good grace and the problem caused at this time little friction between the two countries.[1]

[1] From Lamb, 20 Dec., 1837: *B.P.* On the connection between the commercial treaty and the Danube problem see Puryear, *International Economics*, 132–139, 141–145. He has collected together much interesting information from the Foreign Office Archives to supplement A. Beer, *Die Oesterreichische Handelspolitik im neunzehnten Jahrhundert*. Here, however, as in his study of the Turkish treaty he is apt to give too much political effect to economic motives. For the negotiation of the commercial treaty see A. F. Pribram, *Oesterreichischer Staatsvertrage*, and From Lamb, 3 July, 1838: *F.O. Austria*, 272, an interesting review of the treaty which Prof. Puryear does not seem to have used: and E. B. Chancellor, *Diary of Neumann*, II, 78–82. Aberdeen affected to think the new treaty no different from that of 1829 concluded under his auspices. So he told Princess Lieven. E. Jones-Parry, *Corres. of Princess Lieven and Aberdeen*, I, 121.

4. THE SECOND FAILURE OF THE CONCERT

Throughout these years in spite of the divisions between the Governments there was recognition in every capital that the only alternative to war over the Eastern Question was a new treaty concerning the Straits and the integrity of the Ottoman Empire. The Tsar himself was, it is true, adverse to any step which would enable the Western Powers to share the special position which Russia had acquired by the Treaty of Unkiar Skelessi. But Nesselrode and others were fully conscious of Russia's inability to accept their challenge successfully if it were made. Metternich always dreamed of establishing Vienna as the centre of mediation between Russia and the West so that he could himself find the means by which a new treaty could be negotiated.

In 1835, on the other hand, both Broglie and Palmerston thought that the best course was for Britain and France to make a treaty with the Sultan and thus nullify the Treaty of Unkiar Skelessi. Austria could be associated with it when she had overcome her fear of revolution sufficiently to detach herself from Russia. That Power would then either have to accept a 'European' solution or find herself isolated. If Austria refused, Britain and France together would be able to protect the Sultan from both Mehemet Ali and Russia. In 1835 they made a great effort to achieve this end but neither of them were able to get the consent of their Governments to such a course. The pro-Austrian party in the British Cabinet insisted on Austria being approached before a treaty with France and the Sultan was negotiated, while Louis Philippe insisted on putting forward Talleyrand's old device of a European conference to obtain a treaty not merely to guarantee the Ottoman Empire but the territorial limits of all European states. This suggestion, in spite of its impracticability, seems to have been sincere. But Louis Philippe also used it as part of his manoeuvre to disentangle himself from Britain and draw nearer to the Eastern Powers and especially Austria, as has been described in Chapter VI. The fall of Broglie in February 1836 removed any chance of obtaining a treaty in that year, but Palmerston took up the project once more in 1838 in a new manner adapted to the changed circumstances of that time. He again failed, but his effort prepared the way for his success in 1840.

Metternich was left in 1835 to a régime of Chargés d'Affaires as Palmerston had been in 1834. He justified his conduct to them on the Eastern Question with much allusion to the consistency of his own conduct. The fatality of Navarino had been due to the action of France and England. What could Austria do when they joined Russia? But neither Palmerston nor Broglie believed that Metternich would subscribe to any treaty or declaration which, however phrased, was bound to be considered as aimed at the Treaty of Unkiar Skelessi. All they could expect, Broglie declared, was a *sous-entendu*, a sort of understanding, that cooperation would be possible between the three Powers, if Russia resumed her policy of conquest.[1]

When, therefore, Palmerston first put his plan before the Cabinet in November 1835, his own idea was that Britain and France alone should make a treaty with the Sultan; that the latter should promise not to make any cession of territory and that they should promise to support him. This was clearly a treaty directed against Russia rather than against Mehemet. The Cabinet were in favour of something being done, but Melbourne and others wished that Austria should be invited to be a party to the treaty from the outset. This was far from being Palmerston's view. He was at this time specially indignant with and suspicious of Metternich.

When the plan was communicated to Sébastiani at the beginning of December, that Ambassador agreed with Palmerston that Britain and France should make the offer to the Sultan first and at once wrote to his King and to Broglie. The latter laid the matter before the French Cabinet who were favourable except for a slight hesitation at the moment chosen, because of the dispute then going on with the United States.

Broglie desired, however, a rather different treaty and a rather different procedure. He agreed with Palmerston and Sébastiani that the negotiation should in the first instance be confined to France and Britain, and the resulting treaty then offered to the other Great Powers and the Sultan. He had no hopes that Austria would be ready to sign it immediately and feared that Metternich

---

[1] From Fox-Strangways, 25 Aug., 1835: *B.P.* With memorandum approved by Metternich of his views. He had tried, he said, to remedy the bad position in which the false policy of Joseph II had placed Austria. From Granville, 16 Nov., 1835: *F.O. France*, 505.

might even try to prevent the Sultan from signing it. If that Sovereign, however, was given the treaty at the same time as the other Powers he might be induced to sign it before Russian influence could be brought to bear on him, though Broglie was clearly doubtful also about the Sultan and enquired if Palmerston had any grounds for believing that his signature could be obtained. He, therefore, wished to include an attack by Mehemet Ali in the *casus foederis*, in order to forestall Russian objections that the treaty was solely directed against her and to induce the Sultan to accept the treaty.[1]

It was naturally assumed in London that Louis Philippe approved of Broglie's point of view, but he subsequently denied that he had ever given his consent. It seems clear that Broglie had gone on with the discussions with Palmerston in the hope that an agreement between the two governments would force the King to give way.

Palmerston at once accepted the view that the treaty should only be offered to Austria after Britain and France had signed it. He was less favourable to Broglie's other suggestions. He thought that it was impossible to sign a treaty against the cession of Turkish territory without the Sultan being a party to it. Supposing the Sultan did sign away some territory to Russia, they would have grounds for war both against Russia and against Turkey. There was no need to mention Mehemet Ali, he said, because all the territory the Sultan would ever offer to him was "so many feet of earth as may equal the length of his body".

However he began to discuss these questions with Sébastiani and they seem to have moved far towards agreement on them. The object of the treaty was to be any 'menace' to the 'indepen-

---

[1] To Granville, 8, 15 Dec., 1835, 9 Feb., 1836: B.P. From Granville, 11, 28 Dec., 1835: *Granville P.* This discussion was not recorded in the despatches but dealt with by private letters. Some of these are missing but that of 9 February is a résumé of the whole transaction until February, 1836. I have not been able to find any official letters in the series *Angleterre* of the Archives of the French Foreign Office, but Thureau-Dangin (*Histoire de la Monarchie de Juillet*, II, 421) gives a French point of view from Broglie's private papers. He exaggerates Broglie's reluctance to agree to a treaty. William IV much approved the exclusion of Austria and as usual considered that the treaty should be backed up by the reinforcement of the Mediterranean Squadron. (16 Dec., 1835: *B.P.*) Leopold, whose opinion was asked by Louis Philippe, strongly supported the view that France and Britain should first make a treaty and then offer it to the Sultan. The latter would accept it if it was already made, he insisted, but not it if it were a mere project. The hostility of Russia to Belgium made Leopold desire that France and Britain should unite against her (From Leopold, 22, 29 Dec., 1835; Leopold to Louis Philippe, 12 Dec., 1835: *B.P.*).

dence and integrity' of the Ottoman Empire, whose existence was essential to the balance of power in Europe. The Sultan was to be mentioned as an acceding party in one of the articles. The final drafts do not appear to have been settled, but it seems probable that they could easily have been so had not an obstacle arisen on the question of the exclusion of Austria from being a party to the original treaty.[1]

Palmerston vehemently supported Broglie's view—and surprisingly enough Lamb, who was in London, took the same side. Palmerston's reason was his distrust and dislike of Metternich who he still suspected of casting a greedy eye on Bosnia and desiring a deal with Russia about the Ottoman Empire. But in a cogent memorandum he shewed that whether Austria refused, as he anticipated, or supported the treaty and tried to persuade the Tsar to accede also, the result was likely to be much more satisfactory if France and England had first signed the treaty and asked the Sultan for his adhesion.[2]

He tried for a whole month to get Melbourne to accept this view but failed entirely, though he had a majority in the Cabinet and the King was wholeheartedly on his side. Melbourne, who, it seems likely, did not want anything done at all, consulted Grey. The latter in a verbose reply expressed the opinion that no treaty was necessary, since the danger from Russia was not pressing. He was afraid of the complications which might arise and particularly urged that nothing should be done to assist the Sultan to recover Syria from Mehemet, who he thought might again "become an important element in the future policy of the East". He distrusted both Russia and France. The best thing, therefore, was to shew a readiness to cooperate in resisting any further encroachment on the Ottoman Empire but to avoid any formal engagement. He closed with a reference to Fox's famous quotation, "Iniquissimam pacem justissimo bello antefero." "I am always inclined", he added, "to take the chances of time, which may by their own working prevent that tremendous result."[3]

Palmerston wrote a furious reply to what he considered to be a pusillanimous judgment and the Cabinet seems not to have accepted Grey's policy of appeasement, in which he may have been

[1] So I judge from the drafts of the treaty in the Broadlands Papers, one in English and the other in French.
[2] Memorandum in Palmerston's handwriting dated 1836: *B.P.*
[3] Grey to Melbourne, 8 Jan., 1836: *B.P.*

influenced by Durham. But no doubt it added to the difficulty of getting them to agree to Palmerston's own plan which was far more likely to result in a treaty than one in which Austria was to be consulted first. Melbourne remained sceptical. "The Black Sea and the Caucasus and these great Asiatic Empires", he wrote, "inflame imaginations wonderfully." "I have", Palmerston told Granville, "during the last six weeks used every endeavour in my power and employed every argument I could think of, but in vain; Melbourne remains immoveable and the natural consequence of that is, that other members of the Cabinet who originally agreed with me begin to partake Melbourne's opinion. People who do not follow up questions in the way that the person at the head of the department is obliged to do are generally for the doubting line."[1]

By this time Broglie's Government had fallen and, though Palmerston directed Granville to approach his successor, Thiers, he can have had little hope of success. Granville, though he much regretted that the idea of a treaty with France had been given up, put with much force to Thiers the suggestion that Britain and France should approach Austria with a view to the negotiation of a treaty. When Thiers asked for details Granville could only say that if he agreed to go on with the plan the two governments could discuss the instructions to be sent to their Ambassadors at Vienna on the subject. When Thiers consulted the King he found that Louis Philippe had very different ideas and Granville was soon made aware of them by the King himself. When Granville began to discuss the treaty the King replied "that they must be settled by a conference of the Ministers of the five Powers and that Vienna seemed the natural place for that conference". "This language", suggested Granville, "very much chimes in with Talleyrand's views, who has made no secret of his wish to end his political life in such a conference. The King also seemed desirous to efface any impression that may have been created in England that Talleyrand's predilections for the English Alliance had at all

[1] To Melbourne, 12 Jan., 1836; From Melbourne, 23 Jan., 1836; To Granville, 9 Feb., 1836: *B.P.* Lansdowne was inclined to the bolder course if a more trustworthy French Minister than Thiers could be found, and the rumour that Thiers was to be Broglie's successor probably finally decided the Cabinet (Lansdowne to Melbourne (Tuesday), 1836). Commenting on Grey's letter Lansdowne thought Palmerston had hardly been quite fair, but he agreed with him rather than with Grey. Lord Holland had a plan of his own. William IV was very much on Palmerston's side and rather embarrassed Palmerston by his continual interest in the treaty after it had been dropped. (From Will. IV, 9, 11 Feb., 1 March, 10 April, 1836: *B.P.*)

changed; he said his [Talleyrand's] opinions were the same now as when at the Congress of Vienna in 1815 he exerted himself to unite France with England and Austria against Russia."[1]

The effect of this communication on Palmerston was, of course, to cause him to drop the project altogether. The last thing he would have agreed to at this time was a conference at Vienna which might well have been used to draw Western affairs away from London in addition to giving Metternich the control of the diplomacy concerning the Eastern Question. He told Granville that he would not accept such a conference and, shortly afterwards, to let the whole matter sleep.[2]

Louis Philippe seems to have been sincere in putting forward this fantastic plan of a Treaty of Guarantee for all Europe to be negotiated at a special conference at Vienna. He may well have been persuaded by Talleyrand into a real belief in it. But of his immediate object there can be no doubt. He was already preparing that propitiation of Austria which has already been described in Chapter VI. He had in January informed the Austrian Ambassador of the British scheme, said he would never agree to it and adumbrated his own idea of a territorial guarantee. He kept recurring to the theme throughout this year in his conversations with Apponyi.[3]

Nevertheless the idea of sounding Austria was still in the minds of the Cabinet and especially of Melbourne, who doubted whether Constantinople could be saved from Russia without her cooperation. Thus when Lamb at last began his tardy journey to Vienna in May 1836, he had orders to take the question up there and secure the cooperation of St. Aulaire. As has been seen, he visited Paris on the way and in the course of his conversations discussed the question of the Ottoman Empire both with the King and with Thiers. It was piquant for Lamb to report from the King himself that he had always refused to agree to the separate treaty with Britain, the question on which Palmerston had fought with Melbourne for six weeks on the supposition that it was the considered

---

[1] From Granville, 26, 29 Feb., 1836: *F.O. France*, 520; do., 29 Feb., 1836: *B.P.*

[2] To Granville, 1, 8, 12 March, 1836; To Lord John Russell, 7 March, 1836: *B.P.* To Melbourne, 1 March, 1836: L. C. Sanders, *Lord Melbourne's Papers*, 337.

[3] Apponyi to Metternich, 24 Jan., 1836: *V. St. A. Frankreich.* See on Louis Philippe's communication to Austria my Raleigh lecture in *Proceedings British Academy*, 1934, 143–145.

decision of the French Government! The King and Lamb, however, agreed on their objective, viz., to support the Ottoman Empire by peaceful means, and Lamb was surprised to find Louis Philippe desiring that Syria should be restored to the Sultan, "by the assistance of England, France and if possible Austria, without, however, landing a French soldier in Syria."

But on the question of method the King not only said that Austria needed to be conciliated by the abandonment of the patronage of all 'Propaganda', a hit at British policy in Spain, but began to develop his project for a general treaty of territorial guarantee for all European states. Lamb enjoyed himself in a devastating attack on this idea. Could the King for example, he said, guarantee Poland to Russia? Certainly Britain could not. And he pointed out that the frontiers of Belgium were still to seek. He then found that the King was specially anxious for such a treaty in order to protect Belgium. Leopold's army was unreliable, he said, and he could not go on indefinitely in the present situation. The King's next object was "to prevent the future cessions or sales of territory either in Germany or Italy from which he apprehends the absorption of the smaller states by the larger ones." "What childishness!", was Lamb's comment, and he told Palmerston that he need not, of course, take up these suggestions. At the same time the King had made it so clear that he would never consent to a separate treaty between France and England on the Eastern Question that Lamb advised Palmerston he must abandon that idea whatever Ministry might be in power in France, until he heard that Louis Philippe himself had changed his mind.[1]

Meanwhile Lamb turned to Thiers for a policy and found that they were in pretty close agreement. Austria, Thiers thought, would not sign a treaty and the only thing to do was what Grey had suggested, to see how far Britain and France could get her to come to some understanding with them. He promised that St. Aulaire would work with Lamb to that end. The French Ambassador was well prepared for the task. It had long been Broglie's policy, and St. Aulaire fully shared his views, to lead Metternich back to cooperation with the Western Powers by small concessions, association in mutual conveniences and an assurance that the con-

[1] From Melbourne, 29 Feb., 1836: *B.P. Appendix*, p. 851. From Lamb, 13 May, 6 June, 1836: *B.P.* He told Palmerston he had better not try to find out how the mistake occurred. Clearly he thought Broglie had been disingenuous.

stitutional governments were the only alternative to the revolution in its most extreme form. Louis Philippe himself wanted something more and, as has been seen, it broke up the Anglo-French entente. But for a time Britain and France could on the Eastern Question pursue the same policy towards Austria.[1]

As might have been expected Lamb's discussions at Vienna did not lead to any very tangible result. Metternich reiterated his confidence in the Tsar and asserted once again that any attack by Russia or any other Power on the Ottoman Empire would make Austria join forces with Britain to prevent it. But he refused any suggestion of a treaty which he said was not necessary for such a hypothetical case. The three Eastern Courts, he added, worked perfectly well together without one. In response to skilful questioning by Lamb he said that his guarantees of Russian good faith were given just as much for the Asiatic dominions of the Sultan as for the European, thus answering an old suspicion of Palmerston's. What Metternich wanted was quiet at Constantinople, not the restless activity of Ponsonby—and Lamb shewed how much he agreed with him in this respect. At the same time Metternich saw no reason why Britain should not declare to the Sultan that she would guarantee the integrity of his dominions, a course which Lamb thought might satisfy Ponsonby who was so much against joining with Russia in a Five Power treaty for that purpose. Metternich also was wholeheartedly in favour of supporting the strengthening of Turkey internally. All this, thought Lamb, was excellent. The interests of Austria and Britain were so identical on the Eastern Question that matters could be left to work themselves out. Meanwhile he, like Metternich, was more concerned about Western affairs.[2]

Lamb thought this approach had made a substantial impression on Metternich. But the latter was in fact just as hostile to Palmerston as before. The despatch which Palmerston wrote in the

---

[1] From Lamb, 26 May, 1836: *B.P.* Thureau-Dangin, *Histoire de la Monarchie de Juillet*, II, 421. Even Melbourne was ready to accept a 'general treaty', since it would tend to "break up the union of the three Powers". He added, however: "Treaties of this comprehensive character are very dangerous transactions; they have rarely answered the purpose for which they were formed, and have often involved consequences, which were in no respect foreseen." (5 April, 1836: *B.P.*)

[2] From Lamb, 5 Aug., 1836: *F.O. Austria*, 257; do., 2 Nov., 1836: *B.P.* The first of the two despatches of 5 August was shewn to Metternich and approved by him as a correct account of his attitude after one or two minor alterations.

autumn, of his gratification that the views of Austria on the Eastern Question were the same as those of Britain, only aroused Metternich's suspicions. He was, he told Esterhazy, not susceptible to flattery. As for the Eastern Question, "There is no Eastern Question," he said. Nor was Palmerston satisfied. He had in fact been offered nothing but Lamb's assurances of Metternich's assurances. But he was occupied with Spain and the Eastern Question must be left alone for a time. After all, he told Ponsonby, "Metternich is not immortal.... He will pass away in due time and then we shall have Austria with us on Turkish affairs." Molé was even less anxious to do anything and when Roussin, home on leave, proposed action at the end of the year both Molé and Palmerston agreed that nothing need be done.[1]

Thus nothing had been done when the Eastern Question again became acute in 1838, because Mehemet threatened to declare the independence of all the territories which he controlled. Mehemet, as will be described in Section 5, was stopped by the diplomatic action of the Great Powers. But the Treaty of Unkiar Skelessi still threatened to disturb European peace since Palmerston was determined that Russian forces should not again dominate Constantinople. His idea of making a special treaty with France as a counterbalance to that of Unkiar Skelessi had been shewn to be impossible. He abandoned it, therefore, in favour of an attempt to negotiate, by means of an Ambassadorial conference in London, a European treaty to replace that of Russia.[2]

He was undoubtedly encouraged in this view by the reports which came from Vienna. On two occasions Metternich had agreed that the immediate problem of tackling Mehemet should be settled by an arrangement in London. Lamb had interpreted these remarks as an agreement to the negotiation there of a new treaty or convention about the whole problem. This was far from

---

[1] Metternich to Esterhazy, 29 Nov., 1836: *V. St. A.* To Ponsonby, 7 Nov., 1836: *B.P.* To Lamb, 11 Nov., 1836: *F.O. Austria*, 256. From Granville, 28 Nov., 1836: *F.O. France*, 526. William IV was sorry that Roussin's suggestion was not followed up. He never ceased to regret the dropping of the treaty of guarantee. (11 Dec., 1836: 23 Jan., 1837: *B.P.*)

[2] This incident has been studied in some detail by Mr. Philip E. Mosely from the evidence of the Russian Archives in his *Russian Diplomacy and the Opening of the Eastern Question in 1838 and 1839* (1934). See also my Raleigh Lecture, "Palmerston, Metternich and the European System, 1830–1841," *Proceedings of the British Academy*, 1934, which is based on the British, French and Austrian Archives and Granville papers. The two accounts substantially agree though the emphasis is different. The Broadlands Papers add only a few details.

Metternich's intention. He was concerned with the immediate issue produced by Mehemet's action and not with the negotiation of a substitute for the Treaty of Unkiar Skelessi. He had no intention of allowing the management of the whole Eastern Question to fall into Palmerston's hands. At any rate, as soon as he encountered Nesselrode at Toeplitz he completely altered his tune. He ordered Esterhazy to consider the instructions to Pozzo di Borgo as addressed to himself. This despatch, which Esterhazy thought it most imprudent of Pozzo di Borgo to communicate to Palmerston, indicated that in certain circumstances Russia might find it necessary to base her action on the Treaty of Unkiar Skelessi. Metternich did not of course confess to Lamb how much he had changed. That Ambassador still thought that he would accept a conference if Palmerston insisted, though he would only give "indirect assistance". "He will not face Russia, but will try to lead her into his path; the pushing her into it must come from you." Palmerston did not receive this advice until 15 August, but the previous communications may well have contributed to the decision to take the dramatic step of summoning the Ambassadors to consultation.[1]

Molé, on the other hand, when Lamb's information was communicated to him, roused Granville's indignation by suggesting that the conference should take place in Paris, a more neutral place. Were not the interests of France and Britain identical, asked the Ambassador? But he explained this attitude to Palmerston as due to Molé's extreme jealousy of Sébastiani. Palmerston had seen such objections overcome in 1830 and might hope that he could do so now, especially as Sébastiani now, like Talleyrand then, was wholeheartedly on the British side.[2]

Palmerston persisted in separate negotiations with the Ambassadors until he received on 8 August Nesselrode's despatch to Pozzo di Borgo. He at once pointed out to the Russian Ambassador the alarm that would be caused by separate action on the part of Russia. His attempt to meet the immediate threat from Mehemet had already shewn how difficult it was to arrange

---

[1] From Lamb, 19 June, 1838: *F.O. Austria*, 271; do., 19 July, 10 Aug., 1838: *B.P.* See P. E. Mosely, *Russian Diplomacy*, etc., 76, for the Russian pressure on Metternich. M. Sabry has pointed out (*L'Empire Egyptien*, 416) that Metternich was the first to suggest a conference but he does not realise the issues at stake nor pursue the development of the question.

[2] From Granville, 9 July, 1838: *F.O. France*, 562.

concerted action by an interchange of views between the capitals. But over all lay the menace of separate action by Russia on the basis of her treaty. Her intentions even now were obscure. The only way, therefore, was to endeavour to obtain a negotiation in London to work out a substitute for it and arrange the methods by which common action could be obtained.[1]

It must be admitted that the means by which Palmerston sought to obtain this result were very unorthodox. For Esterhazy, Pozzo di Borgo and Bülow each received on 13 August a little note inviting them all to meet him at the Foreign Office next day. Only Sébastiani had been admitted to Palmerston's confidence. To the others no reason had been given and the subject of discussion might well have been the Belgian Question then under consideration in conference. Palmerston confessed to Sébastiani that he took this course for fear Pozzo di Borgo would stay away if he knew the object of the meeting. The three Ambassadors, however, consulted together and were pretty sure that it was Palmerston's intention to bring the Eastern Question before them. They eventually decided to go, but only after Esterhazy had agreed to see Palmerston first and warn him that he must not ask his visitors to make any statement but simply inform them of the views of his government. Palmerston admitted that his procedure was irregular, but promised that his object was no more than Esterhazy had suggested. He in fact next day expressed to the four Ambassadors the pleasure of the British Government at the unity of ideas manifested in the instructions sent to Alexandria, pointing out, however, that Britain had gone further than the others by declaring that Mehemet's persistence in his determination would mean that he must consider himself in a state of war with Britain. It might be hoped that these declarations would be effective for their purpose. But it would still be desirable to concert together in London as to the measures to be taken by the five Powers in case Mehemet Ali committed an act of aggression against his Sovereign and so disturbed the peace. He asked them to obtain the instructions of their Governments for that purpose. Sébastiani, primed by Palmerston, immediately said that he had such instructions. Esterhazy and Bülow said they would ask for them. Pozzo di Borgo said nothing at all. Perhaps that was what Palmerston anticipated. For his object, according to Sébastiani,

[1] P. E. Mosely, *Russian Diplomacy, etc.*, 79.

who seems to have been much in his confidence at this time, was either to confine Russia more and more in the bonds of a 'concert préalable' or else to force her to reveal clearly by her refusal the true secret of her oriental policy.[1]

Metternich, as we have seen, had already agreed that this particular crisis should be settled at London. Esterhazy tried to make matters easier by insisting that there was no question of setting up a 'conference' in London but only of establishing a 'concert' between them. Both Melbourne and Palmerston, he said, appreciated that point fully. Metternich knew well enough that this distinction of form, which he had often used himself, meant very little. The real question was where the issue between Russia and Britain was to be decided. In any case he was already pledged to Russia, though he could not very well confess this to Lamb. The fact that he had gone to Italy for the coronation ceremonies caused some delay and when Lamb, who went to attend them, pressed him for instructions he always promised them but none were sent. Lamb put this dilatoriness down to old age and feebleness but Metternich knew very well what he was doing.[2]

Meanwhile Pozzo di Borgo had reported the incident in an agony of fear and indignation. Palmerston increased the Ambassador's dismay by following up the meeting with a note in answer to Nesselrode's despatch. It was only at Esterhazy's urgent desire that he omitted from it an explicit reference to the Treaty of Unkiar Skelessi. But he insisted that, though Mehemet had given way on this occasion, he might try again unless means were taken to see that the Five Powers were really united on the Eastern Question. These must not be unprepared in the future. "Unanimity can be arrived at", he stated, "only by previous concert." He pressed Pozzo di Borgo, therefore, to obtain instructions from his Court to enable him to take part in discussions on the subject at London. All this took place while the Persian dispute was beginning and Pozzo di Borgo was frightened to death. But he had little influence on the decisions of his Court who recognised his inadequacy to the occasion.

---

[1] Sébastiani to Molé, 14 Aug., 1838: *A.A.E.* Esterhazy to Metternich, 18 Aug., 1848: *V. St. A.* Molé revealed Sébastiani's despatch to the Russian Envoy, but the motive had been fairly obvious. (P. E. Mosely, *Russian Diplomacy, etc.,* 80.)

[2] Esterhazy to Metternich, 18 Aug., 1838. From Lamb, 25 Oct., 1838: *F.O. Austria*, 272.

The answer which Nesselrode despatched at his master's orders simply reaffirmed the previous note, declared that the British position was perfectly well appreciated by the Emperor and that no 'concert préalable' was necessary. On the contrary, it would be more likely to create differences than produce unanimity. Palmerston now determined to make the issue perfectly clear by explicit reference to the Treaty of Unkiar Skelessi. In a reply, sent to the British Ambassador at St. Petersburg, he reaffirmed with great emphasis his view that "Europe never would endure that the matter should be settled by the single independent and self-regulated interference of any one Power, acting according to its own will or without concert with any other Power." Russia had no doubt acted with the best intentions in 1829 and in 1833. But in each case she had obtained advantages for herself, in the one case increase of territory, in the other the Treaty of Unkiar Skelessi. Britain could not allow such a thing to happen again "to the detriment of other Powers", and he believed that the French government took the same view.

This was plain speaking, indeed. But Palmerston used the opportunity to point the moral. "That, therefore", he went on, "the only way in which the Turkey could be assisted without risking a disturbance of the peace would be by the establishment of that concert between the Five Powers which Her Majesty's Government have proposed." When this despatch was read to Nesselrode he appeared a good deal moved. He protested that Russia considered the Treaty of Unkiar Skelessi a burden and added that the sole condition to their advantage, the closing of the Dardanelles, applied only to a state of war. The acquisition on the Danube had been trifling. He denied that he had ever intimated that Russia would occupy Syria if Mehemet attacked, but only that she would defend the Sultan if Mehemet approached Constantinople. On the question of the concert he was silent. The incident was now closed and only formal despatches followed. But there can be no doubt that Palmerston's emphatic warning had great influence on Russian policy when the crisis came next year.[1]

The attempt to establish a concert to negotiate a new European

---

[1] Esterhazy to Metternich, 10 Sept., 1838: *V. St. A.* To Pozzo di Borgo, 3 Sept., 1838; To Clanricarde, 10 Oct., 1838, From Clanricarde, 20 Nov., 1838: *F.O. Russia*, 247, 243, 244.

treaty was, therefore, again a failure. But, like the attempt to organise joint forces described in Section 5, it was a great contribution towards a settlement. It made clear to the other Governments exactly what the British position was. Russia profited by the warning, France did not. Metternich saw that he could rely on British determination and with that support proposed to follow at Vienna the very course Palmerston had suggested should be taken at London. But there could be no question in anyone's mind, including his critics in the Cabinet and the diplomatic service, that Palmerston had shewn himself more 'European' than any other statesman. He had accepted action with Russia; he had urged France and Austria to join with him. He had abandoned, no doubt largely because France was unreliable, the policy of the two maritime Powers acting together against the three Eastern ones. He had placed British policy on the strongest possible basis. The Eastern Question was for all the Great Powers to decide in concert, not for any one of them to control by a special treaty.

5. THE SULTAN AND HIS VASSAL

The contest for the Sultan's favour revolved round the problem of driving Mehemet Ali out of Syria, the Sultan's passionate desire. Mahmud preferred British help to Russian for that purpose because he knew that Britain wished to preserve the Ottoman Empire and that Russia wished ultimately to destroy it. He relied in the last resource on the British fleet to keep him safe from Russian aggression. He also made effort after effort to induce the British Government to give him help to attack his vassal but always without success. He had, therefore, to keep a way of retreat to Russia who had protected him from the Pasha in 1833 and was bound by treaty to do so again if necessary. But Russia also denied him all help to attack; the Treaty of Unkiar Skelessi was purely defensive. Of the discussions between the Porte and the Russian Ambassador on that question we are not yet very accurately informed, but at any rate the Sultan met with the same refusal at St. Petersburg as in London.

The Sultan often threatened to attack by himself. He thought —and events after his death showed he was right—that the Great Powers would be bound to come to his aid whatever happened. The risk of a defeat was better than the prolongation of the armed hostility that existed between him and the Pasha and the consequent exhaustion of his financial resources. He had to be restrained. Palmerston continually sent peremptory orders to Ponsonby to stop him and inform him that his plan was impossible, that he would be beaten and that an appeal by him to Russia might cause the overthrow of his Empire. Ponsonby carried out these orders in his own way. He always gave hope that the Sultan's desire would one day be carried out. In this sense he encouraged him to keep an attack on Mehemet in mind. But he always advised against the attack at that particular moment. He also preferred, if possible, to allow the representatives of other Courts to take the lead in such action which always angered the Sultan and made him less amenable to advice. Butenev, the Russian Ambassador, acted in exactly the same way, though his quieter methods drew less attention to himself and the Russian Government sometimes managed an affair behind his back so as not to embarrass him.

Ponsonby's recipe for gaining the victory over Russia continued to be the same as he had advocated in 1834, the British fleet in the Sea of Marmora. Once it was there, the Sultan was safe from Russian naval attack and British influence would be established at Constantinople. He continually claimed that Russia would accept this situation without war, though sometimes he—and Palmerston had the same thought occasionally—did not see how the problem could ever be resolved until war came and Russia's supremacy in the Black Sea was destroyed. But Palmerston saw clearly the consequences of such a struggle, and desired to avoid or at any rate postpone it. If Russia insisted on isolated action he would not shrink from war. But he would not be the aggressor and he always had hopes, which ultimately proved to be well founded, that once the situation in the West had been cleared up, he would be able to get without war a solution satisfactory to British interests.

That solution necessarily involved the expulsion of Mehemet from Syria. Ponsonby now vehemently supported the Sultan on that question and Palmerston agreed wholeheartedly. Indeed all the European Powers accepted this view. Even Russia advocated it strongly and Broglie and other French Ministers. Metternich never wavered regarding it. Russia was the most suspect, and Ponsonby was convinced that not only did she wish the Pasha to remain in Syria in order to weaken the Sultan, but even had an agreement with him to that effect, and Palmerston was sometimes almost ready to share that opinion. There is no substance in this charge, but Russia's conduct often seemed suspicious and she always insisted that she had no obligation to defend more of the Ottoman Empire in Asia than the Straits.

Wellington, as we have seen, was shocked at Ponsonby's attitude, which the Ambassador made no effort to change when the Tories came in, and would have dismissed him if he had dared. This judgment was partly due to the summoning of the fleet from Malta to Vourla Bay by Ponsonby because of the situation at Constantinople and the Sultan's determination to break with Mehemet. Wellington told Esterhazy that the summoning of the fleet was a proof of Ponsonby's incapacity. Accordingly he cancelled the general instruction concerning the fleet, which, he said, enabled an Ambassador to involve his country in war. The French Government was immediately informed by him of what he had done.[1]

When Palmerston came back he told Ponsonby that the sending of the fleet to Constantinople would not solve the problem. In any case Britain must tackle first the more pressing one of Spain. Ponsonby for a time said little about it. No doubt he thought the position of the Whig Government precarious. In August, however, he made a frank confession of his views. The new Government, he thought, had not the energy to solve the Eastern Question, though Palmerston's own nerves were strong and his opinion sound. He did not wish to remain at Constantinople if England in fact abandoned the Sultan. "This, I think", he went on, "depends upon accident. It depends upon the decision of the Sultan as to a war with Mehemet Ali. If that takes place the British Government will have no choice; it will be bound to act with arms in its hand or give up the ghost. I think the Sultan will make war on Mehemet Ali. I am certain he ought to do so. He cannot long support the present state of things in comparison with which defeat by Mehemet in the field would be an advantage. . . . Remember I tell you that I think it probable the Sultan will make war and that if so, unless he shall be completely victorious you must interfere, and even if it be so, I doubt if you will be able to avoid taking a strong part."

In the autumn Ponsonby ("that I may acquire a certain responsibility," he explained) began to put these views in rather more guarded language in his despatches. In 1835 the Syrians showed much opposition to Ibrahim's administration and the fanatical Druses of the 'Mountain', Lebanon, had to be repressed. Ponsonby announced that the Sultan was contemplating attack, giving details of movements of Turkish troops and fleet, and implied that the Sultan hoped to bring in the Russians and then the British and French and so emancipate himself from his two enemies at the same time. "It will be madness in you to oppose the Sultan's resolution," he said in a private letter, . . . "I will assert that you will never be able to do any good with Turkey until Mehemet Ali is destroyed and he will be destroyed by any war he shall

[1] Esterhazy to Metternich, 11, 27 March, 1835: *V. St. A.* Wellington to Ponsonby, 16 March, 1835: *F.O. Turkey*, 251. Wellington to Aston, 17 March, 1835: *F.O. France*, 497. Medem told Wellington that if the British fleet went to Constantinople the Russians would attack by land.

make on the Sultan even though he should obtain another great victory."[1]

These prophecies were fulfilled to the letter in 1839, but everything depended on when the crisis would come and what the diplomatic situation would be when it did come. Palmerston, as has been seen, was engaged in endeavouring to produce a treaty which would make it possible for Britain and France to act together at Constantinople and perhaps use their fleets. But these negotiations had hardly begun and clearly it was necessary to wait. Palmerston instructed Ponsonby to use his utmost endeavours to stop the attack. Time, he repeated, was on the Sultan's side. And he ordered him to warn the Turkish Ministers that if the Sultan forced the issue, "the British Government will never allow itself to be thus forced into war by the caprice or wrongheadedness of another Government; and . . . would find means to protect her own interests without regard to those of a Government which would thus have deliberately sought to bring on a general war in Europe for its own selfish interests."[2]

Ponsonby consistently refused to speak in this way to the Sultan's advisers. Such a course, he said, would throw Turkey into the arms of Russia, undermine all his own influence and produce the very result Palmerston was anxious to avoid. But he was able to announce that he had taken steps to make it certain that Turkey would not attack. No doubt one of the means used was to support the mission of M. Blaque which came to such an untimely end. The Sultan promised not to attack until the result of that mission was known. Though the British agent, Richard Wood, reported that Emir Bechir and his subjects were ready to cooperate with the Turks in driving out the Egyptians, the crisis died down.[3]

Ponsonby could be sure of Palmerston's approval so long as the immediate attack was prevented. For he knew that his chief was in sympathy with his main thesis. "You have all along taken a just view of the position of affairs," Palmerston wrote privately,

[1] To Ponsonby, 16 July, 1835: *B.P.* From Ponsonby, 11, 30 Oct., 1835. *F.O. Turkey,* 255, 256; do., 19 Aug., 27 Sept., 1835: *B.P.*

[2] To Ponsonby, 4 Nov., 8 Dec., 1835: *F.O. Turkey,* 251. The strong wording of the first dispatch was partly due to a wish to satisfy Melbourne to whom Ellice had complained after his passage through Constantinople with Durham. To Melbourne, 31 Oct., 1835: *B.P.*

[3] From Ponsonby, 29 Dec., 1835, 4 Jan., 5 Feb., 1836: *F.O. Turkey,* 256, 276. Richard Wood's reports were consistently hostile to Ibrahim and Campbell insisted that he did not do him justice. But the events of 1840 showed that Wood had judged rightly.

"and perhaps you are right in the remedies you propose, that is to say the employment of force, but considerations connected with home affairs and the circumstances of other parts of Europe prevent us from adopting these means. For my part I believe that England alone and unaided by any other power would enable Turkey to defend herself against Russia, for that, if we and Turkey had, as we should have, the command of the Black Sea, Russia would not be able to get access to the Balkans."[1]

Thus encouraged, Ponsonby continued to expound his views in private letters. "In this question", he wrote on 8 April, "the possession of the Sultan is the main spring. If we have him our voluntary and real friend we can so arrange matters as to obtain *against* Russia whatever we may think necessary without giving Russia the least stateable or just cause of complaint." If Russia did oppose, she would expose her whole position. "It is wholly impossible", he went on, "for H.M.'s Govt. to prevent a war between the Sultan and Mehemet Ali, and I think it folly (excuse the word) to attempt it, for in the attempt the sacrifice will be made of the greatest strength we have for the preservation of a general peace, and this will be made clear, by events, to all the world, and the Government be answerable for bringing on that war which they may easily avoid by acting so as to keep the Sultan their fast friend. I have placed you in the situation to obtain this great good. If you do not chuse to avail yourself of it I am not to blame."[2]

Meanwhile there had been an incident which had added to the growing criticism of Ponsonby at the capitals of Europe and of which the Russian representatives, chagrined at the increase of British influence over the Sultan, took full advantage. At the end of January 1836 Roussin told Ponsonby that the Turkish Ministers had informed him that the Russian dragoman had warned them that, convinced that England meditated attack, the Tsar intended to put the Treaty of Unkiar Skelessi into operation and occupy the Dardanelles with Russian troops. Roussin had replied that England and France were united and now consulted Ponsonby as to the necessary action. The latter told his colleague that he was not authorised to act, but that if the crisis came and the Sultan "demanded *privately but officially*" the support of the British

---

[1] To Ponsonby, 15 Dec., 1835: *B.P.*
[2] From Ponsonby, 6 Feb., 8 April, 1836: *B.P.*

squadron, he would write to the Admiral saying that it was necessary to protect the Sultan and would personally take the responsibility.   According to Ponsonby the French Ambassador said
he would do likewise.   Ponsonby reported his action home and
said that if he had done wrong he hoped that he might be informed
in order that he might tell the Sultan to make the best terms he
could with the "victorious Muscovite".   The declaration of Roussin, he added, had done much good in encouraging the Turk and
alarming the Russians.   Austria, he claimed, would side with
England and France, if they showed that they were determined to
resist Russia.

In a private letter, sent at the same time, Ponsonby wrote that
he thought the Russians were convinced that they had lost their
influence over the Sultan, and that they could not accept such a
situation: "I think Nicolas *dares* not lose the game here for fear
of the consequences of his defeat upon his subjects.   I am confident he cannot win the game if he be opposed by the will of the
Sultan and that if he risk any movement unsanctioned by the
Sultan he will be ruined by that measure. . . .   I suspect that a
black cloud hangs over him and will destroy him.   I think Poland
will press him down and finish him, as human, if not poetical,
justice requires should be the case."   He asked for Palmerston's
approbation: "I am certain that if war can be avoided it will be by
the measures I have so long and patiently matured and that the
overthrow of the Russian influence here was necessary to preserve
peace."[1]

When, at Palmerston's desire, Granville asked the French
Ministers about this incident, they at first denied all knowledge of
it, but subsequently Desages produced a report of discussions of a
very different colour.   Roussin did not admit that he had agreed
to act with Ponsonby, but stated that he had warned Ponsonby
that it was his language that was provoking the Russians and that
the Ambassador had replied "that it was true England did not
wish for an immediate war with Russia and that Lord Palmerston
had written to him in this sense in a private communication, but
Lord P[onsonby] said, I will nevertheless bring it about because

[1] From Ponsonby, 7 Feb., 1836: *F.O. Turkey*, 273; do., 8 Feb., 1836: *B.P*
cf. Sabry, *L'Empire Egyptien*, 307.   Professor Puryear (*International Economics,
etc.*, 45), gave Roussin's account of this incident in a note, but did not check it
by the British archives.   Dr. Bolsover had succinctly and correctly reported it
from that source.   (*Slavonic Review*, July, 1934, 12.)

I conceive it to be in the interest of my country." When Roussin said England and France were unprepared for war, Ponsonby insisted that Russia was also unprepared, that he could at any moment order the English Admiral to station his fleet in the Dardanelles and the Admiral would have to bear the responsibility if he refused.

There seems little doubt that this is a garbled account of the interview, possibly due to difficulties of language. It is near enough to Ponsonby's account to make a mistake quite possible. It must also be remembered that Roussin was jealous of Ponsonby's success and that the latter was on far better terms with the French Secretary of Embassy, D'Eyragues, than with Roussin himself. The French Government took little notice of the despatch until Granville made enquiries, though they had hinted on more than one occasion that Ponsonby was not carrying out his orders. They cannot have taken Roussin's report very seriously. Palmerston not only believed Ponsonby but in a sense accepted his point of view. "What we ought to do", he told Granville, "is to sign our treaty, offer it to Turkey, and send our two fleets to the entrance of the Dardanelles, with orders to go up to Constantinople the moment they were invited to do so by the Sultan. We *ought* then to tell Mehemet Ali to evacuate Syria and retire into his proper shell in Egypt. To this many members of our Cabinet would I fear object, and I suspect the French Government is not quite prepared for it. But it is clear that while Mehemet Ali has a great army in Syria, the Sultan must keep the greater part of his forces in Asia Minor, and leave his northern frontier undefended." Thus the Sultan was in the power of Russia and Mehemet, and, while Britain and France could control the latter, they must wait until the Sultan had reorganised his forces before trying to redress the balance against Russia.

But at the same time Palmerston, as he promised Granville, instructed Ponsonby that Britain's aim was peace and for that reason the Sultan must be kept quiet: "Our line is simply this. We wish to maintain peace and shall certainly not provoke war; we hope to keep at peace; but there are certain things we shall not stand; and we are resolved to uphold the integrity and independance of the Turkish Empire. Pray conform your language to this." And then he warned him that he had many detractors who tried "to make out that your language is too warlike," Edward

Ellice among them, and of a "cock and bull story" that Ponsonby had said that "we were determined to go to war with Russia". Though the Ambassador might adapt Palmerston's language if he thought it too severe, he must exhort the Sultan in the strongest measure to keep the peace. This advice he reiterated a month later when he heard of M. Blaque's mission. Until the secret agent arrived he would not give an official answer "upon the subject of the attack which the Sultan contemplates making upon Mehemet Ali." But Mehemet had turned seventy. "Is it not better", he asked Ponsonby, "for the Sultan to wait the cooperation of his sure ally than to risk his own existence by precipitate rashness?"[1]

The proof of Palmerston's confidence that Ponsonby would carry out these orders lies in his renewal of the Ambassador's power to summon the fleet to Constantinople, if the Sultan asked for it. This would be a defensive measure against Russia rather than an aggressive one against Mehemet. It was clear that if Russia did intend to occupy the Dardanelles, which not only the incident at Constantinople, but much information from Russia showed was possible, the situation could only be saved if the British fleet got there first. Palmerston must have had some difficulty in obtaining these instructions, but no record has come down about them and possibly the fear of Russian aggression, which was felt in all quarters at this time, helped the Cabinet to approve an action which was after all only precautionary.

Ponsonby himself had shown no great desire to be given back his instructions and in reporting the incident he had said that he had no need of them. "Have you ever known", he wrote, "the cause why the Duke of Wellington withdrew from me the powers entrusted to me by your instructions of 10th March 1834? I know his reasons and I think them very discreditable, to his understanding at least. I may however be glad to be free from the responsibility they would have laid upon me, were I not always willing to risk everything to serve the Govt. and the country. I think these instructions were like the last trump at Whist and sure to win the game under the circumstances that *they* anticipated. You have now before yourself the facts upon which to act and I have no need of the instructions as things are."

[1] To Granville, 1, 12 March, 1836. From Granville, 11 March, 1836; To Ponsonby [Blank] April, 10 May, 1836: *B.P.*; do., 7 May, 1836: *F.O. Turkey*, 271.

But Palmerston obviously thought it better to regularise the position. Suggestions had been made for the use of the fleets in 1833 and the French Admiral had contemplated going through the Dardanelles. Such a situation might well recur. What was Ponsonby to do if the Sultan appealed to him for aid? There would be no time for reference to London. Power was, therefore, given him with the same restrictions as before. Only if the Sultan himself invited the fleet and only if the Admiral agreed that there was no naval risk could the Ambassador order it to pass the Dardanelles. Ponsonby had already given assurances that his power to summon the fleet would only be used as a last resource to anticipate a Russian entry. Palmerston endorsed this attitude with a solemn warning that the power was only to be used in "case of urgent and demonstrable necessity", because if a precedent were so created the Russian fleet was in a position to take advantage of it more often than the British.[1]

By this time the return of Silistria to the Porte by the Tsar had convinced some of the Cabinet of the truth of Durham's reports and even made an impression on the public, though Ponsonby declared that it was simply done to humbug Britain and France. No doubt this was one of the means by which the Russian Government regained to some extent the confidence of the Sultan. Then occurred the Churchill incident narrated above, which was used by the Russian party for the same purpose, and, as we have seen, Ponsonby's reputation and spirits fell to a low ebb in the autumn of 1836 and winter of 1837.

Palmerston on the other hand was especially anxious to keep things quiet in the East because the struggle in Spain had reached its height. "We are defending Turkey in the Basque Provinces," he wrote, "and John Hay and his squadron are rescuing the Dardanelles from Russia at Passages and St. Sebastian." Ponsonby did keep things quiet, and it seems unlikely that he had any responsibility for the dispatch of the *Vixen* which was entirely due to Urquhart's influence on Bell. Palmerston naturally refused to consider a suggestion derived from Roussin, which Molé made Sébastiani put forward as his own invention, that France should take the initiative in a mediation between the Sultan and Mehemet. He wanted, he said, the *status quo* preserved. Roussin on the

---

[1] From Ponsonby, 8 Feb., 1836: *B.P.* To Ponsonby, 20 June, 1836: *F.O. Turkey*, 271.

other hand was a busybody. He got the Sultan himself to make some sort of approach to Mehemet Ali, and at the end of 1836 Sarim Effendi, an experienced official of the second rank, had been sent to Alexandria to sound the Pasha as to a reconciliation. Some suggestion that he should be guaranteed the succession of his children in Egypt and part of his Syrian dominions seems to have been made in return for the surrender of the rest of his territory, but the negotiation was conducted on the most oriental lines and neither Campbell nor anyone else seems to have discovered what exactly took place.[1]

At any rate no arrangement was arrived at and it is improbable that the Sultan expected any other result. After this failure he made another appeal for help to Ponsonby in vague language which the Ambassador did not press on Palmerston with his usual vigour. It was of course refused. "We can give the Sultan no encouragement in his warlike propensities against Mehemet; and you may extinguish all hope he may entertain of that," wrote Palmerston. Ponsonby as usual altered the terms of the refusal in order to avoid "serious discouragement" of the Sultan. The Sultan remained quiet, but Ponsonby continued to assert throughout the years that he could get the Sultan to allow British ships to enter the Black Sea if Palmerston would permit him to insist on doing so. Austria and Prussia would be only too glad, he claimed, and what could Russia do? Palmerston made no response.[2]

Thus the situation remained until the middle of 1838. The Sultan was enjoined to improve his army and wait. Ponsonby claimed credit for "the exertions I have made to keep the Sultan upon the strictest line of pacific policy consistent with measures of self defence", and for "the counsel I gave him not to permit his

[1] To Ponsonby, 17 Jan., 1837: *B.P.* For the *Vixen* incident see above, p. 571. From Campbell, 20 Dec., 1836, 9, 21, 24, 27 Jan., 7 April, 1837: *F.O. Turkey,* 284, 319. The negotiation broke down on the rank to be accorded to Ibrahim, but there was much communication between Pertev and Mehemet of which little is known. cf. Sabry, *L'Empire Egyptien,* 321–322. Note to Sébastiani, 7 Nov., 1836, Sébastiani to Molé, 11 Nov., 1836, *A.A.E.* Desages wrote long accounts of Roussin's action to Bourqueney, explained how he had ordered D'Eyragues to refute it after Roussin had gone on leave. Sarim Effendi, he wrote, was "un espèce de *moi* ou de Backhouse" (8 Nov., 1836, 14 April, 1837: *Bour. P.*) Metternich's advice to the Porte was to give way on Egypt but on nothing else and to take advantage of Mehemet's refusal to withdraw the offer of Acre. From Lamb, 31 March, 1837: *F.O. Austria,* 264.

[2] To Ponsonby, 11 May, 1837; From Ponsonby, 7 June, 7 July, 1837: *B.P.* Mavrojeni urged the same course on Lamb at Vienna.

army to fight a general action under any circumstances of provo-
cation". The Ambassador continued to insist that Russia was
pushing the Sultan on while at the same time secretly encouraging
Mehemet. This last charge is, of course, not true, but Russia
preferred to leave to Ponsonby the task of restraining the Sultan.
Moreover, we now know that the Russian Government was ready
to seize the Dardanelles and Bosphorus in force if the Sultan were
to call on Britain and France to assist him at Constantinople.
Palmerston's endeavours to obtain a European concert on the
Eastern Question already narrated aroused great suspicions, and
the Tsar put pressure on the Austrian Court during the Toeplitz
meeting of this year to wean Metternich from Lamb's dangerous
influence, while at the same time he behaved in a more conciliatory
manner towards France.[1]

Thus Ponsonby's expectations that he might wake up one morning and find a Russian squadron on the Sea of Marmora were not
quite so foolish as his critics thought. He reluctantly admitted
that Palmerston would not apply his own remedy, a British squadron at Constantinople, before the Russians could get there. But
he was pressing now for the right to apply to the Sultan for
permission for British frigates to pass through the Straits and
explore the Black Sea. He rightly thought that the Tsar intended
the Black Sea to be a *Mare Clausum* and wished that no other
warships sail on it. Since all the Powers were at peace, Russia, he
said, could not object. He wrote Lamb a bullying despatch to
urge Melbourne to accept his plan. That Ambassador was
indignant and suggested that Palmerston should make Ponsonby
realise that it was time enough for Ambassadors to be warlike when
their Governments were. Palmerston had contemplated sending surveying vessels through the straits but he was in no mood
for Ponsonby's plan. "To do what?", he wrote on Ponsonby's
letter. He entirely agreed with Lamb's strictures. He knew
that the diplomatic situation was not yet sufficiently favourable for
action.[2]

Then came the news that Mehemet was about to declare his
independence. Throughout these years Palmerston had grown
more and more hostile to the Pasha and come to regard him as the

[1] From Ponsonby, 11 March, 1838: *B.P.* The Russian policy of this year
has been revealed by P. E. Mosely (*Russian Diplomacy*, 40–42).
[2] From Ponsonby, 27 May, 1838; From Lamb, 4 May, 25 June, 1838: *B.P.*

great stumbling block to the solution of the Eastern Question. Nearly all his agents succumbed to the wiles of Mehemet. The British agents in Syria reported, it is true, the discontent of the population with Ibrahim's rule and especially his methods of conscription. Richard Wood and Farren were especially critical. But Campbell grew more and more favourable to Mehemet and refused to admit the validity of these reports. Though he carried out Palmerston's orders there can be little doubt that his sympathetic attitude had some effect on Mehemet. When Bowring went out in 1838 to investigate the commercial possibilities of Egypt, he too fell under Mehemet's spell and undoubtedly encouraged him to think that he would have some support in Britain for his plans.[1]

Since 1834 Palmerston had supported every move to break down Mehemet's power and to keep him subordinate to the Sultan even though it was not yet possible to turn him out of Syria. He welcomed for that reason the Sultan's abolition of monopolies in the commercial convention. He had already strongly insisted on Mehemet carrying out the abolition of the silk monopoly in Syria. He suspected Mehemet of wishing to annex the Pashalik of Baghdad (quite wrongly for it was not in the Pasha's view worth having) and protested against the occupation of Dair by Ibrahim which he thought was a preliminary to such a plan. He viewed with growing anxiety the Pasha's gradual conquest of the Arabian peninsula which was intensified in 1837. The Government of India in 1838 had already taken steps to exclude Mehemet from further penetration of the Red Sea by the negotiation for the lease of Aden to Britain.[3]

This was the situation when Mehemet suddenly announced to

[1] Palmerston told Campbell to "undo the mischief" Bowring had done (4 Aug., 1838: *B.P.*). Bowring later tried to repudiate the accounts of his language and said Mehemet Ali had misrepresented him, and Campbell reported that Bowring had always told Mehemet that he could not speak for his Government on official questions. The Pasha's move, he claimed, was due to Prokesch and French influence. It was at this time that Campbell sent home Prokesch's report of 1833 first published by M. Sabry (*L'Empire Egyptien*, 271). It was no doubt sent at this time to divert Palmerston's attention from Campbell himself and Bowring, whose attitude Campbell had welcomed.

[2] For the action as to Aden see the admirable account by Dodwell (*The Founder of Modern Egypt*, 145–151) who has used the India Office Papers, and a recent article by Halford L. Hoskins, "Background of the British Position in Arabia," *The Middle East Journal*, April, 1947. Researches are now being made in the Egyptian Archives into this significant but little known activity of Mehemet Ali. For the connection of this problem with the Persian attack on Herat see Chapter VIII, Section 5, p. 749.

the Consuls-General at Alexandria that he intended to declare his independence of the Sultan. The motives which prompted him to do so at this time are not exactly known, but in spite of the fact that his son Ibrahim was strongly against such a step, Mehemet's patience seems at last to have given way and he determined to make an attempt to get his family established, relying on the disunion of the Powers to prevent any action against him. The Sultan was greatly alarmed. If Mehemet became independent, Mahmud would no longer be sovereign of the Holy Cities on which to some extent his whole claim to rule the Ottoman Empire depended.

Palmerston took up the challenge at once. Such a threat might bring on immediate war and the Russian fleet to the Bosphorus. He thought that the crisis which he had so long tried to prevent had come at last and was resolved to use it if he could to clear up the whole Eastern Question. His first thought, in spite of Melbourne's opposition, was joint action by France and England on the lines suggested in 1836. He did not expect Austria to do anything, but a treaty of the two Powers with the Sultan would at any rate legalise the entry of the British and French fleets into the Dardanelles if necessary. Indeed, he wrote, a treaty with Britain alone might be sufficient. He proposed, therefore, a plan to Melbourne for an Anglo-French Turkish convention. But Granville poured cold water on this project which he did not think Molé would accept. And the Cabinet when consulted wished an offer to be made both to Russia and to Austria to join the Maritime Powers in defence of the Sultan. The former might send her fleet to act conjointly with those of Britain and France, while Austria might furnish land forces in Syria, an old idea of Palmerston's, which he had already without much hope of success suggested to Lamb when the first rumours of Mehemet's intentions reached him.[1]

---

[1] From Ponsonby, 25 June, 1838: *F.O. Turkey*, 331. To Granville, 5, 8 June, 1838: *Bulwer*, II, 266–7, and *B.P.* (Bulwer's version gives a very inadequate idea of these letters). To Granville, 16 June, 1838: *B.P.* This letter described a one-article convention by which Britain and France would provide naval aid at any time in the next eight years if Mehemet attacked or declared himself independent. The Sultan was to promise not to ask for aid from any other source except on urgent necessity and with the agreement of the French and British Ambassadors. Melbourne deprecated a treaty. France, he wrote, was an unreliable partner and would merely look after her own interests. "It may be necessary to defend Turkey but I should not like to be bound to defend her. . . . I agree with you that there is every appearance of the coming on of considerable difficulties, but our policy is to have our hands free." (3 June, 1838: *B.P.*)

The first thing, however, was to get all the Powers to protest energetically at Alexandria. This was the more necessary as the French Consul-General was showing every sign of sympathy with Mehemet's demands and Campbell was not much better. In this matter there was no great difficulty. Molé refused, it is true, to make joint representations. But no doubt Desages gave him some good advice. At any rate Molé and Palmerston consulted together and each was entirely satisfied with the despatches of the other. The despatch which Palmerston sent to Alexandria was written in his best manner and warned Mehemet that he was much mistaken if he relied on the jealousies of the European forces to protect him from Britain's wrath. Metternich readily agreed to do likewise, thought Palmerston's despatch admirable and engaged to get Russia to send a similar one at the Toeplitz meeting. Nesselrode did do so, but, in his despatch to Pozzo di Borgo concerning it, he hinted that Russia was in a different position to the other Powers because the Treaty of Unkiar Skelessi bound her to assist the Sultan if he demanded her aid. As has been noted in Section 4 it was this claim which produced such a great effect on Palmerston and led him to make a special effort to force Russia to substitute a general European treaty for that of Unkiar Skelessi.[1]

But meanwhile no common plan for action against Mehemet could be made. Palmerston discussed the problem with Sébastiani, Esterhazy and Pozzo di Borgo in a series of interviews. All were most helpful. Pozzo di Borgo, though he was alarmed about Constantinople, suggested that the British fleet should go to Egypt. Sébastiani not only wished the British and French fleets to cruise together, but agreed with Palmerston and recommended to his Government that a land force might be necessary and that Austrian forces would cause the least jealousy if used for this purpose. He was ready for the Russian fleet to act with the British and French fleets in the Mediterranean. Louis Philippe professed himself delighted at this idea of Austrian troops but unfortunately Molé, whose jealousy of his own Ambassador was almost equal to that which he had had of Talleyrand in 1830, was furious at Sébastiani taking so much on himself. He absolutely

[1] To Campbell, 9 June, 7 July, 1838: *F.O. Turkey*, 343. To Granville, 3 July, 1838: *F.O. France*, 557; do., 6 July, 1838, *Bulwer*, II, 370 and *B.P.* From Granville, 11, 15, 18, 22 June, 1838: *F.O. France*, 562. Esterhazy to Metternich, 26 June, 1838: *V. St. A.* Nesselrode to Pozzo di Borgo, 23 July, 1838: *F.O. Russia*, 247. See above, Section 4, p. 591.

refused to agree, stating that such a move would be unpopular in France, though he professed himself ready for the British and French fleets to act together if Mehemet persisted in his intention. He added that the two Governments might also consider how to reconcile the Sultan and the Pasha on the basis of the hereditary succession of Mehemet's family not only in Egypt but in Syria. These hesitations naturally confirmed all Palmerston's suspicions of French good faith, though Granville and Louis Philippe himself attributed them to Molé's jealousy of Sébastiani. It was in fact, as Louis Philippe well knew, something more than this. Molé was much more ready to get into touch with Russia than with Britain. The effect on Palmerston was apparent, as Esterhazy noted, though with Sébastiani his relations continued to be as intimate as before. Nor could Lamb get anything further out of Metternich who was off to see Nicholas at Toeplitz. The dispute with Russia concerning Persia also complicated matters. In the final result nothing was done but to get the British and Turkish fleets ready.[1]

Thus no international naval action was obtained, and for long Palmerston was very anxious lest Russia should send a force to Constantinople or to Asia Minor at the Sultan's request. This anxiety was increased by the Persian dispute which was now becoming acute. Palmerston was, it is true, prepared to invite a Russian squadron to cruise with the British and French fleets in the Mediterranean. But we know in fact that preparations were being made for isolated action by Russia, and that Pozzo di Borgo himself had already suggested that the right place for the Russian troops was Constantinople and that the task of stopping Mehemet in Asia Minor could be left to others.

Fortunately Mehemet was impressed by the series of warnings received from the Consuls-General and with many protestations and complaints gradually withdrew from his position. Further action was not necessary. But Palmerston's efforts had been worth while. They were to be repeated with better success in 1840 and had taught him much of the manner in which he could obtain

---

[1] To Granville, 3 July, 1838: *F.O. France*, 557; do., 8 June, 6 July: *Bulwer*, II, 268, 270 and *B.P.* From Granville, 11, 15, 18, 22 June, 2, 6, 9, 13, 16 July, 1838: *F.O. France*, 562; do., 2, 9, 16 July, 1838: *B.P.* Esterhazy to Metternich, 26 June, 3, 22 July, 1838: *V. St. A.* Sébastiani to Molé, 12, 29 June, 12, 19 July, 1838; Molé to Sébastiani, 7 July, 1838: *A.A.E.* Esterhazy early noted that Palmerston seemed almost as suspicious of France as of Russia.

his ends without a European war. And his energy, directness and readiness to accept the suggestions of others for a common object had impressed all those with whom he had come into contact.[1]

Meanwhile Ponsonby had made the Sultan keep quiet while his defence was being prepared. The Ambassador believed that Mehemet had been stirred up by Russia, and Palmerston at the outset was inclined to agree, but not because of the reports that the Turkish Ministers thought so. "It is natural", Palmerston wrote on 23 June, "that they who know we are jealous of Russia and also want to set us against Mehemet should tell us that their enemy and ours are secretly friends to each other. But it is in the nature of things that it should be so: and no assertions will make me disbelieve it." Moreover, though British and French fleets could intercept Egyptian vessels if the Sultan ordered them to do so, they could not touch neutrals. He wanted, therefore, the Turkish fleet to cruise with the British and French fleets, after a convention had been made between the two Governments and the Sultan. "Such a convention", he went on, "might lead naturally and without the appearance of any intention hostile to Russia to a part of our squadron coming up to Constantinople either to escort the Turkish ships down, or to help to fit them out, or to accompany them."

Ponsonby had already sent for the British fleet to move from Malta. He sent a letter through the Austrian post which claimed that the Sultan could defeat Mehemet and implied that Mehemet was following Russian advice: "*Disorder* and *difficulties* in Turkey", he wrote "are the means for bringing about Russian ends." But his conduct was otherwise unimpeachable, though, of course, he supported the Sultan's position by every means in his power. Reschid declared that the Sultan would never consent to his vassal's demand, and Ponsonby himself pointed out that Mehemet's assumption of independence would mean that, since the Sultan would no longer be the Sovereign of the Holy Cities, a new Caliph might be set up. He suggested that Chrysanowski should be put in command of the Turkish forces. But even though he was informed that the Russians had offered naval and military forces to the

[1] Sébastiani to Molé, 14, 24 Aug., 1838: *A.A.E.* Pozzo di Borgo to Nesselrode, 3 July, 1838: P. E. Mosely, *Russian Diplomacy, etc.*, 148. From Campbell, 16 Aug., 5 Sept., 1838: *F.O. Turkey*, 343.

Sultan, his conduct was most circumspect. He urged the Sultan
to be quiet and when the French Ambassador objected to the
Turkish squadron going to sea lest it should come into collision
with Mehemet's fleet, he advised that it should go to Tripoli or
Malta and avoid Syria.[1]

He was naturally immensely moved by Palmerston's proposal
for a convention for the defence of the Sultan and immediately
tackled Reschid on the subject. But even here he was, though
verbose, very careful, and while suggesting the employment of a
British fleet if the Sultan entered into the necessary contracts to
obtain it, explained that only if Mehemet persisted was such a
contingency possible and made no mention of the entry of British
ships into the Dardanelles, lest by some leakage Russia should get
to hear of it and use it as an excuse for action. There followed a
series of conferences with Reschid Pasha and Mustapha Kamil
Bey in which the relations with Russia were discussed. The
Sultan authorised the Ministers to declare that he would not apply
for Russian aid, but in return asked for an assurance that England
would protect him from Russian attack. Ponsonby, who of course
had no official authorisation to make any such declaration, handled
the matter very skilfully by appealing to promises made in the
King's speech in Parliament of maintaining the integrity of the
Ottoman Empire and of Palmerston's recent assurances to Reschid
in London which that Minister confirmed. In the end he obtained
a letter from Reschid in which it was stated that the Sultan had not
the slightest intention of asking Russia for help, that none such had
yet been offered and that the Porte was ready to seek British naval
aid along the lines Ponsonby had suggested.

These proceedings, which occurred during the negotiations for
the commercial convention, excited the greatest suspicion of
Roussin who was already very jealous of Ponsonby's success. He
imagined that a loan had been offered as part of a treaty of alliance
and demanded information from Ponsonby. Ponsonby did not
disclose the subject of his meetings and thought that he had
convinced the Ambassador that they were solely concerned with

[1] To Ponsonby, 23 June, 1838: *B.P.* From Ponsonby, 6, 11, 14, 24, 25 June,
1838. *F.O. Turkey*, 331; do., 6ᵗʰ June, 1838: *V. St. A.* Husrev objected to
Chrysanowski's appointment (30 July, 1838: *B.P.*). Ponsonby on several
occasions sent letters by the Austrian courier containing criticisms of Russia.
Lamb protested; but it may be that Ponsonby's apparent carelessness was
calculated.

the commercial convention. Roussin, however, naturally sent home an account of the incident to his Government and made the uncooperative and suspicious Molé still more unready to allow the French and British fleets to act together.

The French Government suspected that in order to obtain the convention Britain had offered an alliance. This is of course untrue, and there is nothing in the communication which Ponsonby made to the Porte different from the plans which Palmerston had for long discussed with the French Government. But the desire to obtain British help in an attack on Mehemet was one of the reasons why the Sultan agreed to the commercial convention, and it is probable that it would not have been obtained at this moment if these discussions had not made it seem more likely that such aid could be obtained.[1]

Since Mehemet withdrew his claims nothing tangible could immediately result. The French fleet did not cooperate with the British but the Turkish fleet did. Palmerston now suggested a joint cruise as a means of showing the friendly relations between the two Governments and exercising the Turkish navy rather than as a demonstration against Mehemet. It served that purpose, but the absence of the French fleet did not go unremarked in Europe.

There was of course no question in Palmerston's mind of the fleet now going up to Constantinople. The danger had passed. Ponsonby refused to believe it and insisted that the *status quo*, rejected by both the Sultan and Mehemet, was only supported by Russia and France for their own interests. The Pasha would act in order to get out of enforcing the commercial convention. Ponsonby still hoped, therefore, to be allowed to bring the fleet up to Constantinople, a course which he claimed was not a breach of the Treaty of Unkiar Skelessi. He was furious when Admiral Stopford refused to stay in the neighbourhood of the Straits in spite of all appeals. "It is one thing to face iron bullets," he wrote, "and that Admirals will always do, but some of them are devilishly afraid of paper bullets." And he urged Palmerston to clinch the

---

[1] From Ponsonby, 30 July, 1838; Reschid Pasha to Ponsonby, 28 July, 1838: B.P. and *Bulwer*, II, 272, who omits the concluding passage. Professor Puryear has given an account of Roussin's suspicions. He, like other historians, found it difficult to account for them, since there is no mention of Ponsonby's discussions with Reschid in the official correspondence. (*International Economics, etc.*, 82–83.)

success just obtained in Persia by sending the British fleet into the Dardanelles. But Palmerston thoroughly approved of Stopford's action and again warned Ponsonby that there was nothing to be gained in getting the fleet to Constantinople unless it had a definite object. Nor when he heard of Reschid's mission to London did he give the slightest encouragement that an offensive treaty could be made. On the contrary he suggested that perhaps the best arrangement was to offer Mehemet the hereditary succession of his family in Egypt in return for the evacuation of Syria.[1]

Thus the action at Constantinople amounted to little more than a joint fleet exercise. But this also contributed to the solution in 1840. It showed the hesitations of France, the possibility of the British fleet acting with the Turkish and thus obtaining a better legal and moral position than if it acted alone, and the fact that the Tsar was not prepared to give the final orders to occupy the Bosphorus even when the Turks were clearly acting under the guidance of Britain in their defence against the Pasha.

The ageing and ailing Sultan, though again disappointed, had noted the vigorous action of Palmerston, more prompt and effective than that of any other Government. He determined to make one more attempt to obtain the countenance and support of Britain before he forced the issue by attacking Mehemet on his sole responsibility. That was, in his mind, the object of Reschid's mission. The Ambassador was to explore the situation at Vienna, Berlin and Paris on his way to London. But it was to Palmerston that the Sultan's appeal was really directed. This step was apparently concerted between Reschid and the Sultan without much consultation with Ponsonby who believed it much more important to get the fleet to Constantinople than to make a treaty. He was afraid of Russia using the threat from Mehemet to reestablish her ascendancy once more. But for the Sultan it was Mehemet and not Russia that was the enemy. He wanted the British fleet on his side, to crush him.

---

[1] To Ponsonby, 15 Sept., 11 Dec., 1838: *F.O. Turkey*, 329A; do., 10 Aug., 13 Sept., 2 Oct., 1838: *B.P.* (*Bulwer*, II, 282, gives part of the letter of 13 Sept.) From Ponsonby, 19, 27 Sept., 3, 13, 20, 29 Oct., 1838: *F.O. Turkey*, 332; do., 27 Sept., 17, 20 Oct., 1838: *B.P.* Ponsonby had, however, told Stopford to keep away from the entrance to the Dardanelles when the Russians complained that his fleet was a threat. V. J. Puryear (*International Economics, etc.*, 94–96) describes Ponsonby's manoeuvres in some detail but does not mention Palmerston's despatch of 11 December approving the Admiral's action. On one private letter of Ponsonby (20 Oct.) Palmerston pencilled 'Stuff'.

Reschid's mission was ill-starred from the beginning. He got no encouragement at Vienna or Berlin on his way. At London he found Palmerston absorbed in other matters and in no mood to respond to the Sultan's entreaties. At the end of December Reschid tried to spur him into action by urging that the Russians had the ear of the Sultan and had persuaded him to refuse all conference on the Eastern Question at London. Britain and France must shew proofs that they were ready to act against Mehemet if they were to prevail. But the discussions still went on slowly while conflicting reports as to the Sultan's intentions came from Constantinople. Reschid of course had to recognise that Palmerston could only consider a defensive treaty. But the exact shape of this was not easy to devise and Palmerston had much other business. Not until the 13 March, 1839, was Palmerston able to tell Ponsonby that the Cabinet had agreed on the principle of the defensive treaty which Reschid had proposed. The fall of Molé, he added, would enable Britain to cooperate with a French Government at Constantinople.

Just at this time Reschid, who seems to have given up hope of action, informed Palmerston that a defensive treaty was now useless since Ibrahim's preparations had caused the Sultan to order an immediate attack. Palmerston sent immediately instructions to Ponsonby to urge the Sultan to remain quiet, while Reschid sent to Constantinople a draft treaty on which he and Palmerston had agreed through of course nothing had been signed. It amounted to no more than an agreement for the British and Turkish fleets to act together in case Mehemet or his sons were 'disobedient'. Nothing was said of depriving him of Syria and his other possessions outside Egypt.[1]

[1] From Reschid Pasha, 28 Dec., 1838, 12 March, 1839; To Ponsonby, 13 March, 1839: *B.P.*; do., 15 March, 1839: *L.P.*, I, No. 7. The best account of Reschid's Mission is in P. E. Mosely, *Russian Diplomacy, etc.*, 120–133. It is founded on what the Turks told the Russian Ambassador about it. There is little about it in the Foreign Office Archives or the Broadland Papers. In an interview with Tsartoriski in March 1839 Reschid dwelt pessimistically on the situation of the Sultan, a cruel tyrant whose camarilla was the worst he ever had and wholly under Russian influence. Though ostensibly advising peace the Russians were secretly urging the Sultan to attack. He himself would not return to Constantinople except with a British fleet. He had no wish for the same fate as Pertev. (*Tsartoriski Archives*, Cracow, XX, No. 5294.) Tsartoriski also had an interview with Palmerston who explained to him him how impossible it was to attack Russia in the Black Sea or to send a British fleet to Constantinople. When Tsartoriski reminded him of British actions at Naples and Copenhagen, Palmerston replied that Britain would only use moral force which, with that of France and Austria would be sufficient to stop Russia. (do.)

Since the Sultan now determined to attack, this proposal was useless. The Turkish Reis Effendi, Nouri Pasha, informed Ponsonby that it would do more harm than good. The Ambassador who knew little of what had passed between Palmerston and Reschid pressed the Sultan's Ministers to accept it, but without avail. Henceforward, as later events were to shew, the Sultan was determined to force the hands of the Great Powers by attacking Ibrahim. Nouri, it is true, asked both Stürmer and Ponsonby for a treaty the object of which should be to deprive Mehemet of his possessions. But this cannot have been done with any expectations that it would be accepted. The intention of the Sultan was more clearly indicated by the anger with which Nouri received Ponsonby's transmission of Palmerston's entreaties not to attack. For once the Ambassador could not make up his mind as to how far Russia was behind these warlike moves. Officially she was reported as urging the Sultan to keep the peace, but Ponsonby suspected, quite erroneously, that her agents were secretly inciting the Sultan and Hafiz Pasha, the Commander-in-Chief, to attack Ibrahim. He had, indeed, lost the Sultan's confidence and was out of touch with what was planned. His faithfulness in carrying out Palmerston's instructions had, as he had so often prophesied would be the case, deprived him at this critical moment of the commanding position which he had enjoyed in the counsels of the Porte.[1]

Meanwhile, had not Peel behaved so stiffly to the Queen over her Ladies, Palmerston would have been no longer Secretary of State. Among the last things he did before the Melbourne Government resigned on 7 May was to get Melbourne to make Lamb Baron Beauvale and reward Ponsonby with a Viscountcy for his great services at Constantinople. Reschid had informed him at the end of April that better news had come from Constantinople and that peace was assured. He prepared, therefore, when the Whigs resumed office, to go on with the negotiations for a defensive treaty with the Sultan in spite of Reschid's insistence that it would not be well received. Reschid had in fact been warned by Pozzo di Borgo and Orlov of the Russian opposition

[1] From Ponsonby, 27 Jan., 12 Feb., 7, 19, 23 March, 7 April, 1839: *F.O. Turkey*, 354–356. All references to Russian policy were cut out in the *Levant Papers*. From Ponsonby, 22 April, 1839: *F.O. Turkey*, 356 (part in *L.P.*, I, No. 26) with minute of draft treaty; do., 1 May, 1839. Nouri Pasha to Ponsonby, 28 April, 1839: *L.P.*, I, No. 37; do., 21 May, 1839: *L.P.*, I, No. 47.

to the treaty and received fresh instructions from Constantinople. Palmerston did not know this, and, as, after much manoeuvring, a new Government had been formed at Paris under Soult, he hoped for French cooperation. Meanwhile the young Tsarevitch was making an excellent impression in London. But Palmerston had hardly begun to take stock of the situation when news came that the Sultan's armies had crossed the Euphrates and the conflict with Mehemet Ali, so long expected and feared, had at last really begun.[1]

[1] From Reschid Pasha, 27 April, 1839: *L.P.*, I, No. 21. P. Mosely, *Russian Diplomacy, etc.*, 132–133. To Ponsonby, 14 May, 1839: *B.P.* "Recid tells me the Sultan will not thank us for any treaty which shall not bind us to turn Ibrahim out of Syria. We shall see. We have got a French Government and France is an European power again, at least for the present." To Granville, 10 May, 1839: "The Grand Duke succeeds here amazingly. . . . I gave him a dinner of fifty people at this office." *Granville P.* T. Schiemann, *Geschichte Russlands*, III, 363. Pozzo di Borgo had tried to stop the visit on the ground that the Tsarevitch would be badly received.

CHAPTER VIII

MEHEMET ALI AND THE STRAITS: THE TRIUMPH IN THE EASTERN QUESTION 1839–1841

1. COOPERATION WITH FRANCE AND AUSTRIA, 1839

2. THE RAPPROCHEMENT WITH RUSSIA, 1839
   - (i) THE FIRST FAILURE
   - (ii) THE TSAR ACCEPTS THE BRITISH CONDITIONS

3. THE CONVENTION OF 15 JULY, 1840

4. THE CONVENTION OF 15 JULY, 1840, IN OPERATION

5. THE CONTEST IN CENTRAL ASIA, 1837–1841

6. THE SETTLEMENT WITH MEHEMET ALI AND THE STRAITS CONVENTION OF 13 JULY, 1841

" Never, I will answer for it, was a great measure undertaken upon a basis of support so slender and so uncertain."
MELBOURNE, 14 September, 1840.

" Mehemet Ali is like a lie and will be destroyed as that is by truth." PONSONBY, 12 August, 1840.

CHAPTER VIII

MEHEMET ALI AND THE STRAITS: THE TRIUMPH IN THE EASTERN QUESTION
1839–1841

THE triumph of Palmerston in 1840 was perhaps the greatest which he ever won in his long connection with foreign affairs. At one time he stood almost alone, not only in Europe but in his own country, for a policy which he thought essential for British interests and the preservation of peace. His energy and resource, both diplomatic and administrative, obtained results which astonished nearly all his contemporaries. At the same time, in the long-drawn-out negotiation he shewed a patience and readiness to wait for the right moment such as he rarely achieved. No British Foreign Minister, save perhaps Canning, won such a diplomatic victory with a Cabinet so divided on the main issue. He wielded every weapon in the diplomatic armoury with unerring skill; intimidation, conciliation, flattery, personal appeal were all employed at the appropriate time. Meagre military resources were used with their maximum effect. Palmerston could not control the appointment of Admirals and Generals. But he got the inadequate military leaders who were supplied by the Admiralty and the Horse Guards provided with more skilful and bold subordinates. At the end even his enemies recognised the greatness of the achievement.

This result was obtained because Palmerston sought ends which in the long run even those who opposed him saw were necessary. The time was not ripe for a dissolution of the Ottoman Empire which would almost certainly have occurred if Palmerston had not had his way. The failure of Mahmud's final fling at his vassal, so disastrous in its results, would have deprived the Porte permanently of the rule of all the Arab-speaking lands, including the Holy Places, unless it had been rescued by European, mainly British, action. Had Mehemet obtained the hereditary rule of these large dominions, the prestige of the Sultan would have been so reduced that his control over the European provinces could hardly have been preserved. Europe was not ready to face such a problem nor were the subject populations of the Porte ready for liberation. It is most probable that the result would have been a war between the Great Powers. All came in time to see the dangers of inaction and the necessary remedies, but it was Palmerston who ensured that they were applied. Amongst them was the closing of the Straits, which by the wise agreement of Palmerston, Metternich and the Tsar's advisers, was for the first time made part of the public law of Europe. No deviation from its principles has ever been successful.

Palmerston succeeded partly because London became the diplomatic centre where these problems were discussed. That advantage was obtained by a policy of self-abnegation which he must have found it hard to apply. He abandoned without protest both his desire to have the problem settled under his personal supervision and his scheme to guarantee the integrity of the Ottoman Empire. He thus won Austria and later Russia to his side. He allowed France to make the running at the start. It seemed at the outset, indeed, that France and Austria would play a far larger part than Britain in the settlement. Both took the initiative and in the early stages of the discussion were far more prominent in devising schemes to meet the danger. Metternich succeeded at last, so he thought, in making Vienna the diplomatic capital of Europe. Louis Philippe had confronted Russia, so he thought, with a combination not only of France and Britain but of Austria and Prussia as well. Palmerston, far from shewing jealousy of either of these two Powers, cooperated wholeheartedly with both of them. In April his Government had fallen and in May, when it was first realised that this time Mahmud meant business, it had scarcely recovered sufficiently for Palmerston to take the lead. He himself seems to have realised rather slowly the gravity of the danger. But though it came somewhat late neither France nor Austria could complain of the support which he gave them when he had obtained Cabinet approval. Vienna was accepted as the place of negotiation and France's desire to check isolated Russian action supported to the full. This close cooperation finally resulted in the five Great Powers undertaking the responsibility of settling the problem in such a manner that the integrity and independence of the Ottoman Empire should be maintained.

Then two things transformed the situation. The complete defeat and death of the Sultan and the skilful propaganda of Mehemet Ali led many Frenchmen to imagine that a great Arab state could be brought into existence under French auspices. The Tsar with some justice suspected that Metternich was as much opposed to Russia as the maritime Powers and preferred to deal directly with Britain. He accepted the view that it was in the best interests of Russia, as well as of Europe, that the Sultan's Empire in Asia Minor should be preserved and that the Straits should be put under European protection. Palmerston had already proclaimed these principles and remained faithful to them so that he was able to come to terms with Russia. France abandoned the first while seeking to enforce the second and thus lost all control over the negotiations. Metternich, made ill by the Tsar's contemptuous dismissal of his services which the Western Powers had accepted, never recovered his powers of decision and vacillated interminably. Palmerston assumed the leadership thus offered him and mastered the appalling difficulties of the situation, not only preserving the Ottoman Empire but winning the respect and cooperation of Russia. This he obtained also as regards Persia and Afghanistan as well as in the decisions concerning the Straits and Asia Minor. He lost, it is true, the *entente* with France, but, as has been seen, that was already worn out. The situation in Western and Central Europe had been stabilised and the greatest threat to British influence there was not that of the Eastern Powers but of France herself.

The story has been told many times, but there are still some parts of it which are difficult to unravel. In Russia the final decisions were taken by the Tsar and the arguments which decided him are not exactly known. Louis Philippe, who decided those of France, was the most prolific talker of all the actors in the drama, but the advice of the permanent civil servants, the gold of Mehemet Ali, the ambitions of French politicians and the pride of the French people had all to be taken into account by him and the rest of the world. Palmerston's hardest fights were in his own Cabinet and with sections of public opinion in Britain, partly inspired by attachment to France and hatred of Russia, partly by personal dislike and jealousy of Palmerston himself.

As courageous men always do he found some devoted and able supporters. Minto and Hobhouse were strong allies in the Cabinet. Much of the Tory opposition under Wellington's patriotic leadership rallied to his side. But in the long run everything depended on the energy and determination of Palmerston himself. In the end all recognised that it was a personal as well as a national triumph.

1. COOPERATION WITH FRANCE AND AUSTRIA
1839

The Sultan's attempt to obtain British support for an attack on Mehemet had been due to his determination to make one in any event in the spring of 1839. However disappointed he might be at the result of the negotiations at London, the attack was still to take place. No doubt Mahmud felt his health failing and that he could not back his own life against the tough old vassal who had so long defied him. He could not continue, as he frequently explained to Ponsonby, to remain indefinitely in a state of armed suspense. Such a situation was worse than the defeat which his friends warned him was likely to come. He continued, therefore, to accumulate men and provisions and prepare his Seraskier, Hafiz Pasha, for an attack on Ibrahim's forces. His hopes of success were increased by the news of unrest in Syria, which might even be optimistically called an insurrection against Ibrahim. But there can also be no doubt that he relied in the last resort on the intervention of the Great Powers, and especially of Britain. He thought that she was bound to come to his aid in a new clash of arms however much Palmerston refused to pledge himself. His diagnosis was a correct one. Though he did not live to see the success of his plan, his final fling was one of the most astute of his long and chequered career.

From the beginning of the year there were indications of the Sultan's intentions in the movements of troops, and indeed he made no secret of them. But all this had been said and done before and for a considerable time they were not taken very seriously by anyone. In the spring both the British and French Governments were in a state of dissolution. In Britain the Whig Cabinet resigned in May on the weak support given by the House to its West Indian policy, but the tactless conduct of Peel and Wellington over the Queen's Ladies had brought it back to office for another two years. It was, however, much shaken and was preoccupied with domestic questions. The Prime Minister was more than ever absorbed in the special problems of his royal mistress and had little time for foreign affairs.

In France there was a long period of intricate negotiation before

Louis Philippe obtained a Cabinet which would satisfy the Chamber while remaining sufficiently obedient to himself. Neither the Doctrinaires nor Thiers were members of it and Soult was both Premier and Foreign Minister. He was a strong Anglophil, for he had been immensely touched by the attention paid to him in London by his old enemies during the coronation festivities. The relief to Palmerston and Granville after dealing with Molé was immense. But Soult was a vain and emotional man who never fully understood the intricate foreign questions with which he had to deal. Policy was as before decided by the King, but the despatches of the officials received even less control from Soult than from either his predecessors or successors. It was only natural that France failed to find a consistent line of action under his leadership. Neither Roussin at Constantinople nor Sébastiani at London were able to interpret to the satisfaction of the Quai d'Orsay the shifts and subtleties of French policy and both had to go. Barante at St. Petersburg shewed excessive zeal. But Soult himself was all for action and under his inspiration France pressed eagerly forward to take control of a problem in which she thought she had a very special position.

Metternich also saw in the crisis an opportunity. He perceived the seriousness of the situation sooner than anyone else and thought that out of the clash of interests he could at last realise his dream of making Vienna once more the diplomatic centre of Europe. Remembering Palmerston's attempt to draw the Eastern Question to London in 1838, he was determined this time to anticipate him and with unusual energy set all his machinery in motion to get the Great Powers to settle it at Vienna, not by a formal conference, for that was not the medium in which he best excelled, but in informal discussions. He expected to be the intermediary between the maritime Powers and Russia and instead of playing the inactive and humiliating role of 1833 to emerge as the dominating figure of European diplomacy. He seems to have been in no doubt that, if France and Britain accepted this position, the Tsar would welcome such assistance from the man who had been most closely associated with him since 1830.

For the Tsar himself the crisis came at a most inconvenient time. He had not yet settled his dispute with Britain over Persia though the tension had eased. But his main attention was concentrated on family affairs. For him the marriage of his daughter

Marie to the Leuchtenberg Prince was an event of great importance, all the more so in that it was ill-received by his German
relations. He was also engaged in considering the marriage of the
Crown Prince whose attachment to a Polish lady was causing him
grave anxiety. For reasons of which the Tsar was unaware the
Prince's choice of a wife had widened the breach with Prussia.[1]
Finally he was preparing to celebrate the unveiling of a memorial
on the field of Borodino with a reproduction of the battle on a
magnificent scale, a task all the more congenial because it was not
likely to please the French. London, Paris and Vienna were all
without a Russian Ambassador and the Chargés d'Affaires were
men of no great ability or influence. All the Tsar and his Ministers
wished was for the Sultan and Mehemet to keep quiet and nothing
could be less true than the suspicions which Ponsonby sent home
by every courier, and which Palmerston for a time shared, that the
crisis had been produced by the secret encouragement of the
Russians in order that they might reestablish their position at
Constantinople before the Treaty of Unkiar Skelessi came to an
end in 1841.

Though Ponsonby's reports grew increasingly alarmist Palmerston took little notice of them. As has been noted he repeated
officially his usual warning to the Sultan not to attack and he was
of course reiterating the same advice to Reschid Pasha in London
while he pressed on him a purely defensive treaty between Britain
and Turkey. He was occupied with the final stages of the Belgian
Question, the dispute with Persia, the question of Afghanistan and
the growing difficulties in Canton. He responded less promptly
than usual to the warnings from Constantinople and made no
diplomatic preparation to implement the policy which he had laid
down in 1838. It may be, though there is no indication of it, that
he thought that his position would be stronger if he allowed others
to take the initiative instead of taking the lead himself as he had
done the previous year. At the same time he was determined, as
we have repeatedly seen, that the situation of 1833 was not to recur.
If Russia attempted to use the Treaty of Unkiar Skelessi to send
her fleets and soldiers once more to Constantinople to protect the
Sultan, the British fleet would go there also. He could be certain

[1] From William Russell, 2 Oct., 1839: *B.P.* The Princess of Hesse Darmstadt was believed by the Prussian Court to be the daughter of a Frenchman, the
tutor of the elder children of her mother, a fact "which has almost brought about
a rupture between the Courts".

that Louis Philippe, after nearly nine years of contemptuous treatment from the Tsar, would be ready for the French fleet to accompany it.

But in addition Palmerston, as Mahmud foresaw, was determined that a solution must also be found for the conflict between
the Sultan and the Pasha and that that could only be the return
of Syria to the Sultan's control. He had made up his mind that
Mehemet possessed so large a portion of the Ottoman Empire
that its very existence was threatened. The relation of Sultan and
vassal was no protection while the Sultan had no control over the
Egyptian army and fleet. The desert must be placed as a frontier
between the Sultan's dominions and Egypt. The latter was in
effect lost to the Sultan as much as the rest of North Africa, and
Mehemet could be allowed to establish his family there. But
Asia Minor was different. There was no barrier to the expansion
of Mehemet's power there and the valley of the Euphrates might
well pass under his control with what Palmerston thought was the
best short route to the East. But even more important than this
was the weakening of the Sultan's power and prestige to such an
extent that he could not perform his function of guarding the
Straits and preserving Balkan Europe from Russian aggression.
To prevent this catastrophe was Palmerston's object from the very
beginning of the crisis and he never departed from it, though
forced to compromise on some points by the opposition of some
of his colleagues. He was almost alone in Europe in thinking it
possible to expel Mehemet from Syria, though Metternich agreed
also from the outset that it was by far the best solution if it could
be obtained.

Early in May news reached Constantinople which made war
appear certain. The Sultan's troops had crossed the Euphrates.
"The Sultan", wrote Ponsonby, "would rather die or be the vassal
of Russia than not endeavour to destroy the rebel subject." His
entourage hoped much from the Syrian revolt but, they added, "if
we should be beaten we are still sure of succour from Russia."
Ponsonby—and it was no bad judgment—thought that Russia
would merely attempt to mediate and settle with Mehemet by
giving him hereditary succession of Syria and such new conquests
that he made. Such a settlement, he said, would destroy the
Ottoman Empire. The only way to prevent it was "that England
should immediately resume the right of *equal interference* with

Russia in the settlement of the question." He made no secret of his opinion that Mehemet should be thrown out of Syria. Palmerston himself from the first thought that the opportunity had come to expel Mehemet from Syria while allowing him to have the hereditary government of Egypt. His colleagues, he told Granville, agreed with him, though the Cabinet had not considered the question formally.

"For my own part," he added, "I hate Mehemet Ali whom I consider as nothing by an ignorant barbarian who by cunning and boldness and mother wit has been successful in rebellion and has turned to his own advantage, by breach of trust, power which was confided to him for other purposes. I look upon his boasted civilization of Egypt as the arrantest humbug; and I believe that he is as great a tyrant and oppressor as ever made a people wretched; but there he is and one can not get rid of him altogether without war and all its concomitant evils." He hoped that Austria and Britain would be able together to bring Russia and France to adopt a common policy.[1]

Soult at any rate wanted action to restrain Russia and it was Paris that acted first. Soult on the 28 May sent his aide-de-camp, Captain Callier, to Mehemet to urge him to keep his armies back and to proceed to Ibrahim's headquarters with orders to that effect. Similar pressure was to be put upon the Sultan at Constantinople. Meanwhile Bourqueney's reports and Granville's private letters shewed that so far as the attitude to Russia was concerned the outlook of France and Britain was very similar. Both wished to use Austria to put pressure on the Tsar to accept joint action at Constantinople by all the Great Powers. Palmerston, it is true, shewed some distrust of Metternich's ability and influence which he thought had deteriorated and even suggested a conference in St. Petersburg, while Louis Philippe was more convinced of the value of Austria's assistance and was obviously more ready than Palmerston to see Metternich take control of the situation. There was also complete agreement on joint naval action by France and Britain to enforce their policy. A vote of credit of ten million francs for the increase of the French fleet was hastily passed through an enthusiastic Chamber. In these circum-

---

[1] From Ponsonby, 20 May, 1839: *F.O. Turkey*, 356. All this is left out in *L.P.* I, No. 44, and the whole character of the despatch is thus changed. To Granville, 10 June, 1839: *Granville P.*

stances the French Government took little notice of Palmerston's emphatic statement to Bourqueney that, whatever the rights and wrongs of the dispute, the Great Powers could not be neutral towards Mehemet Ali. They must settle the question this time by getting him out of Syria altogether. Granville's first opinion on the other hand was that Mehemet must get an increase of power. Soult "who was out of his element as a foreign minister" let the question go by, so eager was he to secure Great Power cooperation against Russia.[1]

At Vienna Lord Beauvale saw at once all the implications of the news from Constantinople. He suggested to Palmerston that a conference would be necessary and that Austria should be called upon to shew her flag in the Orient. This plan he did not communicate to Metternich who had told him that this affair would blow over as others before it. In reality, however, Metternich had already determined to act and by the medium of France. He told St. Aulaire, the French Ambassador, that he had already suggested to the Porte to appeal to the five Powers. That would necessitate a conference, or rather a centre of decision, which Metternich implied could only be Vienna. His Ambassador, Count Apponyi, was ordered on 18 May to make the same suggestion at Paris. For some little time Soult rather demurred and told Granville that he would prefer London or Constantinople. But Metternich knew that he could rely on Louis Philippe's passionate desire to break down the isolation from the Eastern Courts which Nicholas had imposed for so long. Thus France accepted Metternich's offer and it was through the medium of France that Palmerston's consent was first asked unofficially. He found it hard to make up his mind. He sent his apologies for the unavoidable delay adding: "If we could get Russia to join in a conference perhaps there would be no harm in having that conference at Vienna as Soult suggests. There would be some advantage in the nearness of Vienna to Constantinople; on the other hand Russian intrigue would be more powerful at Vienna than elsewhere to the Westward." He was unable to get a Cabinet to consider the question during the first part of June and it was a step to which he could

[1] Bourqueney to Soult, 25 May, 1839: Guizot, *Mémoires*, IV, 479; do. 27 May, 1839: *A.A.E.* From Granville, 27 May, 1839: *B.P.* Soult to Cochelet, 28 May, 1839: E. Driault, *L'Egypte et l'Europe*, I, 34. The Prussian Chargé d'Affaires reported from Paris that the vote of credit was inspired by hostility to Britain rather than Russia. A. Hasenclever, *Die Orientalische Frage*, 39.

hardly agree on his own responsibility. The Cabinet also were doubtful: "We do not know what to say about a conference at Vienna. Metternich is so feeble and timid and tricky and so much swayed by Russia, and by nature so prone to crooked paths, to playing off one party against the other; and so fond of staving off difficulties and putting off the evil day, that I greatly doubt whether a Vienna conference would lead to anything good. On the other hand Russia might perhaps consent to a conference there and not elsewhere, knowing Metternich and reckoning upon the influence which she exerts over him and which is not less real because he and Russia hate and distrust each other."[1]

Metternich had, however, also sent Esterhazy back to London and the Ambassador shewed as usual great understanding and tact. Palmerston told to him as well as to Bourqueney all the doubts and hesitations of the Cabinet and their reluctance to increase Metternich's control of the situation by accepting Vienna as the centre of discussion. He was doubtful, he confessed to Beauvale, whether Metternich would carry through such a plan as he himself thought necessary. The Chancellor was too timid to adopt wholeheartedly the Sultan against Mehemet. But if he could be worked up to 'concert pitch', "he would do more to consolidate the peace of Europe than any man has done since the 18th June 1815." Britain would of course give him enthusiastic support. How could Russia object? And, if so, France would be bound to overcome the resistance of the little cabal at Paris that supported Mehemet.

But Palmerston put great faith not only in Beauvale's ability and energy but in the Ambassador's influence over Metternich. If Austrian support was to be obtained, the Ambassador, who had so long been certain of securing it when the emergency came and whose words now seemed to be justified by Metternich's action, was a suitable instrument of British policy. Thus Esterhazy was at last able to report triumphantly to his chief that he had conquered Palmerston's secret desire to make London the centre of the negotiations on the Eastern Question and obtain over them the same influence that he had exercised over those on Belgium. The result had been obtained, he thought, largely because French

[1] From Beauvale, 21 May, 1839: *B.P.* St. Aulaire, *Souvenirs*, 246. From Granville, 31 May, 1839: *B.P.* To Granville, 10, 19, 21 June, 1839. To Beauvale, 20 June, 1839: *Granville P.*

support had first been secured. The gratified Chancellor noted on the despatch that it was for that very reason he had chosen this method of approach.[1]

Metternich was delighted with the new position in which France and Britain had placed him, and his Ambassador's despatches were covered with enthusiastic comments. There was not to be a 'conference' at Vienna, he explained to everybody concerned, but only a centre of discussion in which joint decisions could be arrived at. He gave as a reason for this insistence the right of Turkey to claim representation at any formal conference by appealing to the Protocol of Aix-la-Chapelle. The Belgian discussions had shewn how little this formal right was respected by the Great Powers. But Metternich had always preferred less formal methods and he seems also to have thought that the Tsar would be more ready for Russia to take part in discussions of that kind. Palmerston was ready to agree for the same reason though he noted that by this method Russia would be less bound than if she became a member of a formal conference. One motive of the British Government, he wrote in a despatch, was their confidence in their Ambassador at Vienna. However, as Soult pointed out, the use of the word conference made little real difference; the great thing was to get Russia to cooperate with the rest of Europe.[2]

At any rate, once the decision was taken it was necessary to make it effective. Palmerston at once suggested that the Ambassadors at Vienna should concert with Metternich joint instructions to the Ambassadors at Constantinople and the Admirals of the fleets. This was my plan, wrote the delighted Chancellor on the despatch, and he informed Esterhazy immediately that he accepted the responsibility of obtaining agreement at the 'point central' of Vienna on the instructions to be sent to Constantinople. Beauvale had been more doubtful. He praised Metternich's energy and pointed out to his critical chief how much had already been done to get things going. But he was very conscious of the difficulties of concentrating all decision in Vienna: "Metternich is really anxious that the term conference should not be applied to the discussions upon Eastern Affairs here. At the same time he

[1] Esterhazy to Metternich, 29 June, 3 July, 1839: *V. St. A.* Bourqueney to Soult, 20, 26, 27 June, 1839: Guizot, *Mémoires*, IV, 493; *A.A.E.* To Beauvale (as previous note).
[2] To Beauvale, 28 June, 1839: *F.O. Austria*, 278. From Granville, 22 June, 1839: *L.P.* I, No. 67.

wants something strong enough to give orders both at Constantinople and Alexandria and be obeyed, and above all if there are affairs of importance to be treated of, he wants everything to proceed from this centre, and the separate French action threatening at Constantinople, stopping the Turkish fleet, protecting and counselling Mehemet Ali at Alexandria, to cease. How this is to be unless you could come here I don't know and I told him so, to which he said that a reunion of the Cabinets would be the best thing. Think about it." This was generous of the Ambassador who much appreciated the importance of his own position in the affair. But it shews the inconsistency of Metternich and that he had not yet grasped all the implications of the position which he had so eagerly seized.[1]

Strangest of all was his delay in approaching Russia. Tatischev, the Russian Ambassador, was at St. Petersburg and his Chargé d'Affaires, Struve, was unable to give Metternich any advice on the subject. Metternich's explanation was that he must first secure the agreement of France and Britain. Once that was done he prepared a monumental expedition for St. Petersburg full of flattery for the Tsar but practically announcing a *fait accompli* which he assumed would be accepted. He recommended that the British and French fleets should join the Russian fleet in the Sea of Marmora if Constantinople were threatened. How ill prepared the Tsar was for this communication will be seen.

But in the intervening month of July there was a real 'Concert' at Vienna which obtained results of the greatest importance. For it was here that the steps were taken to deal with the terribly critical position which arose at Constantinople. Metternich was right in claiming that geography made Vienna the natural seat of operations. Had action had to wait for Paris and London to receive the bad news, it would have been too late. For Ibrahim had routed Hafiz Pasha at Nezib on 24 June. Captain Callier had reached him too late to prevent the clash but it was perhaps his influence that caused Ibrahim to refrain from following up the action immediately.[2] The Sultan himself had died of his many

---

[1] Esterhazy to Metternich, 9 July, 1839; Metternich to Esterhazy, 19 July, 1839: *V. St. A.* From Beauvale, 5 July, 1839: *B.P.*

[2] Thiers stated later that Callier promised Mehemet the hereditary possession of Syria. N. Senior, *Conversations*, I, 4. A. Stern, *Geschichte Europas*, V, 390, stated that no such report is in the French Archives. Callier's report in E. Driault, *L'Egypte et l'Europe*, I, 142, shews that he at any rate encouraged him to hope.

disorders on 1 July even before the news of the battle reached him.
The new Sultan was not yet seventeen years of age. Old Husrev
reestablished the office of Grand Vizir in his own person and
attempted to deal with the situation. But his first thought was
to make a deal at almost any price with the enemy at the gates.
This disposition became something like panic when the Ottoman
Fleet left Constantinople and deserted to the enemy. Instead of
appealing to the Great Powers Husrev prepared to send emissaries to
Mehemet with the offer of almost everything which he demanded.
The British and French Ambassadors were kept in the dark as to
this step as long as possible. When they found out what was going
on they reported on it in the most pessimistic terms. Ponsonby
had already attributed the weakness of the Ministers to Russian
intrigue. Russia would prefer, he thought, that Mehemet Ali
should be satisfied rather than send her fleet to Constantinople to
oppose him. Now that Mahmud was dead there was no one to
whom to appeal, and, though Husrev had promised to do nothing
without the assent of the Great Powers, he could not be trusted.
The only remedy was his usual one of the British fleet at Constantinople whether the Turkish Ministers asked for it or not. On the
26 July Ponsonby sent a despairing despatch. Appeasement had
been decided and he believed not only Russia but Austria would
countenance it. In this he was not far wrong. Russia was trying
to get Mehemet to make peace on the basis of adding Orfa and
Diarbekir to his Syrian territories and Metternich later told
Beauvale that Stürmer had confessed that he had advocated concessions. "I consider", wrote Ponsonby, "the Ottoman Empire
to be delivered over to Mehemet Ali and that Russia has been the
chief director of what has been done."[1]

But at the last moment the situation was saved. For Metternich
had already acted. The 'point central' had from the first shewn
zeal and efficiency. St. Aulaire had cooperated eagerly and Beau-

[1] From Ponsonby, 8, 21, 22, 26 July, 1839: *L.P.* Nos. 149, 216, 225 and *F.O.
Turkey*, 357. These despatches, written with more than usual emotion, were
much mutilated before publication, e.g. "The Liberals of Europe will see what
may be called the fortress of the world placed in the hands of the chief support
and representative of despotism". From Beauvale, 11 July, 1839: *L.P.* I, No.
137. "It is clear that Vienna in its relation to that place [Constantinople] is
nearly a month ahead of London and Petersburgh." From Beauvale, 1 Aug.,
1839: *F.O. Austria*, 282 [as to Stürmer]. Goriainow, *Le Bosphore, etc.*, 58–59.
Nesselrode reported to the Tsar that the Porte had intended to offer the hereditary possession of all his territories to Mehemet Ali—and was angry that this
had been stopped.

vale had of course been zealous to get Palmerston's ideas adopted. He was less confident than his chief of the possibility of throwing Mehemet out of Syria and that negotiation had made little progress. But, in concerting fleet action for entry into the Dardanelles, France and Britain had Austrian support and Austrian ships with an Archduke were to be associated in the joint squadrons. That this demonstration seemed more aimed at Russia than at Mehemet Metternich was shortly to find out, but for the moment the union of the three Powers seemed most cordial and the Russian Chargé d'Affaires was not the man to challenge Metternich. When therefore the bad news came pouring in from Constantinople there was a centre ready to deal with it, as both Metternich and Palmerston had hoped. Afraid that the Sultan's Ministers would come to a separate arrangement with Mehemet, Metternich was determined to act at once. He sent an instruction to Stürmer to warn them that they should entrust the future fate of Turkey to the Great Powers who were agreed to maintain its integrity. The Russian Chargé d'Affaires, Struve, also carried out Metternich's request to write to Butenev. The French and British Ambassadors immediately did likewise, Beauvale, though he felt that he was to some extent exceeding his powers, St. Aulaire, influenced by the desire of retaining Austrian and British support against Russia, who might otherwise act alone. But as Beauvale later insisted, the measure was entirely Metternich's own. The others only followed his lead.[1]

These communications produced an immediate effect at Constantinople. Baron Stürmer, however suspect his previous conduct, took instant action and the Prussian representative, as always, of course followed his lead. The French and British Ambassadors felt authorised by their communications from Vienna to associate themselves with him, and in such circumstances the Russian Minister thought it wise to give his support also. Thus resulted the famous collective Note of 27 July, actually presented by the Dragomans of the Five Powers to the Sultan's Ministers on the

[1] From Beauvale, 24 July, 3, 10 Aug., 1839: *B.P.* St. Aulaire, *Souvenirs*, 253–254. There is no clear account in Beauvale's despatches and consequently none in the *Levant Papers*. Metternich himself, because of the shock from Russia which followed, advertised his action but little. This is one reason why historians have never given him due credit for his energy and foresight at so critical a moment. Ponsonby gave the main praise to Beauvale who disclaimed it. St. Aulaire admits that he yielded to the pressure of Metternich and Beauvale.

28th. This stated that instructions had been received by the five
representatives so that they could inform the Porte that "agreement among the Five Great Powers on the Question of the East is
secured" and "invite it to suspend any definitive resolution without
their concurrence, waiting for the effect of the interest which those
powers feel for it." Ponsonby, recovering from his despair, had
himself taken the first action by sending Chrysanowski at 5 a.m. to
warn the Grand Vizir of the news from Vienna. He reported that
the note had been delivered just in time to prevent Husrev's
resignation and enable him to resist both Mehemet and Russia.
He gave warm praise to his old antagonist Stürmer. Butenev's
signature, he said, did not surpise him: "I have long been convinced that Russia would yield whenever really opposed."[1]

The responsibility of settling the dispute between the Porte
and Mehemet was thus thrown squarely on the Five European
Powers. No solution had been agreed but the Porte had at least
a moral claim for better terms than it could have got for itself.
The Great Powers were bound to one another as well as to the
Porte. The dispute had been recognised by all as one for the
'Concert of Europe'. France through her Ambassadors was
bound by this declaration to this point of view, and Russia also.
The obligations of this step affected all the future course of the
negotiations. None of the Five Powers ventured to denounce the
action of their Ambassadors.

But in actual fact before the news of this important step reached
the capitals of the Powers open differences of opinion on fundamental points had occurred. France and Britain had realised that
their policies towards Mehemet were in contradiction and Russia
had repudiated the use of Vienna as a centre. It is now necessary
to retrace the manner in which these two cleavages occurred.
They were revealed at almost the same time and produced a
diplomatic revolution almost as far-reaching in its effects as the
famous one of the eighteenth century. The cleavage between
France and Britain was to prove the deepest and most intractable,
for in the long run the Tsar accepted Metternich's policy, though

[1] From Ponsonby, 29 July, 1839: *F.O. Turkey*, 357. The version in *L.P.* I,
No. 226, leaves out all mention of Ponsonby's own action and of course of his
remarks on Russia. St. Aulaire places the main responsibility for the prompt-
ness at Constantinople on Roussin, but he could hardly know. Metternich
attributed Butenev's cooperation to long standing orders to follow the Austrian
lead and Struve's letter from Vienna. (From Beauvale, 10 Aug., 1839: *B.P.*)
cf. Hasenclever, *Die orientalische Frage*, 55–56, where Stürmer's report is quoted.

not his conduct of it. But the issue between France and Britain could not be resolved until France was forced to withdraw in humiliation and defeat.

During June and July Palmerston had been full of praise for Soult. The reason for the delay in appreciating the situation is a very simple one. During June and July Palmerston had been as eager as France to prevent Russian isolated action. He had followed the French lead in organising measures to prevent such a step. France had gone ahead both in securing Austrian support and in organising a joint naval squadron in the Eastern Mediterranean which should enter the Dardanelles if Russian ships passed the Bosphorus. Palmerston regarded these fleets as directed against Mehemet also. He had from the first put forward his view that Mehemet should be driven out of Syria, whatever the immediate issue of the struggle between him and the Sultan. Soult had not accepted this view and neither had any of the other Powers though Metternich had gone very far in that direction. But both Soult and Louis Philippe had shewn themselves sympathetic to a reduction of Mehemet's power.

When Russia put forward the view that the contest between the Sultan and Pasha should be left alone provided Ibrahim's armies did not advance across the Taurus, and even suggested that Orfa and Diarbekir should be added to the area under his control, both Soult and Louis Philippe—all the more emphatically since Russia had completely ignored France—shewed sympathy with Palmerston's indignant criticisms. Soult, it is true, said that he could not agree that the whole of Syria should be taken from Mehemet, but at any rate he disapproved the policy of inaction which Russia recommended. Louis Philippe went much further. "He agreed", wrote Granville, "not only on the desirableness of restoring the whole of Syria to the Sultan but with all the arguments you adduce in support of your opinion; he thought that the desert between Egypt and Syria was a better boundary between the possessions of the Sultan and of Mehemet Ali than any that could be found in Syria itself." Louis Philippe had, however, also a reservation as to the possibility of obtaining this desirable end. "He was not prepared to say at present", continued Granville, "that we must go to war with Mehemet Ali rather than not obtain it—much must depend upon the opinion of the other Great Powers; if they were all disposed to make that proposition to the Pasha, France would join in it." This was not an absolute promise of the use of force but it naturally left in Palmerston's mind the conviction that, if he could get Austria to agree, France would not lag behind.

On the news of the death of the Sultan the French Government again took the initiative and sent a circular despatch to the other four Powers suggesting that they should all guarantee the independence and integrity of the Ottoman Empire. Palmerston was quite ready to see his old device brought into the foreground again and hastened to send a favourable reply. It was in response to this overture that he used the often-quoted words "Soult is a jewel". Metternich also gave a favourable reply, and Prussia therefore did the same. The effect on the Tsar of this proposal was very different and was one of the causes of his change of front in the next month. But for the moment it seemed to make France the champion of the Ottoman Empire and Palmerston, who of course printed it in the *Levant Papers*, was often to refer to it in later months.[1]

By "independence and integrity" the French officials, if not Soult himself, meant something very different to Palmerston's interpretation, but, though there was considerable difficulty in establishing exact uniformity in the instructions to the Ambassadors and Admirals, the relations between the two Governments remained on an excellent footing until the end of July when the difference between them was first realised. For the defeat of the Sultan's attack, which he ascribed to Russian scheming, seemed to Palmerston to make the reestablishment of the Ottoman Empire all the more urgent. It could not be divided. They must choose between the Sultan and Mehemet as ruler—and the choice could not be doubtful. At the same time, Soult expressed to Granville an opinion "that neither the disastrous overthrow of the Turkish Army, nor the traitorous conduct of the Capudan Pasha, nor the prostrate attitude of the Divan, should affect the course which the Great Powers of Europe intended to pursue." Granville also re-

---

[1] Nesselrode to Pozzo di Borgo, 3/15 June, 1839: *L.P.*, I, No. 74. To Granville, 29 June, 1839. *F.O. France*, 575; *L.P.*, I, No. 82. From Granville, 2 July, 1839: *F.O. France*, 584; *L.P.*, No. 101; do., 2 July, 1839. *B.P.* Palmerston's suspicions of Russia and his proposals for a combination of the other Great Powers against her are of course not given in the *Levant Papers*. They tended to predispose Louis Philippe in his favour. The vagueness of Soult and Granville as to where the desert was much amused Louis Philippe, who was far better informed, and Granville had to ask Palmerston to correct the despatch after it had arrived in London. Soult to Bourqueney, 17 July, 1839 (circular) *L.P.*, I, No. 128. *Bulwer*, II, 295.

ported that Louis Philippe was ready to follow Austria and Britain as regards the conditions of peace between the Sultan and the Pasha, though he warned him that the French Press took a different view and if action were delayed he might not be able to count on French support. Palmerston was delighted and in an official despatch recorded his Government's rejoicing "at the complete identity of opinion on these most important matters between France and England."[1]

In reality the breach had already occurred, for Soult had already signed, but not read, a despatch written by Desages which took a very different line. Cooperation was, indeed, to be maintained but, it was suggested, Mehemet's victory made it necessary to offer better terms than before if he was to be restrained from further attack. This despatch was clearly in complete contradiction with what Soult had said. Bourqueney reported Palmerston's surprise and indignation. Soult found it difficult to explain his conduct when an outspoken despatch arrived at Paris, though Granville acquitted him of any intentional double dealing. He had intended, Soult said, to ascertain Palmerston's view as to what ought to be done. He himself was still inclined to exclude the Pasha from Syria but account must be taken of the views of Austria and Prussia. Thus, while Palmerston demanded that the French and British fleets should be sent to Alexandria to bring back the Turkish fleet by force if necessary, Soult would agree to nothing of the kind. It would be dangerous, he said, to remove the fleets from the Dardanelles. When Granville saw Louis Philippe he found him in full agreement with his Ministers. He would not be easily induced, thought Granville, to run counter to French public opinion which Mehemet's recent successes had caused to run strongly in his favour. Only if Austria would also agree and thus break up the Triple Alliance against France would Louis Philippe consider taking such a step.[2]

This deadlock continued and the difference of opinion grew deeper and deeper. It was in no way composed by the arrival of the news of the joint note of 27 July. Palmerston was of course

---

[1] To Granville, 23 July, 1839: *Granville P.*; do., 30 July, 1839: *L.P.*, I, No. 157. From Granville, 26 July, 1839: *L.P.*, I, No. 156; do., *B.P.*

[2] Soult to Bourqueney, 26 July, 1839: *L.P.*, I, No. 158. Guizot, *Mémoires*, IV, 519. Bourqueney to Soult, 31 July, 1839: Guizot, *Mémoires*, IV, 523. To Granville, 30 July, 1839: *L.P.*, I, No. 159; do., *B.P.* From Granville, 2, 8 Aug., 1839: *L.P.*, I, Nos., 181, 209; do., 2, 8 Aug., 1839: *B.P.*

delighted with it and claimed that it bound the other Powers to adopt his views. The situation, he told the House of Commons, had been entirely transformed by it and the previous instructions were now out of date. In spite of the reports about the defection of Russia, he still looked to Vienna as the centre of action whence new instructions would be issued.

The French Government on the other hand received the news of the note with some dismay. Soult suggested that Russia would repudiate the action of her Ambassador and obviously hoped she would. He got very excited at the suggestion that instructions should be issued from Vienna to the Admirals to act against Mehemet. And, in spite of Sébastiani's contrary advice, Louis Philippe strongly supported the view of his Cabinet, that the question of the Straits must first be settled, since any action against Alexandria might cause Ibrahim to march on Constantinople. The French Government did not venture to repudiate Roussin's action. But it had already suggested to Palmerston that the two Governments should send new Ambassadors to Constantinople. Palmerston had naturally refused to remove Ponsonby and merely ordered him to cooperate more closely with Roussin. Now the French Government decided to recall their own Ambassador and substitute for him someone less sympathetic to the Sultan and more favourable to Mehemet. Meanwhile they refused with growing impatience all Palmerston's suggestions to send, through the Vienna centre, instructions for action against the Pasha. The French Press began to attack British policy, revealing in the process that they had been given information of the confidential discussions between the two Governments. Soult said he was as pained as Palmerston at these criticisms and the simulacrum of friendship was maintained by the special mention of France in the Queen's Speech, the first time for two years that this had been done.[1]

In these circumstances Palmerston began to look more and more to Vienna for help. There for a short time there had been much

---

[1] To Granville, 16 Aug., 1839; To Bulwer, 20 Aug., 1839: *L.P.*, I, Nos., 223, 236. To Granville, 9, 16 Aug., 1839: *Granville P.* From Granville, 12, 16 Aug., 1839: *B.P.* The suggestion about Roussin and Ponsonby was made in July. Roussin was reprimanded at the beginning of September, for transmitting a letter (which he had not read) to the Commander of the Turkish fleet at Alexandria and recalled a few days later. His successor Pontois was appointed as Minister only, to save Roussin's face. From Granville, 5 July, 1839; From Bulwer, 6, 9 Sept., 1839: *B.P.* Bourqueney to Soult, 13, 15, 20, 27 Aug., 1839: *A.A.E.* To Beauvale, 25 Aug., 1839: *V. St. A. Varia.*

diplomatic activity. Both St. Aulaire and Beauvale were pressing for further measures. St. Aulaire was urging Metternich to join with France in insisting on the entry of the fleets into the Dardanelles to support the Turkish Government. Beauvale did not agree to this step and Metternich also refused it. The British Ambassador, on the other hand, was ready to support Soult's proposal of a declaration of the Great Powers that they would maintain the independence and integrity of the Ottoman Empire, and notes were exchanged on this subject. Metternich was shewing, it is true, much hesitation, but his views concerning Mehemet seemed in harmony with those of Britain. Accordingly Palmerston directed to Beauvale his important despatch of 25 August in which he laid before the Great Powers his opinion that Mehemet must be driven out of Syria and the unity of the Ottoman Empire thus be reestablished. In this he suggested, for the first time officially, that the refusal of one Power to agree to such a course of action need not prevent the others from carrying it out. This was meant, of course, as a warning to France as much as to Russia. The 'Concert' at Vienna was to issue the necessary instructions to the Admirals to go to Alexandria and get back the Turkish fleet, or, if that was not possible, to break off diplomatic relations by recalling the Consuls-General. In the private letter that accompanied the despatch he asserted his belief that Soult and Louis Philippe still wished to act with the other Great Powers, but were prevented by the powerful clique of a few hundred Frenchmen who had vested interests in Mehemet's administration. He hoped, however, that France would be drawn in, if action was taken: "I am still not without hopes that all five may be brought to insist on the evacuation of Syria and I am sanguine in expectation that, if that demand is resolutely made, it will be complied with, not, perhaps, at first, but after some little time, if the five Powers shew by their acts that they are in earnest. If that is done, we can get a treaty of restitution [sic] for the Porte by all five Powers or by three for the next ten years."[1]

But before this despatch reached Vienna the whole situation there had been transformed, the 'Concert' had virtually been

---

[1] From Beauvale, 30 July, 1 Aug., 1839: *F.O. Austria*, 281, 2. *L.P.*, I, Nos. 202, 207. From Beauvale, 24, 25 July, 1839; To Beauvale, 25 Aug., 1839: *L.P.*, I, Nos. 248, 249 (circular); do., *V. St. A. Varia*. The letter, which went on to deny that Turkey was worn out, is quoted by F. S. Rodkey, *Journal of Mod. Hist.*, June, 1930, 202.

dissolved and Metternich had retired a shattered man to recover
his health at Johannisberg. For he had received from St. Petersburg an even more humiliating blow than in 1833. At the beginning of the negotiations at Vienna he had confidently expected
Russian approval to all that he was doing and had constantly told
Beauvale that he would answer for the Tsar. Such news as he had
from St. Petersburg seemed to shew that this was so. When no
official despatch came from his Ambassador, Ficquelmont, he
grew somewhat uneasy. Then immediately after his important
instructions had been sent to Constantinople a courier arrived with
despatches which he for a little time tried to conceal from Beauvale
and St. Aulaire. The contents, vague and mainly concerning the
fêtes and celebrations at St. Petersburg, were disquieting. The
news of the death of the Sultan was considered there to have put
an end to the crisis and ensured peace. More extraordinary still,
Ficquelmont was taking advantage of a leave of absence granted
long before and coming home. "I can understand this from
Russia," wrote Beauvale, "it is her game; but Ficquelmont, the
flower of the Austrian diplomacy, what can it mean from him?"
It seemed clear that Russia did not accept Vienna as the main centre
of discussion. But Metternich refused to believe it. He thought,
Beauvale reported, that he could still drag her along: "Il faut
l'envelopper avec nous et elle marchera." Thus the discussions
about guaranteeing the Ottoman Empire, the entry of the fleets
into the Dardanelles, still went on, but with a good deal less zest
than before. It made it all the more necessary, Beauvale thought,
that France and Britain should be closely united. He might then
be able to detach Austria from Russia and get action taken at
Vienna, if Palmerston would give him the necessary powers.
Metternich, he said, was enchanted with Palmerston's condemnation of Mehemet Ali, though he doubted the possibility of taking
such strong measures against him and thought he should have
some part of his Syrian territories for life.[1]

A few days later when Ficquelmont arrived it was realised that
Russia refused all cooperation at Vienna. Metternich was completely out of favour with the Tsar. He had appeared to join
France and Britain in a menace to Russia. Barante's insistence
on the right of entry into the Dardanelles and the exuberant

---

[1] From Beauvale, 25 July, 1 Aug., 1839: *B.P.*; do., 31 July, 2 Aug., 1839:
F.O. Austria, 282.

claims at Paris that Austria had been entirely won over, prevented the Tsar from sending Tatischev back to Vienna to negotiate there the solution of the Eastern Question. At least that was Metternich's explanation. For some time he tried to bear up under the blow, heartened a little by the news that came from Constantinople of the success of his last effort. He wrote to London and Paris to ask that instructions should be sent to Beauvale and St. Aulaire to work out a common policy at Vienna. He entirely approved Palmerston's attitude towards Mehemet Ali. "He adopts", wrote Beauvale, "all your principles and reasonings but thinks your means of attack upon the Pasha weak."

Discussions still continued for a time between Metternich, St. Aulaire and Beauvale on the different questions. But all the heart had gone out of them. The French and British points of view diverged. The French Ambassador refused to agree to any coercive action against Mehemet. Metternich, deprived of confidence and prestige by the Tsar's attitude, could do nothing to bring them together. How great was the blow to his pride was seen by his sudden collapse on 11 August which rendered him quite incapable of business. He retired to Johannisberg to recover his health. He had designed the Anglophil, Clam, to succeed him, but the Archdukes intervened. They had been much perturbed at the rupture with Russia, and preferred Count Ficquelmont, naturally the most favourable to Russia of all the Austrian diplomats. His first step was to urge that the fleets might be removed from the Dardanelles so that the Tsar might be placated. In these circumstances Beauvale could only assume that the great role he himself had hoped to play in the negotiations was over. He had come to realise as much as Palmerston that Louis Philippe was trying to force Austria into an acceptance of the French view of Mehemet. Both France and Austria were unreliable. Perhaps it was only from Russia herself, the Ambassador even ventured to suggest, that the necessary support for action against Mehemet could be obtained.[1]

---

[1] From Beauvale, 3, 7, 8, 10, 24, 27 Aug., 8, 9 Sept., 1839: *B.P.*; do., 3, 8 Sept., 1839: *F.O. Austria*, 282; *L.P.*, I, No. 301. St. Aulaire to Barante, 10 Aug., 1839: Barante, *Souvenirs*, VI, 298. St. Aulaire, *Souvenirs*, 256–262. There is little of the story in the British despatches, but Beauvale's private letters give all the details which he could find out. Princess Mélanie narrates the course of the illness which at first seemed very serious, and was thought by some to be a kind of stroke. Metternich, *Mémoires*, VI, 327–330. St. Aulaire's *Souvenirs*, written in retrospect, are perhaps not quite trustworthy as to details. He certainly gets his dates wrong.

2. THE RAPPROCHEMENT WITH RUSSIA
1839
(i) The First Failure

There had been less excitement at St. Petersburg over the crisis than at any other capital of the Great Powers. The desire most expressed was to leave matters alone. Neither the Tsar nor his Ministers had any wish to put the Treaty of Unkiar Skelessi into effect and send ships or troops through the Bosphorus. They hoped that the Sultan would again come to some arrangement with his vassal. The autocrat was preoccupied with his family affairs and was much annoyed at this distraction. It was even said that he would have dismissed Nesselrode for not stopping the Sultan had there been anyone to replace him. In addition, owing to his own extravagance and the rapacity of his Ministers and courtiers, his finances were in an exceptionally bad state and in no condition to bear the expenses of an expedition. Nesselrode's formal despatch, therefore, laid it down that there was no need to do anything unless Ibrahim crossed the Taurus. He might even add Orfa and Diarbekir to Mehemet's dominions if he wished. When in response to this Palmerston at last sent Clanricarde information of the British contrary view, Nesselrode admitted that Mehemet ought to give up Syria—and perhaps the Sultan would get it back when his vassal died. When the news came of the death of the Sultan, neither Minister nor Tsar concealed their pleasure and again their first reaction was to hope that a settlement would now be arranged between the Ministers of the Porte and Mehemet.[1]

It was while this was the mood of the Emperor that Nesselrode received from Barante and Ficquelmont the results of the activities of their Courts. Barante, pleased to revenge innumerable slights on his monarch, pressed hard the fact that France would not tolerate the Russian fleet at Constantinople without her own ships going there also. "Thereupon", reported the British Ambassador,

[1] From Clanricarde, 8 June, 1839: *F.O. Russia*, 252. Nesselrode to Pozzo di Borgo, 15 June, 1839: *L.P.*, I, No. 74. From Clanricarde, 15, 18, 27 July, 1839: *L.P.*, I, Nos. 132, 160, 184; *F.O. Russia*, 252; do., 26 June, 3 July, 1839: *B.P.*

"Count Nesselrode changed colour and became violently excited. He said these constant feelings of suspicion and distrust of the Emperor and of his intentions that were evinced by France were unjust and intolerable." The effect of this communication on Nesselrode was indeed so marked, wrote Clanricarde, as to "make him ridiculous to all the Court. . . . And I believe no school-boy ever approached a master with more dread than he will the Emp^r to discuss the subject." Neither the Emperor nor Nessel-rode, he added, had asked him whether similar instructions had been sent to the British fleet and so he remained silent on the subject. The Tsar and Orlov seemed well pleased with him.

It was thus from Austria rather than Britain that support for the insistent Barante seemed to come. Metternich's communication of the agreement of France and Britain to coordinate their actions under his auspices at Vienna could not have been worse timed, especially as Austria seemed to have agreed that her flag should fly with those that threatened the Dardanelles. Metternich was probably right when he ascribed the action of the Tsar to the excessive zeal of the French Ambassador. But Nicholas had shewn more than once that he put no trust in Metternich's view of the Eastern Question and had no desire to make him the arbiter between Russia and the West. He was told—and it was true— that Metternich had claimed that he could answer for the Tsar. The paean of joy at Paris seemed to shew that Metternich thought a solution could be obtained on any terms. The Tsar neither intended nor desired to send ships to the Sea of Marmora and the actions of the Porte gave him plenty of excuse to refuse. But he did not wish to appear as intimidated from action by a Euro-pean combination against him. Nesslerode's dislike of Metter-nich is clearly revealed in his private letters. Thus instead of sending Tatischev back to Vienna to control Metternich, as seems at first to have been the intention of Nesselrode at any rate, the Tsar sent Ficquelmont to inform the Chancellor that the negotiation at Vienna was refused. When Tatischev returned he was only to negotiate with Metternich not with the other Ambassadors at Vienna. Constantinople was suggested instead as the centre where the Ambassadors should act to-gether, but this was before the news of the note of 27 July reached St. Petersburg, which shewed that action there was by no means along the lines which the Russian Government had desired.[1]

On the other hand, in contrast to France, Britain had seemed to shew a desire to get on good terms with the Tsar. The latter was much moved by the reports which now reached him of the great success of his son's visit and had already decided to shew his appreciation by a present to Queen Victoria of a vase at the Hermitage, "the finest specimen of Malachite in the world." In these circumstances it is not surprising to find Nesselrode turning to Clanricarde with confidential assurances which he gave to no other Ambassador. Metternich, reported the British Envoy, is entirely wrong if he thinks he can guide the Tsar. On the contrary all the evidence at St. Petersburg shewed that the Russian Government was aggrieved and irritated at his conduct. "If Austria would separate from France and England," Clanricarde went on, "Russia might lean to her side in a difference of policy. But such would be the case, I believe, in a still greater degree if England were to separate herself from France and Austria or from France alone. Russia fears England more than Austria and therefore she respects her more and is more inclined to court her." This excessive simplification of the position was characteristic of the Ambassador, but it seems obvious that Palmerston's determined conduct in 1838, coupled with the friendly reception of the Tsarevitch, had a considerable effect on the Tsar. At the same time, there can be no doubt that the opportunity presented of driving a wedge between France and Britain by accepting Palmerston's view of the contest with Mehemet appealed strongly to both the Tsar and his Ministers after the affront they considered they had received. "The Emperor", wrote Clanricarde, "is extremely pleased at the sentiments of the British Cabinet with regard to Mehemet Ali which are, he says, in unison with his own. And it has been made very evident that the prospect of any separation between the French Govt. and that of the Queen gave him great satisfaction." Nesselrode assured the Ambassador: "You may be sure that we shall not desert you."[2]

[1] From Clanricarde, 3, 9, 10 Aug., 1839: *F.O. Russia*, 252; do., 3 Aug., 1839: *B.P.* Barante's own accounts, given in vol. VI of his *Souvenirs*, still shewed complacency, but he had become aware to some extent of the effect which he had produced. Nesselrode to Meyendorf, 24 July, 1839: Nesselrode, *Lettres et Papiers*, VII, 287. From Beauvale, 2 Sept., 1839: *F.O. Austria*, 282; do., 29 Aug., 1839: *B.P.*

[2] From Clanricarde, 15, 17, 22 Aug., 1839: *F.O. Russia*, 252 253. (Only small extracts are given in *L.P.*); do., 28 Aug., 1839 (with undated despatch from Medem): *L.P.*, I, No. 292; do., 24 Aug., 1839: *B.P.*

For these reasons the Tsar decided to enter into direct negotiations with Palmerston and for that purpose sent to London Baron
Brunnow, of no higher rank than his Minister at Darmstadt and
Stuttgart, but a man who until recently had been Nesselrode's
principal assistant at St. Petersburg and consequently knew all the
shades of Russian policy and had, as Nesselrode said, "the un-
reserved and entire confidence" of his Government. He was to
arrange matters concerning Persia as well as the Ottoman Empire.
Nesselrode had no doubt, he told Clanricarde, that Brunnow would
be able to satisfy Palmerston on both questions.[1]

The British Ambassador insisted on going to Borodino, where
the Tsar had now encamped, more in order to see the spectacle
than the Tsar. The Tsar had been annoyed at Ponsonby's support of French action at Constantinople in refusing the Russian
request that the fleets should be sent away from the Dardanelles,
but he paid the most flattering attentions to Clanricarde, and an
opportunity was thus given to make him aware of Palmerston's
despatch of 25 August which first laid down uncompromisingly
the necessity of throwing Mehemet out of Syria. The Tsar was
delighted with it and the Ambassador was assured he could reckon
on Russian support for his policy. Nicholas added that "he did
not care a straw if we took and kept Egypt if we liked. He said
it was no business of his, that he should not even interfere to
prevent the French having it, altho' he said he never could look
on the French in the same light as the English." This insidious
suggestion made no appeal to Palmerston; but the Russian view
of French policy was being confirmed by every despatch from
Paris. "The whole gist of the observations of the Emperor and
his Minister on this subject", wrote Clanricarde, "was that France
would while away time in negotiations in order to protect and
strengthen Mehemet Ali and would then laugh at England whose
policy would thus be entirely frustrated." It was clear that the
Russian Government hoped to use this position to get Palmerston
to accept their own views as to the Straits.[2]

Ere Palmerston received these later despatches Brunnow had

[1] The appointment was attributed to the influence of Orlov, whose secretary
Brunnow had been during Orlov's visit to London in 1833. He had since been
one of the six higher officials of the Russian Foreign Office dealing with Western
affairs—all Germans. (T. Schiemann, *Geschichte Russlands*, III, 368.)

[2] From Clanricarde, 27, 31 Aug., 16 Sept., 1839: *F.O. Russia*, 253; do., 10 Sept.,
1839: *B.P.*

arrived in London with the Russian proposals. As to Mehemet Russia not only accepted all Palmerston's views but wished Britain to act at once, whether France—or Austria, though the latter was not mentioned—would join in the action or not. Brunnow even produced a memorandum shewing the necessary steps which the British fleet should take to raise Syria against Mehemet very much on the lines actually put into operation in 1840. He offered full support together with the assurance that if the Russian fleet had to go to Constantinople it would act as the mandatory of Europe, and not under the terms of the Treaty of Unkiar Skelessi. The Russian Government had now fully determined to accept the policy of closing the Straits to all vessels of war, thus securing that the Black Sea should be a *mare clausum* to all but its riparians, which meant Russian supremacy in it.

Palmerston had, as we have seen, already come to the conclusion that because of the nearness of Russia to the Bosphorus the closing of the Straits was also the best policy for Britain. Only if the Porte were the ally of Britain against Russia would a British fleet in the Black Sea be necessary. Thus the Straits would be closed while the Sultan was at peace but not while he was at war. The Russian Government had for a moment hoped that it could get agreement on the closing of the Straits even if the Porte were at war. But it was clear that the Porte could not be denied the right of summoning an ally to defend it if it were attacked. Palmerston always saw this point very clearly but he did not put it in the foreground. It shewed too clearly the advantage of the treaty to Britain. Lastly the Tsar and his advisers were strongly against any general guarantee of the Ottoman Empire by the Great Powers. This might threaten some of the special treaty rights which Russia had secured in the last sixty years, and perhaps prevent Russia from succeeding one day to territories to which she would always aspire even if Constantinople itself were given up. Palmerston had of course only just recently welcomed the French revival of this project, an old one of his. But he may have well thought that the interpretation put on it by the French Ministers made it of little practical value at this juncture. The question of a general guarantee of the Ottoman Empire though raised by him was not pressed, all attention being concentrated on the Straits. As Esterhazy reported, Brunnow tried to keep away from theory and concentrate on the immediate issues.[1]

Palmerston himself was from the first strongly tempted to accept Brunnow's offer in order to obtain the necessary support for his plans against Mehemet Ali. The French attitude towards it drove him further in this direction. The Russian despatch suggesting action against Mehemet had already produced from Louis Philippe a declaration that the Powers would never agree to use force for that purpose. The news of the Brunnow mission produced in the excitable French Prime Minister a veritable phrensy. Bulwer, who was obviously delighted to be left in charge while Granville was on leave, described in detail the emphatic manner in which Soult cried that France would never, never agree to such terms. If England agreed with Russia instead of France, Bulwer added, all the old accusations of perfidy would be brought up once more and the feeling of the country would be little short of fury. The Government's attitude was due to confusion and wounded vanity rather than to any deep-laid scheme of aggrandisement such as Palmerston had suggested to account for the inconsistencies of French conduct. Whatever their vacillation as to Mehemet, they had maintained the same viewpoint on the Straits and they were not likely to abandon it.[2]

Bulwer, like Granville, would at this time have liked to make large concessions to Mehemet to get French agreement, but he was considerably shocked by an interview with Louis Philippe at the end of the month. The King got as excited as his Prime Minister at the idea of Britain breaking the Alliance of which he claimed to be the 'Papa'. In response to Bulwer's expostulations and flattery, he would only say that he could never get a Ministry to join in coercive measures against Mehemet. It was clear also that he already thought that Austria would take the same attitude now that Ficquelmont was in charge at Vienna. Bulwer, reporting the

---

[1] Goriainow, *Le Bosphore, etc.*, 63. T. Schiemann, *Geschichte Russlands*, III, 386. Esterhazy to Metternich, 4 Oct., 1839: *V. St. A.* Goriainow makes it clear that Brunnow was to refuse a guarantee and discusses the point raised by Metternich as to whether the Straits would be closed if the Sultan was at war with Russia. But, with his usual imprecision he mixes up the various questions and it is impossible to know exactly what were discussed with Palmerston. Schiemann also is vague and confused. A. Hasenclever (*Die orientalische Frage*, 92) states on Werther's authority that the question of guarantee was discussed. The account drawn up by Brunnow and accepted by Palmerston at the end of the negotiations (*L.P.*, I, No. 353) deals only with Mehemet Ali.

[2] From Bulwer, 14, 23 Sept., 1839: *B.P.*

situation in long and detailed letters and despatches, could only surmise that it was unlikely that this resolution could be overcome. Even Sébastiani urged the necessity of conceding Syria to Mehemet and the humiliation of allowing Russia to act alone at Constantinople.[1]

Palmerston on the other hand was receiving from Esterhazy assurances that he agreed with all Palmerston's views on the Levant and the opinion that the best way to keep France right was to shew her that the other Powers could get on without her. Esterhazy, whatever the disposition of his Court, abounded in hostility to Mehemet, though he evaded Palmerston's demand for Austrian troops to throw him out of Syria. His main object was to bridge the rift that had grown up between Russia and Austria, and for this purpose he agreed with all Brunnow's conditions and tried to get himself accepted as a co-worker in the negotiation with Palmerston. He had considerable success. He won Brunnow's confidence and the latter confessed to him that his first object had been to exclude Austria from the discussions with Britain, so strongly had Russia resented Austrian participation with the Anglo-French squadrons. But he was glad of the support on the question of the Straits which Esterhazy was able to give to him, for with his usual analytic ability Metternich had always been able to see further into this question than anyone else.

Esterhazy also tried to overcome Russian dislike of Prussian cooperation which had gone so far that Brunnow was not prepared even to discuss matters with young Werther, the Chargé d'Affaires in Bülow's temporary absence. Esterhazy thus turned the negotiation to some extent into a transaction between Britain and the three Eastern Courts, and Palmerston's disposition to agree to Brunnow's demands was increased by the thought that, even if France held aloof, the other Great Powers would be with him. He later told Beauvale that Esterhazy's conduct had been 'perfect' throughout the negotiation.[2]

[1] From Bulwer, 30 Sept., 1839: *B.P.* Sébastiani to Soult, 23 Sept., 1839: *A.A.E.*

[2] Esterhazy to Metternich, 25 Sept., 1, 4, 8 Oct., 1839: *V. St. A.* Metternich's observation on the despatch of 4 Oct. agreed that the Austrian attitude towards the Straits was the main reason for Russian distrust of him. He noted also: "L'employ de force de terre Autrichien en Syrie comme en Egypte est un rêve creux," while he told a French official at Johannisberg that the best thing would be for the Porte to make its own arrangements with Mehemet Ali though no one would dare to suggest such a course (Desages to Bourqueney, 21 Oct., 1839: *Bour. P.*). To Beauvale, 25 Oct., 1839: *B.P.*

In these circumstances Palmerston himself would have accepted the Russian offer, as regards the Straits and Mehemet. He pressed Sébastiani hard to receive them favourably and pointed out that it was not England alone but Europe that France would desert if she refused to agree to any coercion of Mehemet. He was, moreover, still coquetting with the idea of a convention guaranteeing the Ottoman Empire for a period of years. The French Government still held strongly to this plan and Soult desired the guarantee to be perpetual. Palmerston shewed a readiness to agree and produced a draft of his own.[1]

This was of course not something which Brunnow could have accepted, but it was not the main point nor the one on which the negotiation broke down. The Cabinet refused to break with France over the question of the Straits. Palmerston proposed that coercive measures should be taken against Mehemet along the lines which Brunnow had suggested, if necessary without the participation of France. Naval forces were to be used on the Syrian coast and as a last resource troops landed in Egypt itself. Mehemet was to be offered the hereditary governance of Egypt alone and, if he refused to agree, that concession was to be withdrawn and even the temporary possession of Egypt was to be taken from him if he ordered Ibrahim to attack. In this last case the use of Russian ships and troops in Asia Minor to protect Constantinople was envisaged. But the Cabinet unanimously rejected this plan. The strong pro-French section had the powerful argument that in such a case it would be Britain that would be inconsistent, for from the outset Palmerston had supported the French demand that Russian ships must not be allowed to enter the Sea of Marmora without those of the maritime Powers. Until this point was settled discussion of the future regime of the Straits was useless. Other influences working against agreement, reported Esterhazy, were the financial classes interested in Egypt, and the Liberals who could not bear to desert France for the Russian Tsar.[2]

Brunnow, therefore, had to be told that Britain could not agree

[1] Sébastiani to Soult, 14, 17, 27 Sept., 1839: *A.A.E.*; do., 23 Sept., 1839: Guizot, *Mémoires*, IV, 550.

[2] Memorandum, 19 Sept., 1839: *B.P.* It is noted on it in Palmerston's hand that the proposals in it were subsequently almost entirely carried out except the landing of troops in Egypt. Esterhazy to Metternich, 4, 8 Oct., 1839: *V. St. A.* I do not know whether the Memorandum itself was placed before the whole Cabinet or only discussed with Melbourne. The correspondence with him referred to in the Memorandum is missing.

that only Russian ships should enter the Straits even though the Treaty of Unkiar Skelessi was abandoned. In such circumstances, the attack on Mehemet could not be immediately begun, as Russia had suggested, for it might raise the question of the entry into the Straits on which it had not been possible to agree. Brunnow urged that inaction was dangerous. Palmerston did not conceal his sympathy with this point of view and the discussions were throughout marked with the greatest cordiality and frankness. Brunnow, for example, suggested that Palmerston should remove Ponsonby and send Durham to Constantinople. Naturally Palmerston refused this proposal as also Brunnow's suggestion that Britain should take Candia. But he was convinced of the genuine nature of the Russian offer. "I believe that Power to be acting honestly," he told Beauvale, "and I hope we may be able to come to an understanding with her." But neither Palmerston nor Brunnow had the power to accept the indispensable conditions laid down by the other, and all that could be done was for the latter to report to his Court and await the decisions of the Tsar.

On his way back, however, he paid an important visit. He passed through Dover and sought out Wellington. The Duke had long ago in 1835 advised Palmerston of his view that the closing of the Straits was to the interest of Britain. He found no difficulty, therefore, in agreeing with Brunnow on that topic which was not explored in detail. But in addition he was emphatically of the opinion that Mehemet should be confined to Egypt, and he judged the strategic situation much more favourably than the civilians. Ibrahim would never be able to march on Constantinople, he said, if his sea communications were cut and by the same means he could be turned out of Syria. This opinion undoubtedly had an immense effect on Brunnow who regarded it as confirming the wisdom of the plan he had proposed to Palmerston. If it were true, it was unlikely that the question of the entry into the Dardanelles would in fact occur and this seems to have exercised considerable influence on the decision of the Tsar. Brunnow also hastened to inform Esterhazy, as the most delicate way of communicating immediately to the British Government the views of a leader of the Opposition. He also emphasised its importance to the British Minister at Frankfurt and asked him to make sure Palmerston knew about it.[1]

[1] To Beauvale, 25 Oct., 1839: *B.P.* Brunnow to Esterhazy, 15 Oct., 1839, enclosed in Esterhazy to Metternich, 15 Nov., 1839: *V. St. A.*, and in Esterhazy to Palmerston, 15 Oct., 1839: *B.P.* From Abercrombie, 26 Oct., 1839: *B.P.*

The French Government was informed that the rejection of the Russian offer had been done in deference to the French view. If Palmerston hoped to obtain concessions concerning Mehemet by presenting matters in this way he was immediately disappointed. He made, as a result of the Cabinet discussions, an offer to Sébastiani of the Pashalik of Acre to Mehemet for life, without the renowned fortress, and asked if France would support him in imposing such a solution. This perhaps did not go very far. But it was the first time Palmerston had yielded on his desert frontier. The offer was treated at Paris with contempt. No attempt was made to negotiate about it or even to answer Palmerston's arguments. Both Soult and the King refused to consider the exercise of force against Mehemet in any event. Louis Philippe, when reminded by Bulwer that he had long ago agreed that Mehemet should give up the Holy Places, replied, "Mon Dieu, qui les prendra?" Soult, reported Bulwer, had become "irritable and very disagreeable if contradicted". He said that, in fifty years of active life, "it is extraordinary that I have never once been wrong." "Prince Metternich", added Bulwer, "is the only other Providence who would say the same thing."

The French Government denied also that Austria and Prussia accepted Palmerston's plans, and the despatches from Vienna had been so uncertain that they had much material to support their view. It was clear that they thought that now that the Russian negotiation had broken down Palmerston was helpless and must in the long run give way. Now that Brunnow had gone, the Foreign Minister had left London and, reported Sébastiani, diplomatic affairs were in a state of complete stagnation. Many members of the British Cabinet did indeed share the French view. They were sick of the question. At the end of October Melbourne confessed to Esterhazy that he was against the coercion of Mehemet because it was a source of division among the Great Powers, and that he almost wished that the note of 27 July had never been presented since it had prevented direct agreement between the Porte and the Pasha.[1]

Esterhazy delayed his own departure to see Wellington and Peel. The former confirmed these views. Peel on the other hand disagreed with him and shewed much jealousy of Russia. Palmerston had told Bourqueney in July of Wellington's opinion expressed in 1835. Guizot, *Mémoires*, IV, 510. He now passed Brunnow's letter on to several colleagues.

[1] From Bulwer, 14 Oct., 1839: *B.P.* Esterhazy to Metternich, 8 Oct., 1839: *V. St. A.* Sébastiani to Soult, 27 Sept., 1839: *A.A.E.*

Not so Palmerston. His determination to secure his objective was only increased by the intransigeance of France, and the refusal of the Cabinet to accept Brunnow's offer. His first step was to withdraw the offer to France which had been so contemptuously refused. Poor Sébastiani, who tried to keep the negotiation open, found the usually genial Foreign Minister absolutely 'glacial'. The offer was cancelled and Palmerston refused even to discuss it. He was, he told Esterhazy, convinced that there was more to hope from Russia than France.[1]

It was in this mood that he, using for this purpose, during a short stay at Broadlands, the 'stagnation' which Sébastiani had reported, composed the first of the trenchant indictments of French policy which wounded and embittered Louis Philippe and his Ministers all the more deeply because they were practically unanswerable, so vulnerable had the French position become. In response to the pleadings of Granville he twice softened its wording. But, as Melbourne pointed out, these changes made little difference. It was the exposure of the whole trend of French policy rather than any details which was bound to hurt and humiliate France. The survey shewed that France, after joining with the rest of Europe in the agreement to protect the Sultan against Mehemet, now refused to take part in any action necessary to make the promise good.[2]

As Palmerston had, perhaps, expected, this despatch produced no effect at Paris. Louis Philippe professed to be deeply wounded at it and said that it was not the will but the power to overthrow Mehemet that was lacking. Soult's reply was of the lamest and Palmerston had no difficulty in refuting it. But more serious was it that all the efforts of Esterhazy, who spent three weeks at Paris on the way back to Austria, produced absolutely no effect, though he pressed hard all the arguments for action. Public opinion, he said at the end, was less in favour of Mehemet than he had expected but Louis Philippe far more so. The King insisted that Palmerston had a personal grudge against him because of his Spanish

---

[1] Sébastiani to Soult, 10 Oct., 1839: *A.A.E.* do., 3, 10 Oct., 1839: Guizot, *Mémoires*, IV, 553, 555; do., 18 Oct., 1839: *A.A.E.* There is a note in the margin of Sébastiani's despatch of 10 Oct. about Palmerston's offer to the effect that it was absurd to suppose it possible.

[2] From Granville, 1, 8, 15 Nov., 1839; From Melbourne, 16 Nov., 1839: *B.P.* The despatch is dated 29 October (*L.P.*, No. 358) but it not despatched officially until later. Copies of it were sent to the other capitals of the Great Powers.

policy. It was impossible, he added, to coerce Mehemet. Conciliation was the only possible policy. Soult's only concession was to ask Esterhazy to see if he could get Palmerston to renew his offer of the Pashalik of Acre. Esterhazy did his best to find some means of compromise and in a letter to Palmerston himself acquitted the French Government of desiring Mehemet to be established in Syria, even though they refused to employ the slightest threat against him. Before he left he thought he had done some good, but that was not Granville's opinion. The French Government, now that the negotiation with Russia seemed to have ended was convinced that its point of view must prevail. And though Esterhazy had tried to remove the effects of Austrian vacillation they could still hope that Metternich would ultimately come over to their side. Beauvale attempted to defend Metternich's twists of policy but he had himself become defeatist as regards Mehemet. And no one could have been more so than Admiral Stopford who practically refused to take the responsibility for using the fleet to coerce him—a refusal which Lord Holland warmly commended. The Chancellor of the Duchy was only one such in a Cabinet which Palmerston knew was deeply divided and doubtful of his policy.[1]

Encouragement now came from the Porte itself. All through the late summer Ponsonby's despatches had dwelt on the precarious nature of the situation there. He could never be certain whether underground negotiations were not taking place with Mehemet—and in fact in one subterranean channel or another these never ceased. Pontois was reported to be urging the Porte

---

[1] From Granville, 18, 25, 29 Nov., 1839: *L.P.*, Nos. 385, 395, 399; do., 29 Nov., 2, 7 Dec., 1839: *B.P.* To Granville, 22 Nov., 1839: *L.P.*, 386. From Esterhazy, 4 Dec., 1839: *B.P.* Esterhazy to Metternich, 15, 29 Nov., 1839: *V. St. A.* From Beauvale, 19 Nov., 1839: *B.P.* It was at this juncture that the suggestion was made by Ponsonby that the British fleet should find shelter inside the Dardanelles at the White Cliffs. The idea was originally Stopford's to get shelter from the autumn weather. Ponsonby pronounced it inconvenient and Reschid forbade it, but some refuge had to be found for the fleet. Palmerston was for a moment tempted to advocate that course but Melbourne was against it. Wiser counsels prevailed and the fleet was ordered to Smyrna. It could leave the entrance to the Dardanelles, Palmerston explained, because of the new disposition of Russia. Though there had been precedents for using the entry as a haven, the Russians might certainly have suspected an attempt to enter the Sea of Marmora. From Beauvale, 14 Oct., 1839: *B.P.*; do., 8 Nov., 1839: *F.O. Austria*, 282. Ponsonby to Beauvale, 9 Oct., 1839: *B.P.* To Beauvale, 25, Oct., 1839: *B.P.* From Ponsonby, 9, 22 Sept., 8 Oct., 1839: *F.O. Turkey*, 358, 359. To Admiralty, 29 Oct., 1839: *L.P.*, I, No. 356; To Ponsonby, do: *B.P.*

to come to an understanding with the Pasha on the basis which had been put forward in Paris of the return of Adana and the Holy Places to the Sultan. Russian activities were thought to be in the same direction and her Ambassador was also trying to get the fleets away from the entrance of the Dardanelles. Husrev, reported Ponsonby, was too old to cope with all these difficulties and liable to be bought by Russia. Fortunately Stürmer was now working closely with Ponsonby and it was largely by his influence that the dangerous intrigues in the Seraglio connected with the Sultan's Mother were frustrated.[1]

The one hope was the new Foreign Minister, Reschid Pasha, who had been sent for from London by Husrev when the crisis came in July. He arrived on 21 September and at once told Ponsonby of his faith in Britain, his suspicions of Russia and his doubts of France. In less than a month he had got rid of the least reliable of the Turkish Ministers, Nourri, Sarim and Mustapha Kiamil. With Husrev as the figurehead, Reschid got two other pro-British Ministers, Halil and Ahmed, into power, to help him. They warned the Sultan against the intrigues of his Mother. Correspondence with Mehemet still went on and no one was sure of Husrev himself. But though rumours of plots persisted, Ponsonby believed that Stürmer and he could maintain Reschid and Halil in office and prevent the interference of the Seraglio. "The Seraglio", he wrote, "was everything in the time of Sultan Mahmoud. The young Sultan has agreed not to consult with or listen to the men who surround him as domestic officers."[2]

This increase of Reschid's power gave him the opportunity for the grand stroke which he seems to have contemplated ever since his last visit to London. For on 3 November the famous Edict of Gulhané was issued. Reforms of the most drastic character were promised and Ponsonby hailed them as a blow against Mehemet: "It is a victorious answer to those who say that the Empire cannot be saved by its ancient Government and that the spurious regeneration to be worked out by the Pasha of Egypt is its only preservation. The enemies of Turkey and the friends of Mehemet

[1] From Ponsonby, 18, 19, 21, 22 Aug., 1839: *F.O. Turkey*, 358.
[2] From Ponsonby, 10, 23, 30 Sept., 8, 16 Oct., 1839: *F.O. Turkey*, 358–359. Some of this, much emasculated, is printed in *Levant Papers* where is also given the official correspondence between Mehemet and the Porte, which is, however, less important than the hidden intercourse.

Ali are said to feel the weight of the blow that has fallen upon them."[1]

Palmerston also thought the Edict a master stroke. He gave Ponsonby credit for the achievement. "Your Hathi Sheriff", he wrote, "was a grand stroke of policy and it is producing great effect on public feeling both here and in France. I never have despaired of seeing Turkey rear her head again as a substantive element in the balance of power." He warmly commended Reschid, though Melbourne, with some wisdom, thought it safer not to single out a Minister by name. But even more important was the change in Russian policy which rendered the presence of the fleet no longer necessary at the mouth of the Dardanelles. Ponsonby was urged to work as cordially as possible with the Russian Ambassador: "It is not necessary to enquire what the reasons are which have led Russia to adopt her present course, nor to examine whether among them may be a hope that she may thus at least retain some portion of her influence at Constantinople. It is our business to take advantage of her present temper, and to encourage her to work with us for our own objects, as long as she is willing to do so."[2]

(ii) The Tsar accepts the British Conditions

While his sympathetic account of the failure of his first mission was on its way to his master Brunnow returned to his post at Stuttgart via Frankfurt. On his way he paid another important visit. He spent several days with Metternich at Johannisberg and Frankfurt (19–24 Oct.). His tact and authority, which Princess Mélanie reveals in her naïve diary, produced a great effect. It shewed the Chancellor that agreement could be obtained only on the basis laid down at London and made him anxious that these negotiations should be successful. He was ready to second them if the Tsar agreed to go on.[3]

At the same time Metternich was far from accepting all Brunnow's propositions. He emphasised the necessity of recognising the sovereignty of the Sultan over the Straits and won Brunnow's assent to seeking a solution of the problem in this manner. But

[1] From Ponsonby, 5 Nov., 1839: *F.O. Turkey*, 360. For the scene, which Ponsonby and others describe in detail, see H. W. V. Temperley, *Crimea*, 161
[2] To Ponsonby, 29 Oct., (undated) 1839; From Melbourne, 9 Dec., 1839: *B.P.* To Ponsonby, 2 Dec., 1839: *F.O. Turkey*, 353.
[3] Metternich, *Mémoires*, VI, 341–344.

how anxious Metternich was to keep in with all parties was seen in Leopold's report of a conversation which he had at Wiesbaden on the 22 October. The Chancellor was full of suggestions for reconciling the French support of Mehemet with the necessities of the Porte. Metternich, according to Leopold, was anxious to establish Five Power unanimity and saw the danger of using force against the Pasha. Leopold urged him to mediate between France and Britain and at Metternich's suggestion wrote an account of his views to Louis Philippe.

Palmerston no doubt thought that this epistle was not likely to exert much good influence at Paris, and he immediately sent Leopold a terrific indictment of French policy. If France, he wrote, were to be judged by her Press, which was primed with confidential information, she must be considered more dangerous to Europe than Russia. But he was ready to attribute her apparent bad faith more to timidity than worse motives. Mehemet had in his pay five or six leading newspapers, many of the talkers in the Salons and perhaps a friend or two in the Cabinet, and the Government was afraid to stand up to them. But what sort of a figure would France cut when the papers were published as they must be? In Spanish affairs, while secretly betraying Britain, she had preserved appearances. Now she had behaved like a weathercock and substituted a policy of dismembering the Ottoman Empire for that of preserving the integrity which she had promised to defend. Such a course was not even in her own selfish interests. For, even if she did not mind Russia possessing Constantinople, provided that she could establish an Arab Empire, "she would find that if such did come into existence England would have far more influence over it than France, and this for a great many reasons, moral, political, geographical."[1]

Meanwhile the Tsar was awaiting at St. Petersburg Palmerston's confirmation of Brunnow's reports and proposals for a new agreement. Clanricarde recounted the impatience to receive it and Brunnow complained bitterly to Sir George Shee at Stuttgart of Palmerston's neglect to instruct his Ambassador. Meanwhile, he said, the way was left open for French intrigue at St. Petersburg where Barante was insinuating that Britain was not to be relied upon, and had three times pressed Nesselrode to accept the French point of view about Mehemet. Nesselrode had replied

[1] From Leopold, 24 Oct., 1839; To Leopold, 4 Nov., 1839: *B.P.*

with a despatch to Paris which played for time, but which the French Government interpreted as a distinct advance in their direction. Eventually in order to satisfy Nesselrode's impatience Clanricarde used an extract from one of Palmerston's private letters. At last on the 14 November Palmerston's long-awaited despatch arrived.

The result was that the Tsar agreed to the British condition that, if the necessity arose, both fleets should enter the Sea of Marmora. He seems to have grasped quite eagerly at the opportunity of agreement. No doubt the probable effect on France was a strong inducement to him to come to terms with Britain. But there were also other reasons. The effect which might be produced on the struggle in the Caucasus and generally a desire to get things quiet again in the Middle East were also powerful motives. Nesselrode, indeed, insisted that it was no part of the Emperor's intentions to cause a breach between Britain and France. It will be seen, however, that Brunnow's instructions were so drawn as to make that breach almost inevitable unless France gave way completely.[1]

The notice of this change first reached Brunnow at Stuttgart at the beginning of December, in the shape of a private letter from Nesselrode. He at once got in touch with Shee who assured him that Palmerston would be delighted to receive him back in England. The Russian Minister was much pleased with the compliments paid to him by Palmerston in his despatch and was, stated Shee, "*thoroughly English. His eyes seemed quite to fill* when he talked of the probable renewal of friendly feelings between Russia and England." Shortly afterwards a formal despatch authorised him to resume his negotiations in England on a new basis.

Brunnow had hoped to persuade Esterhazy to go back from Paris to London to help him. But as usual that Ambassador was immersed in personal affairs. Metternich, however, as the result of Brunnow's diplomatic handling at Wiesbaden, was completely

---

[1] From Clanricarde, 5, 18 Nov., 1839: *F.O. Russia*, 253. *L.P.*, I, No. 377. To Clanricarde, 25 Oct:, 1839: *L.P.*, I, No. 352. From Shee, 3 Dec., 1839: *B.P.* Palmerston had promised to send to St. Petersburg a report similar to that drawn up by Brunnow. He subsequently said that he accepted Brunnow's as his own. Pressure of work had delayed his sending instructions. Later he said he had expected the Russian Government to make new proposals on the basis of Brunnow's report. There seems to have been a genuine misunderstanding but Palmerston may well have desired to rest his case on Brunnow's report than on one of his own which the Cabinet would have to see.

won over to the necessity of Austrian participation in the discussions at London. He therefore sent Neumann on a special mission
for that purpose. Neumann had left London six years before on
the worst of terms with Palmerston, but all that was forgotten and,
as will be seen, he was to play an important part in assisting
Palmerston to get his way with the Cabinet. Palmerston's agents
abroad had for the most part little confidence that Metternich
would act without France. But from Vienna Beauvale once again
expressed confidence in the Chancellor's resolution, and reported
his advocacy of the conference system. If only Palmerston and
the Tsar could meet—with Metternich himself perhaps to act as
a catalyst—all would go well. But the centre of discussion must
now, Beauvale solemnly pointed out, be at London, a fact which
was apparent to all the world.[1]

The news of Russian agreement naturally caused the greatest
excitement in French circles. Officially both Louis Philippe and
his Minister had to profess to be delighted that the Russians had
given way. The main object of their diplomacy had ostensibly
thus been achieved. But they could not help being aware that
Palmerston, instead of being isolated, was now the centre of a new
negotiation which would be directed against Mehemet Ali. Sébastiani was given no inkling of what was in Palmerston's mind.
But he was congratulated on France's return to the alliance, and
the two agreed on the vacillation and unreliability of Metternich
who had been saying different things to Britain and France.
More significant was it that Sébastiani announced to Hummelauer, who was used to keep a line out to France, that he would be
able to defeat Palmerston's plans by his influence on those
members of the Cabinet whom he knew did not accept the Foreign
Minister's policy as their own.

Neumann shewed wonderful zeal and caught up with Brunnow
at Calais. The two journeyed to London together and won each
other's confidence at the outset, a fact of great importance at the
subsequent negotiations. It was not at London but at Broadlands
that these negotiations began. For on 16 December, two days

<hr/>

[1] From Sir George Shee, 3, 7, 8, 9 Dec., 1839; From Beauvale, 8, 17, 31 Dec.,
1839: *B.P.* Neumann was at first only given instructions as to the Straits
because it was thought that Brunnow was limited to that topic, but when it was
realised he was also to deal with the question of Mehemet he was given further
instructions to enter also into that negotiation. He had at first only a letter to
Palmerston, no Full Powers to negotiate.

before they landed at Dover, Palmerston had married Lady Cowper. He did not, however, allow his honeymoon to interrupt his diplomatic labours. He invited Brunnow and Neumann to visit Broadlands and discuss the situation. Sébastiani thought the action most precipitate and that the Cabinet would disapprove. It had in fact Melbourne's warm approval. Thus at Broadlands on Christmas Day the foundations were laid of all the subsequent negotiations. Palmerston saw Brunnow twice on the 23rd and 24th, discussed matters afterwards with Neumann and spent the first Christmas Day of his married life in going over the whole question with both of them together.[1]

Brunnow's instructions were complicated. The Sultan was not himself to be a party to the treaty which was to be made between the Great Powers, who offered the Sultan their assistance and, after he had accepted it, would proceed to make their help effective. There were many different possibilities according as Austria, France and Britain came to an agreement. A good deal of discretion was, therefore, allowed to Brunnow in the interpretation of his orders and of this permission he was to take full advantage.[2]

There was, however, one cardinal point which brought all the strands of the negotiations together and ensured that the result should be a comprehensive settlement if it were secured at all. It also made almost certain a breach between Britain and France which was always one of the objects of the Tsar even if Nesselrode did not desire it. For Brunnow was instructed to make Russian assent to the entry of the fleets into the Dardanelles depend upon an agreement on the dispute between Mehemet and the Sultan. It was most unlikely that Britain and France would agree on this question and the means might thus be found of completely destroying the Franco-British Alliance. Brunnow from the first insisted that he had no latitude on this point. Neumann made some attempt to get him to divide the two questions when they first

[1] From Hummelauer, 21, 31 Dec., 1839; From Neumann, 21 Dec., 1839: *V. St. A.* Soult to Sébastiani, 9 Dec., 1839: Guizot, *Mémoires*, IV, 556. Sébastiani to Soult, 12, 18 Dec., 1839: *A.A.E.* From Melbourne, 21 Dec., 1839: *B.P.*
[2] Brunnow's Instructions are given in a confused form in Goriainow, *Le Bosphore*, etc., 73–75, and discussed with equal obscurity in T. Schiemann's *Geschichte Russlands*, III, 391–392 and F. Marten's *Recueil*, etc., XII, 111. Neumann's despatches and private letters make them pretty clear. (See *Appendix D.*)

discussed it. But the Russian Minister was adamant and he said the same thing to Palmerston, who of course wished for the same procedure—if he could get his Cabinet to agree.

Subject to this consideration Brunnow was to suggest a definite method by which, if the need arose, the fleets of the different Powers should take up their stations. The British and French fleets, reduced to a few vessels, were to be stationed inside the Dardanelles, the Russian fleet of indefinite number was to take up the same position as in 1833, i.e. on the Asiatic side of the Bosphorus and away from the Dardanelles. Austria's station was not laid down but it was intimated that, true to her role of mediator, she might like to send a vessel or two to lie somewhere between the ships of Russia and those of the maritime Powers.

This was, however, to be a special exception to protect the Sultan from Mehemet Ali. It was not to derogate from a general rule to which Russia was prepared to agree, the closing of the Straits. Here Russian instructions had been much influenced by Metternich's insistence that what had to be done was to recognise the right inherent in the Sultan's sovereignty of closing the Straits rather than to impose any restrictions upon him. Thus the Powers were to agree with one another that they would respect this right and the Sultan was to declare that he meant to uphold it. The words "in peace and in war" still remained but Brunnow already told Neumann that he was prepared to withdraw them if pressed. Nothing was said about any guarantee of the Ottoman Empire as a whole. That had now been abandoned by every Power save France.

Lastly the Powers were to come to agreement about the steps to be taken against Mehemet along the lines laid down in Brunnow's previous memorandum. Here Brunnow was given much latitude. He could of course agree without the assent of France. But he could also in the last resource agree even if Austria did not consent to take part. If, however, the Porte and Mehemet had already come to an agreement—as the news from Constantinople at St. Petersburg when the instructions were written seemed to indicate was possible—he was to do nothing to overthrow this. In this case it was assumed that the crisis would cease to exist.

Palmerston, as might be expected, received all this with the greatest pleasure. He told Neumann that it left nothing to be desired, though, as was soon to be seen, there was much in it which he wished to alter when he had had time to examine the document carefully. But for the moment all that he suggested to Brunnow was that the question of the Straits might be regulated separately in a convention recognising, in the same way as Britain had done in 1809, the Porte's ancient right to close the Straits. But he at once gave up this suggestion when Brunnow told him he was expressly ordered to include everything in one transaction. Neumann was received with equal cordiality and frankness.

Palmerston could not of course pledge the Cabinet. The best method of winning their assent was frankly discussed with the two Envoys, who were well aware of the difficulty and delicacy of the task. The only concession which could be made to Mehemet, said Palmerston, was that which he had made to France and withdrawn, the Pashalik of Acre without the fortress itself. There was much discussion as to the force to be used and Palmerston recurred to an old idea of bringing Indian troops to invade Egypt. The detailed application could not obviously be immediately worked out. Meanwhile it was decided that it would be better for Palmerston himself to lay a plan before the Cabinet rather than merely submit that of Brunnow, and this task he promised to undertake at once. Palmerston pointed out that though Brunnow had the necessary authority to sign the treaty, Neumann, and of course the Prussian representative also, had not received Full Powers for that purpose. He engaged to write to their Courts to obtain them. The two representatives meanwhile promised to do everything possible to assist Palmerston to obtain the assent of the Cabinet.[1]

How necessary such assistance might be was shewn by Sébastiani's conduct. Furious at being left out of the discussions, he forced an invitation to the country house where Palmerston went immediately after this negotiation. There, in response to his insistent enquiries, Palmerston told him little or nothing. He would, the Ambassador assured his Court, wrap himself up in 'calm' and 'indifference'. But he indicated to both Hummelauer and Neumann that he would fight Palmerston in the Cabinet, the majority of which he knew were against a breach with France. Faithful to his promise Neumann spent two days with the Hollands whom he knew were the most likely to be on Sébastiani's side, following Palmerston who had been engaged on the same

[1] Neumann to Metternich, 31 Dec., 1839: *V. St. A. Appendix*, p. 875.

task. He reported that he had had great success in seconding Palmerston's views. Brunnow meanwhile had seen Wellington and received his congratulations on the success of his diplomacy. The French, the Duke said, would be fools if they did not agree also. But all the news from Paris shewed that the French took an entirely different view. And it was under these circumstances that Palmerston began to draft the convention he was to submit to the Cabinet.[1]

[1] Hummelauer to Metternich, 31 Dec., 1839; Neumann to Metternich, 30 Dec., 1839: *V. St. A.* Sébastiani to Soult, 27 Dec., 1839: *A.A.E.* It was noted on the despatch that to be 'calm' was all right but 'indifference' was the last thing Sébastiani ought to shew. On the contrary he ought to make every effort to know all the threads of the negotiation and insist on taking part in it as he had been ordered to do. This was perhaps the last straw which made Soult and Desages determined to overcome Louis Philippe's reluctance to recall Sébastiani and substitute a less Anglophil ambassador. Brunnow told Sébastiani that he had simply come to resume the discussions broken off in October but he admitted that plans were being made to coerce Mehemet as Holland and Portugal had been coerced. (28 Dec., 1839: *A.A.E.* partly in Guichen, *La Crise d'Orient*, 187–188.)

3. THE CONVENTION OF 15 JULY, 1840

The agreement of Russia to share the defence of the Straits with the Western Powers seemed to have removed a major obstacle to agreement. But it was not long before Palmerston found out how many other difficulties lay in the way of that combined action against Mehemet Ali which was necessary to reestablish the Sultan's authority over his Asiatic dominions. The negotiation of the next six months is, indeed, one of the most intricate and curious in the annals of diplomacy. Until the month of July was reached it seemed impossible that a satisfactory result could be obtained. Throughout these months Louis Philippe, the French Government and nearly all their advisers were confident that Palmerston would fail in his primary object, the use of force against Mehemet. More than once Brunnow and Neumann, as well as their chiefs, Nesselrode and Metternich, were ready to give up in despair. At Constantinople intrigue never ceased to obtain a separate arrangement between the Sultan and the Pasha, which would have made Palmerston the laughing-stock of Europe and was only prevented by the ceaseless vigilance and powerful authority of Ponsonby. The majority of the British Cabinet under the leadership of Lord Holland and the new recruit, Clarendon, were always opposed to Palmerston and ruthlessly rejected almost every plan that divided Britain from France. The French Ambassadors were fully informed of their proceedings and assisted many of them with advice. The Prime Minister, though his first desire was to avoid at all hazards a split in the Cabinet and the consequent downfall of his Government, was, so far as he took a determined line at all, on the side of compromise and peace.

But Palmerston himself, though he was forced to manoeuvre and delay, never lost either his courage or his patience. He forbore to force the issue until the situation was such that he could insist on his own way. Then with dramatic intensity he compelled the unwilling Cabinet to follow his advice by the threat of his resignation. He was throughout overwhelmed with work, for there were other important problems to be dealt with, and a Queen's marriage which necessarily threw many duties on him. This was no doubt one reason why events moved so slowly while Neumann chafed impatiently and wrote stinging despatches to his Court. But Palmerston believed, and rightly, that time was on his side and that Mehemet would not dare to forestall him by a vigorous action. The Egyptian army indeed was losing strength all through this period of delay and Ponsonby had begun to overthrow Ibrahim even before the Powers had come to agreement.

Palmerston's first task was to produce a draft for the Cabinet as he had promised to Brunnow and Neumann at Broadlands. As soon as he set himself to examine closely the project which Brunnow had laid before him he found that he was far from agreement on several essential points. In the first place he now adopted the view which Metternich had so constantly put forward that everything must be done in the name of the Sultan. This made it necessary that the Sultan should be a party to the convention and, therefore, that a Turkish Plenipotentiary with Full Powers should come to London, a condition inevitably causing delay. Palmerston was very conscious of this and even before he obtained the assent of Brunnow and Neumann ordered Ponsonby to urge the Porte to send to London its representative at Paris, the 'oaf', Nourri Pasha, who, he assured him, would not have to sign anything which "a good Turk ought to hesitate to subscribe to". Secondly, Palmerston could not accept the Russian proposal that the fleet of the Western Powers should be limited in numbers while that of Russia was unrestricted. He accordingly suggested that the Russian fleet should be equal to the combined strength of France and Britain. Lastly he did not wish at the outset that the military and naval coercion of Mehemet should be too nakedly announced, and confined himself to the promise of aid to the Sultan to cut off supplies to the Syrian army and omitted all mention of an attack on Alexandria. These last two changes were probably more due to the advice of Cabinet colleagues than to Palmerston's own desires, for he consulted some of them informally about his draft. These consultations revealed the intense desire of many members of the Cabinet not to break with France and Palmerston was forced, therefore, to use language which would at least postpone the issue.[1]

For the same reason he entered into communication with

[1] To Beauvale, 26 Jan., 3 Feb., 1840: *B.P.* Neumann to Metternich, 14, 17 Jan., 1840: *V. St. A.* To Ponsonby, 25 Jan., 1840: *L.P.*, I, No. 455; do., *B.P.*

Sébastiani, revealing to him the substance of Brunnow's proposals and asking him to obtain the agreement of his Government to his own modifications of them which took into account French susceptibilities to a much greater degree. This was a bold step for Brunnow had given him no authority to do so, but, after all, Sébastiani was to a large extent himself on Palmerston's side and was likely to find out from other members of the Cabinet what was going on.

All these negotiations took time and it was not until 20 January that Palmerston communicated the result to the impatient Brunnow and Neumann. They were both dissatisfied, but Brunnow was so shocked and indignant at what Palmerston had done that he even refused to discuss the draft with him. There was no need at all to summon a Turkish representative, he said, and thus incur a long delay. But the other two alterations were inexcusable. His master would be insulted at the idea that his ships were to be limited in number, while the communication of the Russian plans to France before they had been officially placed before the British Cabinet, much less accepted by them, was against all the rules of diplomatic behaviour. The lack of precision regarding the coercion of Mehemet was also regrettable. In fact the draft seemed still to be aimed more at Russia than at the rebellious Pasha and his French backer. Neumann felt less strongly on these points, but he thought it necessary to support Brunnow and maintain the Austro-Russian front, and it was he who at Brunnow's request conveyed these criticisms to Palmerston. But Palmerston refused to yield on the first point, the participation of the Sultan. He insisted to Neumann and emphasised in his private letter to Beauvale that he was merely following Metternich's advice. Nor could he admit that Britain and France were to be placed in a different position to Russia as regards entering the Straits. On the question of the coercion of Mehemet he was more ready to listen to Neumann's arguments. He did himself in fact agree with them, but he pointed out that the experience of Spain shewed how difficult it was for an outside Power to exercise the right of blockade in a civil war, and intimated that he could only gradually get his colleagues to accept the full implications of coercion on which indeed he had as yet no very clear idea himself. Neumann had objected to the mention of an Austrian squadron in the draft. It was needed, Palmerston explained, for moral effect

2 U

not material aid. And it was clear that it was on the British Cabinet that moral pressure was most needed.[1]

Neumann criticised severely Palmerston's handling of the Cabinet of which he seems to have been well informed. Since they had approved of the despatches to Clanricarde and Granville of October they had, he insisted, committed themselves to Palmerston's view of French policy. But Palmerston's communication to Sébastiani of Brunnow's proposals had enabled the latter to influence several members of the Cabinet. The effect on Melbourne particularly was very noticeable. The result was that Palmerston was enjoined by his colleagues not to make a separation from France inevitable. Palmerston had shewn them the two drafts and they had preferred his to that of Brunnow. But he was under an illusion, wrote Neumann, if he thought he could overcome their resistance.

Thus, though Palmerston said that he would go on without France, Brunnow, whose instructions were to return to Darmstadt by the middle of February, was already in despair and urging Neumann to leave London at the same time. All that the Austrian envoy could suggest was that Metternich should get Beauvale to use his influence with the Prime Minister. He asked for instructions as to how far he was to go in standing solidly with Brunnow.[2]

Meanwhile nothing had come from Palmerston's approach to Sébastiani and his strong appeal to France to join the other Powers. He had rather to protest at the increase of the French fleet in the Mediterranean and intimated that unless it was stopped Britain would have to follow the French example. Sébastiani's attempt to get his Government to agree met with no response. The debates in the Chambers had shewn them to be strongly in favour of Mehemet and the whole Cabinet was opposed to Sébastiani's advice. Louis Philippe said no French Cabinet could consent to limit the French force for the Dardanelles to two or three ships. Though a clause had been put in the King's Speech in response to the mention of the Alliance in that proroguing the

---

[1] Neumann to Metternich, 21, 23 Jan., 1840; *V. St. A.* To Beauvale, 26 Jan., 3 Feb., 1840: *B.P.*

[2] Neumann to Metternich, 23, 26 Jan., 1840: *V. St. A.* He reported that Baring, the Chancellor of the Exchequer, had personal financial interests in France, Lord Holland thought the French alliance indispensable and Melbourne feared the expense of an expedition to Syria or Egypt.

last session of the British Parliament, many speakers had criticised British policy. A notable exception was Thiers who warmly defended the alliance. But he also had had to advocate Mehemet's cause and he hastened to tell Bulwer that no Ministry could join in sanctions against him, an opinion strongly endorsed by Bulwer himself.[1]

In these circumstances it was only natural that no mention was made of the French alliance in the Queen's Speech opening the new session of the British Parliament. Nevertheless Louis Philippe and his Ministers were very hurt and Granville, who recorded with a kind of melancholy satisfaction the outcome of Palmerston's *démarche* on which he had not been consulted, also reproached his chief. "But how", replied Palmerston, "could we with any truth have talked about our union and alliance with France, when France has left us on the most important question of the day and when no real unity of views continues to exist? Such phrases are worse than unmeaning when they are not in accordance with the truth."[2]

It was not very likely, therefore, that Sébastiani's advocacy would have any success. On the contrary, its principal result was to produce the recall of Sébastiani himself. Soult had long distrusted him and been jealous of his position at London. Now the French Cabinet by a threat of resignation forced Louis Philippe to withdraw his protection from an Ambassador who had been in very intimate relations with himself. All that he could obtain was that Sébastiani should remain to represent France at the Queen's wedding. His successor was to be no less a person than Guizot, and one of the causes of the King's acquiescence was that the appointment gave some prospect of Doctrinaire support in the Chamber for the approaching vote on the grant to the Duc de Nemours; for his son's marriage to a Saxe-Coburg princess ranked in Louis Philippe's mind as of almost equal importance to the Eastern Question. Soult meanwhile could avoid an official refusal by asserting that he had only received an unofficial communication of the new plan. When Granville, who complained that

---

[1] To Sébastiani, 5 Jan., 1840: *B.P.* This is written from Holland House, no doubt after discussion with Lord Holland. It refuses to communicate to Sébastiani the despatch to Brunnow which contained the details of the plan, but Palmerston had shewn it to him previously. To Granville, 3, 7 Jan, 1840: *B.P.* From Granville, 13 Jan., 1840: *L.P.*, I, Nos., 447, 448; do., 17 Jan., 1840, *F.O. France*, 601; do., 3, 6, 10, 13 Jan., 1840; From Bulwer, 13 Jan., 1840: *B.P.*

[2] From Granville, 20 Jan., 1840; To Granville, 23 Jan., 1840: *B.P.*

he himself had little knowledge of what was going on at London, spoke to the King about it, he made the same excuse.[1]

Soult was encouraged in this course by Apponyi, the Austrian Ambassador, who assured him that Metternich did not like the Russian plan. When Sébastiani reported that the British Cabinet had agreed to negotiate a treaty with the Sultan he said it would take two months for a Turkish representative to reach London. The official French answer eventually sent welcomed the new situation with regard to the Straits but insisted that no means existed for the coercion of Mehemet. There was thus no hurry and Guizot, in spite of Palmerston's urgent entreaties, remained at Paris to vote in the debate, and France, since Sébastiani had lost the confidence of his Government, was virtually unrepresented at London. It was clear also that Granville was now an inadequate representative of Palmerston's views, closely connected as he was with the policy of a French alliance. He said that the coercion of Mehemet by Britain might cost Louis Philippe his throne.[2]

Naturally this failure had its repercussions at Vienna and St. Petersburg, but the reaction was very different in the two places. At Vienna it sensibly reduced the boldness of Metternich, who, on the first news of Brunnow's plan, had promised that he would go on even if France refused, had hastened to send Neumann instructions to negotiate a comprehensive treaty and had even talked of sending Austrian troops to Crete. The effect was all the greater because he had heard from St. Aulaire of the refusal of the Cabinet to accept Brunnow's plan long before Neumann had realised all the implications of Palmerston's hesitations. The truth was, explained Beauvale, that members of the Cabinet were betraying its secrets to the French before Palmerston could adjust his official policy to their decisions. Metternich's confidence was shattered and he was now trying harder to repair his bridge with Russia than to press on with the coercion of Mehemet. Unless Palmerston stood firm against France he would find himself

[1] From Granville, 24 Jan., 1840: *L.P.*, I, No., 458; do., 27 Jan., 1840: *F.O. France*, 601; do., 24, 27 Jan., 3, 10, 14 Feb., 1840: *B.P.* Bulwer said that Sébastiani was recalled because he kept the Cabinet in ignorance of what he was doing, Granville that they felt his faculties were impaired, Palmerston, in 1843 (*Bulwer*, III, 429), because he was not sufficiently favourable to Mehemet Ali. Louis Philippe was greatly pleased at the handsome tribute paid to Sébastiani by the British Government and made him a Marshal, but that hardly helped him to exercise much influence when he got back to Paris.

[2] From Granville, 13, 27 Jan., 14 Feb., 1840: *B.P.*; do., 31 Jan., 1840: *L.P.*, I, No. 470. Soult to Sébastiani, 26 Jan., 1840: Guizot, *Mémoires*, IV, 568.

isolated. Beauvale himself dared not entrust his thoughts to an official despatch lest it be seen by members of the Cabinet who would disclose them to the French. Metternich, he added a little later, was sending new instructions to Neumann which he hoped would make Palmerston's task easier. These in fact were of little assistance. They exposed, indeed, the inconsistencies of French policy. But they recommended that the question of the Straits should first be settled separately by the Great Powers and the coercion of Mehemet be postponed until a more favourable moment. This was exactly what the French party in the Cabinet desired and Lord Holland wrote a note strongly urging that Metternich's scheme be accepted.[1]

At St. Petersburg, on the other hand, both the Tsar and his Minister had been made even more bitter against France by the communication by Bloomfield, who was in charge in Clanricarde's temporary absence, of a despatch of Soult strongly critical of Russian policy. They had received Brunnow's reports of his first interviews with great satisfaction, and Orlov said that any attack on the British fleet at the Dardanelles would be looked upon as an attack on Russia itself. Nor did they react so strongly as Brunnow had feared to the changes which Palmerston subsequently proposed. Nesselrode suggested that all mention of the number of ships should be left out of the agreement. But though the Tsar's hatred of France made him ready to accept almost anything that Britain offered, his Ministers, while moved by the same anti-French feelings, were not so complaisant. Nesselrode was shocked at the delay in the negotiations and by a speech of Peel which strongly advocated the French alliance. He also complained of the proposal to send for a Turkish Plenipotentiary. The truth was, confessed Clanricarde, that there were two opposite motives acting on Russian policy. Nesselrode above all wanted peace and talked of making some concession to Mehemet. The Tsar's main object was to isolate France. The communication of Soult's despatch, for which he took full responsibility on his return, alone enabled him to get the necessary action by Russia. But at any rate when this came it was very satisfactory. The Treaty of Unkiar Skelessi was virtually abandoned altogether

---

[1] From Beauvale, 12 Jan., 1840: *L.P.*, I, No. 453; do., 12 Jan., 3 Feb., 1840: *B.P.* Metternich to Neumann, 7 Feb., 1840: *F.O. Austria*, 293, with Minute by Lord Holland, 29 Feb., 1840.

and Britain placed on complete equality with Russia in any action in the Straits. And, most important of all, Brunnow was not to leave London but to remain as Envoy and Minister Extraordinary to carry on the negotiations. Both Tsar and Minister were convinced that France would never agree to action against Mehemet. This fact made the Tsar all the more ready to join with Britain for that purpose.[1]

At London, meanwhile, little could be done because of the new situation in France. On 20 February the refusal of the Chambers to make the grant to the Duc de Nemours drove Louis Philippe to violent expostulation, his wife to tears and the Cabinet to resignation. It was some time before a new Government could be formed. Thiers, in spite of the King's dislike of him, was the obvious successor to Soult. He shewed no great desire to assume the responsibility and tried to get Broglie to become Premier and Foreign Minister. But Broglie would not listen to Thiers whose return to office he was anxious to prevent. Soult was ready to resume office and much hurt that no one else, except the King, thought such a course desirable. The latter devised many other combinations but none were possible and eventually Thiers became President of the Council and Foreign Secretary; for nearly three weeks, however, the precarious nature of his position was almost the sole topic of Parisian society as he and Louis Philippe manoeuvred for position. Thiers' strength lay in the fact that he had control of a considerable portion of the Press, including the *Siècle*, which had a larger circulation than any other French newspaper. At last they came to an understanding, the King stating that Thiers' pacific views and attachment to the British alliance had won him over, and a handsome majority on the very controversial question of the disposal of the secret funds firmly established the new Ministry in office, too firmly indeed for Louis Philippe's liking. He was soon jealous of his Prime Minister.[2]

---

[1] From Clanricarde, 2, 14, 29 Jan., 11, 24 Feb., 3 March, 1840: *L.P.*, I, Nos. 491, 511 and *F.O. Russia*, 260. The dislike of the Russian Government to the inclusion of Turkey in the negotiations is carefully excluded from the *Levant Papers*. Brunnow's rank was not sufficiently high for him to be given the title of Ambassador. T. Schiemann (*Geschichte Russlands*, III, 393) states that it was a speech by Soult in the Chamber concerning Poland that made the Tsar go on.

[2] From Granville, 23 March, 1840: *B.P.* The principal influence on the French Press, however, was at this time Mehemet Ali himself whose subsidies were larger than those of the French Government. "He annually expends", reported Hodges, "350,000 francs on his mission in France over which Mons.

Thiers was later to claim, as Louis Philippe assured Granville at the time, that "the cornerstone of my policy has always been the English alliance".[1] He interpreted his policy, however, in a manner peculiarly his own. He made no concessions himself and expected the rest of Europe to give up their demands entirely. The situation was such that he had no alternative but to refuse to join Britain in the coercion of Mehemet Ali. His policy was, therefore, one of delay and obstruction, a course which, so he later stated, Granville advised him to pursue. But his imagination and energy and the influence on him of his study of the revolutionary and Napoleonic age made it impossible for him merely to remain passive. There is still some doubt as to how far he went in actively promoting a settlement between the Sultan and the Pasha while he was ostensibly still bound to pursue a common policy with the other Great Powers in accordance with the note of 27 July. But it is clear that up to the last minute he hoped to force Palmerston to abandon his policy completely.[2]

Guizot had arrived in London on the 27 February before Thiers came to power and it was for some time uncertain whether he would remain to serve the new Ministry. The advice of his friends on that point was conflicting. But Guizot was anxious to keep out of the melée at Paris for the time being and undoubtedly attracted by the new and unexpected position which he now occupied. He had never before been out of France and had no knowledge of diplomacy—except perhaps what his intimate connection with Princess Lieven had taught him. She was, however, not a very suitable instructress for one of Guizot's habits and temperament. There was much amusement when she followed him across the Channel at the crisis of the negotiations in which, as will be seen, she played no very helpful part. Guizot was enthusiastically received by the Hollands who were delighted to have an Ambassador so cultured and interested in the kind of table talk

Ouvrard presides. I know for a fact that he has given 100,000 fr. to the Journal des Débats, 35,000 to the Semaphore of Marseilles and 20,000 each to those other French newspapers as a remuneration for the advocacy of his cause for 12 months, and I believe that he places more reliance on the sympathies of the French nation as generated and fomented by the above organs than on the virtual support of the Executive Government." (To Palmerston, 23 Jan., 1840: B.P.)

[1] N. W. Senior, Conversations with M. Thiers, M. Guizot, etc., I, 4.

[2] In an interesting article ("La politique de Thiers pendant la crise orientale de 1840", Revue Historique, Jan., 1938, pp. 72–96) Professor C. H. Pouthas comes to conclusions about Thiers very much the same as those put forward here.

that filled the Holland House circle. In other quarters his rather undistinguished mien and stiff bourgeois manners did not make a very powerful impression. But he was always a good foil to the flamboyant Thiers and could be held up by those who attacked Palmerston's policy as a model of pacific and orthodox behaviour. Ostensibly he was on excellent terms with his chief but there was no real confidence between them. Louis Philippe, on the other hand, as the situation developed grew more and more to trust Guizot.

The uncertainty in France and the inevitable delay before the Russian attitude could be known prevented any progress being made in the negotiations in February and March. Brunnow kept himself in the background. The French Ambassador began quietly, explored London society and the London suburbs with a rather naïve curiosity but gradually learnt the cross-currents of the political situation. Neumann's new instructions reached him in the middle of the month and brought him, after a long delay of which he bitterly complained, once more into communication with Palmerston. Metternich's caution had moderated the rather excessive zeal with which Neumann had cooperated with Brunnow while at the same time his support of coercion was toned down. The ostensible instructions were communicated to Palmerston and the Cabinet, where, Neumann reported, they won strong approval. Metternich himself moved steadily in the direction of concession to Mehemet. He would, reported Beauvale in the middle of March, be prepared to give him Syria for his own life. He considered that the policy of coercion had practically been abandoned and that all that the Great Powers could do was to guarantee the Sultan against further attacks and await Mehemet's demise before further action was taken. The death of Clam at the beginning of March was a heavy blow to Metternich and to Beauvale's attempts to get active Austrian cooperation. He had now no means, the Ambassador confessed, of persuading Metternich to allow Austrian troops to join British naval forces.

Meanwhile Guizot had preliminary and non-committal discussions with Palmerston in which the difference between France and England was frankly reviewed. Guizot said that Mehemet could only be coerced with the help of Russia, a greater danger to the Ottoman Empire than the evil it was to remedy. Indeed the Sultan could not govern Syria if it were given back to him and his power did not depend on the extent of his territory. All this was said in as conciliatory a manner as possible in accordance with the advice of Desages who in a friendly note had warned the new envoy not to reproach Palmerston but to help him to find his way back to the alliance. But Palmerston shewed no signs of yielding. He replied that all history showed this last assertion to be false, that Russia would be no danger if controlled by a Concert, but a menace that might well cause war if she were forced to act by herself. But Russian troops would not be necessary. And he proceeded to sketch out a plan for "an expedition to Alexandria to strike at the heart of the Pasha's power. . . . I reminded him that about 13000 English had made good their landing in Egypt in face of a French army of 20 and 30000 men, and that a combined Austrian and Turkish expedition would drive like dust before them the artisans of the dockyard and the wretched Egyptians whom Mehemet Ali has now in Egypt, and that if he brought Mehemet's army from Syria to defend Egypt, the expedition would only have to change its direction and go and take possession of Syria then left defenceless."[1]

Thus it was necessary to look to Austria for help and the prospect there was not too good. Nevertheless Palmerston still saw in Austrian cooperation the main means of influencing the British Cabinet in the right direction. While he waited to see what would happen in France he tried to prepare the way for action. If Guizot refused to cooperate he would go on without France, he told Neumann in February, and he believed that he could get his Cabinet to agree to do so. "Let the French say what they like," he replied to Granville's warnings, "they *cannot* go to war with the Four Powers in support of Mehemet Ali." Brunnow had of course promised him all support. But it was necessary, Palmerston said a little later, to have some Austrian troops, so that it would not seem that the policy of coercion was only approved by Russia. Neumann could not help but admire the patience and persistence with which Palmerston opposed the French party in the Cabinet. Clarendon, he said, was the head of it and indeed

---

[1] Desages to Bourqueney, 2 March, 1840: *Bour. P., Appendix p.* 897. To Beauvale, 12 March, 1840: *B.P.* Guizot's account (5 March) in his *Mémoires* (V, 33–45) attributes to Palmerston the suggestion of a Russo-Turkish expedition, but this was written long afterwards and dressed up the despatch to Soult on which it is founded. (*A.A.E.* and Guichen, *Crise d'Orient,* 213–216, which gives an imperfect summary of it.)

from now on people began to talk of Clarendon as a possible successor to Palmerston. Neumann was induced to assist Palmerston to overcome the reluctance of his colleagues and had conversations with Lansdowne, Minto, Clarendon and Lord Holland. The promise of Austrian help would, Neumann informed Metternich, make all the difference to the situation.[1]

The instructions of Thiers to Guizot were necessarily only a repetition of the usual formula, the impossibility of coercing Mehemet since France could not do so. They went indeed beyond previous instructions for they insisted that it was necessary to take into account not only "l'ambition raisonnable mais encore l'amour propre" of the Pasha. His son, Ibrahim must, therefore, succeed to all Syria. A solemn warning was added that the Alliance depended upon the agreement of Britain and France on a question so fundamental. When Palmerston in answer to this said that he could not give the hereditary possession to Mehemet and take it away from his children, Guizot made a lame reply and, as he reported, the conversation then languished. Palmerston's reticence had the effect which he no doubt desired. Guizot warned Thiers that while the British Government was anxious not to destroy the alliance, they saw in the present situation an opportunity to protect their own interests in the East against both Russia and France which they did not wish to let slip.[2]

Palmerston informed Neumann immediately of this unpromising beginning and told him frankly that everything depended on the attitude of Austria. If she would give some help, say troops to Candia, not only would she satisfy his colleagues and British public opinion which disliked acting with Russia, but France herself would be forced to go with them. He would make a new attempt, he told Neumann, when Nourri arrived. The Turk could appeal with great moral effect to the joint note of 27 July, 1839. Meanwhile he needed, he said, all the help Neumann could give him with the Cabinet. He had, indeed, the latter reported, only four members of it on his side, Lansdowne, Minto, Hob-

---

[1] From Clanricarde, 24 Feb., 1840: *B.P.* Metternich to Neumann, 7 Feb., 1840: *F.O. Austria*, 292. To Granville, 11 Feb., 1840: *B.P.* Neumann to Metternich, 9, 10, 11, 18 Feb., 9, 11 March, 1840: *V. St. A.*
[2] Thiers to Guizot, 12 March, 1840; Guizot to Thiers, 16 March, 1840: *A.A.E.* (small extracts in Guichen, *La Crise d'Orient*, 262–263). The original draft had referred to the 'vanité' of Mehemet which Thiers altered to 'amour propre'.

house and John Russell. All the rest with Lord Holland at their
head refused to break with France. He urged Metternich to give
Palmerston the necessary support.

The test of the Austrian attitude would come when the Turkish
representative appeared. Ponsonby had been able to get Reschid
to send orders to Nourri Pasha to go at once to London while
Chekib, considered a more reliable envoy, would shortly follow
from Constantinople with the ostensible object of congratulating
Queen Victoria on her marriage, a happy thought of the young
Sultan himself. Meanwhile it was encouraging to know that the
Russian representative had received orders from St. Petersburg to
cooperate with Ponsonby in inspiring the Porte with confidence
in the Great Powers, while, though Ponsonby himself wished to
have specific instructions in case of an attack by Ibrahim, Hodges
reported from Alexandria that there were no signs of Mehemet
being bold enough to order his son to advance.[1]

Meanwhile Neumann, who had been warned by Metternich not
to be too intimate with Brunnow, reported with a certain satisfaction the Russian envoy's growing irritation and sense of frustration at the delay. Brunnow had expected to accomplish his
mission in a few weeks. Now he had given up hope and was preparing to return to Darmstadt. But towards the end of March he
received the new instructions from Nesselrode which informed
him of his permanent appointment to London and the acceptance
by his Court of practically all Palmerston's demands. This new
concession which Neumann attributed to the fear of a new clash
with Britain in Central Asia at a time when Russia was especially
weak, was conveyed in a private letter. It was, therefore, some
time before his new position could be made generally known in
London, and Brunnow's influence on the negotiations was to
Neumann's great pleasure sensibly diminished. On the other
hand, Bülow had been sent back to replace the young and inexperi-
enced Werther. In accordance with Metternich's instructions
Neumann did everything possible to bring him into the negotiations. The two determined to work together for a solution of the
Eastern Question by making great concessions to France. At the
same time the *amour propre* of Neumann, who had now such a

[1] Neumann to Metternich, 17, 23 March, 1840: *V. St. A.* From Ponsonby,
26, 28 Jan., 18, 26 Feb., 1840: *L.P.*, I, Nos. 513, 516, and *F.O. Turkey*, 392.
From Hodges, 6 Feb., 1840: *L.P.*, I, No. 504.

central position in the negotiations, made him strive his hardest
to produce a result.[1]

The diplomatic moves were now concentrated on Nourri Pasha,
the rather stupid and somewhat suspect Turkish representative
who came to London from Paris at Reschid's orders. Granville
reported that he was against coercion and he had told Thiers, who
tried to get him to promise to advocate a direct arrangement
between the Sultan and Mehemet, that he had no Full Powers and
would sign nothing. But, as Palmerston had foreseen, once
Nourri got to London he subjected himself entirely to the advice
of those on the spot. "Poor old Nourri", he told Beauvale, "is
a perfect cipher but he can hold his pen and sign his name."
This is exactly what Nourri did. He had indeed some difficult
moments. Palmerston advised him to appeal to the note of 27 July
and claim the support of the Powers because the Porte had been
so weakened since Navarino by the Great Powers themselves. To
draft such a note was far beyond Nourri's powers and he had no
capable assistant. In this extremity he turned to Neumann who
was delighted to supply the necessary document. Neumann left
out, it would seem wisely, all reference to Navarino, but drafted
a vigorous note. Palmerston, unaware of the real author, made one
important alteration and so Nourri was able to send a compelling
appeal to the representatives of the Great Powers. It emphasised
the promises made by them to the Porte, narrated the nefarious
conduct of Mehemet, and demanded their cooperation in order to
put an end to evils of so serious a nature, for which purpose, Nourri
informed them, he was empowered to conclude a Convention. It
was expressly said that Mehemet ought to surrender all territory
outside Egypt. This claim was due to Palmerston for Neumann
had tried to leave the way open to the largest possible concessions.[2]

This was an important step forward but what difficulties still
remained were seen when the Powers came to consider how it
should be answered. Palmerston invited Guizot to join the other
four Powers in a conference to draft a joint reply. Guizot of
course could do no more than acknowledge the receipt of the note

[1] Neumann to Metternich, 24 March, 1840: *V. St. A.*
[2] Neumann to Metternich, 11 April, 1840: *V. St. A.* In order to leave nothing
in his handwriting Neumann dictated the note to Nourri's interpreter. Guizot
saw that Nourri could not have drafted it himself and thought that Palmerston
had done it. (Guizot to Thiers, 13 April, 1840: *A.A.E.*) Bülow alone was told
the truth. Nourri to Palmerston, 7 April, 1840: *L.P.*, I, No. 541.

and refer it to his Government. Thiers at first said that no answer would be given. He refused, he told Guizot, to take it seriously. It simply repeated the old arguments which had been so often refuted. Whatever France meant by her signature of the note of 27 July she did not mean what Nourri demanded. And if she were criticised for not going on with the others at London, had she not the same right to withdraw, if she were in a minority. as Russia had to refuse to negotiate at Vienna? This would indeed have let the other Powers know exactly where France stood and Guizot with great wisdom refused to act on it. It would simply leave open the way for a Four Power treaty without France. But though no formal answer was made by Guizot, Thiers stated frankly to Granville that France must refuse to enter into any conference to discuss the coercion of Mehemet Ali because her views on that subject differed so radically from those of the other four Powers.[1]

Even agreement between the Four was, however, found to be difficult. Brunnow had disliked bringing in a Turk, partly, so Neumann alleged, because it deprived him of the premier role in the negotiations. He joined with Palmerston in wishing to emphasise the threat of sanctions in the reply, but Neumann and Bülow, who met his violent and insistent tone with a concerted coolness of manner, insisted that the cooperation of the Powers to implement the note of 27 July should only be stated in the most general terms in order to enable France to subscribe to it. "The negotiation is thus well launched," wrote Palmerston, "and I hope it may be brought to a satisfactory end, *with* France, if possible, but *without* France, if she will not concur." But when France made her vague response nothing had really been agreed by the rest and it could hardly be claimed that much progress had been made.[2]

Events in other parts of the world now threw obstacles in the way of agreement. The violent quarrel which had arisen between

[1] From Granville, 13, 17 April, 1840: *F.O. France*, 602 (*L.P.*, I, Nos. 545, 547). Thiers to Guizot, 14 April, 1840: *A.A.E.* Guizot, *Mémoires*, V, 78. Granville's despatch of the 17 April was often used by Palmerston in later discussions of the French attitude at this time.

[2] Guizot to Thiers, 7 April, 1840: Guizot, *Mémoires*, V, 76. Neumann to Metternich, 11 April, 1840: *V. St. A.* Palmerston to Nourri Effendi, 11 April, 1840: *L.P.*, I, No. 543. Neumann wrote that Palmerston insisted on the word 'immediately' and redrafted the note so that it enabled the other Powers to act together without France.

Britain and Naples over the British sulphur mines alarmed Metternich and made him still more pacific on the Eastern Question,
while it gave Thiers an opportunity for shewing his friendship
for England by acting as mediator. The situation in Central Asia
was causing both Britain and Russia anxiety. Bülow indeed
informed Neumann that according to Russian information both
Nesselrode and Orlov were sick of the Eastern Question and only
the Tsar's hatred of Louis Philippe, on which Brunnow played in
his despatches, prevented them from giving way to France. The
Tsar himself showed some impatience at the long delay and
told Clanricarde that moderation so far from bringing France in
would have the contrary effect.[1]

Palmerston, while maintaining his position in all essentials
during this period and urging that the Four should find a way to
act without France, had necessarily to wait on events. His principal object was to keep Austria firm and here he had but indifferent success. Metternich told Beauvale that he had come to the
conclusion that coercion at this time was impossible, that Mehemet
had better be given Syria for life, care being taken that it was on
his death split up amongst his descendants. Meanwhile the Great
Powers should guarantee the *status quo* and prevent any attack.
He promised to await Palmerston's reply before stating this view
definitely to the other Powers, but on 25 April in a long and
pessimistic review he shewed behind a mass of verbiage his conviction that the situation was hopeless if France did not join the
other Powers. Palmerston meanwhile used every effort to shew
Neumann that the coercion of Mehemet was perfectly feasible
without France. He was encouraged in this view by the optimistic
reports and letters which Ponsonby was sending from Constantinople.[2]

Ponsonby had, it is true, plenty of difficulties to cope with. His
confidence in the good effects of the new reforms ebbed rapidly
and it was soon seen that they increased rather than diminished
the rapacity and corruption of the provincial governors. The
combination of the modern Reschid with Husrev and the old gang
at the Porte was an uneasy one, and Ponsonby was soon once more

---

[1] Neumann to Metternich, 3 May, 1840: *V. St. A.* From Clanricarde,
4 May, 1840: *F.O. Russia*, 260.
[2] Neumann to Metternich, 3, 8 May, 1840: *V. St. A.* Metternich to Neumann, 25 April, 1840: Metternich, *Mémoires*, VI, 454. From Beauvale, 24,
25 April, 1840: *F.O. Austria*, 290.

in the thick of intricate manoeuvres concerned with changes in the Ministry. Reschid himself was surrounded by Frenchmen, and Ponsonby occasionally suspected his complete loyalty to the British view. But on the main point of holding the Porte firm on the question of Mehemet Ali he was always able to report satisfactorily. The negotiations and intrigues between Alexandria and Constantinople never ceased, and on occasion Mehemet seemed to have made some progress. But Ponsonby was always able to pull back the Sultan's Ministers on to the right line by an exertion of his vigorous personality. Thus, when Reschid wished to make a vague reply to Mehemet's official offers to restore the fleet if the rest of his demands were conceded, he insisted on the despatch of an uncompromising rejoinder. Though he reported more than once that Pontois was urging Reschid to come to a separate arrangement with the Pasha, that Minister always informed him at once of the approaches made to him. Husrev, however, though in the eyes of the world the symbol of opposition to Mehemet, could not be trusted. Mehemet was gradually penetrating the Harem of the new Sultan who proved to be no less susceptible to the influence of favourites than his predecessors, and the Sultan's Mother was very suspect. But no one was found courageous enough to defy the Ambassador, especially as he now had the support of the representatives of the Eastern Powers.

Ponsonby was also using all his energy not only to make the Porte safe from attack by Ibrahim but even to prepare the way for an offensive against him. By incessant pressure he got troops collected to oppose any advance of the Egyptian forces and Chrysanowski placed, though unofficially, in control of them. This necessitated the removal of both the Commander-in-Chief and the Minister of War, and it was not until the end of May that the process was completed and Ponsonby could advise Palmerston that Constantinople was safe from attack by Ibrahim.[1]

But in addition Ponsonby began to prepare for the attack on Mehemet, and his foresight and energy and the advice which he now gave to Palmerston contributed greatly to the rapid success of the autumn. He assured Palmerston at an early stage that the

[1] From Ponsonby, 15, 22, 27 April: *B.P.*; do., 26, 28 Jan., 7, 23 March, 10, 25, 26 April, 7, 14, 15, 17, 26 May, 1840: *F.O. Turkey*, 392–396. *L.P.*, I (Nos. 494–496, 504, 513, 526, 530, 570, 571, 582–588) leaves a great deal out.

Sultan would facilitate the establishment of a blockade and be able to send ships to join in it. Even at the beginning of January he claimed "I will raise the Druses against Ibrahim if you choose" Then reports began to come in of the growing discontent of the Syrians, in which the powerful chief Emir Bechir shared, at the enforcement of conscription and other arbitrary measures of Ibrahim. As early as March the Druses, the most warlike of the tribes, secretly appealed to British agents for help from Britain. Ponsonby suggested that he should get the Porte to promise them their ancient rights and perhaps the city of Acre. The reply given to them was that Britain was the upholder of the Sultan's authority, but Ponsonby had no doubt that he could raise the whole country if Britain shewed that she intended to act. "I could if you direct it bring this [unrest] to a head," he wrote in March . . . "I know how to act upon the Druses. I think it much to be desired that the inhabitants of Lebanon should have privileges secured to them by our aid and I think it could be done." He admitted that it was essential for either France or Russia to be on the British side so that the other would be held in check. In that case the task was an easy one. "Neither will stir and whatever we desire can be done. As to the power of Mehemet I think it is despicable. I have told you I can raise the Druses. All Syrians that can get a musket will act against the Pasha. The Sultan's flag united with the English will bring all Mussulmen to our side." This was an exact prophecy of what was to take place later on, but at this period Ponsonby almost alone of those in a position of responsibility believed such a course to be possible.[1]

Hodges, indeed, was sending in his private letters a somewhat similar view. According to him Mehemet was depending on the dissensions of the Great Powers which he thought would prevent effective action. The Russian Consul, Medem, spoke Turkish and had many private interviews with the Pasha, and to a late date Hodges continued to reiterate his suspicions that Russia was behind Mehemet's obstinacy. But at the same time he asserted that Mehemet would not stand up to Britain if she acted alone. He deprecated an attack on Alexandria which would need 15,000 troops, but naval action would he thought intimidate the Pasha.

---

[1] From Ponsonby, 8 Jan., 23 March, 8 April, 1840: *B.P.*; do., 3 March, 1840 (with Consul Moore to Ponsonby, 21 Feb., 1840), *L.P.*, I, 526; do., 3 March, 1840: *F.O. Turkey*, 392.

Hodges' judgments are emotional and rash but he also foresaw that Mehemet could be easily defeated.[1]

Palmerston had need of all the encouragement that Ponsonby could give during the next six weeks. He got little from other sources and those on whom he had counted most were most urgent that he should give way. Guizot was allowed by his chief to negotiate, though not to take part in a conference, but every communication from Paris shewed that Thiers would not accept less than Mehemet demanded. Palmerston had agreed immediately to Thiers' request to bring back the remains of Napoleon from St. Helena and hoped the French would be more malleable: "This will amuse the public mind for six months to come and make those full grown children think less of other things." Neumann told Metternich that he by no means shared Palmerston's illusion that effective sanctions could be taken without the assistance of France. He and Palmerston, however, were still working closely together and it was at his insistence that a new and important offer was made to Guizot.

The new offer was better than that made and withdrawn in October, 1839—not only the Pashalik of Acre, but the fortress and part of lower Syria to Beirut to Mehemet for life. The French official answer was that Mehemet Ali must be consulted before they could reply, but Thiers told Guizot that he would not accept it. No other reply was made until June when it was said that Syria could not be cut in two. Palmerston attributed this obstinacy to the influence of Edward Ellice, who, whatever his language to Granville, had been intriguing against Palmerston at Paris. The Embassy staff also, he said, was not without blame, a remark at which Granville was much hurt. Thiers, he wrote, had given his reason for the refusal, the impossibility of coercing Mehemet, and Granville clearly agreed with him.

Neumann was indignant at French intransigeance, but Palmerston said there was nothing to do but wait. He would go on without France if she refused, he told Neumann. But for the Cabinet, the latter thought, he would do so at once. In order to overcome the Cabinet's reluctance Austrian cooperation in sanctions must be obtained. The real difficulty lay not in Paris or Alexandria but in London itself. When Palmerston warmly defended Russia's good faith in the House, his opponents in the

---

[1] From Hodges, 23 Jan., 1, 21 April, 1840: *B.P.*

Cabinet said that he was being duped by her. Melbourne told him that, though the "large majority" of the Cabinet would support him, it would be with fear and reluctance. It was true that Brunnow was doing everything he could to prevent an arrangement with France. Thus Neumann had to report complete failure to his chief, though, as will be seen, the fact that this offer was made and rejected in such a manner had an important effect on the last stage of the discussions. But Metternich by no means approved the step. The offer should only have been made, he said, after it had been agreed to by the other three and the British Cabinet. He scolded Neumann for taking so much on himself. Nevertheless the incident seems to have produced considerable effect. Metternich noted on Neumann's despatches that Britain and Russia had the means of action if they chose to employ them and that while the cooperation of Russia was indispensable to success that of France was not.[1]

This situation came to a head in June when Chekib Pasha arrived from Constantinople to replace Nourri who was only too glad to get back to Paris. Chekib, who was from the first anxious for a settlement, received shortly after his arrival new instructions which seemed to make one urgent and was ready for almost any concession to obtain it. He claimed with some reason that Britain ought by now to have settled what action should be taken. Neumann agreed with him and determined to use Chekib to force a solution on Palmerston even if it meant conceding the whole of Syria. Thus after Palmerston and Brunnow had told Chekib that there was no necessity for haste, Neumann and Bülow gave him contrary advice and without Palmerston's knowledge Neumann drafted a note from him to the Great Powers, and another to Palmerston, pressing for a decision. The note made no stipulations but the language used implied that great concessions to the Pasha would be made. Since Palmerston knew that he could not get the reply to Chekib's communication which he desired, he played for delay and refused to do anything, in spite of a stiff note

[1] To Beauvale, 12, 19 May, 1840: B.P.; do., 20 May, 1840: L.P., I, No. 575 and F.O. Austria, 288. Neumann to Metternich, 9, 12, (Appendix, p. 876–7), 19, 22 May, 10 June, 1840: V. St. A. with Metternich's notes. Guizot, Mémoires, V, 85–88, 189–190. To Granville, 29 May, 1840; From Granville, 1 June, 1840: B.P. "I have seen a great deal of Ellice," wrote Princess Lieven to Earl Grey, 19 May, 1840 (G. Le Strange, Corres. Princess Lieven and Grey, III, 317). From Melbourne, 7 June, 1840: B.P. Lord Holland was already talking of recording a minute of protest.

sent to him by Neumann which enclosed his official report to
Metternich of the urgent necessity of immediate action. Chekib
himself was rebuked by Palmerston for telling the other representatives that he would settle at any price, a thing he protested he
had never done. Neumann's exasperation and frustration were so
great that he prepared to appeal to Melbourne and the Cabinet.
They should at least be made aware, he said, how far Austria was
prepared to go to obtain French assent and thus a pacific solution
of the whole matter. And in his desire for action he took an even
graver step. For, in a private and unofficial conversation with
Guizot, he offered him the whole of Syria including Aleppo and
Scanderoon, though of course not with hereditary tenure. When
Guizot transmitted this offer to Thiers he obviously thought that
France had won the game. He told Neumann that if Palmerston delayed much longer he would send Chekib an answer
himself.[1]

When the situation was at this critical stage, more critical
perhaps than was realised by Palmerston, who never lost his confidence or sangfroid, it was transformed by further news from
Constantinople and a change in Metternich's attitude. From
Constantinople came reports of three important alterations in the
situation. First the deposition of Husrev, which had been foreseen
and indeed welcomed by Ponsonby, who thought that the old
man's "persevering venality and corruption" entirely justified it.
But by the world it was regarded as a symbol that the Porte was
going at last to make terms with Mehemet, and the Vice-Roy
himself received the news of the fall of his old enemy with loud
demonstrations of joy. He sent at once an emissary, Sami Bey, to
offer to return the Turkish fleet. He had high hopes that he would
be able to retain all his conquests and obtain the hereditary
possession of Syria. The situation at Constantinople was at any

---

[1] Neumann to Metternich, 10, 12, 15 June, 1840: *V. St. A.* Guizot, *Mémoires*, V, 197–201. (Neumann made the offer on the 12 June, Guizot reported
it on the 15 June, Thiers on the 19 sent a reply which was not clear, Guizot
asked for an explanation on the 24 June, Thiers replied on the 30 June that he
could only accept hereditary Syria which he had meant in his previous reply.)
Chekib to Palmerston, 31 May, 1840: *L.P.*, I, No. 580. This was addressed to
the representatives of all the Great Powers. There is another addressed to
Palmerston personally (do., No. 579) asking for quick action. From Neumann,
10 June, 1840, (with his ostensible despatch of 10 June): *B.P.* In a letter of
15 August Neumann confessed to Palmerston that he had offered the Pashalik
of Aleppo to Guizot who had demanded it 'hereditarily' which he had refused.
F.O. Austria, 292.

rate growing more serious and the Russian and Austrian Ambassadors reported on it to their courts with far more alarm than Ponsonby himself at first shewed.

The British Ambassador, however, added more definite information on a topic to which he had previously alluded, the endeavours of M. Coste, a French journalist, on intimate terms with Thiers, to persuade Reschid to make a deal with Mehemet Ali. Though the final proof is not extant it is almost certain that Thiers was cognisant of and had perhaps inspired this attempt to defeat the negotiation at London on which France was still ostensibly engaged. It was at any rate one of the main reasons why he refused Guizot's advice to accept the offer of Syria for life and told him that, now that Husrev was gone, the matter would soon be arranged at Constantinople.

Lastly, Ponsonby was able to report that the Syrian insurrection had begun, that the insurgents were appealing to England and France and that he had advised Reschid to encourage the revolt and promised to try to get the British Admiral to send ships to Beirut. Since the mission of Sami Bey was supported by the Sultan's mother and the Sultan was anxious to get back his fleet, the situation was not without danger, though he and Stürmer hoped to prevent any yielding to Mehemet.[1]

The news of these events had important effects both at St. Petersburg and Vienna. They likewise startled Brunnow, who also received peremptory orders from Nesselrode, and made him almost as anxious as Neumann to bring the negotiation to an end. He had, hitherto, like Palmerston, been playing for time. He now joined Neumann in urging Palmerston to force the issue. But above all they helped Metternich to a decision, which he seems to have been contemplating for some time, to contribute Austrian

---

[1] From Ponsonby, 20 May, 23 June, 1840: *B.P.*; do., 29 May, 8, 9, 23 June, 1840: *L.P.*, I, No. 613, and *F.O. Turkey*, 394. For M. Coste's intrigue see Major John Hall, *England and the Orleans Monarchy*, 270–272. These letters were obtained by the ubiquitous Vogorides. (From Ponsonby, 13 Sept., 1840: *B.P.*) Thiers always denied that he had tried to make a separate arrangement between the Porte and Mehemet and no doubt this was true so far as official action was concerned. For his confident belief that it would ensue see Guizot, *Mémoires*, V, 206, and his comment: "C'était précisément là le vœu du cabinet français, et le but vers lequel il tendait constamment en dépit des entraves que lui imposait l'engagement d'action commune contracté entre les cinq puissances par la note du 27 juillet 1839." Cochelet to Thiers, 26 May, 1840: E. Driault, *L'Egypte et l'Europe*, 1839–1841, II, 295. In June Thiers tried to send Bresson to Constantinople but that wily diplomat, one of Louis Philippe's personal appointments, refused to go. (From Will. Russell, 24 June, 1840: *B.P.*)

forces for joint coercive action even if France would not agree to associate herself with the other Powers.[1]

Palmerston himself, though imperfectly aware of the intentions of Neumann and Bülow, could not help but be moved by the insistence from so many quarters that the decision must be taken. For long he resisted all their attempts to make concessions to France. When asked for an alternative plan he confessed that he had not got one but was waiting on events. Finally he agreed that part of Syria should be offered to Mehemet and the fact stated in the reply to Chekib. Neumann meant that part to extend to Aleppo and hoped that, if the Cabinet agreed, France would then be forced to come in by the threat that the Four Powers were united and would go on without her. He then with great energy tried to influence all the various parties whose consent was indispensable. He urged on Melbourne the necessity of Cabinet backing for Palmerston if France was to be brought in. Melbourne, however, was most pessimistic and said that without France it would be impossible to get more than Adana from the Pasha, perhaps not even that. He talked of the dangers from Russia and was in no way comforted when Neumann tried to shew him that there was every prospect of obtaining agreement. With other members of the Cabinet Neumann had more success and got them to agree that they would consent to such a plan as he had proposed if Palmerston put it before them.

Guizot, as he had long threatened to do, now replied to Chekib himself in a note which promised nothing at all. He could not say more because Thiers refused to make any concessions. This was a mistake on Guizot's part as it emphasised the isolation of France. But when Neumann pointed out how much Palmerston's reputation was involved, Guizot promised to do his utmost to get a new offer accepted. It looked both to Guizot and to Neumann as if agreement was in sight on the basis of giving to Mehemet all

[1] Neumann to Metternich, 12 June, 1840: *V. St. A.* The fall of Husrev was not reported officially by Ponsonby until the 8 June, but he had indicated it must happen on the 24 May. The news seems to have reached London on 11 June. The reports of the Austrian and Russian Ambassadors had been pessimistic before the final denouément and it must have been before the news of Husrev's fall reached him that Nesselrode instructed Brunnow to press for a decision. Bloomfield knew nothing of this and reported on the 20 June that the Russian Government had become 'indifferent' to the subject. *F.O. Russia,* 261.

Syria for life, as Metternich had proposed in April, if France would agree to ensure Mehemet's acceptance.[1]

It is improbable that Palmerston would ever have consented to have gone so far, but Neumann had in fact pressed his scheme too fast. Chekib himself, indeed, professed satisfaction and Bülow was assisting Neumann with all his power. But Brunnow said that he refused to pass under the Caudine Forks of France. He urged Palmerston not to give way. Even more important was it that Guizot could not get his chief to move an inch from his position. Thiers naturally refused contemptuously, when Guizot at Palmerston's request pressed for an answer, the offer of the Pashalik of Acre, thus giving official proof of refusal to compromise which Palmerston could lay before the Cabinet. But he also would have nothing to do with the suggestion that Neumann and Bülow were putting forward with Chekib's consent of all Syria, though without hereditary possession. The news of Husrev's fall confirmed him in the belief that the question would be settled at Constantinople. There was no hurry, he told Guizot. Both his Ambassador and Neumann were helpless. In his *Mémoires* Guizot claims that he himself was aware of the danger of the situation. He does not mention what provoked the mingled amusement and irritation of the Diplomatic Corps, that Princess Lieven had arrived from Paris to join the pedantic but obviously lovesick Ambassador. What advice she gave is not exactly known but it seems certain that she led Guizot astray on one all important point. For the King of Prussia had died on 7 June, and she extracted from Bülow the information that he had not received Full Powers from his new monarch and deduced from that fact that a treaty could not be signed at once.

Thus the Austrian plan could not go forward with the prospect that France would accept it. Nevertheless Neumann insisted that the Cabinet should be informed of how far Austria was prepared to go, and Palmerston promised that if they would not accept his own line he would put the other before them, though he did not say he would support it himself. Since Brunnow declared that the Austrian plan was nothing less than the French plan in disguise he was backing Palmerston strongly. On the 30 June Neumann had

---

[1] Neumann to Metternich, 22, (*Appendix*, p. 878) 23, 26 June, 1840: *V. St. A.* Note of Guizot to Chekib, 21 June, 1840: Guizot, *Mémoires*, V, 443. A. Hasenclever, *Die orientalische Frage*, 155–156, gives Bülow's account of the intricate negotiations of these days.

little hopes of what to him would seem a satisfactory result. In either case Russia stood to gain. If the Cabinet accepted Palmerston's plan, France would be isolated, secretly the real desire of Russia. If not, then the affair would most probably fall into Russian hands to settle at some future date.[1]

But Palmerston was by no means in despair. The news of the Syrian revolt had at last revealed a method of expelling Ibrahim from Syria, if the chance were taken at once. "I will fairly own", he wrote later to Ponsonby, "that till this insurrection broke out I did not clearly see my way as to the means by which we could drive Mehemet out of Syria." Now that had appeared he was most eager of all to get an agreement and ready to force the issue with the Cabinet. And Neumann just in time was given hope by receiving from Metternich the new instructions which authorised him to offer Austrian assistance in coercion without the participation of France. He at once communicated the despatch to Palmerston for use with his colleagues at the meeting of the Cabinet, where it had a decisive influence on the course of events.[2]

The discussions had now reached an acute stage. When Palmerston pressed for a decision, Melbourne was now of the opinion that the majority of the Cabinet would not agree to his plan. A meeting on 5 July shewed that this forecast was correct. Clarendon, who with Holland was the most intractable, complained to Melbourne that it was too vague. Palmerston immediately sent his resignation to Melbourne who, however, entreated him to await another Cabinet before he finally made up his mind. The Cabinet, he added with characteristic insouciance, might very likely be forced to resign on another difficulty, and was that not better than revealing their differences over the Eastern Question? He suggested that Palmerston should wait for the result of next day's division.

[1] Neumann to Metternich, 29, 30 June, 1840: *V. St. A.* Guizot, *Mémoires*, V, 199–203. Neumann's acid comments on Princess Lieven were no doubt specially meant to please her old lover. He says that she in vain tried to pump Lady Palmerston and to extract information from Bülow.

[2] To Ponsonby, 15 July, 1840: *B.P.* Metternich to Neumann, 24 June, 1840: *F.O. Austria*, 292. Palmerston received on 28 June a despatch of 10 June from Ponsonby (*L.P.*, I, No. 596), giving Hodges' opinion that Mehemet could be overcome by naval action on the Syrian coast and confirming the news which had already been sent of the discontent in Syria. This seems to have been the information to which he alludes in his letter. Much previous information had already come in of a less definitive kind. Moore's report of 10 June, as sent by Ponsonby did not arrive till 12 July, but it may have reached Palmerston earlier by another route. (*L.P.*, I, No. 613.)

Palmerston's reply was crushing. His letter reviewed the whole course of the negotiation and came to the conclusion that if Britain now refused to go forward with the three Governments the Ottoman Empire would be divided into two parts, one of which would be under the control of Russia and the other of France. Twice before, in 1833 and in 1835, had Palmerston been overruled by the Cabinet when he tried to find means to preserve the Ottoman Empire. He was so certain now that he was right that, if he were wrong on this, he could, he wrote, be of no further use to the Cabinet.

Melbourne was at last fully aroused to the gravity of the situation. He entreated Palmerston to await the result of another Cabinet before he took the fatal step. This Palmerston agreed to do stating that he had thought it fairer to give Melbourne a free hand and had not thought his resignation would necessarily break up the Cabinet. To this Melbourne replied in a note obviously written in great haste and agitation, that his resignation would dissolve the Government. A last attempt by Lord John Russell to find some compromise seems to have had no effect at all.

A further Cabinet was held on the 8th and this time, after a long discussion, Palmerston was triumphant. Melbourne's endeavours to prevent a rupture at the last minute may have influenced Lord Holland and Clarendon. Palmerston's threat to break up the Cabinet was no doubt the most important factor in forcing the decision. But the news of the Syrian insurrection gave him a powerful reason for acting immediately. The official refusal of France to agree to the scheme which Palmerston and Neumann had proposed shewed that he had made concessions which had been contemptuously put on one side. He was also able to shew, partly by means of a despatch of Apponyi, that Thiers was playing false and seeking to make a separate arrangement at Constantinople. And the news that Austria would join in coercive action without France made just that extra bit of difference that turned the scale. There were no resignations. Holland and Clarendon contented themselves with adding a formal record of their dissent to the Minute which, in view of the gravity of the decision, was submitted to the Queen.[1]

[1] To Melbourne, 5, 6 July, 1840: *Bulwer*, II, 356, 361. The draft at Broadlands of the first of these shews how carefully Palmerston prepared one of the most trenchant of his letters. From Melbourne, 4, 6, 7, 8 July, 1840: *B.P. Appendix*, p. 857. The letters between Melbourne and Clarendon, 6, 7 July, is

The representatives of the other Powers were summoned to hear the details on 9 July in an atmosphere of mutual congratulation. Chekib, whose name signified 'patience', was overjoyed, thus, as Palmerston told Ponsonby, refuting by his manner the allegations that he was pro-Mehemet. Palmerston congratulated the others on their patience also as he informed them that he had been given authority to draw up a convention by the Cabinet.

Now that he had gained his object Palmerston moved at a pace which astonished Neumann. He and Bülow agreed immediately to all Palmerston's proposals which were worked out with the greatest clarity. Brunnow was far more afraid of responsibility and wanted to insert once more the exact number of ships to be employed in the Sea of Marmora, and to refer the whole question to St. Petersburg. But Bülow and Neumann got him to agree by promising to force Palmerston to accept such an arrangement over the Straits as would ensure him against censure from his Court. This was done by means of a note from Palmerston assuring Brunnow that only a small number of British ships would be sent through the Dardanelles in any event. Neumann wrote in pity and contempt of Brunnow's senile fears and the miserable life of a Russian agent who must always be afraid of the anger of the Tsar if he made a false move. As for Princess Lieven, he added, after recounting her attempt to extract information from Bülow, she had indeed fallen from the high position that she once held in Society.[1]

In Palmerston's view, however, the agreement to close the Straits to warships satisfied the interests of both Britain and

in Sir H. Maxwell, *Clarendon*, I, 194–195. To Beauvale, 9 July, 1840: *B.P.*, in which Palmerston lays special stress on the refusal by Thiers of the offer, which he said had much influence in the Cabinet, but this may have been due to a desire to shield Neumann who had acted in this way without Metternich's instructions. The authority for the minute of Lord Holland and Clarendon is given by Professor Bell (*Palmerston*, I, 485) as Windsor Archives, and Professor Temperley (*Crimea*, 486) actually printed it as an appendix from that source, but it had of course long been in print in Sir H. Maxwell, *Clarendon*, I, 196. Nor is it as is stated (*Crimea*, 113) "almost unprecedented", though such minutes and dissenting opinions were only used infrequently. Neumann to Metternich, 9 July, 1840, who had an account of the Cabinet discussion from Lord Normanby, stresses the points made above and adds that even Lord Holland had admitted that Austria had given the "casting vote". *V. St. A., Appendix*, p. 878. From Minto, 6 July, 1840: *B.P.* pressing Palmerston to get a decision. Broughton, *Recollections*, V, 277.

[1] To Beauvale, 15 July, 1840; To Ponsonby, 15 July, 1840: *B.P.* To Brunnow, 15 July, 1840: *L.P.*, I, No. 622. Neumann to Metternich, 16 July, 1840: *V. St. A. Appendix*, p. 883.

Russia. "What the Emperor really wanted in all this transaction", he told Beauvale, "is the article about ships of war not passing the Dardanelles and I do not think that Brunnow would have lightly run the chance of losing that by postponing signature till he could refer to the Emperor. On our part I consider this article as an advantage gained. We were bound to this by the Treaty of 1809 but Russia was free; now both are bound alike and the Porte is as secure as paper can make her against uninvited visitors from the Black Sea. Notwithstanding all the clamour raised for an opposite system, I much prefer that the Straights should be closed rather than that there should be a thoroughfare. It is an additional security for peace."

This general rule, of course, remained suspended during the immediate emergency which was the occasion of the convention. This was mainly directed to the coercion of Mehemet, should he refuse the conditions offered to him by the Sultan of which the Powers had approved. His communications were to be cut by British and Austrian naval forces. Should he advance on Constantinople all the Powers were entitled to come to the Sultan's defence. This act was, however, to be an exception to the ancient rule of the Ottoman Empire that, "as long as the Porte is at peace", no foreign warship should pass the Bosphorus or the Dardanelles.

In another convention the terms to be offered to Mehemet Ali were laid down in a very Palmerstonian manner, the hereditary rule of Egypt and the Pashalik of Acre for life if he at once accepted. If he did not do so in ten days the offer of the Pashalik was to be withdrawn. If he did not do so in another ten days the offer as regards Egypt itself was no longer valid. All other possessions of Mehemet were to be given up and the Turkish fleet with its crews and equipment was to be returned to the Sultan. It was also expressly provided that the laws of the Ottoman Empire were to apply to Mehemet's possessions and that his army and fleet were to be part of the Imperial forces. Egypt would thus be a province of the Empire, even if hereditarily ruled, and not independent as it had been, save for the payment of tribute, during Mehemet Ali's Pashalik.

In a separate Protocol, due entirely to Palmerston, it was laid down that action could be taken on the treaty before it was ratified. This was unprecedented and it was the most courageous action of the signatories. "Success alone could justify a resolution so bold and energetic," wrote Neumann, and added that Palmerston might have to get a bill of indemnity from Parliament. The British Constitution did not make such a step necessary, and the wisdom of immediate action was obvious for it was necessary to take advantage of the rising in Syria before Ibrahim could put it down. One can imagine, however, how such a measure would have been criticised if Mehemet had been able to make a successful resistance.

Finally it was agreed that the convention should not be disclosed to France. Nothing was said to Guizot until the messengers were well on their way with the fateful despatches. Then Palmerston gave him a Memorandum which informed him in most general terms of what had been agreed upon.[1]

Whatever Guizot had suspected he was clearly quite unprepared for such an announcement. He had assumed that France would be informed before the treaty was signed and given a last chance to join the other Powers. No doubt he had been preparing himself for a final struggle against Palmerston. The latter said that the four Powers were only putting into force a plan which Guizot's predecessor had at one time proposed to him. Since France had refused to contemplate force in any event the others would have to act without her. Guizot denied both assertions. He said that Sébastiani had only acted in his own name and Palmerston had to admit that there was no official record, but implied that Louis Philippe himself had authorised the offer. When Guizot denied that France had refused all use of force and had always offered to defend Constantinople, Palmerston said this was not coercion and added that "many believed that France aims at dismembering the Turkish Empire and erecting a new and independent state to consist of Egypt, Arabia and Syria." Guizot was taken aback when Palmerston said the action would begin immediately and not await an answer from Alexandria. He indicated that France would need to be in great force in the Levant to protect her interests. Palmerston trusted that she would give no encouragement to Mehemet to resist. When Guizot regretted

---

[1] The Conventions of 15 July were of course printed in *L.P.*, I, No. 615, and have often since been published. There was also a Protocol regulating the admission of light vessels of war in the service of the Legations (*L.P.*, I, No. 617), a topic which was often to be a subject of discussion in later years. To Beauvale, 15 July, 1840: *B.P.* Neumann to Metternich, 16 July, 1840: *V. St. A. Appendix*, p. 881.

that such serious consequences had arisen out of "three or four wretched pashaliks in Syria", Palmerston said their value could be judged by the tenacity with which Mehemet Ali clung to them. The Ambassador retired in high dudgeon and maintained in Society his attitude of cold hostility, which his mistress also displayed. "Guizot and Madame de Lieven have looked as cross as the devil for the last few days," wrote Palmerston. The representatives of the three Powers, he added, accused the Princess of betraying her country and becoming the tool of France.[1]

It was only natural that Guizot should take such a line. Palmerston had expected it. He continued to assert in despatches to every capital that France would not resist by force the decision of the Powers, and awaited with complete calm the reaction of the French Government and people to the measures which had at last been taken.

[1] To Bulwer, 21, 22 July, 1840: *F.O. France*, 600A, and *L.P.*, II, Nos. 10, 11, do., 21, 22 July, 1840: *Bulwer*, II, 315, 318, and *B.P.* Guizot, *Mémoires*, V, 220 ff. In recounting the interview Neumann insisted that only after every effort to get France to come in had failed did Palmerston suggest they should act without her. (To Metternich, 25 July, 1840: *V. St. A.*) Both Brunnow and Neumann were following the Princess's actions closely. Brunnow after watching her at a reception warned Neumann in a hasty note that she was already intriguing with the Opposition against the convention and urged him to use his influence with the Tory chiefs to frustrate her plans—a task which he immediately carried out with great success. She told Neumann that her Russian heart rejoiced in the fact that the old Quadruple Alliance had been reconstructed, at the same time remarking that Palmerston had undone the work of Canning by recreating the Holy Alliance. She was much taken aback when Neumann said he for his part was sorry that France had left the Alliance and especially when he told her that the final step had been taken by Guizot himself in his reply to Chekib of the 21 June (25 July: *V. St. A.*). Bulwer cut out all references to the Princess in his *Palmerston*. He wrote at this time from Paris that she was accused there of misleading Guizot.

4. THE CONVENTION OF 15 JULY, 1840
IN OPERATION

That the convention obtained with so much effort was carried out in its entirety was due to the strong will, steadfast courage and sustained energy of Palmerston. It is perhaps the incident in the whole of his long career which best displays these qualities. He had to overcome obstacles that seemed certain to wreck the plan. He had to contend with the opposition of those who had joined with him to make it, both Cabinet colleagues and continental allies, while the instruments chosen for him to apply the necessary force in Asia Minor were hesitant and unimaginative and did not believe in the possibility of success. To cope with the former Palmerston had the consistent backing of the Tsar; the Admiral and General were supplemented by more capable younger men whom Palmerston himself selected for the purpose. They were spurred into action by the faithful Ponsonby and still more by Palmerston's own urging and that of Minto, who was his greatest support in Britain during the crisis. But the essential thing was that Palmerston himself saw the situation more clearly than anyone else, knew exactly what he wanted to do, and never doubted that he could do it.

The convention was not signed until five o'clock and was followed by a Cabinet dinner, but late that same night Palmerston had already written despatches and letters to Vienna and next day the instructions were sent off to Constantinople to set the naval and military forces in action, and a long series of despatches and letters to the other Courts followed in rapid succession. Speedy ratification was essential in order to deprive France of the last opportunity to delay and thus frustrate Palmerston's plans. It was secured from all the signatories with ease except in one case— Prussia. Palmerston had urged that she should give money, expert officers and artillery. Werther's answer was "that Prussia would contribute nothing, nothing whatever." The ratification was accompanied with the reservation that she was not bound to use force. This was the Minister's decision rather than the King's, who promised Metternich shortly afterwards at Dresden to withdraw it. But Austria was little more helpful, her main addition to Bandiera's small squadron being the young Archduke Frederick, the son of the Archduke Charles. She would promise nothing more. The Tsar, who was delighted with the convention, was far more eager; an expedition was got ready in the Black Sea. But this was for use only if Mehemet threatened Constantinople; neither the Tsar nor Palmerston wished it to be employed in Asia Minor. All depended, therefore, on the Turks themselves, the British fleet and the insurrection of the Lebanese, and it was not long before news came that this last had miscarried and that Ibrahim's authority had been reestablished.[1]

When Thiers received the news of the convention he did not at first shew more surprise and indignation than Guizot had done. He complained bitterly that a final offer had not been made to France, though in the same breath he admitted that he would have refused it, an attitude which Metternich thought was nonsensical. He had told Bulwer only a day or two before that he had not in any way endeavoured to get the Sultan to yield to Mehemet Ali's demands, so he could hardly claim that the convention had prevented an arrangement being made at Constantinople. But Thiers, like Desages and indeed most people in Europe, believed that Mehemet could not be deprived of Syria without French assistance. The *entente* he bitterly insisted was at an end. He poured out to Bulwer a flood of expostulations and explanations of his own conduct, but, though he made vague statements as to the actions that France might take to protect her interests, the reception was better than might have been expected, as Palmerston himself confessed. The first treatment of the news in the organs of the French Press controlled by Thiers, while angry and hostile, was not threatening, and the official memorandum that was sent in reply on 24 July was moderate and pacific in tone. In fact Leopold told Palmerston a little later that Thiers would have accepted Palmerston's memorandum as a friendly gesture

[1] To Beauvale, 15 July, 1840: *B.P.* From William Russell, 29 July, 1840: *F.O. Prussia*, 229. From Bloomfield, 30 July, 1840: *F.O. Russia*, 261; do., 8 Aug., 1840: *B.P.* The Tsar shewed his personal enthusiasm for the convention by sending Brunnow the order of the White Eagle and a year's salary, and decorating every member of his mission. Guichen, *La Crise d'Orient*, 336. From Beauvale, 25 July, 1840; Metternich to Beauvale, 22, 28 July, 1840: *B.P.* Metternich chuckled over Princess Lieven's failure to find out that the convention was to be made, boasted that Palmerston had used Austria to overcome the opposition in the Cabinet and was full of praise for both Palmerston and Ponsonby, but explained he could not give arms, money or officers. He suggested Prussia might send an officer to join the Austrian Flagship.

if he had not been stirred up by Palmerston's opponents in England.[1]

However that may be, it was not long before a storm of passionate protest arose in France in which the whole nation joined and which neither Thiers nor Louis Philippe could have ignored had they wished to do so. They joined, therefore, in an uneasy alliance to direct and control it, each suspecting the other of the intention of using it for his own personal ends. Thiers began, as Bulwer said, to breathe fire and flames, and threats began to be uttered about Malta or some coup in Spain. Louis Philippe would never countenance such action, Bulwer believed, but he dared not openly shew himself too peaceful. "The position of the King and Minister is indeed most curious," he wrote. "Playing the game together as partners, each is jealous of the cards and skill of the other and afraid that he will find some means of pocketing the whole of the stake which should be divided between them."[2]

But though the King openly backed the arming of France, the increase of the fleet and, most discussed project of all, the circling of Paris with fortifications, his tone to Bulwer was more of grief than anger and he added that he had already himself sent off to Alexandria a messenger to prevent Ibrahim from crossing the Taurus and precipating a crisis. He had to arm, he said, to satisfy the nation. Nor could he get rid of Thiers who would be more dangerous in opposition than in office. In a private letter Bulwer told Palmerston that while the King was pacific, he must be prepared for anything.[3]

Granville, who came back to his post at the end of July, reluc-

[1] From Bulwer, 20 July, 1840: F.O. France, 604. L.P., II, No. 9; do., 20 July, 1840: B.P. To Granville, 12 Aug., 1840: B.P. Metternich's note on Neumann's despatch (25 July, 1840), giving the assertion of Thiers that France should have been asked though he would certainly have refused, was 'fort sot'. V. St. A. French Note of 24 July: L.P., II, No. 17. Leopold told Bülow, however, that it was the sarcastic letters of Princess Lieven and Mme Flahaut's assertion that he had been tricked that caused Thiers to take the line he did. (Neumann to Metternich, 15 Aug., 1840: V. St. A.)

[2] From Bulwer, 27 July, 1840: F.O. France, 604. L.P., II, Nos. 33, 34; do., 25, 26, 27, 31 July, 1840: B.P.

[3] From Bulwer, 27 July, 1840: F.O. France, 604. This despatch and all other references to Louis Philippe himself are left out of the Levant Papers. Statements by him are sometimes attributed to the "French Government", From Bulwer, 2 Aug., 1840: B.P. The project for fortifying Paris has generally been ascribed to the desire of the King to have protection against internal disorder. But the forts certainly were an important contribution to the defence of France as 1870 was to reveal, and in 1840 the Prussian soldiers emphasised the fact that Paris would no longer be liable to immediate capture by an invading army. (From Lord William Russell, 25 Nov., 1840: F.O. Prussia, 229.)

tantly and full of gout, was much more perturbed and pessimistic.
If the King dismissed his Minister, he said, he might lose his
throne so strong was the feeling of the country. The publication
of the British memorandum had done good and so had Palmerston's
moderate and friendly speech in Parliament, but the Prorogation
Queen's Speech, by eulogising the convention and not mentioning
France, had reawakened the storm. Ordinances had proclaimed
an increase in the army and navy, though Granville was sure
crews could not be found for the 16 sail of the line and 9 steamers
contemplated in them. James Rothschild, in the first of many
interviews of these days, was quite trembling with the idea that the
warlike feeling of the public would force the Government into
war, and pleaded for a conciliatory word. Then, as the King left
for Eu, Granville also went off to the seaside to nurse his gout and
apprehensions which grew daily more painful. Macaulay, who
paid a short visit to France, shared these fears and, though agreeing with Palmerston on the necessity of carrying out the treaty,
"thinks war very probable".[1]

Bulwer's reports continued the story in a more cautious strain.
Though he warned Palmerston of the possibility of an 'Anconade'
against Malta or Crete, he made more of the arguments for peace.
The fury was not always sustained at the highest pitch, the papers
had been ordered not to attack Palmerston personally and only one
or two had repeated the accusations of Attwood and the absurd
crew of Urquhart's friends who had come over to Paris. Moreover the persistent rumours that Thiers had made money on the
crisis by stock-jobbing had done him much harm with the public,
though Bulwer himself did not believe them.

Meanwhile the news had come that the Syrian insurrection had
failed and the communications from Vienna were so vague and
contradictory that Thiers described them as 'twaddle' and Apponyi had confessed to Granville that he did not know what they
meant. In these circumstances it was natural that Thiers should
hope for some new offer from Britain, especially as his British
visitors all assured him that Palmerston represented only himself
and not the feeling of his country. He told Bulwer unofficially

[1] From Granville, 3, 5, 7, 10 Aug., 1840: *F.O. France*, 604, partly in *L.P.*,
II, Nos., 48, 56, 61; do., 6, 10, 14, 17 Aug., 1840: *B.P.* Palmerston's replies
to attacks by Hume and Leader had described the failure of the negotiation with
France in such friendly terms that Brunnow was quite alarmed. (Neumann to
Metternich, 9 Aug., 1840: *V. St. A.*)

that he would accept the temporary occupation of Syria for the lives of Mehemet and his son. He would not promise coercion if Mehemet refused the offer, but he indicated that it would not be necessary. Louis Philippe also reiterated his desire for peace and said he would aim at preventing Ibrahim from crossing the Taurus, or the French fleet from going into a dangerous zone. He hoped for a compromise and promised to dismiss any Minister who refused what he considered to be a reasonable one. Since the continual Bourse rumours had weakened Thiers' position, it was Bulwer's opinion that the King would prevail if such a clash came.[1]

Palmerston received these reports with equanimity. Bulwer was told to leave Thiers alone if he was rude—and to let him know the reason. It was the influence of Ellice, furious at having failed to dictate British policy, which had caused Thiers to act thus, Palmerston thought. But he was not afraid of the combination: "There are other clever people in the world besides Thiers and Ellice. Of course both Thiers and his English jackal are much disappointed, and for a time will both of them try to make as much mischief as they can; but we must stand them both." If the French threatened to use their temporarily superior naval force in the Mediterranean, he would, he said, summon the Russian fleet—and they would be challenging Austria too. Thiers, he wrote a week later, had, he knew, been warned by Guizot of the probable consequences of his policy and if "he has pinned his faith on Ellice instead of Guizot or if he has deliberately preferred that France should be left by herself, he has no right to blame anybody but himself." Meanwhile he urged that the defences of Malta should be looked to and worked in close conjunction with Minto. The latter shewed great zeal and energy. By the end of the month the British had 15 sail of the line and six steamers in commission in the Mediterranean, and Palmerston told everybody they could now feel safe that France would not put her threats into action; with an army in Algiers and no superiority of naval force it would simply be madness, and, though Thiers might talk loudly, he was not mad enough to act thus—and still less so was Louis Philippe.[2]

[1] From Granville, 10 Aug., 1840: *B.P.* From Bulwer, 21, 28 Aug., 1840: *F.O. France*, 604, 605. *L.P.*, II, Nos. 72, 78; do., 17, 21, 22, 28 Aug., 1840: *B.P.*

[2] To Bulwer, 22, 29 July, 1840: *B.P. Bulwer*, II, 318, gives the first but leaves out the sentence quoted. Princess Lieven had written to Lady Palmerston on 7 May: "I have reason to believe that Ellice has been his [Thiers] sole informant about your political situation." (Sudley, *Corres. Princess Lieven—Lady Palmerston*, 188.) To John Russell, 5, 11 Aug., 1840. To Sir Hussey Vivian,

Unfortunately Thiers had made a far greater impression on others, both in Britain and abroad, and Palmerston's tone grew more dogmatic and bitter as he realised that so many people refused to accept what to him seemed so certain. He had to reiterate his convictions in letter after letter to his Cabinet colleagues and his representatives abroad. Hardly one except Ponsonby believed him, though the majority were as yet prepared to take the risk of war. Melbourne himself quite early began to shew his uneasiness and forwarded a letter from Lord Spencer condemning Palmerston for breaking up the whole system on which British foreign policy had been conducted during the last ten years.

This attitude was probably due to Ellice, Palmerston replied, but added that it was characteristic of Lord Spencer. Melbourne, however, continued to send hints and warnings. Louis Philippe, he wrote, had still a good deal of Jemappes in him. Towards the end of the month Lord John Russell had begun to press the same point of view in a series of notes and to demand a new approach to France through Austria.[1]

At Holland House these views were already openly stated and Bourqueney, left in charge while Guizot went back to France to consult the King, was able to report them to Thiers and, what was just as important, to Desages. When Guizot came back he found Leopold on the scene and began to concert action with him to get a new treaty by which Mehemet should be given possession of Syria for life. Leopold said he had prepared the way for the Ambassador in long interviews with Palmerston and Melbourne. When Guizot himself went into action he naturally got no concession on these lines. But Palmerston treated him with the greatest friendliness. He told him that the convention must be carried out, but that no commercial blockade of Syria would be instituted and that Russian troops would not be used.[2]

12 Aug., 1840: *B.P.* Minto in an able review of the naval situation stated that the real difficulty was not the ships but the crews. They were difficult to obtain in summer without a Press. Minto to Melbourne, 23 Aug., 1840: Lloyd Sanders, *Lord Melbourne's Papers*, 464.
[1] Spencer to Melbourne, 7 Aug., 1840. To Melbourne, 8 Aug., 1840; From Melbourne, 8, 12, 25 Aug., 1840; *Appendix*, p. 858. John Russell to Melbourne, 24 Aug., 1840: *B.P.*
[2] Bourqueney to Thiers, 8, 11 Aug., 1840; Guizot to Thiers, 22 Aug., 1840: Guizot, *Mémoires*, V, 286, and *A.A.E.* Neumann described how Palmerston gave a little dinner not only to Guizot and himself but also to Princess Lieven, taking Guizot aside to explain to him how impossible it was to negotiate a new convention (25 Aug., 1840: *V. St. A.*). Guizot does not mention the other guests.

These decisions had been made for other reasons and were only communicated to Guizot because Palmerston thought that the Ambassador would take a more reasonable view of the situation than Thiers. He now drafted a trenchant despatch designed to stop the protests in the Cabinet as much as the loud complaints of Thiers. It was another long review of the past conduct of France. The French Government, he pointed out, had refused all the offers made to them and secretly pressed the Porte to negotiate with Mehemet Ali. "I hope," he told Bulwer, it "will undeceive Thiers as to his notion that we are going to give up our Treaty of July 15. . . . Does Thiers imagine that such menaces and revilings that he has been pleased to deal out through his irresponsible organs have made the slightest change in our determination and intentions? If he does, he has yet much to learn as to the character and habits of the English nation." Melbourne at once admitted the cogency of this indictment: "It is a capital paper and completely proves that France has no right to complain of offence or surprise or of anything else in the game which has been done." But the French Cabinet were far from considering that they must accept defeat. Guizot had seen in Palmerston's moderation a desire to compromise and found many members of the Government more afraid of the use of Russian troops than of Mehemet himself. It was the challenge to the Euphrates route, he wrote, which had brought about the situation. Let the Pasha keep away from that part of Asia Minor. Desages was also writing with great confidence at this period. The Lebanon insurrection had been put down and he did not see how Palmerston could succeed with the means at his disposal. Meanwhile the French Consul-General, Cochelet, had persuaded Mehemet not to proclaim a holy war and to be content with assuring Ibrahim's supplies by means of a camel corps. Time was on France's side, Desages thought, and Leopold's intervention was not needed. He was the more inclined to think Palmerston's position was a weak one because of the half-hearted defence of the treaty that came from Austria. This illusion lasted for nearly a month until Desages realised that Palmerston not only intended to carry out the convention but had the means to do so.[1]

[1] From Melbourne, 29 Aug., 1840: *B.P.* To Bulwer, 31 Aug., 1840: *F.O. France*, 600A. *L.P.*, II, No. 91; do., 1 Sept., 1840: *B.P.* Guizot to Thiers, 21, 22, 31 Aug., 1840: *A.A.E.* (Extracts in Guichen, *La Crise Orientale*, 351, 355.) Desages to Bourqueney, 7, 17, 20 Aug., 1840: *Bour. P.*

Desages' belief that Metternich was not too steadfast in attachment to the convention was unfortunately only too well-founded
and the same was true of Werther at Berlin. Throughout the
month of August Beauvale and William Russell managed to keep
both Foreign Ministers up to the mark, but it was significant that
they already had to seek help from outside. Metternich shewed
signs of yielding to the insistent pressure of St. Aulaire who had
hastened to Königswart where as usual Metternich was holding
his little court during the midsummer months. The Chancellor
pleaded that he could do nothing away from Vienna. This was a
strange excuse and Beauvale accordingly appealed to Esterhazy
for help to get the Archdukes to take action. The presence of
the young Archduke Frederic in the Austrian fleet was a great
argument in his favour. But neither money, arms nor officers
could be obtained. It was at any rate satisfactory that Metternich
had refused the suggestion already made by Leopold and Bülow
to transfer the conference to Vienna. He was far too comfortable
at Königswart. And, when the news reached him of the threats
Pontois, the French Minister, had made at Constantinople, he
sent a severe despatch to Paris which Palmerston of course
endorsed with a strong protest of his own. Metternich also
wrote a letter to Leopold which stated in firm language the necessity of France accepting the situation, though it did not meet
all Palmerston's wishes, since it implied some sort of concession to
French demands, and the resumption of negotiations concerning
the Eastern Question.[1]

Similarly Lord William Russell had appealed from Werther to
the King, whom he had insisted on seeing personally, and found
cool and collected. The Austrian and Prussian soldiers were
already at least talking of collaborating against France. But
Werther himself was clearly unreliable and Bülow, with his
countenance, was already in collaboration with Leopold who, with
a pretence of seeking Belgian interests, was exploring every means

[1] From Beauvale, 27, 29, Aug., 1840: *F.O. Austria*, 291A; do., 4, 9, 11, 12,
23, 25, 31 Aug., 1840: *B.P.* The Archduke Charles was delighted at the
opportunity his son had to go into action with the British fleet. Palmerston
naturally at once refused Bülow's suggestion which would have reflected on
himself and told him not to mention it again. (To Beauvale, 5 Sept., 1840:
B.P.) Metternich, *Mémoires*, VI, 412. St. Aulaire gives a vivid picture of the
scene at Königswart, where the Eastern Question was discussed interminably
day and night by the Ambassadors of the three Courts, Esterhazy and Ficquelmont. (*Souvenirs*, 301.)

to obtain concessions for France, while at Bresson's instigation he was considering doubling his army. It was clear that the resolution of both Austria and Prussia had visibly weakened in the face of the threats of France—and this was bound to encourage Thiers to go on in the course he had chosen.[1]

Much, therefore, would obviously depend on how well and how fast affairs went in Syria. Palmerston was fully conscious of the value of the advice which Guizot himself had given to Melbourne at the outset—to get the thing over as quickly as possible. But to organise an attack on an army of 50,000 men with the resources at Palmerston's disposal was no light task. Fortunately at Constantinople was a man as determined and energetic as Palmerston himself and the situation was really much better than anyone in Western Europe imagined. But the offer to Mehemet had first to be made and a means of attack found if he refused. News took two or three weeks to come, and during September there was not much good that came, and the uncertainty entirely undermined the faith both of the Cabinet and Metternich in Palmerston's promise that all would ultimately be attained. The Syrian insurrection, Ponsonby reported, had failed because the Turk had shewed no sign of giving help and Emir Bechir, the King of the Mountain, had therefore taken the side of Ibrahim who had wreaked savage reprisals on the Christians and burnt monks alive. When the convention arrived, therefore, the Admiral, Stopford, had considered his instructions to support the insurrection no longer valid. This weak and hesitating approach to a problem which could only be solved by prompt and confident action was the first of a long series which drove Ponsonby nearly frantic and was condemned by both Palmerston and Minto. "A superannuated twaddler," Palmerston called Stopford on 30 August. It was held to be impossible, however, to change the command in the middle of the operation. All that could be done was to send orders to act as energetically as possible, orders difficult to frame, since their execution depended on local circumstances which could not be accurately known at London. These ultimately produced their effect on the mind of the Admiral, a man seventy years of age, whose courage was stout enough but matched by an excessive

[1] From Lord William Russell, 5, 12, 22, 26 Aug., 1840: *B.P.* do., 5, Aug., 1840: *F.O. Prussia*, 229. Lord William Russell had already written to his brother John to leave the Eastern Question to Palmerston.

prudence. Already Ponsonby relied more on Napier, in command of a squadron of the fleet, than on the Admiral himself.[1]

But Ponsonby himself was sure that the convention could be carried out in its entirety. He only regretted that its terms were too lenient to Mehemet Ali, hoped he would reject them and consequently lose not only all Syria but also Egypt as the convention threatened would then ensue. He was confident that the Pasha's power could easily be destroyed because of the weakness of his moral position. He stated this opinion in a remarkable letter, a sentence of which is at the head of this chapter: "Mehemet Ali is like a lie and will be destroyed as that is by truth. He is believed to be strong and that belief has given him strength. He is weak and it will now be seen and felt that he is so and all those who seek to be on the strongest side will turn away from him. Despair is the origin of the insurrection in Syria. Despair cannot be cured by Mehemet who has created it, and when a chance of succour is offered to the Syrians they must wish to seize it. *That is doing. It will soon be done.* It almost appears as if people were not aware of the power of *opinion.* The greatest men and nations fall before it and now Mehemet Ali has it against him to the highest degree in his own country. . . . I have no doubt of success attending your plans if they [the instructions] are acted upon with spirit by our people and I hope that will be the case."[2]

This notable judgment was entirely accurate. No other diplomatist either at Constantinople or in Europe had made it and no one believed it but Palmerston himself. Ponsonby immediately used all his energy and resource to make it come true. Even before the negotiation at Alexandria took place arms and money were sent to the Lebanon mountaineers and Richard Wood sent back to complete the work he had already begun. The Grand

[1] From Ponsonby, 1, 5, 12 Aug., 1840; Stopford to Ponsonby, 3 Aug., 1840: *B.P.* The convention arrived at Constantinople on the 3 August. The details of the subsequent engagements are given in dramatic detail in Professor Temperley's *Crimea*, 123–135. The author studied the campaign on the ground. He was concerned to defend Stopford from the strictures of Palmerston and Napier. No doubt the responsibility was a great one but there can be little doubt that it was only the orders from Britain and the enterprise of Napier that enabled the campaign to be finished so quickly. Stopford would not have begun, would have removed the fleet at the end of October and refused to attack Acre urless others had forced him to do so. To Minto, 30 Aug., 1840: *B.P.* Stopford was "quite unfit for the mixed political and naval duties" he had to perform, Palmerston wrote (do., 2 Sept., *B.P.*).
[2] From Ponsonby, 12 Aug., 1840: *B.P.*

Vizir was persuaded to send a letter to the Emir Bechir promising the Sultan's forgiveness and countenance. A constant succession of notes was sent to Stopford urging action. There would be no need to employ Russian troops, Ponsonby asserted. The Turkish army, suitably advised, and the British fleet would be quite sufficient. Chrysanowski was used to give counsel to the Turks, though he soon found he could do little more now that action had superseded preparation. Even more remarkable was it that Captain Walker was put in command of the small Turkish fleet, all that was left to the Sultan outside Alexandria.[1]

Meanwhile Stopford himself had gone with a squadron to Alexandria where the Consuls-General of the Four Powers were pressing Mehemet to agree to the terms of the convention. They could get nothing out of him. His answers were given with characteristic reserve and mystery. The violence of Colonel Hodges did not fit in well with the suave manoeuvres of the others who carried out their orders with no great zeal. The real negotiation was taking place with the special envoy of Thiers, Walewski, and Cochelet, the French Consul-General. The latter, a sincere admirer of Mehemet, was urging his Government to support the Pasha wholeheartedly, but the supple Walewski succeeded in getting a request for French mediation without in any way committing his Government. Meanwhile the news came from Constantinople that, as Mehemet had not accepted the convention in the time limit laid down, the Sultan had deposed him from the Pashalik of Egypt, and named his successor. Ponsonby had certainly been the main influence in obtaining this decision but the Austrian and Prussian representatives, though not the Russian, Titov, had supported him. The Ambassador was well aware of what he was doing and defended his conduct in a vigorous despatch and private letter on the ground of the effect that it would produce on opinion in the East: "Half measures will be ruinous; one of our best arms is the prerogative of the Sultan. People will never believe in the sincerity and force of the Porte, if Mehemet be spared. Everybody knows the Sultan can exert his sovereign authority against him and will *suspect* that things are not right if it be not exerted. There is a vast deference paid by all the people

---

[1] From Ponsonby, 5, 8, 16 Aug., 1 Sept., 1840: *F.O. Turkey*, 395, 396; *L.P.*, II, Nos. 91, 94. Walker was also put in command of the transports for 5500 men and all the officers ordered to obey him. "No Giaour has ever commanded the Turks," added Ponsonby triumphantly.

to the Sultan's acts of a solemn nature, for religious feelings are by no means fallen in the way some superficial observers assert. I am told that the Ulemas are really offended at the pretentions of Mehemet Ali to be the Protector of Islam."

That there was much truth in this judgment events were to shew. Mehemet Ali, it is true, laughed off the move. It had happened before, he said. But the threat was there and it was against France as well as Mehemet. The news caused another storm of vituperation in France and Palmerston's colleagues and allies were indignant with Ponsonby. Nesselrode was displeased and Metternich and Werther were horrified. Palmerston himself would have liked to get rid of Mehemet Ali altogether as he more than once confessed. But he was aware that it was impossible to do so. The Cabinet, he later told Ponsonby, would never allow him to attack Egypt. But the move served him well; it was both a threat and something that could be used to make a concession to the importunities of colleagues without injuring the essential object, the removal of Mehemet Ali from all Syria. It was to be of use at a critical moment in the negotiations.[1]

Just as essential was it to reassure the Turkish Government. The French Minister, Pontois, had been ordered to do his best to intimidate them and if possible to prevent the ratification of the convention. With such ardour did he carry out his task that Reschid appealed in great alarm to the representatives of the Four Powers for protection. They hastened to reassure him, Ponsonby foremost but Titov and Stürmer shewing similar zeal. Pontois later denied that he had used the threats attributed to him by Reschid and was supported by the French Government, but Desages confessed to Bourqueney that he had been ordered to

---

[1] Professor Dodwell has described the negotiation at Alexandria from Medem's reports as well as Hodges' despatches. He is too hostile to the latter, who, however, was not the man to handle so delicate a negotiation. The French reports have subsequently been published in E. Driault, *La Crise Orientale, 1839–1841*, vol. III, but there must have been many private letters to Thiers and Desages which are not yet known. M. Sabry had already shewn from the French Archives the equivocal conduct of France. (*L'Empire Egyptien*, 499–509.) From Ponsonby, 3 Sept., 1840: *B.P.*; do: *F.O. Turkey*, 396. To Ponsonby, 5, 27 Oct., 1840: *B.P.* Palmerston's only criticism of Ponsonby was that in a matter of such importance he should have sent home the Protocol of the meeting between Reschid and the Ambassadors in which the deposition of Mehemet was determined so that the attacks on his conduct could be answered. To Beauvale, 5 Oct., 1840: *B.P.* Greville (*Memoirs*, IV, 312) recounts the row in the Cabinet when news came from Vienna that the Ambassadors had not been unanimous.

abuse (malmener) and intimidate Reschid, and there can be no
doubt that his dragoman, Cor, used violent language. At any rate
the opportunity was given to shew the solidarity of the Four, and
the incident did France no good and made even more unlikely
the success of M. Coste who was still engaged in his endeavours to get the Turks to use French assistance to settle the
dispute.[1]

All this was reassuring but there was still no proof that Ibrahim
was likely to be driven out of Syria, while during the next month
the clamour in France shewed no signs of ceasing, and produced
considerable effect on the minds of the European peoples and
statesmen. The impression was in any case a false one. Louis
Philippe and the majority of the French Government never
intended to go to war and by the end of the month Desages was
warning Bourqueney of the probable result. But they had got
into a difficult position and Thiers at any rate hoped that the high
tone he adopted would frighten the Four Powers into a compromise, and was ready for that purpose to risk allowing the situation
to get out of control. He would have succeeded in his object if
Palmerston had not resisted all attempts to shake the position of
the Four Powers.

It was Bulwer who reported the scene at Paris in a flood of
despatches and letters, while Granville remained on leave. The
French Press and the President of the Council grew more and more
bellicose. When Walewski reported that he had induced the
Pasha to give up both Candia and Adana and accept Syria for his
lifetime, Thiers indicated that France would feel bound to support a ruler who had made such concessions at French insistence.
But such threats were still conveyed in the vaguest manner and
Thiers always avoided making any definite statement as to what
would cause France to take up arms. Meanwhile reports had
come from Alexandria that Mehemet Ali might well have accepted
the offer of the Four Powers if he had not been deterred by the
joint efforts of Cochelet and Walewski, and the accusation was
openly made in Palmerston's organ, the *Morning Chronicle*.
Thiers hotly denied this and of course Granville supported him.
But Bulwer, who penetrated into the secrets of the Quai d'Orsay
far more deeply than his valetudinarian chief, was not far wrong

---

[1] From Ponsonby, 17, 19 Aug., 1840: *F.O. Turkey*, 396. *L.P.*, II, Nos. 96,
111. Desages to Bourqueney, 8 Sept., 1840: *Bour. P.*

when he explained the incident as arising from the reluctance of Mehemet Ali to place himself in French hands and his preference to use language which could be interpreted later according to events. As it was the French envoys only secured with great difficulty the request for French mediation which they referred to Thiers.

The French Government only intended to accept the position of mediator if they knew that the Four Powers would offer better terms than were contained in the convention. It was towards this end that all their efforts were now directed. But the majority of the French Cabinet never intended to oppose the Four Powers if they failed to secure it. They relied on a prolonged resistance by the Egyptian forces. This, they thought, would gradually force the compromise on Palmerston which France could proclaim to the world as a victory made in the teeth of all Europe. In order to achieve this end Thiers began to make vague threats that it was not in the East but on the French frontiers that France would attack. Italy especially was ripe for invasion. The German people received these threats with a patriotic outburst of indignation that surprised both France and Europe. But an impression was certainly made on Metternich.[1]

The pacific resolution that underlay these threats was in the nature of things as Palmerston realised. France could not declare war on all Europe to oppose an end which she had herself previously endorsed. But the situation was made perfectly safe by the attitude of the King. He allowed just as much bombast and solid preparation as would satisfy public opinion, reported Bulwer in a private letter, but refused to sanction any steps which would allow of war. The French fleet which Cochelet naïvely thought might be sent to shadow the British fleet was kept at Salamis away from the theatre of war. Thiers wanted to send it to Candia but even there it would have done little harm.

The King played his part in frightening the timid Granville by telling him that the concessions of Mehemet had been bought at too high a price, thus insinuating that France had promised to fight for them. The Ambassador's entreaties to Palmerston grew more and more insistent as the month drew to a close. Bulwer,

---

[1] Many of the most important despatches of Granville and Bulwer appear in *Levant Papers*. But they give a misleading impression because all reference to the attitude of Louis Philippe is omitted. Granville, who returned on the 21 September, was much more positive of the danger of war than Bulwer.

on the other hand, who had pretty well sized up the situation, now told Palmerston that war would be more likely to result if he gave way to France's threats. The French nation would then be so exalted that it would demand impossible concessions. By this time the cooler heads in France had come to realise the folly of Thiers. Roussin prophesied that Ibrahim would not be able to hold out for long and Desages now warned Bourqueney that, however outrageous Palmerston's conduct was, he was likely to be successful. There was, he said, no real danger of war. "Lord P. n'y croit pas et moi non plus."[1]

Palmerston had not the slightest intention of giving way. In measured language to Granville and in the Palmerstonian extravagances to Bulwer, so often quoted, he told his envoys to make the French Government and the French King realise that Britain could not be intimidated by threats. That this judgment was true enough was eventually to be proved, but meanwhile the majority of Palmerston's colleagues adopted an attitude which inspired justifiable hopes in Guizot on his return from France. He could rely also on the help of Leopold whom he had visited on his journey, and he could soon report that Bülow and even Neumann were anxious that something should be done. Palmerston again peremptorily refused to give Mehemet Syria for life. But a much smaller concession would suffice to content France, Guizot told his British friends, and doubtless this was true, though Thiers continued to insist that Mehemet must at least have all Syria.[2]

The ramifications of the pro-French party extended in every direction. Greville's subterranean moves, surely disgraceful in a Clerk to the Privy Council, have been revealed by himself. His principal confidant was Clarendon, who, however, professed to Palmerston to have fully accepted the situation and sent him

---

[1] From Granville, 25 Sept., 1840. *F.O. France*, 606. *L.P.*, No. 168; do., 21, 23, 25, 28 Sept., 1840: *B.P.* From Bulwer, 11, 14, 18, 25 Sept., 1840: *B.P.* The last written apparently without Granville's knowledge gave his theory as to what had happened at Alexandria and his advice not to give way. The despatches of Cochelet and Walewski (E. Driault, *L'Egypte et l'Europe, La Crise orientale*, 1839–1841, III, Nos. 45, 48, 50, 70, 71) shew the manoeuvres of the two envoys to obtain the request of Mehemet for mediation. Walewski was careful to point out that their reply committed France to nothing. Desages to Bourqueney, 29 Sept., 1 Oct., 1840 (*Appendix*, p. 899): *A.A.E.* If a conflict came between Thiers and the King, Desages had no doubt who would prevail.

[2] To Granville, 22, 25 Sept., 1840: *B.P.* To Bulwer, 22 Sept., 1840: *Bulwer*, II, 327. (The celebrated letter which says that in a war Mehemet will "just be chucked into the Nile".) Guizot, *Mémoires*, V, 317–323.

objective reports received from Paris. Greville also was continually spurring on Lord John Russell and the Duke of Bedford to
oppose Palmerston. He was in close touch with Barnes and
through his protégé, Henry Reeves, who had just been brought
into the service of *The Times*, hoped to wield that powerful
weapon against Palmerston. Meanwhile Spencer, Morpeth, the
Duke of Bedford and other Peers continually wrote pessimistic
and disquieting epistles to one another and canvassed what could
be done. They hoped to persuade Lansdowne to move and in the
end even induced the phlegmatic and reserved Nestor of the
Whigs to take alarm. The main centre of intrigue was Holland
House where Guizot went nearly every day, to get his tears dried,
Neumann said, and discussed how Palmerston could be forced to
make some concession to France. Lord Holland no doubt did not
realise all that he and Lady Holland revealed to their friendly
and soft-spoken guest, but the Cabinet controversies thus became
known to the French Government and were used by some of these
to play with French bankers on the Stock Exchange. Beauvale
wrote that Metternich had news of British policy in this way
before Neumann could report on it from London. Palmerston protested to Melbourne against these leakages only to draw
from the Prime Minister the admission that he could not stop
them.[1]

But all this, with Minto and Hobhouse backing him wholeheartedly, Palmerston could overcome and his own control of the

[1] To Melbourne, 16 Sept., 1840: *B.P.* (and part in Lloyd Sanders, *Melbourne
Papers*, 475). From Melbourne, 17 Sept., 1840; From Beauvale, 13 Oct., 1840:
B.P. Neither in his diary nor in his letters to Henry Reeve did Greville shew
any shame or consciousness that he was acting unworthily. His accounts of
what the various actors said to him cannot be trusted, but he clearly knew a
great deal. Ashley reported to Palmerston on him and Palmerston's bitter
notes on the letters shew that he knew what Greville was doing. Clarendon
wrote a number of letters to Palmerston giving news from French correspon-
dents. Melbourne summed up Holland House as follows: "The talking at
Holland House is irremediable. They do not know how much they talk themselves. The table and constant Salon there are great advantages. They form a
great point of union for the party. But they have also their disadvantages and
this perpetual talking is one and a great one. I begin to think that a Minister
should never talk much promiscuously either about Politics or anything else.
He loses something by this both as to what he may hear and what he may teach,
but he gains more in point of safety. Nobody can talk much and be really
prudent unless he be such a compound of skill and mystery as nature seldom
produces, and then, if he is, he is liable to misconception and misrepresentation
which will make him utter follies, even if he has not done so." He eventually
warned Lord Holland that his indiscretions were being used for stockjobbing
(Ilchester, *Chronicles*, 282). If so, they were obviously also known to the French
Government.

Press ensured that all efforts in that direction would fail. But it was essential for him to have the support of the Prime Minister and Lord John Russell, the leader of the House, as well as Secretary of State for War, with whose assistance he had got the convention through the Cabinet. Unfortunately both of them began to lose their nerve and Lord John Russell started an active campaign to compel Palmerston to give way. Lady Palmerston was so alarmed that she urged Beauvale to come back from Königswart to get their brother into a better frame of mind, but the Ambassador was needed to keep Metternich straight.

Melbourne's conduct at this time displayed his characteristic qualities to the highest degree. He never took the initiative himself and answered the heated epistles of his colleagues with cool and detached little notes which pointed out their inconsistencies. He insisted that Palmerston's policy should be tried out but he obviously had no great belief that it would be successful and his natural disposition to compromise made him seek a way out. He was also preoccupied with the condition of the Queen, now far gone with her first child, and this anxiety must have been increased by the fact that an illness in October kept him for some time from his usual place at her side. Thus he was constantly expressing to Palmerston his scepticism and urging him to accept the suggestions of his colleagues though he always gave way when Palmerston, as was nearly always the case, refused to agree. But, as in July, at the last moment he took vigorous action which helped to save the situation.[1]

Lord John Russell's behaviour was far worse, especially as he had been amongst the strongest supporters of the convention. Some of it seems to have come from jealousy of Palmerston's commanding position, for in September he claimed the supervision of the operations on the Syrian coast. Palmerston settled this point by a courteous and moderate reply, which pointed out that Britain was not at war and that he had the same position now as in the Spanish question. At the same time Russell began an attack on Ponsonby and pressed that some more moderate man should

---

[1] Neumann to Metternich, 17 Sept., 1840: *V. St. A.* From Beauvale, 24 Sept., 1840: *B.P.* He had in June asked for leave of absence but he was now strongly of the opinion that he must stay near Metternich. Both Palmerston and his wife eventually agreed. The presence at Königswart of Maltzahn's daughter, whom Beauvale was to marry in 1841, may have contributed to his determination not to come home.

be sent out to Constantinople to conduct the negotiations. For some time Palmerston ignored this impertinence which was as much an attack on himself as on Ponsonby. Then in response to repeated reminders from Melbourne he sent a devastating reply. He refused of course to subject Ponsonby to such a mark of lack of confidence. But in addition he pointed out that his critics were all the while assuming the failure of operations which had not yet even been begun. Let them at least wait until the policy which they had supported in the Cabinet had been tried out.

This argument was indeed unanswerable, as even the Duke of Bedford told his brother, and for a little time it silenced Palmerston's opponents in the Cabinet, except Lord Holland whom, however, Palmerston treated with the greatest courtesy in spite of the harm which his indiscretions were producing. Though we know from other letters that Palmerston was indignant at being subjected to these attacks while he was directing a political and strategic campaign of such importance, his letters to his colleagues are couched in most temperate language when they are made. But he often evaded or ignored their suggestions, believing that time was on his side.

To win sufficient time to bring his forces into action was the main object to which he directed all his diplomatic resources—and it was clear that he could not wait too long, as Melbourne told him in one of his most pessimistic epistles. The dissolution of the Cabinet was threatened, he warned Palmerston on 14 September. The policy had been adopted against the will of two members of it and several others had only given it lukewarm support. "Never, I will answer for it was a great measure undertaken upon a basis of support so slender and so uncertain. The present state of things unless you can find a way out of it or something that will open a prospect of a speedy termination to it, will lead to a dissolution of the Government. This will be an evil for the country because it will appear, and it will be, that the English Government will have been changed by the outcry of the Press and populace of Paris and by the mere apprehension of a serious difference with France. What a prospect for the country and for those who are hereafter to administer its affairs!"[1]

[1] From Melbourne, 14, 16, 17, 19, 24, 30 Sept., 1840: *B.P.* To Melbourne, 22 Sept., 1840: *B.P.* From Lord Holland, 17 Sept., 1840. To Lord Holland, 19 Sept., 1840: *B.P.* Palmerston used the device of telling Lord Holland his answers to an unnamed correspondent who had expressed views which were

The attempts to prevent Palmerston directing operations in the East were easily overcome. But parallel to these was another line of attack which was more difficult to resist. Not only Lord Holland but all the Whig pundits, and foremost amongst them John Russell, began to urge that some new approach should be made to France to satisfy her wounded pride. What exactly was to be done was variously and vaguely hinted, but some concession was to be made and France thus brought back into the Concert of Europe. This is what Guizot had come back to obtain, and what was soon to be urged by both Prussia and Austria as their alarm grew. Leopold was already pressing it on the Queen in a series of avuncular letters in which high politics were mingled with family news, as well as on Palmerston himself. Palmerston was determined to resist it. The next move would be to suspend operations while discussion took place. The reaction in Syria and Turkey would be incalculable. Consequently, he used to the full his commanding position as the channel of communication to prevent any such move taking place. He had a strong technical position. He was able at once to get rid of John Russell's suggestion that the convention, now that it had been ratified, should be communicated officially by the Four Powers to France. Neumann objected that there was no collective body at London to take such a step and Melbourne at once agreed. This suggestion was meant to be the beginning of a negotiation with France as was another proposal to conclude a self-denying ordinance not to take territory which Palmerston also rejected as unnecessary and unwise. But Melbourne responded in characteristic fashion to his complaints of those who had pressed this course on him: "I agree with you as to the manner in which people, who have concurred in a measure which they do not approve, ought to act. But people do not act as they ought. You calculate a little too much upon nations and individuals following reason, right and a just view of their own interest. I do not say that these are not the great considerations which actuate individuals, but there are other motives which exercise at least equal power and influence."[1]

identical with those of Lord Holland himself. Lord Holland replied that he did not desire a 'boxing match' with Palmerston. Memorandum by Lord John Russell, 18 Sept., 1840; To Lord John Russell, 23 Sept., 1840: G.P. Gooch, *Later Correspondence*, I, 15, 19.

[1] For Lord John Russell's attitude see G. P. Gooch, *Later Correspondence*, I, 12–18, and Spencer Walpole, *Lord John Russell*, I, 348 ff. The correspondence with Leopold is given in *Queen Victoria Letters*, I, 288, 293. He pressed

This attack would have probably been no more dangerous than the first had not it received support from abroad. But early in September Metternich began to shew signs of weakness and it took all the efforts of Beauvale to keep him from giving way altogether. He began to despair of carrying out the convention without the aid of France and consequently wanted concessions to be made to her. He was prepared to leave the insurgents to their fate and accept Mehemet's rule over Syria for life. Kolowrat was as usual opposing his policy and Metternich was at first too comfortable at his country estate to go to Vienna and face him. The Chancellor gradually became really alarmed. He was much exercised about the condition of Italy which Thiers threatened to make the first objective of a continental campaign. He recommended a conciliatory gesture to France in order to prevent a general war. The Ottoman Empire, he said, would be destroyed in the course of it. He actually wrote a private letter to Neumann threatening to separate Austria from the other Powers in certain eventualities and only Beauvale's protests and scoldings prevented him from sending it. Gradually Kolowrat came out in open opposition to resistance to France. Eichof, who managed the finances, was altogether on the same side and said that war would mean that Austria must choose between Kolowrat and Metternich and there was no doubt what the decision would be. Beauvale, indeed, had to admit that Austrian public opinion, which cared little about Asia Minor, was on Kolowrat's side. Metternich refused Beauvale's advice to challenge his critic in the Council with the Archdukes, and the action of a Great Empire, lamented the Ambassador, was thus paralysed. "Metternich told me last night in as many words", he wrote on the 30 September, "that not only he should lose the confidence of Germany and Italy if he went to war, but, appealing to me, added 'you know enough of the position of this Empire to be aware that in such a case I should risk my situation in the interior'." A week later Metternich proposed that there should be a conference at Wiesbaden under his auspices. He could, explained the Ambassador in a bitter letter, manage it comfortably from Johannisberg. He was determined if possible to take shelter behind the neutrality of the Confederation

the same view on Palmerston in letters of 13, 19 Sept. from Wiesbaden (*B.P.*).
From Melbourne, 17, 29, Sept., 1840: *B.P.* Neumann to Metternich, 6 Sept.,
1840: *V. St. A.*

and Sardinia if war ensued as a result of the landing in Beirut of which news had just come.[1]

Nor during this month was the news from Prussia much more comforting. Bresson's activity and violence were increasing and Werther was visibly impressed. He was worried at the reported increase of Belgian armaments which was, he said, the clearest indication that war was intended. He was much alarmed also at the deposition of Mehemet, which Bresson told him would mean war, and discontented with the conduct of his own Minister at Constantinople. Lord William Russell placed all his hopes on the King but, though that monarch was braver than his Minister, he was clearly angry at Prussia being placed in a position of danger for a question in which she had no direct interest. Bülow on his return to Berlin wrote a pessimistic letter to Palmerston. Werther, he said, would not even discuss affairs with him, and the King while kind was visibly embarrassed. The country had not yet made up its mind to incur the expense of arming against France. If the matter was allowed to drag on he could not answer for Prussia's steadfastness. "It would suit us here", wrote William Russell in an accompanying letter, "if you could end the Oriental affair. We have a weak King and a pusillanimous Government."[2]

The Tsar of course remained as determined as ever and this attitude was reflected in his Minister at London. A Baltic fleet was got ready and it must have given Nicholas great satisfaction to offer it for the defence of the country which had protested against it for so long. But Nesselrode was by no means as firm as his master. He was perturbed at the deposition of Mehemet which he had not expected. His despatches to Vienna and elsewhere indicated more readiness to make some overture to France than might have been expected.[3]

[1] From Beauvale, 5, 11, 15, 20, 25, 30 Sept., 1, 8 Oct., 1840: *B.P.*; do., 25 Sept., 8 Oct., 1840: *F.O. Austria*, 291B. The long private letters give in detail the intricacies of the internal situation, and are full of interesting reflections on it. There is much less in the despatches on the subject. The two noted above recount Metternich's desire for a new offer to France, a meeting with France on the Rhine and to remain neutral. The Ambassador had necessarily to send a official account of these views since Metternich was putting them in despatches to Neumann. Palmerston wrote to him a little later: "the less you can put his [Metternich's] back-slidings into your despatches the better; for these things are caught hold of by those who are on the look out for difficulties, and are turned to bad account." (4 Nov., 1840: *B.P.*)

[2] From William Russell, 22, 30 Sept., 8 Oct., 1840; from Bülow, 7 Oct., 1840: *B.P.* From William Russell, 2, 23, 30 Sept., 7 Oct., 1840: *F.O. Prussia*, 229.

[3] From Bloomfield, 29 Aug., 12, 18, 26 Sept., 2 Oct., 1840: *F.O. Russia*, 261, 262.

Naturally the Austrian attitude became known in London even though Beauvale was careful to say as little as possible in his despatches. St. Aulaire was sending accounts of it to Paris and Guizot was informing his faithful friends in the Cabinet. Gradually the pro-French party began to look to Austria to force Palmerston to yield. In these circumstances it can be imagined how anxiously he was watching for news from the Near East which would convince his colleagues and allies that he could perform what he had set out to do. It came in time, thanks to the energy and foresight of Ponsonby and the boldness of Napier, but it might have been too late if Palmerston himself had not shewn great address and dexterity as well as determination and courage.

At Constantinople Ponsonby wore himself out in collecting money, arms and stores for the Turkish expeditionary force, as well as maintaining the courage of the timid Reschid and the other Ministers, and counteracting the intrigues in the Harem in which both Mehemet and the French still saw a means of obtaining their ends. Napier had appeared off the coast while Stopford was at Alexandria and begun to stir up the inhabitants of the Lebanon and blockade the ports before Mehemet's answer was known, thus producing a violent French protest of which Palmerston took no notice. When Stopford took over, the technical part of his job seems to have been done with great skill. The fleet was so distributed that Suliman Pasha did not know which part of the coast to defend, and Ibrahim shewed himself quite incapable of concentrating his forces. This was partly owing to the fact that a good part of them were unreliable and this was due to the work of Wood and others who got in touch with the men of the Mountain. Soliman Pasha placed a price on his head, and neither Stopford nor Hodges, who arrived later on, would take notice of him, but his work had been well done and deserved the warm praise which Ponsonby gave him. Nor would the Turkish troops have fought as they did if Ponsonby had not obtained the virtual command for Sir Charles Smith and Jochmus. Napier, as in Portugal, shewed that he was a soldier as well as a sailor. When the first Egyptian defeats came all hastened to get on the winning side, the Emir Bechir too late to save himself from having to give way to his nephew. Thus by 10 October Ibrahim had been driven from the coast, the inhabitants of the Lebanon were rising everywhere and the Egyptian army was doomed unless Acre maintained its usual reputation for prolonged resistance and winter weather drove the conquering fleet from the coast.[1]

The news of the first bombardment, though it caused an extra outburst of wrath in the French Press, gave little assurance of victory. But the fall of Beirut precipitated the final crisis. Palmerston had then to face the combination of all the forces arrayed against his policy. There was of course no real danger of a continental war though Beauvale wrote on 25 September that only a miracle could prevent it. But there was always a chance that Palmerston's enemies and allies would force him to compromise before the hollow nature of the French position had been revealed. Granville was completely taken in by the French Government and in his private letters constantly urged concessions to France on the ground that otherwise war was almost inevitable Thiers, he said, could not give way completely after all his boasting. According to Broglie, who was brokenhearted at the situation, if the King dismissed Thiers he would be brought back in triumph when the Chambers met. If the Egyptians were beaten then France would seize some place for herself as a protection of her interests, Candia perhaps, or the Balearic Isles. The news that the French fleet had been brought back to Toulon seemed ominous though the move was in fact only due to the King's desire to keep it out of harm's way. Thiers still believed that the expedition to Syria would fail. The King was using all his power to prevent war and had stopped an angry note on the deposition of Mehemet Ali. But he could not dictate to the French Cabinet which in its turn was responsive to the great surge of public opinion in France.[2]

---

[1] From Ponsonby, 8, 14, 15, 23, 26, 28 Sept., 1840; Wood to Ponsonby, 7 Sept., 1840; Ponsonby to Stopford, 8 Oct., 1840: *B.P.* (protesting against the intention of leaving the coast). Ponsonby's condemnation of Smith as a General and Stopford for dilatoriness was endorsed by Palmerston and Minto. The other side of the case is given by Professor Temperley (*Crimea*, 119-130). Smith, however, had a sort of apoplectic stroke (To Fitzroy Somerset, 17 Oct., 1840: *B.P.*), and this in itself was surely sufficient cause for his removal. See also p. 726, note. "A man who does not expect success rarely gets it," wrote Minto on 4 October, and on the 27th: "Old Stopford will be the death of me," though he was not quite so bad as Ponsonby made out. (From Minto, 6, 27 Oct., 1840: *B.P.*)

[2] From Granville, 5, 8, 9, 12 Oct., 1840: *F.O. France* 606, part in *L.P.*, II, Nos. 207, 214, 215; do., 5, 9, 11 Oct., 1840: *B.P.* Palmerston was much exercised about the French fleet and ordered Granville to use his Secret Service money to find out about it. Was it to be used to attack the Russian fleet if it came West or to seize the Balearic Isles? A member of the Thiers' Cabinet was later so foolhardy as to confess in the Chamber that the latter idea was in their

Bulwer's private letters to Palmerston were not nearly so alar-mist. The heads of the army and navy, he reported, had backed up the King in opposing Thiers in the Cabinet. Bulwer recom-mended Palmerston to threaten to take away Egypt and then make a handsome concession about it. Palmerston had some such idea in mind. But he was in no mood to make any such concessions as Granville demanded. He told him to warn Louis Philippe that an 'Anconade' would mean war and a Russian fleet in Western Europe, a warning Granville refused to give, because, he said, Louis Philippe's conduct had already shewn that it was unnecessary, thus incurring Palmerston's official displeasure and almost com-pletely losing his confidence.[1]

The pressure on Palmerston had much increased in intensity at the end of September and the Queen and Prince Albert, who had been continually urged to do something by Uncle Leopold, now at last began to use their influence with Melbourne to make Palmerston give way. The Queen wished some overture to be made to France, Melbourne told Palmerston on the 24 September, and he might as well do it as it would not affect the result. Prince Albert added his entreaties to hers and Lansdowne, inspired, Palmerston later said, by Broglie, also pleaded with Melbourne. Leopold himself joined in the attack on Melbourne with a por-tentous letter which, with many underlinings in the true Coburg style, argued the necessity of preserving the throne of Louis Philippe. He suggested that Granville should be told to propose to Thiers a general consultation on the Eastern Question, and the Queen and Prince Albert, at his prompting, repeatedly urged the same course on Melbourne, though always answering Leopold in language suggested by the Prime Minister.[2]

It was to Lord John Russell that all these critics looked for a lead. He had first threatened Melbourne with his resignation on

mind, but there does not seem to have been any real plan about it. Nevertheless at Palmerston's orders Granville sent post-haste to Madrid to warn the Spanish Government, and a messenger was sent off to Gen. Espartero who promised to take the necessary precautions. On the whole subject see C. N. Scott, *France and the Balearic Isles in 1840*, *Eng. Hist. Rev.*, April, 1912.

[1] From Bulwer, 5, 7, 8, 9 Oct., 1840; to Granville, 7, 8, 20 Oct., 1940: *B.P.* The letters of 7, 8 Oct. in *Bulwer*, II, 337, 339, are much emasculated. From Granville, 11 Oct., 1840: *B.P.*

[2] From Melbourne, 29, 30 Sept., 1840, enclosing Prince Albert to Melbourne, undated, and Lansdowne to Melbourne, "Tuesday night". "The inclination of my mind at present is very much to take John Russell's view"; do., 6, 10 Oct. 1840; *Appendix*, p. 860. Leopold to Melbourne, 1 Oct., 1840: *B.P.*

10 September. Since then he had been bombarded by letters from the Whig pundits and particularly Lord Spencer, who, as Althorp, had always been the most pusillanimous of Cabinet Ministers. He had seen Guizot who had also poured out his heart to other Whigs whom he met at Holland House or elsewhere. Russell now insisted on the whole question being brought before the Cabinet. It was perhaps only Melbourne's appeal to him to respect the condition of the Queen that prevented him from resigning forthwith. Lord Spencer had told him that if Britain went to war the Melbourne Government would at once be overthrown in the House of Commons. But the Queen made a personal appeal and when the Cabinet met he was not yet prepared to press his resignation.

This decision may well have been influenced by the fact that in spite of the croakings of the Whig peers increasing support for resistance to France was coming from many sides. The British people had taken longer than those on the Continent to resent the threats of Thiers and the expansion of French armaments on sea as well as on land. They regretted the rupture of the 'Alliance' as it was still called. But the conduct of France had at last begun to take effect. The Tory party was by now almost unanimously on Palmerston's side. Greville and Henry Reeve suddenly found that Barnes had swung *The Times* round to the same side, a change as much due to his deep-seated patriotism as to the advice given him by Aberdeen, now one of the strongest defenders of Palmerston amongst the Tories. Peel was almost as decided and though the Duke made an imprudent remark to Bourqueney that France ought to be consulted, which was much quoted by Palmerston's enemies, he was really entirely of Palmerston's view. The Whig Press was of course all on Palmerston's side and represented a good deal of the rank and file of the Party. Considerable effect had been produced on the more religious of both parties by the proposal to find some means of helping the Jews to get back to Palestine, an element of public opinion to which Palmerston himself paid great attention. Only the Radicals still clung to their opposition to the 'Holy Alliance', not very comfortable allies for Lord John Russell and his aristocratic supporters.[1]

The series of Cabinets began on the 28 September. A comic

---

[1] Spencer Walpole, *Lord John Russell*, I, 348–354. Neumann to Metternich, 30 Sept., 1840: *V. St. A.* On the question of the Jews and Protestant interest in the settlement see below Sec. 6, p. 761.

turn was given to the proceedings by the fact that in each Minister's place was a copy of the letter written by Urquhart to Melbourne accusing Palmerston of High Treason. Palmerston used the incident to warn Russell that the Cabinet discussions would soon be known, if in distorted form, at Paris and Alexandria. The Cabinet arrived only slowly and reluctantly in London and some were absent from the first meetings. Palmerston tried to shew his colleagues that matters were going well enough and they had better leave them alone. But when the opposition refused to agree and insisted on a friendly reply to the conciliatory note which Guizot had communicated on 10 October, he made what seemed at first a great concession. He offered to concert with the signatories of the July Convention a soothing communication to France on the lines long ago laid down by Metternich in his letter to Leopold. This would have committed him to very little, but it might have led to dangerous discussions. It was, however, much less than was now insistently demanded by Lord John Russell, who had if not a majority at least a strong minority of the Cabinet with him. It was done, according to Neumann, after pressure from Melbourne who was now seriously alarmed at the effect of the crisis on the health of the Queen.

Whether Palmerston anticipated the result is not known. He certainly never intended to make any real concession about Syria. At any rate, when he summoned the Allied representatives to the Foreign Office and submitted his draft to them, Brunnow strongly objected. He could not, he said, take such a step without direct authorisation from the Tsar. Neumann, who had reflected the pessimistic attitude current at this moment in Vienna, wished something to be done. But he and others, including later Metternich himself, had to admit that there was no conference in existence at London from which a joint communication could be made to the French Government. Palmerston was thus able to report that it was impossible to do what the Cabinet wanted without a fresh negotiation with the other Great Powers. More time was thus gained and this was of vital importance. In a few days news had come which, if it for the moment increased the French fury, shewed the Cabinet that a serious impression had already been made on Ibrahim's defences.[1]

[1] See my article, "Urquhart, Ponsonby and Palmerston," *Eng. Hist. Rev.*, July 1947. Greville's (*Memoirs*, IV, 299–319) long reports of these cabinets

This situation was, as has been noted, influenced by the two French despatches which arrived in London at this time, the result of a long struggle in the French Cabinet. One dated 3 October was a belated official reply to Palmerston's despatch of the 31 August. It gave a French view of the course of the negotiations in a manner far too moderate for many of Thiers' supporters. It stressed the value to Europe of the Franco-British *entente* during the last ten years. It also tried to embarrass Palmerston by recalling the previous agreements made between France and Britain for action in the Straits against Russia. At the last minute, on the news of the Sultan's deposition of Mehemet Ali, there was added a declaration made in a second despatch dated 8 October. This stated more vigorously that France would regard such an act as a menace to the balance of power, but even here no explicit threat was made. These despatches were indeed a curious commentary on the violence of Thiers and the French Press during the preceding two months. Palmerston might have rated the first more highly than he did if it had not been published in *The Times* within a few hours of his receiving it, and before he could make it known to the Queen and the Prime Minister.

For Guizot communicated to Palmerston on 10 October the second despatch about the deposition before using the first one, of which he was thoroughly ashamed. This he only gave to Palmerston on 12 October. The publication of the latter, indeed, rather dismayed the 'French party' as they were beginning to be called. It seemed to justify Palmerston's estimate of French intentions. The Cabinet, however, still under the influence of the French threats, insisted so strongly that something should be done that Palmerston felt it necessary to make some concession to their alarm.[1]

shew that Palmerston's warning was only too justified. It is impossible to trust completely Greville's account which includes the famous statement that Melbourne fell asleep during the discussions, almost certainly untrue, unless it was a calculated action to lower the temperature. He can be checked by Melbourne's reports to the Queen given in *Queen Victoria Letters*, I, 293–304. From Melbourne, 10, 12 Oct., 1840: *B.P.*, *Appendix*, pp. 860. Neumann to Metternich, 5 Oct., 7 Nov., 1840: *V. St. A.* Guizot to Thiers, 29 Sept., 1840: *A.A.E.*

[1] Thiers to Guizot, 3, 8 Oct., 1840: *L.P.*, II, Nos. 217, 213. Guizot, *Mémoires*, V, 336–337. The first draft of the French despatch of 3 October had been made by Viel Castel (Desages to Bourqueney, 8 Sept., 1840: *Bour. P.*). There had been prolonged disputes about it in the French Cabinet and Louis Philippe himself had insisted on toning it down. Guizot does not comment on the fact, but there is no doubt that he presented the second despatch first. It was the despatch of 3 October that Thiers gave to Reeve and which he published in

The French note of 8 October had indicated, though not explicitly, that France would fight if Mehemet were turned out of Egypt. The other three Courts had shewn their dislike of the deposition of the Pasha when it was first announced, though as will be seen, Metternich was later to take a new line about it. Palmerston accordingly now saw Guizot and told him that the deposition of Mehemet was not a final decision and wrote a despatch to that effect to Granville. Palmerston had already told Ponsonby in private letters that he could not see his way to expel the Pasha from Egypt so he would have to be left there, though the nature of the hereditary tenure could still be determined in a manner most calculated to establish the Sultan's authority. The Ambassador now received a definite instruction to get the deposition reversed, while the French Government were immediately informed that this had been done. Since Palmerston had hardly dared to hope that he would secure Egypt for the Sultan no great concession had been made; the move served its purpose at this critical moment in quietening the Cabinet and shewing Louis Philippe that there was one extremity at least that he would not have to face at present.[1]

That harassed monarch had probably already determined to get rid of his bellicose minister but his resolution was certainly aided by a sudden move by Melbourne who, with one of the spasmodic acts of energy which he sometimes shewed, determined to make the situation quite clear. This action seems to have been as much due to his desire to protect the Queen from the constant pressure of her relatives, as to fear of war. Unknown to all his colleagues he wrote a letter in reply to Leopold's long epistles of October in which he roundly told him that Britain could no longer tolerate

---

The Times but in his note in Greville's *Memoirs* (IV, 314) Reeve mixed up the two despatches. He does not state whether Thiers gave him permission to do so, but though Granville later reported that the publication was not intended (19 Oct., 1840: *B.P.*) it seems likely that Thiers wished it. He probably thought, however, that it would be in Palmerston's hands two or three days before publication. It was the speed of Reeve and Barnes and the delay of Guizot that caused the incident. Guizot told Greville that he had never expected to receive anything so weak and inconsistent as the despatch of 3 October. Lady Palmerston told Princess Lieven that the revelation of the proposed measures against Russia had helped Palmerston with public opinion at home (Sudley, *Corres. Lieven-Palmerston*, 192).

[1] Guizot to Thiers, 4, 10, 16 Oct., 1840: Guizot, *Mémoires*, V, 329, 338, and *A.A.E.* Guichen, *La Crise Orientale*, 399. To Ponsonby, 17 Oct., 1840: *B.P;*. do., 15 Oct., 1840: *F.O. Turkey*, 391 and *L.P.*, II, No. 230. To Granville, 17 Oct., 1840: *F.O. France*, 600B and *L.P.*, II, No. 231.

the threats of France and still less her increase of armaments. If they persisted he would summon Parliament and demand the means to resist them. This letter was, as he knew it would be, immediately forwarded to Louis Philippe and contributed a good deal to the decision which the latter made a few days later. Louis Philippe's first step was to send for Guizot to assist him with the debates in the Chambers now about to meet, and on the 21 October he refused to accept the warlike speech with which Thiers proposed to open them and forced the resignation of his Ministry. Bülow, who saw Melbourne's letter when he passed through Brussels, told Palmerston later that he believed Louis Philippe's action was due to it, and Beauvale, informed from Prussian sources, wrote that it acted like a charm. "He never did a better thing than in writing it," he added, and Palmerston, far from taking umbrage at the concealment of such an important action from himself, seems to have been of the same opinion.[1]

The resignation of Thiers, the appointment of a new Ministry of which Soult was the nominal but Guizot the real head, and the news that soon came from the East ended the crisis. Henceforward Palmerston's attackers could do little. For another month, however, he still had an anxious time. For though the energy of Napier and Jochmus and the defection of the Maronites had defeated Ibrahim's armies and obtained possession of the sea coast, Acre was still there with its ominous reputation for long

---

[1] From Melbourne, 25th Oct., 1840; Leopold to Melbourne, 23 Oct., 1840: *B.P.* described the use made of the letter but implied that he would still keep Thiers in office. The fact of the letter has long been known. (Sir T. Martin, *Life of the Prince Consort*, I, 231.) To Beauvale, 4 Nov., 1840; from Beauvale, 14 Nov., 1840: *B.P.* "Melbourne did not mention to me that he had written to this effect," Palmerston wrote. But Melbourne had in fact communicated its general tenour on 25 October: "My letter to him [Leopold] was principally to urge upon him the bad effect of the French military and naval preparations and of the necessity of which they would lay us under of arming upon our part. I also shewed to him the poverty of the ground which Thiers had taken in asserting that the power of Mehemet was a necessary constituent part of the balance of power and these are the two points of the difference which has taken place between the King and Thiers." The exact contents of the letter are variously described, but all agree that it was very strongly worded. Bülow, who saw it at Brussels, told Neumann that part of it ran as follows: "I will lay before it [Parliament] the conduct of France, ask for supplies in order to increase our fleets. I will take care that they shall be placed upon the largest footing,—this is in a word, War, Sir. If I do take such a responsibility upon myself in the state in which is now Her Majesty, I know that the interests and honour of my country require it and that I will be approved by the whole nation." Neumann to Metternich, 7 Nov., 1840: *V. St. A.*; (in English in the original). cf. A. Hasenclever, *Die Orientalische Frage*, 228–229. Raikes (*Journal, New Edn.*, II, 262) noted the references in the French Press but completely misconceived the purpose of the letter.

resistance and winter was coming on.   Stopford had for some time threatened to take the fleet away in spite of frantic appeals from Ponsonby.   Bandiera, the Austrian Admiral, was strongly in favour of such a course.   Many thought it inevitable, including Guizot's advisers in Paris, who still hoped to obtain something for the Pasha to satisfy French opinion and establish the new Ministry firmly in its place.   Louis Philippe and Guizot, indeed, seemed to think it obvious that concessions should now be made for this purpose which had been refused to the threats of Thiers. Granville pressed this point of view with all his strength.   If the Left came into power, he insisted, there would be war.[1]

That was not Palmerston's view.   British policy, he always insisted, was founded on the necessities of the situation in Asia Minor and had nothing to do with the question of who was to be in power in France.   He warmly praised Ponsonby for getting 10,000 more Turks despatched to Syria and continued to send all the aid he could.   He authorised him to get the Porte to remove Sir Charles Smith and sent a capable engineering officer in his place, together with expert ordnance officers.   He depleted the British arsenals to supply muskets for the Turkish troops.   He stressed especially the necessity of adequate commissariat and medical arrangements and sent out officers to assist the Turks with these problems.   He hoped that their advice would not only help to overcome Mehemet but establish new and better services in Turkey.   He continued to urge Metternich to send help also. He did his best to get the bankers to back the Sultan though he had to refuse the British guarantee of a loan, which, like all their kind, they immediately demanded.[2]

Palmerston had already strongly supported Ponsonby's appeal

[1] From Ponsonby, 3, 7 Oct., 1840; from Beauvale, 13 Oct., 1840; from Granville, 2, 6 Nov., 1840: B.P. Ponsonby, in order to increase the ardour of the Sultan and the public morale, presented a standard captured by Napier's forces as one taken by the Turkish Army. The object of the Ambassador, in which he had great success, was hardly appreciated by Napier—or by some historians who have considered the incident.

[2] To Ponsonby, 17, 23, 27 Oct., 4 Nov., 1840: B.P. "I hope at Vienna they will feel ashamed to leave a young Prince of the Imperial Family fighting in the Levant with not two hundred men at his back. Put this strongly to Stürmer and get him to write to this effect to Vienna." When the Turks were asked to pay for the arms sent the total value was estimated at £41,928. (F.O. Turkey, 391.) "I hope our medical men will be able to make arrangements which will be useful to Turkey beyond the present crisis" (4 Nov.). By the time the missions arrived the fighting was over, the Turks received them coldly and they were able to effect nothing. cf. F. E. Bailey, British Policy and the Turkish Reform Movement, 203, n. 87.

to keep the fleet on the coast, even if it had sometimes to withdraw a little. The steamers at any rate could remain without danger, and Palmerston pointed out that Mehemet had kept his fleet there during the winter. It was difficult to frame explicit instructions on such a question at so great a distance. The Admiralty were naturally cautious, but Minto was altogether of Palmerston's view and wrote to Stopford that the attack was to continue. "I hope", Palmerston wrote on the 5 October, "that by this time our squadron has taken Acre. But I send an instruction to Stopford to attack it if he can do so with a prospect of success, in order to satisfy him that he was right, if he has done so already, and to spur him on, if he has hesitated. He is a brave and honourable man and a good officer; but rather old and worn out in mind, and I should think weak in judgment and liable to take a wrong turn, but I am sure that when he learnt, as he will have done from Minto, the wishes and intentions of his Govt. he will have set himself to work in good earnest to carry them into effect."

The official instructions signed by Palmerston reached Stopford on the 29th. They were no doubt the result of much consultation in London and their careful wording, which placed on Stopford himself the final responsibility for the attack, reflected the caution of the Admiralty and other members of the Cabinet more than Palmerston's own optimism. Melbourne, indeed, strongly advised against action and seems to have given way only at the last moment. A whole series of communications could have already left no doubt in the Admiral's mind of the intense desire to obtain Acre as soon as possible. Stopford was, however, still hesitating when the instructions reached him and it was not only Palmerston's firm conviction but also the opinion of many who had followed the events closely that they decided him to make the attack on 4 November. It was amazingly successful. Aided by the blowing up of the powder magazine by a chance shot, the fortress fell in a single day, the young Archduke of Austria being amongst the first to enter by the breach. Ibrahim had no alternative now but to get his army back to Egypt across the desert route. Had the attack been pressed as Ponsonby desired he might have lost the whole of it. Sir Charles Smith was eventually removed from his position as Turkish Chief of Staff. But though Jochmus did his best he got little support from Stopford, while Napier had been sent to Alexandria to summon Mehemet to surrender, a mission with surprising results. For two months longer Ibrahim kept his army in Syria while Mehemet negotiated for its safety. It was finally allowed to go without pressure. The bulk of the routed army thus at last reached Egypt in safety with their commander, a broken and despairing man, who sought refuge in the bottle from the consequences of his defeat.[1]

The news of the fall of Acre did not reach the Western capitals

[1] To Ponsonby, 5 Oct., 1840; from Melbourne, 4 Oct., 1840: *B.P.* Broughton, *Recollections*, V, 298. The whole question is discussed in great detail in Appendix III of H. W. V. Temperley's *Crimea*, where the instructions of 5 October are printed, and all that can be said in defence of Stopford and Sir Charles Smith will be found skilfully marshalled. Professor Temperley rightly pointed out the responsibility thrown on the Admiral and attacked Napier's conduct during the bombardment where he took up a position contrary to the Admiral's orders. Though Napier demanded a court martial, which was refused, it was he who was sent to Alexandria to summon Mehemet to surrender. Much of the information on which Palmerston relied was sent in private letters. Much of this was *ex parte* evidence from Napier and Jochmus who were strongly supported by Ponsonby. Ponsonby's letters were as usual written very freely and by Palmerston's direction only short extracts were put on official record, but he placed in the F.O. Archives part of the letter of Jochmus of 23 October in which he summed up Smith: "I never saw a person less qualified for his present station, from nervous affection irascibility indolence and, as it appears, to me a *decidedly narrow scope of mind*, than the man now unfortunately charged with directing the movements of this war. He seems entirely incapable of comprehending the description of people he has to deal with and the nature and genius of this mountain warfare, and, what is more, from fear of showing that he does not, he wont consult others who do or who are capable to act. He has shown the most unwarrantable jealousy of Commodore Napier for no other earthly reason than that the latter has been fortunate enough to succeed on shore. . . . If your Excy wants to establish some probability of victory the Admiral must go off Alexandria or into some winter Post where he can waver without injury to the cause: Sir Charles Smith must be recalled to Constantinople to be consulted on the general campaign and remain there or go to England, and Commodore Napier and myself left to fight *in Syria*." (*F.O. Turkey*, 398 and *B.P.*)

Jochmus, while personally interested in the result, was an experienced and loyal officer and this letter is convincing.

Palmerston gave Ponsonby only conditional instructions to get the Porte to remove Smith and substitute Jochmus on 17 October but Ponsonby promptly put them into effect, though Jochmus did not receive his Firman giving him the command until 15 December. (Wood to Ponsonby, 16 Dec., 1840: *F.O. Turkey*, 399.) The letter to Smith himself seems to have been more equivocal and the latter protested bitterly to Ponsonby for the speed at which he had acted. Melbourne certainly thought no decision had been taken (18 Nov.: *B.P. Appendix*, p. 861). Jochmus later complained that his own despatches were not published and in a secret report threw on Smith the blame for allowing Ibrahim's troops to escape to Egypt. Napier, it is true, considered the position at that time critical, but he was defending his own conduct at Alexandria. The whole question of these operations demands more extended treatment than can be given here, but it would seem that the conclusion of Professor Temperley cannot be accepted without further consideration of all the evidence available. To Ponsonby, 17 Oct., 1840; from Ponsonby, 9 Dec., 1840 (enclosing Smith to Ponsonby, 25 Nov.). *F.O. Turkey*, 391, 399. Jochmus to Ponsonby, 12 May, 1841 (with secret report): *B.P.* and *F.O. Turkey*, 434.

until 24 November. In the meanwhile Palmerston had to resist another attempt to make him give Mehemet something more than Egypt—Candia or some portion of the Acre Pashalik. Some concession, Guizot reiterated in his appeals to his Whig friends, was surely due to him for taking up his burden and was necessary to ensure the stability of the new Government about to face the Chambers where Thiers was expected to make a furious attack. Louis Philippe and Leopold began a new campaign to obtain this end and were supported by most of those in England who had previously worked for France including Clarendon and Greville. Lord Holland's sudden death on 22 October deprived them of the great centre of cabal and intrigue, but the Whig peers and Greville and his friends were as persistent as before.

It was no doubt partly to counter these moves that Palmerston now sent to Guizot the despatch which he had prepared in answer to Thiers' note of 8 October. This was another incisive exposure of French inconsistencies and took no account of the fact that Thiers had been thrown out of office. Since Thiers' had published a despatch in *The Times*, Palmerston had his published in the *Morning Chronicle*, thus adding to the chagrin of Guizot and his British allies. This step was perhaps a little vindictive. But Guizot was already intriguing with members of the Cabinet, and Palmerston wished to provide ammunition against Thiers for the debates in the Chambers, a purpose the despatch served very well. It caused, however, a 'great sensation' at Paris where in some quarters it was regarded as a threat that Mehemet Ali might lose Egypt as well as Syria. Guizot told the sympathetic Granville that he was sure that Palmerston, who had been so nice to him on his departure from London, could not have conceived the damage it would do to the new Government.[1]

The attack in London had this time been led by Bülow, who, after being indoctrinated by Werther at Berlin, had come back via Brussels where he and Leopold had planned the new campaign together. He was to tackle Melbourne and other Cabinet members before Palmerston, and the suggestion was that an armistice should be immediately proclaimed in Syria and that the Pasha

---

[1] To Granville, 2 Nov., 1840: *L.P.*, II, No. 262. From Granville, 13 Nov., 1840: *F.O. France*, 607; do., 16 Nov., 1840. Palmerston blandly replied to Granville's protests that pressure of work had prevented him from completing the despatch in time to send it to Thiers. To Melbourne, 26 Oct., 1840: *B.P. Appendix*, p. 848.

might be allowed to possess for life such territory as he still held. Guizot meanwhile had been demanding much more from Granville. This offer, he said, was not good enough. Ibrahim's armies were still intact and their hold on the interior could not be shaken. The British fleet would have to leave the coast. Bourqueney was loth to take part in operations behind Palmerston's back which he knew would be regarded as underhand. He preferred to tackle him directly and of course got nothing but friendly conversation. He held back Guizot's despatches, however, until Bülow could make his approach to Melbourne and the Cabinet so that Palmerston could not conceal them. There was in fact an intrigue to undermine Palmerston's position.[1]

Clarendon and Greville had lent themselves to this intrigue with the same ardour as on previous occasions, though a severe attack of gout prevented the latter from doing very much. Clarendon discussed the possibilities with Bourqueney in a frank conversation in which he told him that Lord John Russell and Lansdowne shared his own desire to make concessions. Austria and Prussia would move with Britain, he said, if she left Russia to draw nearer to France. The Tsar had wished to provoke a European war and a revolution in France and he and his friends would leave the Cabinet before they allowed such a thing to occur. He promised that they would do everything possible in the Cabinet to assist Guizot. Bourqueney had even to remind him that it was with Palmerston that he must transact his business rather than with Clarendon and his colleagues.[2]

In order to obtain a result it was above all necessary that some concrete proposal should be at once made by Guizot that his friends in the Cabinet could support. That Minister was prolific in suggestions in unofficial conversations with Granville and in private letters to Bourqueney. But, either by design or through sheer ineptitude, he gave to neither any explicit or official proposal. When Bourqueney went to Palmerston in the expectation that he had already received from Granville Guizot's definite plan, the Secretary of State was able to show him that the despatch contained nothing of the kind. The Chargé d'Affaires dared not take

[1] From Granville, 6 Nov., 1840: *F.O. France*, 606. Bourqueney to Guizot, 2 Nov., 1840; Guizot to Bourqueney, 4, 7 Nov., 1840: *A.A.E.* Part of the last letter was shewn to Greville (*Memoirs*, IV, 328). Neumann to Metternich, 7 Nov., 1840: *V. St. A.*

[2] Bourqueney to Guizot, 28 Oct., 1840: *A.A.E.*

the responsibility on himself. Thus, though the Cabinet had decided that any such offer must be seriously considered, Palmerston was able to inform them that none had been received. When Granville inquired of Guizot what the situation was, the answer was that Bourqueney's informal approach had shewn that nothing worth while could be obtained and that consequently no official proposal would be made.[1]

In any case the news from Syria destroyed Bülow's effort almost as soon as it had begun. The population there had clearly declared itself on the Turkish side. The Ambassador's discomfiture was completed by the attitude of Metternich. For at Vienna the Court had become very warlike. The Archduke Charles was radiant at the conduct of his son. Kolowrat found he could get no support and abandoned his opposition. Once the danger from France had died down Metternich plucked up courage to be defiant. The uproar in Germany forced both the Prussian and Austrian Government to take the question of the defence of the Confederation seriously. There was much consultation amongst the soldiers and Prussia proposed that the defence of the Confederation should be extended to Piedmont, thus covering Italy about which Metternich had been so nervous.

Metternich now began to consider the extent of Austrian interests in the Levant and proposals began to be made for Austria to become the Protector of the Catholics in Syria. A promise was made to send arms for the Turks and even reinforcements of marines for the Austrian squadron. The result of all this was, wrote Beauvale, exulting in the successes in the East, that "We are now as bold as lions and have forgot we were ever afraid."[2]

This new strength was already reflected in Metternich's despatches. He was not only against any concession in Syria but would not even do what Palmerston had agreed to do, press the Sultan to withdraw the deposition of Mehemet. That, he said, could be left until the Pasha made his submission. Bülow, reported Bourqueney, was 'atterré' by this news. The Ambassa-

[1] From Bourqueney, 2, 6, 8, 9, 10 Nov., 1840: *A.A.E.* His embarrassment and chagrin are clearly revealed in the despatches. From Granville, 6, 9, 13 Nov., 1840: *F.O. France*, 666, 607. To Granville, 12, 13 Nov., 1840: *F.O. France*, 600, B. Greville (*Memoirs*, IV, 323–334) though ill with the gout, got most of the story from Clarendon and Bourqueney, and his advice helped Guizot to decide to do nothing.
[2] From Beauvale, 19, 27, 31 Oct., 14 Nov., 1840: *B.P.*

dor hastened to beat a retreat and, by an abject apology that he had mistaken the situation, to make his peace with Palmerston. Palmerston was easily appeased but he complained to Berlin that, as Prussia had done nothing, he had at least the right to her full moral support. The King was much pained at this complaint for he considered that the stout attitude of the German people had done a great deal to keep France from pressing her demands. Bourqueney and Desages began to fear that the grant of heredity for Egypt would be lost. The only comfort that the former could give Guizot was to stress the fact that Stopford had insisted that most of the fleet should go to Malta for the winter, and that Sir Charles Smith had reported that the whole Turkish army must be reorganised before it could attack again. There would thus be a long delay and meanwhile Metternich might change his mind again as he had so often done before and Prussia would assuredly follow his lead.[1]

It was at this juncture that the debates began in the French Chambers. They were a complete vindication of Palmerston's policy. Guizot used all the arguments that Palmerston himself had employed to shew that France had not been treated in such a manner as necessitated Thier's policy. Thiers in an effort to defend himself explained that he meant to attack Europe when French armaments were completed. The discomfiture of the Whig coterie was completed by Thiers' eulogy of Lord Holland who, he openly insinuated, had worked for France in the British Cabinet. Guizot also described how he had found allies among Palmerston's colleagues. "What a painful picture does the French Ambassador give of the British Cabinet", Palmerston commented, "when he quietly relates his cooperation with different members of it for the purpose of thwarting the Secretary of State for Foreign Affairs and to prevent him from promoting and securing the interests of England; and how much must Privy Counsellors have kept the secrets of the Cabinet when Guizot says that he knew almost everything from day to day that passed in our deliberations!"

But the effect of the whole debate was to justify Palmerston even in the eyes of his most determined critics. "I really think

---

[1] Bourqueney to Guizot, 13, 17 Nov., 1840: *A.A.E.* To Bülow, 9 Nov. 1840; From Bülow, 11 Nov., 1840: *B.P.* To Lord William Russell, 17 Nov., 1840: *B.P.*; do., 16 Nov., 1840; from Lord William Russell, 25 Nov., 1840: *F.O. Prussia*, 227, 229.

you must have had Thiers in your pay during the last 3 weeks,"
wrote Clarendon, "for even in every lie he has told he seemed to
have no other object but to make out a good case for you," Lord
Lansdowne made the same jest. "He says", reported Macaulay,
"that he now sees where all your Secret Service money has gone.
It has been distributed amongst the opposition orators in the
Chamber of Deputies." Though the Left applauded Thiers and
Odillon Barrot, who also used warlike language, French public
opinion was not impressed and realised the futility of Thiers'
policy. It turned its attention to other matters. The reception
of Napoleon's remains was a great and moving spectacle but the
ordinary citizen was even more diverted by the sensational trial
of Madame Lefarge who, according to some cynical observers,
had done more to reduce the temperature of the political discussions than any of the statesmen.[1]

The result was a complete and unexpected triumph of Guizot
in the Chamber, Thiers' final discomfiture being increased by the
news of the total defeat of Ibrahim. The debate and the taking of
Acre finally also routed all Palmerston's opponents in Britain.
One and all had to confess that the facts had shewn him to be
right. Some grudgingly attributed his success to luck, but for the
most part it was admitted that the triumph was well deserved and
due as much to Palmerston's own energy and judgment as to the
unexpected weakness of his opponents. Thiers himself told Lord
Beauvale that he regarded Palmerston "as the first Statesman of
this age and perhaps of any other". Even Greville had to reverse
all his ideas and in his diary compare Palmerston to Chatham, a
standard which Disraeli was later to accept in *Tancred*. The most
portentous congratulation came from Wellesley who had nothing

---

[1] From Granville, 13, 20, 27 Nov., 4 Dec., 1840: *F.O. France*, 607. From
Clarendon, 6 Dec., 1840; From Macaulay (undated); To Granville, 30 Nov.,
1840: *B.P. Bulwer*, II, 365, leaves out this passage and a trenchant criticism
of French honesty and ability in foreign affairs. Lady Holland was much dis-
tressed at the implication that Lord Holland had betrayed Cabinet secrets, a
charge that was repeated in *The Times*. She wrote a number of letters about it,
including one to Palmerston asking for refutation. Lord Holland's friends took
a similar line. Unfortunately, as has been seen, there was too much truth in the
statement for any very convincing denial to be made. Lady Holland was
reduced to appealing to Bourqueney to get a letter from Guizot stating that
Lord Holland had never betrayed his country. (Bourqueney to Guizot, 29 Dec.,
1840: *A.A.E.*) But Palmerston's letters about Lord Holland to his colleagues
and Ambassadors were couched in the friendliest terms. Thureau-Dangon
(*Histoire de la Monarchie de Juillet*, iv, 384–403) gives the details of the debates.
Granville was not allowed to appear officially at the reception of Napoleon's
remains and watched the ceremony from afar.

to retract and nothing to gain from Palmerston's favours and came to his conclusion before the final dénouement was known. After recounting his long experience of political life, which included the careers of both Pitt and Fox, he wrote: "It is a complete and most splendid justification of your policy; and is the most important, and I trust will prove the most salutary event which has happened in the civilised world for the last half century or more. But I must go further . . . and I sincerely declare that this is the ablest act both of diplomatic and military policy that within my memory has proceeded from the British Cabinet."[1]

Many Frenchmen thought likewise and Palmerston had incurred their deep hostility because of the vigour and insight with which he had resisted France. Those most deeply chagrined were those who like Broglie and de Tocqueville had been most attached to the *entente* with Britain. Previous opponents like Molé were much less critical. And the more realistic members of the official class saw that the sooner France got back to her normal position in Europe the better for her interests. The question of Mehemet Ali, Desages advised Bourqueney, should be regarded as only an incident, like the Quadruple Alliance or the Treaty of 1827 concerning Greece. In due course the common interests of France and Britain in some other question would bring them together again. Unfortunately this was not Guizot's attitude, and he no doubt reflected the view of the majority of Frenchmen. He still pressed for some special recognition of France and as Bourqueney did not seem zealous enough in the cause sent a special envoy, Mounier, to expound his views, much to Bourqueney's distress. Mounier had no more success than the Chargé d'Affaires and the problem of bringing France back to her proper place in the European polity was, therefore, yet to be solved and it was to prove much more difficult than anyone yet realised.[2]

[1] Beauvale to Lady Palmerston, 5 Jan., 1846: Airlie, *Lady Palmerston*, II, 105. From Wellesley, 4 Nov., 1840. "This", wrote Palmerston to Melbourne, "is to be taken with the allowance which is always to be made for Lord Wellesley's high flown style; but . . . I have good reason to believe that an immense majority of the British nation will likewise approve the conduct of the Government in this affair." *B.P.* Lord Spencer wrote a private letter to Palmerston admitting that he had been wrong and paid a tribute to him in the House of Lords. Lord Morpeth, who had been an insistent critic, now wrote a handsome letter of congratulation.

[2] Guizot to Bourqueney, 20, 29 Nov., 11 Dec., 1840; Bourqueney to Guizot, 24, 26 Nov., 2 Dec., 1840: *A.A.E.* He was deeply hurt at what would be considered as a 'supercession' of his functions and asked for a mark of confidence to be inserted in the *Journal Officiel*. Desages to Bourqueney, 4 Nov., 1840: *A.A.E.*

Meanwhile Palmerston himself had been much exercised about the grant of hereditary tenure to Mehemet. He had begun to regret the concession already made and wished it to be limited as far as was possible. These views he communicated to Ponsonby in private letters, for the whole question was still hypothetical and he had no definite plan to put before the Cabinet. Already on 27 October he suggested that the grant of heredity might perhaps be limited to Ibrahim alone. But he had to admit that the Cabinet would not allow the British fleet to attack Egypt and it hardly seemed possible to force on Mehemet such a treaty in any other way. Metternich's unexpected attitude, however, encouraged his hopes of getting more than he had anticipated. The Sultan, he pointed out, could make his own laws about the kind of heredity to be granted, and in the act attached to the convention it had been agreed that Mehemet must accept and apply the laws of the Ottoman Empire. Yet he was anxious to get Mehemet's submission before the autumn gales. That would be difficult unless Acre was taken and in view of Stopford's hesitations he hardly dared hope that could be done. But the attempt was worth making. Accordingly on 14 November Stopford was instructed to send an emissary to Mehemet to tell him that if he surrendered all his conquests outside Egypt and handed back the Turkish fleet, the Powers would recommend the Sultan to re-appoint him to the Governorship of Egypt. Nothing was said of hereditary tenure, but in a separate instruction the officer was authorised to convey Mehemet's reply to Constantinople if he insisted on it. As Palmerston explained to Ponsonby: "If he makes his submission as we invite him to do he must have the hereditary Pashalik of Egypt; subject of course to all the restrictions mentioned in the separate act and annexed to the Treaty [of 15 July]. If he refuses and goes on fighting then the Sultan will be doubly free to do what he pleases." Palmerston did not communicate these reservations and interpretations to the Cabinet or his Allies and this is perhaps the most equivocal step which he took in all these years. The attitude which he took towards Mehemet was naturally welcomed by Ponsonby and accounts for all his subsequent conduct in the question of the grant of hereditary tenure. Palmerston did not in fact press his policy to its logical conclusion and, though he never admits it, it is probable that he regretted it during the long period which ensued before the final settlement with Mehemet was made.[1]

The envoy sent to Mehemet, however, was imbued with very different ideas. Stopford had chosen Napier for this mission because he found him so hard to control in the Syrian operations. But Napier fell like other Englishmen under the Pasha's spell and tried to settle matters with his usual recklessness and flamboyance. Mehemet had for long seen that the game was up, and for some time it had taken all the efforts of Walewski and Cochelet to prevent him from throwing over the French and appealing to the Allied Powers. He received Napier with open arms and the two were soon on excellent terms. Napier went far beyond his instructions by negotiating a convention which gave Mehemet all that he could now hope to get. In return for a promise to recall his armies an immediate armistice was to be granted, thus ensuring the safety of Ibrahim's remaining troops, of which the bulk were to come by sea. Further Mehemet promised to make his submission to the Sultan and return the Ottoman fleet on condition that the Four Powers guaranteed to him the hereditary possession of Egypt. With his usual bombast Napier expounded what he had done in extravagant language and alluded to the Ptolemies looking down on the new state. "I have done", he wrote, "what I think you wish." Ponsonby was of course horrified and Stopford without consulting Constantinople promptly disavowed his subordinate. He had just received Palmerston's instruction and private letter of 14 November. He offered Mehemet Egypt, with no mention of hereditary tenure, if he would surrender the fleet.

Palmerston and Melbourne were also taken aback at Napier's action and laughed at the language used. But though Palmerston at once pointed out that the four Powers could not guarantee the hereditary possession but only advise the Sultan to grant it, he was ready to accept in substance what had been done. The Sultan, however, had already refused the submission under these conditions and the whole question had to be reconsidered. Austria and Prussia, reported Beauvale, saw in Napier's convention a sign that Britain was merely looking to her own interests now that the struggle was over.[2]

[1] To Ponsonby, 27 Oct., 14, 15 Nov., 1840: *B.P.* To Admiralty, 14 Nov., 1840: *L.P.*, II, Nos. 22, 23. Beauvale told Palmerston that Metternich would never agree to hereditary succession. (14 Nov., 1840: *B.P.*).
[2] From Napier, 26 Nov., 1840: *L.P.*, III, Nos. 85–87: 28 Nov., 1840: *B.P.* From Ponsonby, 8, 9 Dec., 1840: *B.P.* To Ponsonby, 12 Dec., 1840: *B.P.*

The news that followed from the East was, however, more cheering. Though the reply to Stopford contained some equivocal phrases it was so far satisfactory that Stopford's emissary, Captain Fanshawe, declared himself ready to convey it to the Porte. Shortly afterwards Captain Walker hoisted the Sultan's flag in the Ottoman fleet in Alexandria and prepared to take it to Constantinople. There was still some doubt as to Ibrahim's movements but he seemed to be making preparations to retire to Egypt. Provided the Porte did not impose impossible terms on Mehemet in granting the hereditary tenure of Egypt to him and his family, peace would be assured and the negotiation with France could be begun at once, the settlement of the Eastern Question be put into a treaty of the Five Powers with the Sultan and, even more important, the situation in Western Europe brought back to normal.[1]

For France still refused to reduce her armaments. Guizot had really shown in his speeches that they were not necessary but he would not abandon them at the behest of the other European Powers. After a great fight in the Chambers the fortifications bills were finally passed, though Soult shewed very clearly that he did not approve of them. Some Frenchmen were even talking of the possibility of a Franco-Russian alliance, a fact which Granville reported in great alarm only to get from Palmerston the reply that it was a quite natural development but would not come yet awhile. When Metternich proposed to begin discussions for a mutual return to a peace footing, Guizot warned him that such a negotiation would have the worst effect on French public opinion. All that must wait, he said, until France could be sure that the Eastern Question had been finally settled and Mehemet Ali's

From Beauvale, 26 Dec., 1840: *B.P.* To Beauvale, 4, 19 Dec., 1840: *B.P.* Esterhazy to Metternich, 4, 12 Dec., 1840: *V. St. A.* From Melbourne, 15 Dec., 1840: *B.P.* Melbourne was the only person able to discuss the appositeness of the allusion to the Ptolemies: "I do not recollect much of the nature of the power of the Ptolemies but I dare say it was in the first instance a delegated and dependant authority under the Roman General in Macedonia." Palmerston criticised the form and said it was 'diamond cut diamond' for Napier would not have attacked and Mehemet had already ordered his troops to return. Napier vigorously defended himself. The title given to Mehemet was a bad translation due to the haste necessary to prevent French intrigues; he would have attacked; the order had not been given; Ibrahim had concentrated his army and the Turkish troops were dispersed so that the issue was still doubtful. To Napier, 12 Jan., 1841; From Napier, 26 March, 1841: *B.P.*

[1] Much detail on all this is given in *L.P.*, III, Nos. 115, 117 and in E. Driault, *La Crise Orientale*, III, Nos. 1–42.

position in Egypt assured. He also desired the other Powers to
state that this position was due to their regard for France, "or
rather from fear of her", as Melbourne commented, "which is
what she desires to be understood. Never heard of such a thing
before."[1]

In Europe the alarm caused by Thiers' threats and armaments
took some time to die down. The Prussian soldiers had been
afraid that France would postpone her attack until the Eastern
Question was finished and Britain had not the same interest in
defending Central Europe. They had even in great secrecy asked
the Duke of Wellington to command the European armies if the
breach came, an offer which Wellington had seemed disposed to
accept. This was done without the British Cabinet being consulted. But the Prussian Government also put forward the idea
of creating a permanent alliance against France amongst the Four
Powers. This was naturally welcomed by the Tsar but Palmerston would have nothing to do with it. He had no desire to make
permanent the present situation. He was not afraid of France and
had no desire to encourage the Central Powers to think that he
would be on their side in all circumstances. The project, therefore, was soon abandoned though, as will be seen, it was to come
up again when the Eastern Question was finally settled.[2]

Nor would either Palmerston or Melbourne give the slightest
encouragement to a "very secret" scheme of Metternich to win
back France to the Concert by recognising her position in Algiers.
Such a concession, Palmerston wrote, would turn the "salutary
moral humiliation" of France into a veritable triumph and undo
all the good that had been done. Palmerston was determined that
France should be compelled to accept such terms as he thought
reasonable and right. He refused to see the advantage of concili-
ating her now that he had obtained all that was essential. And,
as he a little later told Esterhazy, Algiers would be a hostage in the
hands of her enemies if France again made war on Europe, a
threat that would be less strong if her sovereignty had been recog-

[1] From Granville, 4, 7, 11, 25 Dec., 1840: *B.P.* A flock of Russian ladies
including Mme Nesselrode had descended on Paris—but they were not allowed
to go to Court. To Granville, 8, 29 Dec., 1840; to Beauvale, 19, 26 Dec.,
1840; from Beauvale, 4, 15 Dec., 1840; from Melbourne, 15 Dec., 1840: *B.P.*
[2] From Lord William Russell, 21 Oct., 25 Nov., 16 Dec., 1840, 20 Jan., 1841:
B.P. I have nowhere else found any allusion to the offer to Wellington but
Russell reports it in the private letters of 16 Dec. and 20 Jan. in such a manner
as seems to leave no doubt but that it took place, though of course informally.

nised by the Great Powers. Melbourne agreed entirely. To give France Algiers "would be treating her like a child", and make it more difficult to guard against the real danger in North Africa— further extension of French power.[1]

Thus, though the year closed for Palmerston in great triumph, he had still tangled and difficult negotiations in front of him which were to try the patience of the Cabinet and the European Allies for many months to come. Nor perhaps was he unconscious of the fact that he had incurred the bitter hostility not only of Guizot and Louis Philippe but of Leopold whose mediatory efforts he had treated so roughly. That he had expected, but it had consequences in Britain itself. For Queen Victoria and Prince Albert and especially the latter, now in full control of the royal prerogative, could not help but be influenced by the insinuations which Leopold conveyed to them in his avuncular letters. "Rex and autocrat" was the phrase applied by him to Palmerston in a specially damaging letter to Prince Albert. Meanwhile not only was Lord John Russell complaining to Melbourne that Palmerston did not keep him reasonably informed of what he was doing, but Queen Victoria, now entirely in the hands of her husband so far as public business was concerned, began to demand that the important despatches should be sent in good time so that they could be considered properly before they were sent off. This was Albert's first move to establish the Crown in that position of authority which it held in the minds of his tutors, Stockmar and Leopold.[2]

[1] From Beauvale, 15 Dec., 1840; to Beauvale, 26 Dec., 1840; from Melbourne, 28 Dec., 1840: *B.P.* Esterhazy to Metternich, 7 Jan., 1841: *V. St. A.* Palmerston said the British Government would declare to France that they would not allow her to do in Morocco what she had done in Algiers.   For his watchful eye on that country see R. Flournoy, *British Policy towards Morocco in the age of Palmerston (1830–1865)*, chap. III.
[2] Leopold to Prince Albert, 26 Nov., 1840. *Queen Victoria Letters*, I, 315. The significance of the letter is brought out by Professor Bell (*Palmerston*, I, 320). A similar phrase, "King and Minister", had long been in Leopold's mind and its connection with the reestablishment of the royal power is more clearly shewn in an account by Lord Burghersh of an interview with Leopold at Laeken on 12 October. R. Weigall, *Corres. of Lord Burghersh*, 286. At this same period, reviewing her visit to England, Princess Lieven wrote to her brother, "Lord Palmerston *gouverne.*" (15 Nov., 1840: *Lie MSS.*) From Melbourne, 28 Nov., 14 Dec., 1840: *B.P.*

5. THE CONTEST IN CENTRAL ASIA[1]
1837–1841

Palmerston recognised that he had obtained all his objectives in the Eastern Question with the cooperation of the Tsar who had supported him more consistently than any other person in Europe. His conduct, Palmerston avowed, had been 'perfect'. But all this time Britain was engaged in another struggle with Russia for power and influence which might ultimately have as important results as that concerning the Ottoman Empire. The whole future of Central Asia was at stake and to some minds that meant the future of India as well. At any rate great areas including Persia, Khiva, Bokhara, Afghanistan and even Sind and the Punjaub, were concerned. The two great empires in Asia were advancing towards one another. No one knew how fast they would go or where the contact would be made. In the employ of both countries were active and imaginative men, who were beginning to realise the possibilities of the situation. The old oriental despotisms clearly could not resist the pressure of the disciplined armies of the European Empires when these could be brought to bear on them. The distances were great, the conditions imperfectly known, the movements of armies or even of traders difficult and hazardous. The contest was largely one of logistics. The risks were great, but the prizes were dazzling and attracted many adventurous as well as patriotic men. The Governments as always lagged cautiously behind, but in these also were some who thought that the time had come for bold and prompt action.

Amongst these was certainly Palmerston, who was one of the foremost advocates of a forward policy. He summed up his position in a letter to Hobhouse in 1840:

"It seems pretty clear that sooner or later the Cossak [sic] and the Sepoy, the man from the Baltic and he from the British islands

[1] There were several Blue books on Persia and Afghanistan reprinted in *B.F.S.P.*, vols. XXV–XXVIII. There is also a large literature on this theme which H. W. C. Davis surveyed in his remarkable Raleigh lecture, "The Great Game in Central Asia", *Proceedings, British Academy*, 1927. There is a wealth of material from British actors in India. Here only an outline can be given of policies for which Palmerston was only partly responsible and the execution of which he did not control. The private correspondence at Broadlands on this subject is not extensive but has some significant letters.

will meet in the centre of Asia. It should be our business to take
care that the meeting should be as far off from our Indian possessions as may be convenient and advantageous to us. But the
meeting will not be avoided by our staying at home to receive the
visit."[1]

This was written when he had in his mind the Russian expedition
to Khiva which he thought would soon extend to Bokhara. His
policy had originally been determined by the Russian action in
Persia. It was only gradually that the wider possibilities of the
situation became clear to him.

In Persia Palmerston inherited a position of great weakness due
to the neglect and parsimony of the British Governments in London and India. During the Napoleonic Wars Britain had established her influence in Persia to thwart the French attempt to use
it as a base for an attack on India. For that purpose Britain could
either use force in the Persian Gulf or offer money to the corrupt
and avaricious rulers of Persia. The latter method was by far the
cheapest in the long run, and by the Treaty of 1814 Britain had
agreed to give a subsidy to the Shah if Persia was subjected to
attack, while in return Persia agreed to prevent hostile armies from
advancing towards India. The Persians readily accepted the
treaty, not only for the sake of the money, but also because they
considered that the two Powers had a common interest in opposing
Russia. The consequences of Russian control over Persia, however, had not been imagined and guarded against by British governments as the French schemes had been. When the Russo-Persian
war took place in 1826 Canning had insisted that Persia was the
aggressor. He was engaged at the time in establishing close
relations with Russia in his attempt to solve the problem of Greece.
Persia was given no support. Russia in the Treaty of Turko-
manchai of 1828 obtained the boundary of the Araxes which has
ever since been that between the two countries on that side of the
Caspian Sea. Persia had also to pay a heavy indemnity and
Britain took advantage of this fact to obtain the cancellation of her
promise of subsidy by one immediate payment which could be
used to propitiate Russia. Abbaz Mirza, who had borne all the
burden of defence, had to accept this convenient relief, though his

---

[1] To Hobhouse, 14 Feb., 1840: *B.P.* With his practised eye for a telling
phrase Philip Guedalla quoted this sentence from the letter which he found in
the Broughton Papers (*Palmerston*, 225).

father, Fath Ali, who would provide no other funds to meet the
Russian indemnity, for long refused to agree to the suggestion.
The result was that Russia became supreme at Teheran, the
Persians feeling completely abandoned by Britain. Metternich
told Lamb that this weakness was even worse than the policy
which had permitted the Russo-Turkish war of 1828.

There had always been a conflict between the Indian and
London administrations as to which should control relations with
Persia. Serious harm had been done to British interests by this
rivalry. The British Government had of course always the final
decision if it cared to exercise its power. But when Palmerston
came into office the British representative, Sir John Campbell,
was under the orders of India and but little interest was taken
there as to what was happening in Persia by those with most
influence on affairs. Its Government was absorbed in the problems brought about by its contact with the Sikh power in the
Punjaub and the congeries of weak states that comprised Sind and
Baluchistan, many of them under the nominal suzerainty of
Afghanistan which itself was convulsed by civil war. Sir John
Campbell's recipe was a renewal of the subsidy. "If we want
Persia, My Lord," he wrote, "we must pay the price of her
alliance."[1]

One consequence of Persia's defeat by Russia was to drive her
to seek compensation in the North-east for what she had lost in the
North-west. She had plenty of excuse, for the Khans on her
frontiers lived by raiding her territory. Abbas Mirza, the Shah's
son, who had had to yield to the Russians, had considerable
success and the Russian Minister at Teheran encouraged the
Shah to exploit it. Persia was thus pressing on the frontier of
Afghanistan just as the British were extending their power from
the south and seeking trading outlets with central Asia through
the Indus River. The Indian government had an uneasy alliance
with Ranjit Singh, the great Sikh ruler of the Punjaub, now aged
and in decline. On his flank the Indus ran through Sind to
Afghanistan. Ranjit Singh was in conflict with his Afghan
neighbours and had taken Peshawar from Dost Mohammed, the
Afghan Khan, who ruled in Kabul. In 1833 he had made a treaty
with Shuja Khan, the deposed ruler of Afghanistan, and a weak
and unsuccessful attempt was made to put him back into power.

[1] From Sir John Campbell, 23 Sept., 1834: *B.P.*

Palmerston had little time for this problem in his first period of office. His gaze hardly went beyond the Ottoman Empire. Nor did he realise the danger to India from Russian penetration and control. Indeed in 1834 on the death of Fath Ali, the Russian and British Ministers at Teheran combined together to put on the throne his grandson, Mohammed Shah, the son of Abbas Mirza who had himself died a year previously. They did a great service to Persia in preventing a civil war, but the new ruler was young, ambitious and altogether under Russian influence. The Government of India had so far recognised the situation as to send a military mission, but its able officers, Stoddart, Sheil, Todd and others, were not well received and could do little. Sir H. L. Bethune sent out from London was somewhat more successful, and played a role in the decisions of 1834. But it was to Russia that Mohammed Shah looked for support in his plans.

When Palmerston came back in 1835 a change was made in the control of the British Mission in Persia which now depended on the Foreign Office. Sir Henry Ellis, who had succeeded Sir John Campbell on a special mission, had adopted a defeatist attitude. Persia, he wrote, was no use as a defence to India. She was more likely to side with Britain's enemies. An attack on Herat, a key town on the Afghan-Persian frontier, was already planned and the Russian Minister was urging the Shah to undertake it. In the face of Russian opposition it was not likely that the Shah would grant the commercial treaty which Palmerston had made one of the principal objects of the mission.[1]

In addition, as soon as he came back in 1835, Palmerston saw danger in a Russian advance across the Caspian to Khiva. "Once in possession of Khiva", he told Durham, "they command the Oxus which is navigable till you come very near the spot where the Indus is navigable, and this would be the route they would take to attack or threaten our Indian possessions." This would also threaten the independence of Persia, "and the independence of Persia is a great object to us not merely with reference to India, but as connected with the independence of Turkey. Russia pursues the same system of strategy against Persia and Turkey; she creeps down the Black Sea and wants to do the same down the

---

[1] *B.F.S.P.*, XXIII, 860–865. From Ellis, 6 Oct., 1835, 15 Jan., 17, 20 Feb., 1836: *B.P.* Ellis also objected to Sir Henry Bethune controlling the military mission because he did not belong to the Indian army.

Caspian and to take both Persia and Turkey on each of their flanks."

This was certainly thinking very far ahead, but at any rate a more vigorous policy and a more vigorous envoy were needed in Persia. Ellis was not anxious to return and Palmerston put in his place John McNeill, who had already had a subordinate position in the British mission to Persia. He was a man in touch with Urquhart and a good Russian hater. In 1836 he published anonymously a pamphlet directed against her. But it was not this, as is often said, that made Palmerston appoint him. McNeill was chosen as the most energetic and strong personality amongst those who had knowledge of Persia. He set out in June 1836 and was soon in the thick of a great controversy with the Tsar and the Russian Minister, Simonich.[1]

Meanwhile the Whig Government had refused to accept the nomination of Lord Heytesbury whom the Tories had appointed to succeed Lord William Bentinck as Governor-General. Lord Auckland was sent in his stead because he was reckoned to be a 'safe' and reliable man. He had worked well with Palmerston while First Lord of the Admiralty and the two were on excellent terms.

The threatened attack on Herat awakened all Palmerston's fears. He at once protested vigorously to St. Petersburg and secured a promise from Nesselrode that Simonich would be recalled. It was more than a year, however, before the promise was made good, and suspicions of Russian designs continued to grow. Durham himself at first deprecated such suspicions, but soon came to share them. It was the only part of Russian policy against which he warned his chief. The danger of Russian expansion towards India was, he thought, real and inevitable. Palmerston must prepare to meet it. Both the British and Indian Governments were indeed now fully alive to what the capture of Herat might mean. If Persia remained under Russian influence

---

[1] To Durham, 27 Oct., 1835; to McNeill, 21 Feb., 1836: *B.P.* Palmerston deprecated the publication of a pamphlet written in such a tone as likely to detract from McNeill's authority in Persia; "to give your acts the greatest weight," he wrote, "they should appear to be the fulfilment of a duty and an obedience to the orders of your Govt, and not the supererogatory works of individual animosity." *The Memoir of Sir John McNeill*, written by his granddaughter, contains a few of the not very numerous letters in the Broadlands Papers. McNeill attributed his appointment partly to Baillie Frazer who worked under Hammond in the Turkish department of the Foreign Office (*Memoir*, 180).

a forward base for the attack on India could be established there. All the contending rulers of Northern India were watching what would happen and there was talk in the bazaars that the end of the Company's rule in India was at hand.[1]

McNeill did his best to stop the Shah by every kind of persuasion and intimidation. His position was all the more difficult since by Article IX of the Treaty of 1814 Britain had promised not to interfere in quarrels between Persia and Afghanistan unless invited to do so by both sides. He nearly succeeded however and went himself to the Shah's camp before Herat and thence into the town itself to arrange a truce with its defenders. But the Russian Ambassador had the last word and the attack went on. Herat was saved by the bravery of its Afghan defenders under Yar Mohammed Khan, the energetic Minister of its weak ruler Kamran, and the encouragement given to them by the young lieutenant, Eldred Pottinger, whose more famous uncle had sent him to the town as the siege began. A grand attack on 24 June 1838 was beaten back with great slaughter and at last the Shah sullenly withdrew his starving armies. Ghorian, of almost equal strategic importance, still remained in Persian hands. Meanwhile, however, relations with the British Government had been broken off. A messenger to McNeill from Herat had been molested, and all reparation refused. Conscious that his prestige and that of his country was at stake, McNeill withdrew to Tabriz and threatened the grave displeasure of his Government. After waiting there for a long period he eventually returned home via Constantinople and St. Petersburg. The Shah, alarmed at what he had done, despatched an envoy, Hussein Khan, to get into direct touch with the British Government.[2]

Meanwhile in the spring of 1838 the Indian Government had at the demand of McNeill decided to put pressure on the Shah by

[1] From Durham, 21 Feb., 19 Dec., 1836: 24 Feb., 25 May, 1837: *F.O. Russia*, 223, 226, 233–234. The last considered in detail the Russian routes for an attack on India.

[2] *B.F.S.P.*, XXV, 1218–1299. The story of this famous siege in which Pottinger played so admirable a part has often been told. Mr. Archbold calls Yar Mohammed Khan "one of the vilest wretches in Asia". (*Cambridge History of India*, IV, 493) Hussein Khan's journey was reported by the British envoys as he made his way to Britain. Milbanke discovered that his interpreter had been bribed by the Russians to send them accounts of all his interviews. Hussein had, however, enough English to make himself understood alone. He said his main object was to obtain the recall of McNeill (18 Jan., 1839: *F.O. Austria*, 280). He was badly treated by the Shah after his failure, suffering corporal punishment.

the usual method of sending a naval force to the Gulf to occupy a strategic position. The island of Karrak was seized. But the Gulf was far off Teheran and, though the Princes of the South could no doubt be raised in revolt, the result might only be to play into Russia's hands. The decision was,.therefore, come to almost simultaneously at Calcutta and London that the Persian menace must be warded off by some new arrangement with Afghanistan itself, the threatened point from which an attack on India might be based. This decision was indeed obvious enough. The Sikh Kingdom by itself was not a sufficient barrier and could be out-flanked. The Afghan feuds provided great opportunities to their enemies. Their Khans were treacherous and unreliable.

Alexander Burnes, who had already made an adventurous journey through Afghanistan, had been sent back in 1836 to Kabul on a 'commercial' mission, whence he reported on the attitude of its ruler Dost Mohammed towards the attack on Herat. Dost Mohammed had promised assistance to its ruler, Kamran, if he were given back Peshawar. But this was just what the Indian Government could not do unless it was prepared to quarrel with Ranjit Singh, the ruler of the Sikhs. Accordingly Dost Mohammed reinsured himself by offers to Persia. Moreover, to Kabul had come a Russian envoy, Vikovich, to whom he seemed to be paying great attention. This 'commercial' agent had been despatched by Simonich to get Dost Mohammed's help in the attack on Herat. In these circumstances Lord Auckland, inspired by his Secretary of Council, Macnaghten, determined to recreate the alliance between the deposed ruler Shah Shuja and the Sikhs, and eventually to assist them with a British force. By this means it was hoped Afghanistan would become a friendly state under British influence, and thus be a barrier to Persian penetration behind which was the more dangerous Russian advance.[1]

---

[1] The despatches on these negotiations including Burnes' reports were laid before Parliament in 1839. They are the famous garbled despatches, for the reports of Burnes favourable to Dost Mohammed were omitted, and the unfavourable evidence left in. When this became known through Burnes' papers Palmerston was challenged in the House, but said the omissions were unimportant. Eventually in Palmerston's old age in 1859 the publication was obtained and Bright made in 1861 the tremendous indictment which has impressed itself on history. But omissions of inconvenient evidence were common in such publications. There is almost as significant evidence concerning Russia left out of the *Levant Papers*. It was the unfortunate end of the occupation that created the necessary emotional background for the attack on Palmerston, not the essential facts of the case.

This is the famous decision which has been the theme of so many pens, most of them roundly condemning the action of the Indian Government. The policy was certainly determined by Lord Auckland at Simla without the advice of many of those best qualified to pronounce on it, and some at the time and many more after the Afghan disaster were critical of it. It was clear, however, that something had to be done and an alternative policy was hard to find. It may be that it would have been better to risk Sikh displeasure and accept the first offers of Dost Mohammed. The abandonment of the siege of Herat might have been considered a sufficient reason at least to postpone the expedition. But that was hardly clear at that time. Indeed political and strategic points that later became obvious were then necessarily obscure. Even the geography was imperfectly known. The right line to which British government should advance and what its relations should be with its turbulent and treacherous neighbours could only be found out by experiment. The real criticism of the policy followed in 1838–1839 is not the decision itself, but of the manner in which it was carried out and especially after it had attained such signal success.

But even before the Indian Government had come to its decision a similar one had been taken by the Melbourne Government. In the autumn Ministers began to be much exercised at the threat to India. Grey was consulted about it by Lord John Russell, who received from Lord Howick the answer that his father, while unable to judge the immediate situation, had "for many years been convinced that sooner or later it would be necessary to resist the encroachments of Russia by force". If action was intended, now was the time while the Russian fleet in the Baltic was frozen in. Howick himself was far from agreeing with these bellicose opinions. On the contrary he avowed that if the decision to take Karrak had not already been made by Auckland on his own responsibility he would have resigned rather than agree to it. The Cabinet were neither so warlike as Grey nor so pacifist as his son. Its members were of course as usual scattered in the autumn, but the position was considered so serious that a meeting of seven Ministers was held at Windsor early in October at which it was decided to instruct Auckland to act in Afghanistan rather than in the South. The expedition to Herat was considered to be only one part of a Russian scheme to advance in Central Asia.

"It is evident", Palmerston told Clanricarde, "that the Schah's expedition against Herat was part of a scheme planned some time ago for extending Persian and therefore Russian influence all over Afghanistan; for the first steps had been taken previous to the Schah's expedition by endeavouring to establish a political connection between Cambul and Candahar and Persia. . . . But Auckland has been told to take Afghanistan in hand and make it a British dependency and there is no doubt of his being able to accomplish that object. We have long declined to meddle with the Afghans and have purposely left them independent, but if the Russians try to make them Russian we must take care that they become British."[1]

Meanwhile Palmerston had already sent a stern protest to Russia through Pozzo di Borgo who was so alarmed at his menacing tone that he became quite ill. This warning was now reinforced with a note which Clanricarde was ordered to deliver, recounting all the misdeeds in Persia. This was no doubt meant to be laid before Parliament eventually as, indeed, it was next year. "Russia", wrote Palmerston in his private letter, "does not I believe wish to go to war with us, but is always trying to push on just to the extreme point of encroachment and aggression to which she may be allowed to go without war. She then halts to take breath and waits till people are looking another way to make another step or two forward." However that may be the British attitude had immediate effect. Even before this despatch reached him Nesselrode had sent to Pozzo di Borgo a despatch which, if inaccurate as to past events, contained satisfactory assurances for the future, so that Palmerston was able to make a friendly reply. Pozzo di Borgo "has been an altered man," he wrote, "has cast his physic to the winds and hung his face with smiles." "This", Palmerston went on, "is a proof of two things. First that poor old Pozzo is in his dotage, which is the Emperor's affair not ours: secondly that as you say Russia fears above all things a war with England." Nesselrode had admitted, he said, that Simonich had "projected an entirely new organization of Afghanistan close to our frontier." However, he was quite prepared to bury the past and resume friendly relations with both Russia and Persia provided

[1] Howick to Lord John Russell, 8 Oct., 1838. To Clanricarde, 26 Oct., 1838: *B.P.* Lloyd Sanders, *Melbourne*, 452-454. W. M. Torrens, *Melbourne*, 463, 464. The seven Ministers were Melbourne, Palmerston, Hobhouse, the Lord Chancellor, Lord John Russell, Lord Lansdowne and Lord Glenelg.

these declarations were carried out. The recall of Simonich which now took place was a proof that they were sincerely meant, and Clanricarde was "convinced that no intention is entertained by this Govt. of taking any direct part in the hostile movements which agitate Asia."[1]

But neither the abandonment of the siege of Herat by Persia, nor the assurances of the Russian Government, were sufficient to cause the expedition to Afghanistan to be given up. That decision was taken in India but it was fully approved in London. Hobhouse was primarily responsible but Palmerston was strongly on his side, and no doubt helped him to a decision. There were indeed after what had happened strong arguments that British influence in the North needed to be reestablished by some special action. Palmerston considered the Russian withdrawal only a truce and wished to take advantage of it before her advance began again. The Persian Government also needed a lesson. The occupation of Karrak was maintained and Palmerston pressed the necessity for reparation so hard that Nesselrode protested on the ground that he might overturn the Shah altogether and throw Persia into a state of anarchy.

There was of course no intention of occupying Afghanistan permanently. "The measure", Palmerston told Lamb, "has been forced on us by the aggression and intrigues of others; it is purely defensive on our part, but we shall probably not carry our operations beyond the limits which effective defence may prescribe. We do not want to make Afghanistan a British province, but we must have it an ally upon whom we can depend." Afghanistan must be 'English' not Persian, he told Hussein Khan, but went on to promise that British troops would retire "as soon as Shah Shoojah [sic] was firm on the throne".[2]

---

[1] Nesselrode to Pozzo di Borgo, 1 Nov., 1838: *B.F.S.P.*, XXVII, 174. To Clanricarde, 20 Nov., 1838, *B.P.* W. M. Torrens, *Melbourne*, 466. From Clanricarde, 20 Nov., 1838: *F.O. Russia*, 244. At the beginning of 1839 Wellington informed the Cabinet of a plan for Russia to send her Baltic fleet with a large force to attack India. This information was communicated to him by a Hampshire gentleman who had a son in the service of the Emperor. The Cabinet did not take the story very seriously. Palmerston pointed out that it was too good to be true, though there might possibly be some idea of sending the Baltic fleet to the Mediterranean. (To Clanricarde, 12 March, 1839. Wellington to Melbourne, 2 March, 1839: *B.P.*) This in fact had been the Tsar's intention in 1838, cf. P. E. Mosely, *Russian Diplomacy, etc., Appendix* A.

[2] To Lamb, 13 July, 1839: *B.P.* Memorandum of a Conference between Palmerston and Hoosein [sic] Khan, 13 July, 1839: *B.F.S.P.*, XXVIII, 85. The Secret Committee of the Indian Board of Control insisted that instructions should be sent to Auckland whom they suspected of wishing to make the occupation permanent. (From Hobhouse, 10 July, 1839: *B.P.*)

Whatever its merits the enterprise against Afghanistan had an immediate success. By August Shah Shuja had been replaced on his throne and Dost Mohammed was a fugitive. A year afterwards the latter surrendered to the Indian Government, a fact which Palmerston thought was "more honorable to the British name than a great victory". Herat, it is true, was still well outside the orbit of British control and Yar Mohammed was suspected of a wish to intrigue with the Persian Government against Britain. But the effect of the entry of a British force into Afghanistan naturally made itself felt throughout all Central Asia. One consequence was to move Russia in the autumn of 1839 to attempt a similar expedition against Khiva, whose Khan by raiding caravans and enslaving Russian subjects had given her plenty of excuse for such action.

Palmerston got news of this just as he had begun the discussions with Brunnow at the beginning of 1840. He at once strongly protested against this new threat to approach the frontiers of India. Russia, he said, had been defeated when she tried to use Persia as a base; now she was making a second attempt along another route. The Indian Government, he warned Brunnow, would be forced to reply by a more active policy in Central Asia. The Ambassador insisted that the expedition had no political object but was merely meant to free the slaves and prevent the attacks on the Russian caravans. He even offered to see the Duke of Wellington about it and ask him to keep the Tories quiet—a course to which Palmerston took strong exception. Brunnow was told that the Emperor and Nesselrode should make the official assurances of their intentions in a formal manner to Clanricarde and then the British Government would see what they would do about it.[1]

It was this situation which led Palmerston to make to Hobhouse the epigram about the meeting of the Cossack and the Sepoy already quoted. He did not believe, he said, that Russia would try to conquer Khiva but she would set up a puppet Khan there. After Khiva would come Bokhara and the way to Afghanistan and India would then be open. The Government of India had also been alarmed. A British officer, Captain Abbott, was sent to Khiva to try to get the Russian slaves released and prevent the

---

[1] To Auckland, 22 Jan., 1841; to Melbourne, 2 Jan., 1840: *B.P.* To Clanricarde, 24 Jan., 1840: *F.O. Russia*, 258.

necessity for Russian armies going there. When Brunnow demanded explanations of this conduct both Hobhouse and Palmerston spoke with the greatest frankness, and even truculence, all the more surprising since Russia was their main support in the negotiation concerning Mehemet Ali. Hobhouse said that if the two Empires should meet in Central Asia he should regret it, but had no doubt as to the result. Palmerston warned Brunnow that if Russia went to Khiva he did not know how far north of the Hindoo Koosh Auckland might be compelled to go. The only way to avoid such embarrassments was for Russia to leave Khiva alone. "All we want of Khiva", he added, "is that it should be a non-conducting body interposed between Russia and British India, and separated from both by a considerable interval of space."[1]

The Russian Government were of course never for one moment prepared to accept the position that, while British influence should be supreme in Afghanistan, Russia should have no more interest in Khiva and Bokhara than Britain. But their expedition was a failure and had to stop 250 miles from Khiva. The British emissaries, sent from Herat to obtain from its ruler the release of the Russian captives, insisted on going on to St. Petersburg with Khivan envoys which the Russian soldiers had hitherto always turned back. By these means a sort of truce was patched up. It was indeed thirty years before Russian power was able to penetrate so far.[2]

Auckland meanwhile had been much less disturbed by the Khiva expedition. He was far more preoccupied at this time with the expansion of Mehemet Ali's influence in the Persian Gulf. He considered that Karrak should not be given up until Russian and Persian policy had been further defined. The surrender of Ghorian would be more convincing evidence of their goodwill

---

[1] To Melbourne, 2 Jan., 1840; to Hobhouse, 25 May, 1840; to Bloomfield, 23 June, 1840: *B.P.* To Clanricarde, 24 Jan., 24 March, 1840: *F.O. Russia*, 258. The Russians, reported Clanricarde, intended to control Khiva but not to attack India. (24 Feb., 1840: *F.O. Russia*, 260.)

[2] The appearance on the Russian frontier of Captain Abbott and later of Captain Shakespeare with news of the release of the prisoners and accompanied by Khivan envoys is amusingly recorded in the despatches. The Russians were clearly disconcerted at so much having been accomplished. The unfortunate envoy of Khiva was practically chased out of the British Embassy by the Russians when he tried to pay a visit there. With the ferocious ruler of Bokhara the British envoys were not so fortunate. Colonel Stoddart after a long captivity and the young Captain Connolly were both put to death by him as Palmerston noted in his own hand on the last letter he received from Stoddart.

than any number of fair words. The Russian expedition to Khiva, he thought—and thought rightly—would find the task a difficult one, but even if it succeeded with dangerous repercussions in Bokhara, the advance would be contained by the growing strength and prestige of Shah Shuja in Afghanistan, if that developed as he hoped and intended it should. He was above all anxious to avoid the necessity of sending a British force to Herat. There he reiterated they must depend on Yar Mohammed Khan who he hoped would be intimidated by the British position in Afghanistan from betraying them. Ghorian he considered so important that he even told Major Todd, who had succeeded Pottinger in Herat, that his Government would support him if he managed to get hold of it by a *coup de main*. The maintenance of the position in central Afghanistan was thus the pivot on which all his policy depended. If Russia would limit her own advance he thought Britain should not look beyond the Hindu Koosh, which ran across Afghanistan. Relying on the strength of prestige obtained in Afghanistan he hoped to maintain British interests in Khiva and Herat through negotiation.[1]

These views reiterated in private letters in the course of the year 1840 did not satisfy Palmerston. Elated with the success of his campaign in Asia Minor he pressed for vigorous measures in Central Asia. After a survey of the European situation, where he pointed out France had been humbled and Russia and Austria become the allies of Britain, he urged on Auckland that now was the time to make good the British position in Central Asia. "Make fast what you have gained in Afghanistan," he wrote; "secure the Kingdom of Cabul and make yourself sure of Herat." Everything should also be done to find new markets for British commerce by sending missions to Arabia and even Abyssinia. In a striking passage he stressed the duty of the Government to work for this end:

"The rivalship of European manufactures is fast excluding our productions from the markets of Europe, and we must unremittingly endeavour to find in other parts of the world new vents for the produce of our industry. The world is large enough and the wants of the human race ample enough to afford a demand for all we can manufacture; but it is the business of the Govern-

---

[1] From Auckland, 16 Feb., 20 April, 11 July, 14 Sept., 20 Nov., 1840; Auckland to Hobhouse, 20 Nov., 1840: *B.P.*

ment to open and to secure the roads for the merchant. Will the
navigation of the Indus turn out to be as great a help as was
expected for our commerce? If it does, and if we succeed in our
China expedition, Abyssinia, Arabia, the countries on the Indus
and the new markets in China, will at no distant period give a most
important extension to the range of our foreign commerce, and,
though in regard to the quickness of the returns, markets nearer
home might be better, yet on a political point of view it must be
remembered that these distant transactions not only employ our
manufacturers but form our sailors."

The opportunity was all the more apparent because the weakness of Russia would compel her to keep on good terms with
Britain for some years and was the explanation of her excellent
conduct during the past year in Europe. "The fact is," he
claimed, "she is fitter for shew than for action; she is apparently
of gigantic strength, but really weak. Her finances are in a state
of great embarrassment and she could not well undertake an
expensive war; the whole system of her internal administration is
a mass of abuse, mismanagement, roguery and peculation, her
nobles are dissatisfied and her army discontented, being hard
worked, ill paid and looked after, and governed with revolting
severity." The Russian failure in Circassia and the new strength
given to the Sultan by the overthrow of Mehemet Ali's power
should render Constantinople safe. Only a Russian-French
Alliance could again bring a threatening situation in Europe, and
this was not likely so long as Louis Philippe and Nicholas lived
and even if it eventually occurred could be met by the union of
Britain with the German Powers.[1]

This optimistic survey had much truth in it. And it had
seemed to be fulfilled, so far as Central Asia was concerned, by
the failure of the Russian expedition to Khiva. But Palmerston
was writing about countries of which he really knew very little,
and shewed here, as in his dealings with Mehemet Ali in 1841,
signs that he was perhaps somewhat too elated by his triumph
and losing the sense of proportion and the realistic approach
which he had hitherto shewn. Auckland was by no means ready
to send out further expeditions. He refused to the end to send a
British force to Herat as Palmerston desired, and when Yar
Mohammed quarrelled with Major Todd, who wished to put down

[1] To Auckland, 22 Jan., 1841: *B.P.*

the Slave Trade and other iniquities, was disposed to blame his envoy rather than the Khan. Even here, however, the British object was soon afterwards achieved. For ultimately the Persian pressure died down, Russian again cooperated with Britain, and, though it came too late for Palmerston to claim the credit, he was able at the beginning of 1842 to write to McNeill, who had returned to his post, to congratulate him on at last obtaining the commercial treaty which Palmerston had put in the forefront of his instructions in 1836.[1]

Then came the news of the shattering blow of the collapse of the British position in Afghanistan, the murder of Burnes and, finally, that of Sir William Macnaghten himself and the destruction of a brigade of British troops. For the blunders and bad leadership that caused this disaster Palmerston was in no sense responsible. But it was of course the result of the forward policy which he had supported, and he can be fairly charged with having adopted it without counting all the risks. On the other hand, events also soon made it clear that the whole position in Northern India had to be transformed. The position in Afghanistan was soon retrieved and its ruler, the restored Dost Mohammed, looked for a time to India for protection and advice. In a few more years both Sind and the Punjaub were annexed. All that Palmerston had desired was in fact obtained. Though Russia was still unable to penetrate the natural obstacles that lay between her dominion and the strategic frontier thus given to India, her expansion was, as Durham and many others pointed out, only a question of time. In due course Russia did annex both Khiva and Bokhara and then Afghanistan became of vital importance, as Palmerston and indeed all sensible men always knew. Whether the same objectives could have been obtained with less bloodshed and intrigue is a question of Indian strategy and politics and not of British foreign policy.

---

[1] From Auckland, 24 March, 21 April, 20 August, 1841: *B.P.* In the last he wrote: "I know that you and others think that I have over-rated the difficulties of an advance on Herat and still more that I have over-rated the store of embarrassment which would await us if we were in possession of that city before the tranquillity of Afghanistan had been perfectly settled and secured." To McNeill, 31 Jan., 1842: *Memoir of Sir J. McNeill*, 257.

6. THE SETTLEMENT WITH MEHEMET ALI AND THE STRAITS CONVENTION OF 13 JULY, 1841

The struggle with Mehemet had threatened the total overthrow of the Ottoman Empire and it was only natural that it should take considerable time to settle the problems raised by it. 'Hereditary tenure' for a Pasha was in a sense a contradiction in terms for a Pasha was no more than the slave of the Sultan. Moreover, in an Oriental country where polygamy was the law, succession as often as not went to others than the eldest son, of whom the father was usually jealous, and whose life was often in danger. The relations between the Sultan and his vassal had also necessarily to be more exactly defined than had been done hitherto. Mehemet's enemies, including both Palmerston and Ponsonby, hoped to take advantage of this necessity to reduce his power to the lowest possible point, even if they could not get rid of him altogether. Reschid had already sent a despatch to London protesting against any grant of hereditary tenure. Meanwhile all kinds of plans were being hastily composed in Paris and Vienna about Syria, now brought once more under the control of the Sultan. Until all this was settled France would not resume her normal attitude. Guizot had peremptorily refused to discuss with Austria and Prussia the question of armaments before the Eastern Question was concluded. He made the same answer to a very mild remonstrance from Granville. And he also refused to sign a treaty on any aspect of the Eastern Question until the Sultan and the Four Powers solemnly declared that the object of the Convention of 15 July, 1840, had been attained, and that consequently there no longer existed any tie between them from which France was excluded.[1]

Neither Palmerston nor the Tsar was particularly eager for a speedy settlement. But Austria and Prussia felt the challenge of

[1] From Granville, 4 Jan., 1841: *F.O. France*, 622. Until the end of March Granville worked zealously to overcome the difficulties that prevented the convention from being signed. Then he had a serious illness which was thought to be a stroke and henceforward Bulwer took complete charge. It had been decided to replace Granville with a new Ambassador, but he recovered somewhat, and nothing had been done when the Whig Ministry fell and Granville consequently retired from his post.

France's armaments and were anxious therefore to conclude some arrangement as soon as possible. It was Metternich's opposition, it is true, which had prevented the grant of hereditary tenure from being peremptorily urged on the Turkish Ministers before the final defeat of Ibrahim. Metternich, however, had only wanted delay as a means to force Mehemet to give in. As soon as Ibrahim had been driven out of Syria he was urgent that the Sultan should grant Mehemet favourable terms so that France might resume her normal position in Europe and reduce the armaments which had so alarmed the German States. Austrian opinion, reported Lamb, was completely unable to understand how one British agent could sign a convention with Mehemet Ali and another promptly disavow it. Metternich, while agreeing that the convention was a mistake, insisted that the Porte must be made to act at once. Both he and Beauvale regretted that the centre of action was so far removed from Constantinople that Palmerston's instructions could not catch up with events.[1]

Palmerston meanwhile had been subjected to pressure from Esterhazy and Neumann to send instructions to Constantinople to force the Sultan to give in, and Brunnow had joined them. Palmerston had conceded the principle of hereditary tenure because, as he told Beauvale, his Cabinet would not take any other line. But, though he had approved the substance of Napier's convention, he now argued that that instrument only dealt with the immediate problem of the armistice and that the main question was still open. France, he insisted, would not fight for the hereditary tenure and the idea of compelling the Sultan by force to grant it was nonsense. "Hereditary tenure of delegated authority", he wrote, "is objectionable and inconsistent," and for a short time he had some hopes that Metternich would take that view. But letters from Vienna soon shewed that Metternich had now an entirely different opinion. Esterhazy and Neumann plied Palmerston with despatches from Stürmer which accused Ponsonby of encouraging the Porte to resist, and threatened that Austria would withdraw all moral and material support from the Sultan.

Palmerston's indignant reply to the charge that Britain was responsible for the delay was made in a despatch to Beauvale of so incisive a character that the Ambassador refused to communicate

[1] From Beauvale, 26 Dec., 1840: *B.P.*

it to Metternich as he was instructed to do. Metternich's insinuations against Britain were, Palmerston wrote, "entirely opposed to facts and to truth." Ponsonby alone of the representatives of the Four Powers at Constantinople had had instructions to advise the Porte to grant hereditary tenure to Mehemet. Metternich, who had been mainly responsible for the delay by refusing to support Palmerston's note of 15 October, had suddenly changed his tactics, a course which, Palmerston indicated in no very veiled language, was simply due to fear of France and not to a consideration of all the circumstances of the problem.[1]

Ponsonby had in fact only carried out the instructions, which Palmerston had given him in the autumn, to define the hereditary tenure in such a manner as to reduce Mehemet's power. But Palmerston, while he defended Ponsonby to his critics, saw that he must not press his advantage too far. Before the end of January he had written to Constantinople that, as the representatives of the Four Powers had already told Chekib in London, the Sultan must give way on the main issue. "Pray get this matter settled as soon as you can," he wrote, "and then let us set to work to organise the Turkish system, military, naval and financial."[2]

But the decision at Constantinople had been taken before these instructions arrived. Ponsonby had in fact loyally advised the Porte to grant the hereditary tenure as soon as he had received instructions to do so. But he had worked out with the Porte's Ministers an elaborate set of conditions "that will be", as he told Palmerston, "the performance of your engagements to the French to give Mehemet the hereditary right and at the same time will preserve intact the sovereignty of the Sultan." "It will be the Sultan's fault", he concluded, "if he does not take proper care to secure himself against the future rebellion of Mehemet Ali and to protect his Egyptian subjects from an aggression worse than slavery or death." The result was a Hatti Sheriff of the 13 February which not only gave the Sultan the choice of a successor

---

[1] From Beauvale, 17 Jan., 1841: *L.P.*, III, No. 136; do., 1, 6, 13 Jan., 1841: *B.P.* To Beauvale, 26 Jan., 1841: *F.O. Austria*, 296; do., *L.P.*, III, No. 138; do., 7, 26 Jan., 1841: *B.P.* From Neumann and Esterhazy, 25 Jan., 1841: *F.O. Austria*, 301, with Stürmer to Metternich, 10 Dec., 1840: "Ld Ponsonby ne cesse de nourrir l'espoir que le Sultan se refusera à accorder l'hérédité de l'Egypte à Mehemet Ali. Il a fait jouer tous les ressorts pour déterminer Reschid Pasha à entrer dans ses vues." Neumann to Metternich, 1 Feb., 1841: *V. St. A.*

[2] To Ponsonby, 29 Jan., 1841: *L.P.*, III, No. 144; do., 26 Jan., 1841: *B.P.*

among the children of Mehemet Ali but also laid down that Mehemet was not to have more power than other Pashas, that his army was to be restricted to 18,000 men and the nomination of all officers above the grade of captain to be in the hands of the Sultan, that he was to build no ships, and, of course, that he be bound by the laws of the Ottoman Empire including the Edict of Gulhané. Moreover, a point to which Ponsonby himself attached the highest importance, the collection of the revenue was to be under the special supervision of the Porte. A quarter of it was to be paid to the Sultan as tribute. It was only natural that Mehemet immediately refused to submit on these terms, a course he was strongly advised to take by Napier who was now one of his greatest admirers and believed that the Pasha was now disillusioned about France and could be made into a strong supporter of Britain.[1]

Meanwhile, as is narrated below, the Four Powers and France had been working out the terms of the treaty which should mark the return of France to the Concert. By reducing it to the sole question of the Straits they had come to agreement when the news of the Sultan's action reached them. Since it prevented the signature of the treaty with France there were loud complaints from all those concerned and Ponsonby was again bitterly attacked as the man mainly responsible for the Hatti Sheriff. Metternich was especially indignant and Beauvale, reflecting this attitude, went further in his attack on Ponsonby than he had ever previously ventured. The Russian and Prussian representatives at Constantinople, he claimed, blamed Ponsonby as much as Stürmer did. He supported Stürmer's accusations that Ponsonby had deliberately deceived both his colleagues and his Government, thus playing Russia's game by keeping France outside the Concert. At the end of March he wrote to the Prime Minister urging that Ponsonby be removed forthwith. Melbourne accepted his brother's view and told Palmerston that when Ponsonby did not like his instructions he simply ignored them and that the Eastern Question would never be settled while it was in the hands of such an Ambassador.[2]

---

[1] From Ponsonby, 10 Jan., 1, 4, 14 Feb., 1840: *L.P.*, III, Nos. 154, 162, 163, 171; do., 4, 11, 27 Jan., 1841: *B.P.* From Napier, 26 March, 1841: *B.P.* Beauvale took the same view as Napier about the possibility of drawing Mehemet closer to Britain but Palmerston rejected the idea as impossible.

[2] From Beauvale, 5 March, 1841; Beauvale to Melbourne, 30 March, 1841; From Melbourne, 9, 13 April, 1841: *B.P.*

Palmerston of course refused to give up Ponsonby who after all had only been carrying out his own wishes by encouraging the Porte to establish the Sultan's authority in Egypt to the greatest possible extent. He continued to insist that the Ottoman law and treaties must prevail throughout the whole of the Sultan's dominions, especially the Edict of Gulhané. But he realised that Mehemet would never agree that the Sultan should choose his successor, and, while genuinely puzzled for a considerable time as to what was the best method of dealing with this delicate question in an oriental country, eventually accepted Esterhazy's advice that the succession should go to the eldest direct heir as in European countries. Some of the other points, he thought, were not worth pressing too far. The Egyptian army was organised on the French model, which was better than that of the Turks who might well imitate it, and the Pasha must be able to appoint the field officers. The tribute was a matter for negotiation and would no doubt be eventually settled by prolonged bargaining in the oriental manner. He had, reported Esterhazy, been tempted by the wholehearted support of Russia to go too far, but he was now coming back to a sane position. At any rate Palmerston pressed these points on Ponsonby during March and April in both private letters and public despatches. Austria was not reliable, he explained, and might back out altogether at any moment. He even threatened that Britain might have to do likewise if the Sultan proved too obstinate. The Sultan must fulfil, therefore, his promise to grant heredity. It was to his advantage to settle the question as soon as possible. It could be reopened at a later date, Palmerston added, if the situation became more favourable.[1]

Metternich was mollified by this attitude and scolded Stürmer for not carrying out his instructions properly. He urged that a settlement should be made as soon as possible. There was nothing more for the conference at London to do, he said, and it should be dissolved. Palmerston considered that the threat of

[1] To Beauvale, 2 April, 1841: *L.P.*, III, No. 210; do., 9, 16 March, 1841: *B.P.* Esterhazy to Metternich, 29 March, 10, 20 April, 1841: *V. St. A.* Palmerston was especially exercised about the difficulty caused if a minor should succeed. "A regency for a minor Pasha would be nonsense, you might as well appoint an infant to be Lord Lieut. of Ireland, and then have a Regent over him." (9 March.) Esterhazy drew up a table of Mehemet's descendants to shew that there was no likelihood of a minor succeeding. He had also a shrewd idea that Palmerston's private letters might have been couched in different language to his public despatches. To Ponsonby, 16 March, 1841: *L.P.* III, No. 186; do., 21 April: *F.O. Turkey*, 428; do., 11, 16 March, 2, 19 April, 1841: *B.P.*

action against Mehemet must be maintained, especially after he had learnt of his rather arrogant reply to the Hatti Sheriff. Metternich was forced to agree and meanwhile the four representatives at Constantinople were able to advise the Sultan, when the news of Mehemet's refusal to accept the Firman reached them, to consult his allies before making a reply. This caused further delay and the news that came at this time of the fall of Reschid caused much perturbation in Vienna. The answer of the Allies was of course not in doubt and was drawn up on the lines already agreed upon. It eventually produced its due effect on the Porte where it was seen that no support could be obtained to enforce the last Firman. Another Firman was issued which granted Mehemet's main demands and though there was to be a long wrangle about the tribute, agreement on all essential points had been obtained by the middle of June. Mehemet sent an emissary with rich gifts to Constantinople. He intended to settle the question of the tribute in the usual manner—by bribery He was glad, he said, that the European Powers had ceased to meddle, he could now handle affairs in the true oriental manner. In August the Consuls-General at last returned to Constantinople and relations with Egypt became normal again.[1]

Meanwhile the Four Powers and France had long concluded their negotiations as to the new instrument which they should sign with the Sultan. These resulted in the middle of March in a convention which dealt with the question of the Straits. But for a considerable period all kinds of schemes were canvassed, some of them bordering on the fantastic. Guizot at first thought that France should celebrate her reentry into the European Concert by a comprehensive treaty. Foremost among his demands was one for a Five Power guarantee of the integrity and independence of the Ottoman Empire. The Russians would of course have never consented to sign such a treaty. They had always refused to commit themselves not to obtain some part of the Ottoman Empire. Apart from this, Palmerston, remembering Thiers' interpretation of such a promise, saw no advantage in it. Metter-

[1] From Beauvale, 22 April, 3 May, 1841: *L.P.*, No. 242, *F.O. Austria*, 299. To Beauvale, 4, 8 May, 1841: *F.O. Austria*, 297. Four Powers to Chekib, 10 May, 1841: *L.P.*, III, No. 249. From Ponsonby, 22 May, 1841: *L.P.*, III, No. 278; do., 19 May, 1841: *B.P.* Ponsonby, true to his principles, refused to approve the new Firman, but he did not oppose its despatch. Mehemet Ali's final moves are given in E. Driault, *La Crise Orientale*, V, 126–224.

nich was even more hostile. Guizot suggested that the Powers might at least recognise it in the Preamble as had been done in the Convention of 15 July, 1840, in order to link it up with the Note of 27 July, 1839, but even in this mild form the proposal found no favour anywhere. Bourqueney had soon to explain to Guizot that it was impossible. The Porte in spite of this shewed some inclination to revive the idea at a later stage when Metternich wrote a specially incisive despatch. "A state placed under a guarantee", he wrote, "becomes a mediatised state . . . and if one protector, to say the least of it, is inconvenient, many protectors become an insupportable burden." Palmerston rather demurred at this, pointing to the success of the guarantee of Belgian neutrality. But such a guarantee of the Ottoman Empire was no longer necessary, he thought, now that the Sultan had reestablished his power in Asia Minor.

A more curious guarantee was suggested by Guizot, that of the routes across the Ottoman Empire to the East. He seems to have thought that in this way he would satisfy a main British interest while preventing her from obtaining political control of Turkish or Egyptian territory in order to obtain it. Metternich supported the idea as regards the isthmus of Suez and Palmerston was tempted to do something about it. Eventually however Guizot himself abandoned it, partly because its negotiation would have delayed the agreement which all were seeking to obtain.[1]

Far more eagerly canvassed by all the Powers were the proposals for some kind of European protection of the non-Moslem inhabitants of Syria—Catholics, Jews and the pilgrims to the Holy City —Protestant as well as the others. The idea seems first to have occurred to the French Government and to have been deliberately adopted as a means of countering the Russian influence exercised through the Orthodox Church. It looks forward, therefore, to the famous controversy which was a prelude to the Crimean War.

---

[1] Guizot, *Mémoires*, VI, 73, 84. Guizot to Bourqueney, 15, 23 Feb., 1841; Bourqueney to Guizot, 19, 25 Feb., 1841: *A.A.E.* From Beauvale, 22 April, 1841; to Beauvale, 10 May, 1841: *L.P.*, III, Nos. 244, 248. Esterhazy to Metternich, 14 March, 1841: *V. St. A.* This of course was a guarantee of the Suez overland route, though the idea of a canal was already being freely canvassed. Palmerston said he could not support Guizot's proposal because it would look as if Britain were seeking special advantage in the treaty. Palmerston was not at this time opposed to a canal for political reasons. He thought that it would be so costly to construct that the money could not be raised for it. (To Ponsonby, 25 April, 1841: *B.P.*) He long held this idea, cf. H. L. Hoskins, *British Routes to India*, 295–299.

But in Guizot's Protestant mind it became connected with the Holy City. "Guizot", wrote Granville, "has been expatiating with quite religious fervour in his conversations with Pahlen upon a project of making Jerusalem a Christian city separated from the Pachalik and guaranteed by all the European Powers." Granville poured scorn on the idea but he warned Palmerston that it might appeal to some religious enthusiasts in England. In reply to his chief's cynical comments on French motives he admitted that the suggestion of a Christian free city at Jerusalem "after the manner of Cracow or Frankfort" had been made as one means of reestablishing French influence in the Levant: "France always assumed a sort of protectorate of the Roman Catholic Christians but . . . the idea of huddling them together within the precincts of Jerusalem seems to be the most wild and impracticable of schemes." Louis Philippe held the same view while Nesselrode and Orlov ridiculed this suggestion of a "Cracovie religieuse". Nevertheless the idea was canvassed quite widely and Palmerston was startled to receive from Castelcicala, the Neapolitan Minister, the suggestion from the King of Naples that his brother, the Prince of Capua, should be made the ruler of the new Christian State of Palestine which the Four Powers intended to set up.

Meanwhile Austria evinced a similar desire to assume the protection of the Catholic Church in the Levant. The idea had long been in Metternich's mind and discussions took place between the two Governments which did not get very far, but might conceivably have resulted in some form of general guarantee by the Powers of the rights of the inhabitants of Syria and the pilgrims to the Holy Land. Metternich suggested the appointment of a special Turkish emissary at Jerusalem to safeguard Christian interests there[1]

But the subject became complicated by the interest of Palmerston in the Jews and the desire of the new King of Prussia to

[1] Guizot to Bourqueney, 15, 16 Feb., 1841: *A.A.E.* Guizot, *Mémoires*, VI, 77, 79. To Granville, 7 Jan., 1841; from Granville, 4, 11, 24 Jan., 19 Feb., 1841: *B.P.* Guichen, *La Crise d'Orient*, 469, 471. "I assured Castelcicala that we mean to preserve the integrity of the Turkish Empire and not to dismember it; but he said the French had made very serious proposals and communications on this subject at Naples; and I could hardly persuade him that his master had been bamboozled by Louis Philippe." (To Beauvale, 26 Feb., 1841: *B.P.*) Esterhazy to Metternich, 13 Feb., 1841: *V. St. A.* Beauvale later reported that France had sent 100,000 francs for distribution amongst the Maronites while Austria had sent money to rebuild houses and churches, 100,000 francs having been collected for that purpose in the Churches of Vienna (5 May, 1841: *B.P.*).

establish a Protestant bishopric at Jerusalem. Palmerston was from the first afraid that any guarantee of the rights of the inhabitants of Syria would lead to undue interference by the Great Powers in their own advantage. But as has been seen, the interest of evangelical Britain in the Holy Land was a factor in public opinion during the crisis in the autumn of which Palmerston tried to take full advantage. In this he was assisted by Lord Ashley, naturally, as Lady Palmerston's son-in-law, admitted to close friendship though a member of the Tory party. This fervent evangelical was as much under the influence of Biblical prophesy as the King of Prussia himself, and had since 1838 been crusading for the return of the Jews to Palestine under some Great Power protection. Moreover, Palmerston seems to have had a genuine desire to protect the Jews in Palestine for humanitarian reasons as well as for the advantage which he thought might thus be obtained both for the Sultan and for Britain.

The ill-treatment of the Jews in Rhodes and Damascus in April, 1840, seems first to have increased interest in their position in the Holy Land. The Jews in the West were much moved by it and used their influence at the capitals of Europe to help their co-religionists. Thiers, who refused to admit that the French Consul at Damascus had shewn callousness, had a serious quarrel with James Rothschild about it, though it did not prevent the French Bourse from financing the French armaments. Ponsonby, on the other hand, shewed much indignation at the pogrom at Damascus which had occurred under Mehemet's administration, and Palmerston of course strongly supported his protests. In England, however, the subject took a wider aspect in evangelical circles and became connected with a mystical idea, never altogether lost in the nineteenth century, that Britain was to be the chosen instrument of God to bring back the Jews to the Holy Land. "We have on our side", Lady Palmerston told Princess Lieven on 13 November, 1840, "the fanatical and religious elements, and you know what a following they have in this country. They are absolutely determined that Jerusalem and the whole of Palestine shall be reserved for the Jews to return to; this is their only longing (to restore the Jews)."[1]

[1] From Granville, 22 June, 9, 12 Oct., 1840: *B.P.* Corti, *The Reign of the House of Rothschild*, 223. James was moved to protest by the Austrian Rothschild, for Laurin had sent to Vienna long reports on the incident and Metternich at once took action. Sudley, *Corres. Lieven-Palmerston*, 196. Thiers claimed

Lady Palmerston must have written with the knowledge that her husband, in response to this feeling, had already in August instructed Ponsonby to get the Sultan to respond to the Jewish idea that the time was approaching for their nation to return to Palestine by the promulgation of special laws in their favour. This would not only be a blow against Mehemet Ali but even if it did not attract many immigrants would spread a friendly disposition towards the Sultan among the Jews of Europe. The importance he attached to the subject is shewn by the manner in which he kept coming back to it in his private letters. "Pray don't lose sight of my recommendation to the Porte", he wrote in September, "to invite the Jews to return to Palestine. You can have no idea how much such a measure would tend to interest in the Sultan's cause all the religious party in this country, and their influence is great and their connexion extensive. The measure moreover in itself would be highly advantageous to the Sultan, by bringing into his dominions a great number of wealthy capitalists who would employ the people and enrich the Empire." And a little later he developed the idea in a wider manner: "The establishment of a good school of Medicine at Constantinople would have a great effect upon public opinion in Europe; and so would an edict giving security and encouragement to all Jews who might chuse to return to Palestine or to any other part of the Turkish Empire. The late barbarities at Rhodes and Damascus would afford the Sultan a good occasion for issuing such an edict, as he might say that being desirous of preventing the recurrence of such scenes, and being determined to give to the Jews full security for person and property within his dominions, he had thought fit to publish an edict declaring that the Jews should henceforth enjoy within his dominions all the securities which have been granted by law to his other subjects. I think it would be best that the Sultan should not place the Jews formally under the protection of foreign Consuls, because the principle of foreign interference between a sovereign and his subjects is bad; and Jews coming to settle in Turkey ought to be considered as subjects of the Sultan. But if any arrangement could be devised by means of which they could be sure of having their complaints brought to the knowledge of the

that the Jews had murdered a French priest and were responsible for the outbreak (22 June). This episode is rather sketchily discussed in N. Sokolow's *History of Zionism*, I, 115–132. Lord Ashley's well-known views are given in E. Hodder, *Life and Work of the Seventh Lord Shaftesbury*, I, 307–319.

Turkish Govt. it would be good; such arrangement, however, should be local. For if there was a Jewish High Priest or other representative established at Constantinople he would, like the Greek Patriarch, be liable to be bought by some foreign Power and through him the Jewish population might be influenced; but if some Turkish Minister of the Porte were bound to receive Jewish complaints, that evil would not be created; and our English Consuls might be instructed to make known to our Ambassador at Constantinople any causes of just complaint for which no speedy redress was obtained.

"The Jews and the Medical men of Europe are each a sort of Free Mason fraternity whose good word would be useful to the Sultan."[1]

The Porte did not then respond to this overture and Ponsonby gave it little support. But when the question of the future of Syria was discussed in the spring of 1841 Palmerston continued for some time to press that the British Vice-Consul recently established in Jerusalem should be used as the agent to transmit to the Porte the representations of the Jewish body, though without any success. The right thing, replied Ponsonby, was for the Porte to secure justice for all its subjects, not for any special section of them, and there is no doubt but that Palmerston felt as strongly as his Ambassador the danger to the Porte of allowing other Powers to have rights of interference in the internal affairs of Turkey. It was the eternal dilemma which he was to face all his life, the impossibility of reforming the Ottoman Empire without such interference as would destroy it.[2]

Palmerston had gone so far in this matter partly for reasons of humanity but mainly to satisfy an important section of public opinion. He was not a man to be moved by any mystical ideas about the future of Palestine. His action to obtain the establishment of a Protestant Bishopric in Jerusalem was determined by similar motives. The protagonist in this movement was the King of Prussia, the pupil of Ancillon, whose biblical instruction now bore rather strange fruit. For the King desired that the Protestant

---

[1] For Palmerston's despatches on this subject see F. S. Rodkey, "Lord Palmerston and the Rejuvenation of Turkey, 1839–1841." *Journal of Modern History*, June 1930, where they are all conveniently brought together. To Ponsonby, 4 Sept., 4 Nov., 1840: *B.P.*

[2] For the details see the article by F. S. Rodkey given in the last note. "Let me recommend the Jews to your special care," Palmerston wrote to Ponsonby on 26 Feb., 1841 (*B.P.*).

Church should share in the special rights of the other Christian sects in the Holy Places, for which armed guards should be provided by the Great Powers. Metternich was much annoyed at this suggestion which, he told Beauvale, threw the whole question into confusion, substituting for his own practical scheme of the appointment of a Turkish official proposals which would not be accepted by the Pope and would cause great controversy between the Christian Powers. He harped on the necessity of checking Russia, who desired to get a monopoly of such rights in the Turkish Empire for the Orthodox Church, and France, who was planning to use the Catholic Christians for her own purposes.[1]

Palmerston sympathised with Metternich's desire to check the pretensions of both Russia and France. But he had to go warily on the question of Protestant representation. The subject was in any case too complicated, he said, to be dealt with in the new convention and must be treated separately. Melbourne on the other hand had incautiously admitted the special position of Russia and France in a speech in the House of Lords, much to the indignation of Wellington. But Melbourne like Palmerston soon saw that the claims of the Protestant Churches must be taken seriously. The subject became a burning one later in the spring when Bunsen was summoned by the King of Prussia from Rome and sent to London to urge the cooperation of the two Protestant Powers. He had an enthusiastic reception from the English Church, both High and Low. The diplomats, it is true, looked a little askance and Melbourne at first thought that more trouble was in store for him. But both he and Palmerston eventually won high praise from Bunsen for their sympathy and cooperation. Palmerston did his best to put the scheme on a practical basis before he handed it over to his successor. He had joined Austria in urging the Sultan to ensure adequate protection for all Christian creeds in Syria and had got Bunsen to agree that Prussia should do no more than this. The special Protestant claim, meanwhile, had been reduced to an agreement to establish a Bishopric at Jerusalem under the joint auspices of the Prussian and English Churches, a Protestant combination that helped to drive Newman into the Catholic Church. Palmerston set Ponsonby to work to get the

[1] From Esterhazy, 31 March, 1841, with Memorandum shewing difference between Metternich's proposals of 3 February and those in the Prussian Memoir, *F.O. Austria*, 301. Esterhazy to Metternich, 30 March, 1841: *V. St. A.*

necessary Firman from the Porte to build a Protestant Church in Jerusalem. It was not an easy task and the delay aroused the anger of the zealous Lord Ashley. He suspected the hidden hands of Rome and the Tsar. Pisani, the interpreter, was a fervent Catholic and as has been noted, his brother worked for the Russian Embassy. "We have thus", he lamented, "a double interest against us. I must say this is a sad issue to all our achievements in Syria. Can you not leave on record an opinion that the thing is just and ought to be completed." Palmerston complied with the request and one of his last communications to his faithful Ambassador was to pass on this warning: "I hope you will be able to manage the matter to which Bunsen's proposition relates," he wrote. "It is a matter which will excite great interest in this country and all through Protestant Germany." Great credit could be gained by ensuring its success. However sacred the object, Palmerston was fully aware that it was mundane considerations that would count most at Constantinople. "And if a thousand pounds of Secret Service money would carry the point," he added, "do not scruple to draw."[1]

All this effort in favour of the sects distracted attention from the central question of how to ensure for all the inhabitants of the Ottoman Empire the benefits of the new reforms. For it was already clear that the Edict of Gulhané, which Palmerston was so insistent must be applied in Egypt, was not producing the expected results in the rest of the Empire. The old Turk party had re-established its position as soon as the danger from Mehemet was past and the assistance of the Western Powers no longer necessary. The Sultan's first representative in Syria, Izzet Pasha, turned out to be even worse than had been expected and he had done much harm by his rapacity and cruelty before Ponsonby could effect his recall. Since then the British Consuls and soldiers had in vain tried

[1] Bunsen's mission is described in Baroness Bunsen, *Memoirs of Baron Bunsen*, I, 593–637. From Lord William Russell, 21 May, 1841: *B.P.* "He is very English. . . . If his Syrian propositions dont please you treat them with great indulgence for the King has set his heart on them"; do., 22 May, 1841: *F.O. Prussia*, 283. Neumann to Metternich, 18 Aug., 1841: *V. St. A.* Wellington thought there ought to be a centre for oriental affairs at Vienna, another working under it at Constantinople and a third under this at Jerusalem where consular agents would watch over the security of the Christians, so Neumann at any rate reported. From Ponsonby, 11, 27 July, 1841: *F.O. Turkey*, 432. Later reports were more hopeful (2, 8 Sept.). From Lord Ashley, 14 Aug., 1841: *B.P.* E. Hodder, *Lord Shaftesbury*, I, 364–380. To Ponsonby, 16 Aug., 1841: *B.P.* The whole subject has been illuminated by an article by R. W. Greaves, "The Jerusalem Bishopric, 1841" (*Eng. Hist. Rev.*, July, 1949).

to overcome the disposition of the Ottoman troops to treat the Syrians as a hostile and conquered population. The Albanian levies had been especially brutal and they had only gradually been removed. Wood had played a big role in all these efforts, but he had not the authority necessary for his task in spite of the energetic support he got from Ponsonby.[1]

Even more ominous was it that the author of the great reform fell from office in spite of the zealous defence of no less a person than Metternich himself. It was one of the charges brought against Ponsonby by Beauvale and Metternich that he had failed to give Reschid the support that so good a friend might be expected to have from the British Ambassador. This was true enough, though they were never able to substantiate their accusation. Ponsonby had come to the conclusion that Reschid's usefulness was over, that he had not the energy and courage necessary to get the reform working. Moreover, Reschid was surrounded by Frenchmen and seemed disposed to listen to Stürmer more than to Ponsonby himself. "It is not to be denied", Ponsonby told Palmerston, "that Reschid looks more towards others than towards us, notwithstanding, or it may be on account of, the fact that *I made him* what he is. I am therefore not inclined to lose the Sultan by attempts (that would be ineffectual also) to support a man who is not our man, however much I might be inclined to do Reschid good by the sort of personal partiality I have for him, and I hope after all that I shall do him essential good, if he must fall."[2]

Palmerston, while puzzled at Metternich's zeal for a reformer, thought it expedient to support Reschid officially and he did so in an instruction which was communicated to Vienna and received warm thanks. But in a private letter, though he summed up in Reschid's favour, he agreed with Ponsonby that it was not worth risking the loss of all influence with the Sultan in order to save him. His weakness and the fact that he had fallen under influences unfriendly to England were obvious enough. But Reschid was westernised and if he could carry out his ideas Turkey would be regenerated. Palmerston surveyed the problem in its widest aspect in words which shew perhaps more clearly than any others his general attitude towards the reform of the Ottoman Empire:

[1] There is much in the *Levant Papers*, III, on the situation in Syria in 1840–1841.

[2] From Ponsonby, 14, 26 Feb., 1841: *B.P.* From Beauvale, 5 March, 1841: *F.O. Austria*, 298; do., 31 March, 1841: *B.P.*

"It is difficult enough for a large political party in an enlightened country like England with abundance of instruments to work with, to carry into execution any great measures of reform; but how much more difficult must it be for a single man to accomplish such things in a benighted country like Turkey! . . . Though paper reforms are of course incomplete until they are carried out in practice yet it would be a mistake to suppose them to be *nothing*. It is a great step gained when the sanction of the sovereign in a despotic country has been obtained for the promulgation of any great measure of reform or for the practical enforcement of any great principle of justice; and though such laws may be a dead letter at first, it is far more easy afterwards to invoke them and to call them into activity than it would be at that later period to get them issued for the first time . . . and, if after we have done so much, our protégés the Turks were to sink back into their former lethargy we should lose much of the credit we have gained and we should not obtain that European security which was the great object and the main justification of all our proceedings."[1]

Before the instruction and this letter reached Constantinople Reschid had fallen as a result of the attacks of the old Turks. His reforming colleague, Ahmed Fethi Pasha, fell with him and Rifaat Pasha had his place and power. "Baron Stürmer weeps over his removal", wrote Ponsonby, "as if it was to occasion the advent of the day of judgment. You know that I have had my doubts of Reschid's honesty a long time past. I am now convinced that he is wholly unworthy to be trusted and I rejoice at his fall and I consider it as a *respite* for this Empire from the full establishment of French influence over its counsels." The reason for Ponsonby's attitude is evident enough, but Reschid's later career shewed that the Ambassador had not mistaken the character of the man whom he had done more than anyone else to elevate. Nor was Ponsonby ungrateful for what Reschid had done. It was largely due to his action that Reschid was protected from further molestation and his safety secured by his appointment once more to the Paris Embassy.[2]

[1] To Ponsonby, 1 April, 1841: *F.O. Turkey*, 427; do., 2 April, 1841; To Beauvale, 1 April, 1841: *B.P.* Many people were puzzled at the fall of Reschid. The French attributed it to Metternich and Palmerston himself was later, in view of Austrian support of Rifaat, inclined to think so. But Beauvale insisted that Metternich had always desired Reschid to remain in office. To Beauvale, 2 June, 1841; from Beauvale, 7 Aug., 1841: *F.O. Austria*, 297, 299.

[2] From Ponsonby, 7 April, 1841: *F.O. Turkey*, 433; do., 29 March, 27 April, 1841: *B.P.* Palmerston on the news of Reschid's fall instructed Ponsonby to

Chekib, Reschid's protégé and friend, tactfully told Palmerston that the change was "just as if in this country the Whigs were to go out and the Tories were to come in." For Palmerston that meant reaction and he expressed his alarm in public and private communications. "This would be very unfortunate," he told Ponsonby, "and would do the Sultan's cause great injury all over Europe; and it would also give great advantage to Mehemet Ali's partisans who hold him up as a pattern of an enlightened and regenerating Mussulman."[1] Chekib was, however, only too accurate a prophet. A period of reaction followed in which the reforms laid down in the Gulhané decree were completely forgotten.

In the short interval left to him Palmerston did what he could to stem the tide. But it was of little use and it was left to Stratford Canning, Ponsonby's successor in 1842, to resume the ungrateful and, indeed, impossible task of reforming the Ottoman Empire. Beauvale, who studied with care Stürmer's reports as well as those of Ponsonby, perhaps stated the real truth with more accuracy than anyone else dared use:

"Reschid Pasha's fall was intended to lead to the fall of his system, and will do so. Rifaat told Stürmer that the Edict of Gulhané would be kept in force in as far as it secures life and property, but that in as far as it limits the power of the Sultan it will be suffered to fall into disuse. Rifaat you will observe is a mere Secretary having no power of any sort. Now as nothing limits the power of the Sultan more than securing life and property, I conclude that no part of the Hatti Sheriff will last. It has been executed nowhere because it cannot be. Its execution demands a police, a graduated system of uncorrupted tribunals, an honest magistracy and all of them backed by a paid, obedient and disciplined force; which of all these things exists in Turkey? The existing discontent in Syria has its rise chiefly in the open shameless extorting corruption of all Turkish authorities from high to low. Go and reform this by an Edict! Where no principle of honour no feeling of shame exist, by what are you to govern if not by force? The question is how to substitute for this weak and faulty principle of Government a better and a stronger one, and the solution of this question is the work of centurys. By

protect his life. Stürmer had told Metternich it was in danger. But Ponsonby had already done far more than this. He had got the Sultan to give Reschid a large grant of money and promise him employment abroad.
[1] To Ponsonby, 22 April, 1841: *B.P.*

rapid sweeping reforms, imitated from countrys quite otherwise
constituted, there is nothing but mischief to be done and no good,
and the less we call upon them to execute the hasty and crude
conceptions, into which they have run without knowing what
they were about, the better. My belief is that the Empire is
falling to pieces by a gradual dissolving process which nothing
can arrest. The problem will be to retard it as long as may
be, and where inevitable to direct it in the least mischievous
course."

Palmerston did not accept this pessimistic judgment. His whole
moral position in the Near Eastern Question depended on the
supposition that the Ottoman Empire could be reformed. But in
these last months of office he had to admit that his immediate
hopes had been disappointed.[1]

But if Palmerston had failed to obtain the necessary basis of
reform in Turkey, he had at last complete success in the question
of the Straits. As has been seen, all the proposals to introduce
other questions into the final document had failed. They were all
too controversial or too complicated to secure agreement. And
the convention as to the Straits was drawn up almost exactly as
Palmerston himself desired, though Brunnow did a good deal of
the drafting. Palmerston indeed claimed that there was nothing
new in it. It simply repeated, with the all-important addition of
French support, what had already been laid down in the Convention of 15 July, 1840. Guizot continued to insist that France
would only sign the new convention after the Great Powers had
solemnly asserted that the aims of the Convention of 15 July,
1840, had been attained, and that consequently its operation was
over. The only representative of the Four Powers who seemed
disposed to refuse these terms was Brunnow who, both Neumann
and Bourqueney reported, wished to prevent a reconciliation with
France. But he was isolated; Austria and Prussia were pressing
strongly for an agreement, while the British people were anxious,
to get on good terms with France once more. The debate in the
House of Commons at the beginning of the Session surprised and
pleased the French Government and people by its cordial tone,
coming as it did after all the revelations in the French Chambers.

---

[1] From Beauvale, 5 May, 1841: *B.P.* Guizot also spoke most pessimistically
about the future of the Ottoman Empire, and said that he meant to do something
about it, but he did no more than order his agents to report all incidents. (From
Bulwer, 4 June, 1841: *F.O. France*, 625.)

Brunnow who had so often spoken of the funeral of the Franco-British Alliance, did not, reported Bourqueney, know what to do about it.[1]

Brunnow continued to make difficulties throughout February and March and was reluctant to sign the agreement when it was at last made. He thought it made too great a concession to France. Palmerston, on the other hand, was anxious to get the signature of France to a document while Guizot was still in power. He did not consider that there had been any undue yielding. On the contrary, he told Clanricarde, "the convention contains nothing but the stipulation about the Straights taken almost verbatim from our Convention of July [1840] and therefore it is virtually and indirectly an acknowledgement of that convention by France." And he put great pressure on Brunnow to sign without specific authority from St. Petersburg, "because on the one hand the treaty is just what the Emperor wished it to be, that is to say a 'transaction' confined within the narrowest limits, and because . . . if we were to let slip this opportunity of binding France, Guizot might go out and then we should have fresh difficulties. For England and Russia this would not much signify, for it is to us a matter of comparative indifference whether France signs or not, but to our German allies it is a matter of importance."[2]

Brunnow gave way and thus by the middle of March Bourqueney had agreed with the others not only on the new convention about the Straits but on the Protocol which the Four were to sign concerning the end of the Convention of 15 July, 1840. But the news that came from Constantinople and Alexandria of the Sultan's Hatti Sheriff and the refusal of Mehemet to accept it prevented the signature of the Protocol. The German Powers would have signed it, but Palmerston refused to do so before the submission of Mehemet was complete. He suspected the French of planning to get rid of the Convention of 15 July, 1840, and then to encourage Mehemet Ali to demand impossible terms after the means of coercion had thus been destroyed. Since the Protocol could not be signed, the new convention could not be signed

[1] Bourqueney to Guizot, 29 Jan., 1841: *A.A.E.* From Granville, 1 Feb., 1841: *F.O. France*, 622.
[2] To Clanricarde, 12 March, 1841: *B.P.* From Granville, 19 March, 1841: *F.O. France*, 623. Bourqueney, reported Granville, "renders full justice to the zealous exertions of Yr. Ldship. to overcome the reluctance felt by Baron Brunnow to put his initials to the draft of the convention."

either. All that could be done was to initial the document as an agreed one, and there was no further change in it.

The uneasy situation in Europe, therefore, persisted. Palmerston was not much disturbed. Brunnow also was naturally not much disappointed. But Austria and Prussia and the friends of France in Britain were exasperated and heaped abuse on Ponsonby as the main cause of the delay. There was, however, nothing to be done until the new Hatti Sheriff was issued and it was seen whether Mehemet would accept it. When it came, it did, as has been seen, grant all Mehemet's main demands and in June it seemed as if the Protocol and the convention could be signed at once. But again Palmerston hesitated. He was still suspicious, Neumann reported, that France and Mehemet would play some trick if he formally stated that the obligations of the Convention of 15 July, 1840, were at an end. He could not, he told Bourqueney, do so until Mehemet himself had shewn that the convention was no longer necessary, and Guizot had to admit that his position was logical and consistent. It was not, therefore, until the news came from Alexandria in July that Mehemet had accepted the new offer (or at least almost all of it—for the tribute was not really settled) that the Protocol and convention could be signed. On 13 July the representatives of the Five and Turkey met for that purpose, Palmerston being especially cordial to Bourqueney and even Brunnow shewing no signs of repugnance.[1]

Thus came into existence the agreement of all the Great Powers concerning the Straits which determined that problem for the rest of the nineteenth century, and indeed in all its essentials the twentieth century as well. There was some alteration from the phraseology of the previuos year. The substance was however the same. The Sultan declared his intention of maintaining the ancient rule by which warships of foreign Powers were forbidden to enter the Straits and that he would admit no such ships "while the Porte was at peace". Brunnow did not renew the attempt, defeated in 1840, to substitute for this last condition "whether the Sultan is at peace or war", which would have left the Sultan to the Tsar's mercy in case of rupture. It was clear that if Russia were to go to war with the Sultan nothing could prevent him from

---

[1] Bourqueney to Guizot, 2, 5, 16 March, 14, 25 June, 1841; Guizot to Bourqueney, 8, 14 March, 1841: *A.A.E.* Guizot, *Mémoires*, VI, 72–117. Esterhazy to Metternich, 3, 14, 16 March, 8, 29 June, 13 July, 1841; Neumann to Metternich, 6 June, 1841: *V. St. A.*

inviting the assistance of other Powers and, if these were ready to give it, it shewed that they were ready to defend him by force of arms. The only sanction for such a clause was the threat of war by Russia and that was useless after war had already been determined upon by the other Powers.

But so long as the Sultan remained at peace Russia was protected from naval attack from the Mediterranean and this to the Tsar and his advisers seemed a considerable advantage. They gave up of course the right to attack in the Mediterranean. But this they had not possessed even under the Treaty of Unkiar Skelessi. Under that treaty, however, the Sultan had promised to consult the Tsar when a state of emergency arose, and it was this stipulation that to Palmerston was the most obnoxious part of the treaty. That privileged position was now lost and the Sultan was free to deal with all the Great Powers according to his own interests. Russia still possessed her special rights concerning the Orthodox subjects of the Porte and she had succeeded in preventing any reference to the territorial independence and integrity of the Ottoman Empire in the convention, even in the Preamble. The way was thus still open to that absorption of Turkish territory at the proper moment which it cannot be doubted was never absent from the mind of the Tsar and his advisers.[1]

But Palmerston also was satisfied with what had been done. He had secured complete equality with Russia as regards the Straits, and since Russia was so much nearer to Turkey than Britain the closing of the Straits was to the advantage of the latter. Moreover, Britain had no intention of attacking the Ottoman Empire and desired none of its territories. She was not likely therefore to go to war with the Sultan, and his control over the Straits was thus likely to be exercised in her favour so long as the Sultan was free to act according to his own desires. On the other hand the Sultan had the right to summon the British fleet to protect him if Russia went to war with him. How important this was was to be seen in 1854 and 1878.

Two variations from the Convention of 15 July, 1840, were both due to Russia. Brunnow not only insisted on adding the clause which enabled the Sultan to permit light vessels of war to

[1] Goriainow's long analysis of the treaty in *Le Bosphore et les Dardanelles*, 82–91, is designed to prove the Russian case concerning the outbreak of the Crimean war and the situation in 1877–1878.

pass through the Straits but made a special declaration on the subject for the record. It was, he said, necessary for Russian communications with Greece. It was due to Brunnow also that a clause was added allowing the Sultan to invite all the other Powers with whom the Porte was in friendly relations to accede to the treaty. This was an unusual step and the reason for it is not quite clear. None of the smaller Powers was likely to cause trouble at Constantinople. But Russia seems to have thought that the protection given by the treaty would be increased if all the smaller maritime Powers bound themselves to recognise it as the Great Powers had done. For the obligation which the signatories undertook was of course to one another as well as to the Sultan. They could not be released from it by any action on his part contrary to the treaty.[1]

At any rate both the Tsar and Palmerston were satisfied at the result of the long contest between them. Indeed the success of Palmerston's handling of the Tsar had already been shewn in dramatic fashion at the end of 1840. The armaments and threats of France had necessarily produced a great effect on Europe and, as has already been mentioned, the possibility of renewing the Quadruple Alliance against her had occurred to some of the Prussian soldiers and statesmen. But the Tsar's relations with Prussia had grown much cooler, even hostile, though this was largely due to the attitude of the Prussian Court towards the marriage of his son. He was also more suspicious of Metternich than he had ever been. He spoke of him to Clanricarde with the greatest contempt and distrust. It was to Britain, therefore, that he made the suggestion of a special Four Power Alliance against France, indicating in no uncertain fashion to Clanricarde that he had more confidence in her than in any other of the Great Powers. In a later discussion he explained the reason for this trust. "The fundamental principle", reported Clanricarde, "of His Imperial Majesty's Government—felt to be such by himself and his people —was their religion and their religious duty. . . . We [the British] maintained our respect for the principles of religion and of good order and of good faith throughout all our changes of opinion upon matters of policy." The danger from France was

---

[1] That these additions were mainly due to Brunnow is made clear by Goriainow (see previous note). Palmerston wrote, "Brunnow has been of great use to us all with his pen." (To Clanricarde, 12 March, 1841: *B.P.*)

apparent and Britain ought, therefore, to make common cause with the other nations of Europe against her. "Such an engagement," the Tsar said, "no matter how contracted, verbally or otherwise, would make peace certain." Nesselrode subsequently made the offer more formally to Clanricarde in a much less enthusiastic manner, dwelling on the importance of the Treaty of Vienna with a hint that Poland was included in it, an approach that the Ambassador thought somewhat impertinent.

But of course Palmerston could not in any case accept such an offer. He took advantage of it, indeed, to explain the attitude of Britain towards such an alliance in a despatch which is reminiscent of the State Papers of Castlereagh and Canning. The doctrine of non-intervention was restated in unequivocal terms and the impossibility of a Parliamentary Government undertaking indefinite obligations was again laid down. At the same time it was once more affirmed that Britain would play her part in maintaining the balance of power in Europe. Perhaps the Tsar had not expected much more. At any rate he took no umbrage and continued to assure Clanricarde of the absurdity of the reports of a Franco-Russian rapprochement which were then rife in Western Europe. Palmerston warned the Russian Government not to encroach on Norway and the Tsar and his Ministers shewed some anxiety lest Britain should absorb too much of the Chinese trade. But these suspicions were overcome by frank explanations on both sides. As recounted in Section 5, the tension concerning Persia and Afghanistan was also by now sensibly reduced. The Ambassador had no doubt as to the Tsar's good faith which indeed all his actions seemed to prove. And as a final mark of his friendship Nicholas paid an informal visit to a party at the Ambassador's residence, an unprecedented condescension, such as Durham had never received.[1]

If the Tsar saw in Britain the key to European peace Metternich also looked to Palmerston to help him to reestablish a new system

---

[1] F. S. Rodkey, "Anglo-Russian negotiations about a 'Permanent' Quadruple Alliance", *American Historical Review*, Jan., 1931, gives the details of the Russian offer and Palmerston's reply, but omits the passage above quoted. From Clanricarde, 18 Jan., 1841: *F.O. Russia*, 271; do., 13 Jan., 24 Feb., 9, 23 March, 20 April, 1841: *B.P.* The private letters add nothing to the despatches except the remark: "You see they have formally made the Holy Alliance proposition. I think Nesselrode's allusion to the Treaties of Vienna impudent. But I don't like to say much about it because the Emperor is more violent than ever about the Poles." To Clanricarde, 2 March, 1841: *F.O. Russia*, 269.

of European diplomacy. He took advantage of the Porte's desire
to obtain a guarantee to propose his own remedies. And, so
Beauvale explained, since he had at last been cured of his strange
illusion that he could answer for the Tsar, it was to Palmerston
that he turned for help. He proposed once more the old device,
once brought forward by Talleyrand in 1833, of a self-denying
ordinance of the Five Powers such as they had given concerning
Greece, a promise that they would not themselves acquire any
Turkish territory. Palmerston knew that the Tsar would refuse
such a proposition which he must consider as aimed at Russia,
and would have nothing to do with it. Nor would he listen to the
hints given by Metternich to Beauvale which the Ambassador said
were feelers after his real object, the establishment at Vienna of a
centre to deal with Oriental affairs. So little had Metternich learnt
from his experience in 1840! Palmerston gave the proposal short
shrift. Austrian policy, he wrote, had not been marked with such
steadiness and consistency as to give her a claim to be trusted by
the British Government. Moreover, such a centre was only
useful and necessary when common action had to be taken to
carry out treaty engagements. Metternich was much disappointed
at the failure of this final attempt to make Vienna the centre of
European diplomacy and roundly abused Palmerston to the Russian Chargé d'Affaires. He hoped to disrupt the cordial relations
established between Russia and Britain, but his abuse did nothing
to lower Palmerston in the opinion of the Tsar.[1]

Prussia made no such definite advances but it was clear that the
Prussian King and the Prussian soldiers looked to Britain more
than to any other state. With only one Power was Palmerston
the stumbling block to better relations—France, whom he had
defeated and humiliated. And it must be admitted that Palmerston himself did little to heal the breach. On the contrary he
widened it in the last weeks of his tenure of office by a speech to
his constituents at Tiverton which contrasted the success of Britain
in India with the failure of France in Algiers, a failure which
he attributed to the barbarous methods employed by the French
soldiers. This was all the more wounding in that there was
some truth in the accusation. The attack was no doubt drawn
from Palmerston in the heat of the contest and not meant to

---

[1] The details are given in my "Palmerston, Metternich and the European
System," in *Proceedings of the British Academy*, 1934.

attract the attention which it obtained. But it is a sign that his success had caused him to lose some of the restraint and tact necessary for the conduct of foreign affairs. Such an outburst might be defended if it was calculated and had some object in view. But Palmerston had nothing to gain by it. On the contrary, he was anxious to obtain Guizot's signature to a Five Power Slave Trade treaty on which he had spent a great deal of time and thought, and which would have been a fitting recognition of the unceasing effort he had made on that subject throughout his period of office. It is not surprising that, in spite of Palmerston's elaborate explanation to Bulwer, which however fell short of a real apology, Guizot refused to allow Palmerston to have this satis-faction.[1]

This was an unnecessary and humiliating setback. But, though the French Government naturally disliked Palmerston himself, they recognised that his policy had been justified by events and were anxious to renew the *entente cordiale*. Aberdeen, who had been one of the most zealous supporters of Palmerston's policy in 1840, had no difficulty in establishing the old relation of the early eighteen thirties with Louis Philippe and Guizot as soon as he had come into office.

[1] The details of this well-known incident are in *Bulwer*, II, 376–383. Palmerston's explanation was made at Bulwer's suggestion. After his failure Bulwer wrote: "I can only say I had good reason to think what I did and our first conversation on the subject entitled me to think even more than I did . . . and tho' I am much hurt and dissatisfied at the present little spiteful proceeding, I must say that Guizot himself always speaks of you, your public service and ability with respect and liking." (27 Aug., 1841: *B.P.*) He also altered for publication his own letter. For example, he had expressed his *conviction* not his *belief* that Guizot would change his decision on receipt of a letter of explanation to Bulwer and he omitted the sentence "Guizot is a Frenchman and like all Frenchmen vain and susceptible".

CHAPTER IX

THE CONTRIBUTION OF PALMERSTON TO BRITISH FOREIGN POLICY
1830–1841

" The system of England ought to be to maintain the liberties and independence of all other nations ; out of the conflicting interests of all other countries to secure her own independence ; to throw her moral weight into the scale of any people who are spontaneously striving for freedom, by which I mean rational government, and to extend as far and as fast as possible civilisation all over the world. I am sure this is our interest, I am certain it must redound to our honour ; I am convinced we have within ourselves the strength to pursue this course, if we have only the will to do so ; and in your humble servant that will is strong and persevering." PALMERSTON, 21 March, 1838.

CHAPTER IX

THE CONTRIBUTION OF PALMERSTON TO BRITISH FOREIGN POLICY, 1830–1841

ALL estimates of these eleven years have necessarily been influenced by Palmerston's later career. He was nearly fifty seven at the close of this period and when he came back to the Foreign Office five years later he was still in full vigour. He shewed no signs of loss of energy when he became Prime Minister at the age of seventy. He had, however, the misfortune to spend nearly all the next ten years in that office. Palmerston wore out more slowly than anyone except Gladstone, but few men are fit for such responsibility after the age of seventy-five and Palmerston's reputation suffered from the mistakes which he made at the end of his life.

Moreover, he had himself to deal with the consequences of the actions of these years. Castlereagh died while the great experiment of the European Alliance was in the balance, and that fact is given as one of the explanations of its failure. Canning joined Russia in an attack on Turkish power and assisted to bring France and Russia together, a combination dangerous to his country. But he died just as this was accomplished and historians have generally thought that if he had lived he would have mastered the difficult situation which he had helped to create. But Palmerston had himself to face in 1848 the revolutions in Europe, which his work in the eighteen thirties had been designed to prevent, and in 1854 he was a member of a Cabinet which began the war against Russia which he had then so successfully guarded against—and there were many other subordinate parts of his policy which he had to reconsider and adapt to new circumstances. Instead of a Liberal France he had to work with an Emperor. It was inevitable that some of his later policy should seem inconsistent with that of his former period of office.

Palmerston also made enemies of some of the most active and influential individuals of this time. The fact is to his credit. He defeated manoeuvres that would have injured not only himself but his country. But Talleyrand and Princess Lieven were attractive personalities and have left voluminous records behind them designed to deceive. Their insinuations and falsehoods have been believed to a far greater degree than they deserved. Both have repeatedly been shewn to be deliberate liars, yet their assertions have often been accepted in the most uncritical fashion by historians of repute and become part of the stock of text-book makers. The legends of the nineteenth century have done more to obscure the truth than those of the Middle Ages, because they have not been examined with the same scepticism and historical technique. Greville's diary also has had an immense influence on British historiography of the nineteenth century. It is written with such an air of candour that it has often been accepted without question. Yet it is full of misleading statements, and, though Greville was compelled at the end of this period to pay a great tribute to Palmerston's abilities, he sometimes had all the rancour of a man whose shafts have missed their mark. Urquhart's accusations were so absurd that they did little injury to Palmerston, even though some of them were repeated by no less a figure than Karl Marx. All this denigration was, however, only very partially answered in the official biography of Bulwer who never took the trouble to examine more than a fraction of the voluminous evidence left in Palmerston's private papers.

Palmerston himself certainly did much to injure his own reputation by the manner of his writings. His private letters often contain extravagant assertions. They were written in the heat of the moment to convey an immediate reaction. Unless they are set beside the official despatches which went with them they give a misleading impression of his attitude towards the problems with which he had to deal. But the despatches also are more direct and uncompromising than most of their kind. Palmerston was in these years always in conflict not only with foreign but with domestic opponents and all his writings bear the mark of the struggle. That is true of nearly all Foreign Ministers in some degree, but it is more apparent in Palmerston's case than in that of any other.

But, whatever judgment be formed on it, it is clear that Palmerston's work during this period was of immense importance. He set the course of British foreign policy for a generation. He signed the two treaties which throughout the century were most important to the position of Britain in Europe—the one securing the neutrality of Belgium and the other the closing of the Straits. But he took an interest in every part of the Continent. His attitude towards Europe in these years was indeed more that of Castlereagh than of Canning. But to Castlereagh's conception of a Concert of the Great Powers he added that protection of Liberalism which Canning had threatened but never carried out. The combination was a difficult if not an impossible one. Yet Palmerston had an extraordinary degree of success.

In method he was of course as different to Castlereagh as it was possible to be and much nearer to Canning. In this respect indeed he can be regarded as that disciple of Canning as he is so often rather mistakenly described. Only in energy and perseverance throughout a long period of office is there any similarity between Castlereagh and Palmerston. Castlereagh who, it is true, in addition led the House of Commons, a task Palmerston escaped until he was seventy, died of the effects of his toil. Palmerston's freshness, resilience and eagerness to continue in office at the end of this period shew what his powers of resistance were. He could hardly perhaps have remained so had he not, so far as possible, confined himself to foreign affairs or questions closely connected with them. He was of course much interested in those of Ireland, but he seems to have succeeded in staying outside the controversies which arose about them in these years. When he did concern himself with them it was always to urge compromise and moderation.

This concentration, necessary for efficiency, had its disadvantages. He sometimes forgot that his colleagues could not be so conscious of the importance of what he was doing as he was himself. But generally Palmerston recognised as fully as anyone who ever held his office the limitations placed on his work by the processes of Cabinet Government. "There are very few public men in England", he wrote in 1838, "who follow up foreign affairs sufficiently to foresee the consequences of events which have not happened."[1]

The art of diplomacy depends upon timing as much as on anything else. But the right moment may come by preparation as well as by opportunity. Sometimes it is possible to take advantage of a fortunate combination of circumstances, but it is also possible to create them. Palmerston was perhaps better at the first than the

[1] To Granville, 5 June, 1838: *Bulwer*, II, 266.

second. He rarely missed an opportunity. But he also shewed great patience and skill in the gradual process of preparation which ultimately leads to success. His conduct of the Belgian negotiation as well as that of the Eastern Question in 1839–1840 shew his exceptional skill in this respect.

Palmerston's directness of approach and clarity of exposition in speech and writing have not often been surpassed in his office. His State Papers are indeed not the equal of those of Canning. They do not lead the reader irresistibly to the conclusion of the writer. They are not so profound nor so subtle. But they are for the most part models of clear and incisive language. They come straight to the point, and the facts on which Palmerston relies are marshalled with great force. They perhaps do not take sufficiently into account the arguments on the other side. Palmerston could use effectively at times the method of stating the opposing case fairly and powerfully, but in such a manner that it could be demolished at a later stage of the argument, one of the best methods of convincing those to whom argument appeals at all. But, as he was always working against time, it was generally as much as he could do to state his own case. His despatches and letters are also often directed against prejudice and jealousy which he knew that he could not overcome. He certainly, however, devoted too much time to abuse and complaint of his opponents. He also tended to labour too much a point which was already won. Both Grey and Melbourne often pointed this fault out to him.

Palmerston's realisation of the strength and importance of public opinion in foreign affairs he undoubtedly learnt from watching Canning at work. He was not naturally an orator either in Parliament or on a public platform. This had been one of the reasons which kept him out of high office and he long refused to make the effort to attain to distinction in this field. But when he devoted sufficient preparation to a speech it could be very effective indeed. He much increased his reputation by this means during the Wellington Administration. When he came into office, however, he was less successful in impressing the House of Commons than might have been expected. This was partly due to its absorption in domestic affairs. But Palmerston seems to have learnt slowly the art of combining the responsibility of office with the ability to make a popular appeal. On the other hand, in informing public opinion by the publication of documents and communication with the Press he set entirely new standards. He was ahead of any other Minister in Europe in this respect. In this way he helped to create an informed public opinion not only in Britain but on the continent of Europe which was of immense advantage to his work.

He could not have done this so well had he not possessed complete mastery over all the complicated problems with which he had to deal. Of some he had a greater knowledge than anyone else in Europe. He was so superior to all his colleagues in the Cabinets that they could never really engage in argument with him. Even Lord Grey, who more than anyone else entered into the problems of the foreign office, relied on Palmerston entirely for the facts on which he based his conclusions. The Lievens or colleagues like Holland or friends abroad were in constant correspondence with the Prime Minister, but it is clear that he trusted Palmerston's reports on and analysis of situations far more than anything he could get elsewhere. When other colleagues made complaints Palmerston could nearly always tear their case to pieces. No other Foreign Minister had a greater command of the information of his office.

The same was true when he met foreign diplomats either in conference or *tête à tête*. He had always all the business at his finger ends. They were overwhelmed by the completeness and certainty of his knowledge. This is clear in their reports which naturally try to make the best of their own share of the discussion. Palmerston's accounts of his conversations similarly give his own point of view, but they shew how terrific he could be in attack and how ruthlessly he could expose the weak side of his opponent's case. This ascendancy had its disadvantages. It cut Palmerston off from one source of information and influence. It was his own policy that he defended and generally obtained. But he had not the gift of stating his own aims in such a manner that others thought they had originated them. In this he was inferior to Castlereagh and Salisbury whose most important achievements sometimes passed without notice and became part of the common stock.

In all that part of his work which depended on technical skill rather than character Palmerston was above almost all holders of his office. His gift of language enabled him to talk to diplomats as easily in French as in English. When it was a question of drafting he could with speed and certainty do all that was necessary in either language. He could master a complicated question with unusual rapidity when he gave his mind to it. He was not a lawyer but he knew much international law and kept the books on that subject constantly in use. "Some people not unqualified to judge", wrote Bagehot, "have said that his opinion on such matters was as good as any law officer's."[1] This was written about his later career but it applies to this period where more than one witness noticed his exceptional knowledge of this aspect of his work. The essays on political economy which appear at regular intervals, if a little naïve, are much more advanced than most statesmen of his time could have written.

The final impression is one of immense energy, power of con-centration, courage and resilience. Palmerston faced combinations of internal and external foes that would have killed most men. A similar combination helped to kill Canning. No one could help but admire the resource and tenacity of his resistance. It is best seen in the final triumph in the Eastern Question, but is hardly less apparent in the problems of Belgium and the Peninsula. His optimism was unfailing. He always believed he could win—and he nearly always did. Clarendon, whose technique was pessimism, was irritated by this trait. "He always reckons that that *is* which he wishes," he told his brother.[2] But for Palmerston that was a method of obtaining what he wanted. He was more aware of the difficulties than he would confess to others—or even to himself.

But Palmerston must be judged by the ends to which these exceptional qualities were directed, by what he achieved for Britain and Europe. No one has ever questioned his devotion to his country's interests. He had indeed often been criticised for an excessive nationalism. This implies that he sought objects to the injury of the legitimate interests of other countries and did not take sufficient regard to the general interests of Europe. This is certainly untrue of this period. The objects which Palmerston tried to obtain were naturally those which he considered to be calculated to promote British interests. No Foreign Minister could hold office on any other terms. But he also pursued policies which were in the general interests of Europe. This may perhaps be disputed as regards the Eastern Question. It can be

---

[1] W. Bagehot, *Biographical Sketches*, 341. This is a hasty and inadequate sketch written two days after Palmerston's death but it contains some pregnant sentences.

[2] Sir H. Maxwell, *Clarendon*, I, 145.

claimed, though the balance of evidence is in the other direction, that the general interests of the world would have been better served if the Ottoman Empire had been allowed to disintegrate at this time. But in its defence Palmerston claimed no territory or special privilege for Britain. His policy in the Eastern Question was more European than that of any other Minister. And in Belgium, the Peninsula, Greece, Switzerland and Italy, he advocated policies which were meant to establish free, independent, prosperous states. There is no other period in British history of the nineteenth century where so much was done in peace time for objects in Europe, of which the benefits to Britain were only the indirect ones that come from the advantages of others. In China and India there was, it is true, the use of force for an immediate interest, in the one case commercial expansion, in the other the protection of the Indian Empire. But both these actions were the result of policies long pursued by Britain as by all other maritime states, and any criticism of Palmerston is one of the whole method by which Western civilisation spread over the world. British relations with the United States were during the greater part of this period exceptionally good, Palmerston was eager to help France and the United States to resume normal relations in 1834–1836 and certainly assisted to obtain the settlement of their unfortunate dispute. The Slave Trade, the United States' attitude to Canada and the Maine frontier problem disturbed their harmony in the last two years of this period, but the record is a remarkable one.

It is, however, his work in Europe which is surveyed in this book. Palmerston is more open to the charge that he interfered too much in European questions in which Britain had no real interest, or that he subordinated immediate British interests to general causes. This was the criticism constantly levelled at him by Frederick Lamb and his even more cynical brother, Lord Melbourne. Melbourne had no policy but doing nothing, but Lamb constantly suggested that Palmerston ought to make a deal with Austria whose interests were identical with those of Britain, instead of pursuing a quixotic policy of supporting the constitutional cause in Europe and driving the three Eastern Powers more closely together. France, the country with which Palmerston was associated, was the rival of Britain overseas and the greatest danger to British security. Central Europe was the natural ally of Britain against both France and Russia.

As has been seen, Palmerston had to take a view somewhat similar to this on his entry into office. He was uncertain of France and used the Eastern Powers to control her policy in Belgium. He was like others afraid that the aggressive policy of the first French Revolution might be repeated. But once that danger was shewn to be, if not entirely absent, more easily checked by cooperation with France, is it to be maintained that he should have subordinated his policy in the West to the necessities of Metternich? It is clear that he could have had a close alliance with Austria and Prussia at the cost of giving up all support to Liberalism. But even if such a course had been to the interests of Britain Palmerston could not have pursued it. No British Government could have supported a policy of repression in Europe.

But Palmerston had no doubt that British interests were entirely on the other side. In his opinion revolution could only be prevented by the progress of Liberalism and revolution was bound to threaten the peace of the Continent—the greatest interest of Britain. He tried hard to avoid the dilemma either of sacrificing British interests in the East or abandoning his position in the West, and it is possible that with a little more effort and financial expenditure the Eastern Question could have been tackled before the position in Western Europe was stabilised. Palmerston sometimes thought so, though perhaps his recognition of the dangers in the East came somewhat late. But if a choice had to be made he preferred to maintain the position in the West, and he was proved right in the end by securing most of his objects in both areas.

For in spite of the dramatic reversal of alliances Palmerston never gave up his defence of constitutional Government in Western Europe and Greece. He continued to the end to insist that its existence was necessary for both European and British interests. Melbourne often challenged this view. "All these Chambers and free Presses in other countries", he told Palmerston, "are very fine things, but depend upon it, they are full as hostile to England as the old Governments."[1] But Palmerston's belief in constitutional government was just as strong at the end of this period as at the beginning. He made some notable expressions of this belief, two of which deserve some quotation here for they sum up the faith that inspired his actions in these years.

[1] From Melbourne, 11 Feb., 1838: *B.P.*

As late as 1841, he replied to the never-ceasing criticism of his Ambassador at Vienna: "you say that a constitution is but a means to an end and the end is good government; but the experence of mankind shews that this is the only road by which the goal can be reached and that it is impossible without a constitution fully to develop the natural resources of a country and to ensure for the nation security for life, liberty and property. I hold that there is no instance in past or present times under a despotic government where these objects have been attained."[1]

This judgment was made in the intimacy of a private letter, but Palmerston wrote just as strongly a little later in an official despatch on the struggle in Greece which committed Melbourne and the Cabinet as well as himself: "It is always easy to say with regard to any country in which men do not wish to see constitutional government established that such a country is not fit for it and that it would not work there; but Her Majesty's Government do not happen to recollect any country in which a constitutional system of government has been established that has not on the whole been better off in consequence of that system than it had been before."[2]

It is of course true that Palmerston did not really succeed in establishing constitutionalism in Western Europe. Of all the countries with which Palmerston was concerned only in Belgium has the Liberal State maintained a continuing existence. Elsewhere it has often failed to cope with its difficulties, and been undermined by the corruption of its followers. But, though there have been intervals of autocracy or dictatorship, the conception of the Liberal state has remained for all Western Europe as the norm to which the body politic should return, as well as for those parts of the world to which the influence of Western Europe has extended. The failure of Liberalism to emerge in the new unified Germany has been a major cause of the two world wars of the twentieth century. Even in this period Palmerston was weakest in dealing with Germany and later on he was to shew that he did not realise how much depended on the manner by which its unity was brought about. But elsewhere he did a great deal to make possible the existence of constitutional Government. Its preservation is still the greatest issue in the world today. In the

---

[1] To Beauvale, 31 Jan., 1841: *B.P.*
[2] To Granville, 19 March, 1841: *F.O. France*, 619.

eighteen twenties Britain had put forward the doctrine of non-intervention but stood aside when it was disregarded.   In the eighteen thirties Britain interpreted the doctrine of non-intervention in another manner.   She claimed the right to protect the Liberal Movement if the Eastern Powers attacked it.   She never did so much again in the nineteenth century.   That so much was done even with imperfect success was mainly due to Palmerston.

The success of Liberalism in this period was in the first place due to France, a fact to which Palmerston gave full recognition. Indeed to the end of the period he believed that the French people were genuinely attached to the idea of the Liberal state, however Louis Philippe and some of his Ministers behaved.   But he had the right to complain that the French King, who in the long run determined French policy, had deserted the cause which had given him his crown.   Louis Philippe's policy in Spain was indeed treacherous and his relations with Austria, revealed in the Austrian archives, were in a sense a betrayal of the *entente*.   Louis Philippe himself constantly attributed Palmerston's attitude towards France in 1840 to the latter's indignation at French policy in Spain.   This is not true.   Palmerston eagerly welcomed the apparently cooperative attitude of Soult's Government in 1839.   But it is true that Palmerston considered that it was only the support of Britain that enabled the constitutional cause to triumph in the Peninsula, and the record of events given in Chapter VI would appear to prove him right.   The rivalry of maritime and overseas power, and the fear of France of British commercial domination of the continent of Europe certainly contributed to this failure of the two countries to work together for a common end in which the mass of the peoples of both states believed.   Palmerston's unfounded suspicions and immoderate language undoubtedly helped to divide them.   But it has been seen that he genuinely desired to continue the cooperation with France.   It was Louis Philippe and not Palmerston who destroyed the *entente*.

Palmerston's great contribution to the Liberal Movement has not received the attention which it deserved whatever opinion be held about it.   But Palmerston's handling of the Eastern Question has been the theme of many pens.   They have, however, concentrated on the attempt to modernise the Turkish Empire, and the vigorous opposition to Russian expansion.   They have all been influenced by the fact that the Crimean War occurred and that

Palmerston shared the responsibility for it. How far the weakness and pacifism of Aberdeen was not more responsible for Britain's part in what is sometimes crudely called an unnecessary war is beyond the scope of this book. But it is in any case irrelevant to the issue of these years when Palmerston's success has to be admitted by all. That involved the protection of the Ottoman Empire and the limitation of Russian expansion and power of interference. But it should be noted that Palmerston's object was to do this by means of the European Concert. The problem of the Straits was in a sense solved by this means during these years. The solemn recognition by the Great Powers that the ruler of Constantinople was to keep the Straits closed except when he was himself at war was one of the great acts of the nineteenth century.

As in the case of Belgium this achievement was the result of statesmanship in a number of different countries. Russia shewed a wise restraint and Metternich, in spite of his vacillation, made a real contribution to the solution. But Palmerston can claim a great share of the credit. He felt his way rather slowly, but without the energy and courage that he shewed in the years 1838–1840 it could not have been obtained. The overthrow of Mehemet Ali was a necessary preliminary, for the Sultan could not have been accepted as the guardian of the gate if he were under a perpetual threat from the South. Palmerston accomplished that task almost singlehanded. But he never lost sight of the greater objective, the safeguarding of the Straits, and was the first to insist that the solution should be a European one. For long it is true he almost despaired of Russia accepting such a solution, but he always thought that if the rest of Europe shewed the necessary resolution she would be compelled to take part. When the Tsar evinced his readiness to do so, nothing could have been better than Palmerston's immediate resolve to take advantage of the opportunity. The conflict that arose with France is now recognised by French historians to be largely due to the faults of Thiers, though they condemn Palmerston's methods, hardly realising that they were necessary under the circumstances to obtain the desired ends. But on the whole the course of history and the analysis of historians have shewn that Palmerston deserved the admiration and praise that he then received in such large measure from all Europe.

He did not then obtain the larger objective, which Castlereagh

had been the first to attempt, of a guarantee of the independence
and integrity of the Ottoman Empire. His readiness to abandon
it was due to the opposition of Russia and it clearly could not have
been obtained without her defeat in war. But it is also true that
he had by 1840 come to regard it as something of much less
importance than what it symbolised, the recognition that the
fate of the Ottoman Empire was of supreme importance to all the
European community of nations and that any changes in it should
be worked out round the Council table and not produced by the
unilateral action of one Power as had happened in 1829 and 1833.
This is the real issue with Russia both in 1854 and 1877 and
Palmerston's policy was the same as that which Salisbury laid
down in the great despatch of 1 April, 1878.

Palmerston considered that he had obtained the cooperation of
Russia by shewing her the determination not only of the Government but of the people of Britain to resist her encroachments on
the Turkish Empire or her control of the Straits. All the evidence
goes to shew that this judgment was correct. No doubt the Tsar
was glad to take advantage of the opportunity to humiliate Louis
Philippe and separate Britain from France. But it can hardly be
doubted that the impression made on him and his advisers by the
attitude of the British people as well as by Palmerston's action in
1838 was a major factor in causing him to take the course he did.

It must be remembered also that the British resistance extended
to Central Asia. No other European power could have anything
to say in that quarter. But as regards the Ottoman Empire
Palmerston had always offered a European solution, while making
it absolutely clear that Britain would fight rather than allow any
unilateral action. Never was a policy more successful. Palmerston won from Russia such cooperation and respect as was never
attained again in the nineteenth century. The course of history
might have been changed had he been able to represent Britain
to the Tsar in 1844 instead of the weak and incompetent Aberdeen.

With this policy of resistance to Russia Palmerston combined
that of reforming the Ottoman Empire. It is obvious that he did
not understand this problem and critics have fastened on this
weakness. Palmerston himself shewed some dismay as the evidence accumulated that once the Turk was out of immediate
danger he was just as corrupt and tyrannical as he had ever been.
He admitted that Britain shared in the discredit because she had

been the principal instrument in preserving the Empire intact. But there was in fact nothing else to do but to persist in the policy of reform and Stratford Canning made his great attempt to accomplish the impossible in the immediately succeeding years. Had Palmerston then been his chief more success might have been obtained but the final result could not have been very different. It was, however, at that period impossible to apply to the Ottoman Empire the policy of later years. Time was needed before the subject races of the Balkans could create viable states and even in 1919 those in Asia Minor were not ready for self-government. This dilemma, the defence of a state which denied the elementary human rights to its subjects, persisted throughout the century. Lord Salisbury's conscience was to suffer from it. But it has still to be seen how far the division of the Ottoman Empire into separate states will secure the independence and welfare of the inhabitants of the Balkans and Asia Minor.

It is surely obvious that Palmerston was a good European as well as a patriotic Minister of Britain. He came near at this time to devising for Europe some permanent form of Council to express its common interests. The success of the Belgian negotiation and the obvious need for a European policy on the Eastern Question drove him in this direction. Modern apologists for Metternich sometimes paint him as the only really European minister in the first half of the nineteenth century. But Palmerston like Castlereagh was well aware of the complexity of European problems, the interest of Britain in them all and the need of some machinery to deal with them. If, like Canning, he inveighed against the "Holy Alliance" he meant merely the use of the Alliance as a means to repress Liberal institutions. He did not adopt Canning's dictum of no more congresses. On the contrary, as has been seen he wished to develop the conference system. Metternich indeed accused him of a design to make the Belgian Conference a sort of permanent Council of Europe. Palmerston himself hardly thought on those lines. But he obviously wished to repeat in another field the success that he had had in the Belgian question. Like Metternich he attached too much importance to his own position in the scheme. Partly for this reason, but apparently still more because of the opposition of the Cabinet, he abandoned the attempt. He tried once more in 1838 to make London the centre of negotiation. But in 1839 he surrendered the control of the machine because he was so convinced of its necessity. The acceptance of Vienna as the centre in 1839 was one of his wisest acts in these years. The subsequent events are perhaps sufficient excuse for his refusal to consider at the end of this period any suggestion for the creation of a permanent centre. Europe was not yet ready for such a scheme and he would have had no support in Britain. But Palmerston at this time went further in accepting the idea of a permanent European Concert than any of his successors until the First Great War. It was one of his greatest failures in the eighteen sixties that he reacted so violently to the proposals of Napoleon III to use the method of conference as an alternative to war.

Like Castlereagh Palmerston regarded a balance of power in Europe as indispensable to British interests. But Castlereagh's conception of Europe was far more static than Palmerston's. Palmerston realised that change must come. But he relied on the balance of power to prevent aggression and in that he was in full agreement with his predecessor. His skill in creating the combinations to defeat the schemes of France, Austria, Russia and France again is a remarkable piece of diplomacy. He was aware that the ideological basis of the earlier years could not always persist. He foresaw the combination of France and Russia which was so dreaded, but believed that Central Europe would be able to resist it with British help. His famous phrase in the debate of 1849 that no country was either the eternal ally or the perpetual enemy of England but "that with every British Minister the interests of England ought to be the shibboleth of his policy" came to him partly as a result of the experience of this period. But it is often forgotten that that expression of national egotism was preceded by a recognition of ethical values which Gladstone himself could not have bettered: "As long as she [England] sympathises with right and justice she will never find herself altogether alone. She is sure to find some other state of sufficient power, influence and weight to support and aid her."[1] It would be a mistake to think such a statement to be mere hypocrisy, any more than the sentences which are placed at the head of this chapter. In all he did at this time Palmerston was fully convinced that right and justice were on his side. And by the end of this period, if many Courts and Cabinets disliked him, his name was already known all over

[1] E. Ashley, *Palmerston*, I, 62–63.

Europe as that of a Minister who had often been the foe of tyrants and the champion of the oppressed.

Two views of Palmerston have often been put forward which are contradictory of one another. There is clearly some truth in both of them. Mr. Philip Guedalla ended his brilliant summary of Palmerston's long career with a phrase that has often been quoted, "the last candle of the Eighteenth Century was out."[1] But this was surely mainly true as regards externals and accidentals. In manners and social habits Palmerston retained the outlook of a previous age. But, in his attitude to Liberalism, to nationality and to economics, Palmerston was a true Victorian though he may have tempered his beliefs with some of the pragmatism of the earlier century.

But Palmerston has also been described as a typical John Bull who expressed the outlook of the British middle classes. He certainly became their idol. The Russian exile, Alexander Herzen, wrote of "the finest meteorological instrument in England, Palmerston, who indicated with the greatest fidelity the temperature of the middle classes."[2] Palmerston did indeed share many of their prejudices as well as their belief in themselves and their determination to get their own way. But no one could have been further removed from their insularity and ignorance of Europe. Palmerston was passionately interested in the Continent and at times commented bitterly on the inability of Parliament and public opinion to realise the great issues at stake both in the West and East of Europe. Nevertheless the Victorian age that was just beginning was a great age of enterprise and adventure, and Palmerston's enthusiasm and self-confidence were shared by many of his countrymen.

It was this intensity of feeling that caused Palmerston to use the language which did his reputation so much harm. The charge that it led him into unnecessary interference, by advice and criticism, of the actions of other countries is not justified, at any rate in this period. He was entitled to make his views known by the treaties which Britain had not only signed but largely devised. He had a right—some might say a duty—to express his opinion about the affairs of Italy, the German Confederation or Cracow. The states concerned had been brought into existence largely by

[1] P. Guedalla, *Palmerston*, 459.
[2] A. Herzen, *Memoirs* (translation by Constance Garnett), IV, 281.

the effort of Britain. But the manner and method of his interference was often unfortunate. It gave him an appearance of
arrogance which was not really a true expression of his feelings.
He was genuinely indignant at acts of cruelty and repression.
But the language which he used about Metternich or Otto of
Greece or Mehemet Ali, though not meant for other than intimate
friends or colleagues, cannot be defended. And that which he
used in despatches and letters which he meant foreign statesmen
to see was often unnecessarily offensive and far too insistent.
And at the end this verbal extravagance became something more
dangerous. He shewed some sign of losing the balance and sense
of reality which he displays in these years. His pressure on
France and Mehemet Ali was unnecessary, his eagerness to obtain
all the advantages of the forward move in Asia was excessive. He
shewed the same excess of zeal in later dealings with Greece and
after the victory of the Crimean War. This was a great defect in
his character but in this period it is not apparent until the end.

Final judgment on Palmerston must wait until the whole of his
career is further explored. But surely enough is known of the
period considered in this book to place him very high on the list of
British Foreign Ministers. During the years between the Great
Wars when pacifism and appeasement were rated highly as methods
of obtaining peace Palmerston's work and character were often
unduly deprecated. The Liberalism which he helped to establish
in Europe also had few defenders in an age in which the bourgeois
state was fiercely attacked and its undoubted weaknesses revealed.
The danger of Russian aggression was imperfectly appreciated.
The realisation of national self-government to which, though
mainly in a later period of his career, Palmerston also made a great
contribution, was thought to have brought as much evil as good.
Palmerston's work was not as unknown as that of Castlereagh for
it had been done much more in the open. But a good deal of it
in this period was overshadowed by the more dramatic revolutions
of 1848. Palmerston himself worked for immediate ends and the
last thing that he expected was any recognition of what he had
done. "The gratitude of individuals may be reckoned upon
sometimes," he wrote at the end of this period, "that of masses of
men or even of any number of men in a corporate capacity never."[1]
This is one of the harsh utterances that he sometimes made in a

[1] To Beauvale, 1 April, 1841: *B.P.*

bitter moment, and it is fortunately not entirely true. But whether gratitude is due to him or not, there are some important things in the world which owe much to Palmerston's influence. If the substantive is to have any meaning in social democracy, if Belgium and the Straits are to remain as independent areas, if the colossal mass of Russia can be contained and fitted into a world system, if effective international cooperation is to be obtained by the use of the Council table, these results will be due in part to Palmerston's work in these years.

APPENDICES

APPENDIX A

LETTERS FROM PALMERSTON TO WILLIAM IV[1]
1832–1837
(i)

Foreign Office, 5 *August*, 1832.[2]

. . . Viscount Palmerston would humbly submit that the measures which Your Majesty has been advised to adopt in your Majesty's character of King of Hanover, are no bar to the course which, as King of Great Britain, Your Majesty is now advised to pursue.

It is well known throughout Europe that the Kingdoms of Great Britain and Hanover have little in common, except the Sovereign whom both have the happiness to obey. That, placed geographically in situations essentially different, they must frequently have interests and engagements differing no less; and that to expect that Hanover should submit her policy to the decision of Great Britain or that Great Britain should make hers follow the guidance of the Hanoverian Cabinet would be to require that, which would be equally repugnant to the feelings of both nations. But the object of your Majesty's Servants, being to preserve things as they are in the German States, Viscount Palmerston humbly conceives that the spirit in which they are desirous of acting, is the same which has guided the Hanoverian councils; and that the only difference between the two Cabinets lies, in the different anticipations which they form of the probable effect of certain measures.

Viscount Palmerston would rejoice to find that he has taken an exaggerated view of the aim of those who have planned these measures, or that he has over-estimated the effects which those measures may possibly produce; but in either case Viscount Palmerston would humbly submit, that no inconvenience can arise from the communications which he proposes to Your Majesty to authorize him to make. It is better that the British Cabinet should be taxed with entertaining groundless or premature apprehensions, than that it should be accused of blind indifference to events which might place the peace of Europe in jeopardy.

Viscount Palmerston begs further most humbly to submit that the course proposed to be pursued is by no means inconsistent with the doctrine, properly understood, of not interfering in the internal affairs of other countries. The interference in the internal affairs of other States, which your Majesty's Servants object to, upon principle, is an interference by force of arms; such an interference as France exercised in

---

[1] From the Broadlands Papers. The correspondence is, of course, always in the third person.
[2] The first part of this letter is in *Bulwer*, II, 415–418, with no indication that anything is omitted.

Spain and Austria in Naples ;[1] and such as the latter of these two Powers seems at present disposed to exert, in Italy, in Swisserland, and in Germany. Such an interference has for its object to subject the will of an independent nation to the military dictation of a powerful neighbour; it is founded on injustice, and leads to the destruction of the balance of power. But an interference which consists merely of friendly advice, tendered by one ally to another, upon questions of general interest, which may at will be accepted or declined, which has for its object to prevent the collision of arms, and to dissuade from measures of force by which peace is disturbed, such an interference, Viscount Palmerston humbly submits, is sanctioned by the most approved principles of international law, and is consistent with the strictest regard for the rights of independent states.

Viscount Palmerston wishes to abstain from any minute examination of the Resolutions of the Frankfort Diet, because the object of the communication which he has humbly submitted to Your Majesty, is rather the possible consequences of those Resolutions if pushed to their full application, than their accordance with the spirit of the Acts, by which the Confederation was constituted. But upon that latter point the recent despatches from your Majestys Ministers at several of the German Courts shew that the general opinion is not favourable to those Resolutions. . . .

It appears, therefore, to be the opinion of Mr. Cartwright[2] judging from personal observation on the spot, that the immediate effect of these Resolutions will be, to create a serious breach between the constitutional Sovereigns and the great mass of their subjects, upon questions of the deepest national importance, and which call into action the strongest passions of mankind, a state of things which cannot exist in any country without serious inconvenience and great danger, even if that country were entirely cut off from all external contact. But Mr. Cartwright goes on to point out a probable result, which it must be far from the wish of Your Majesty to see realized, and he says that "the *mass of the inhabitants* of the constitutional states finding their own Governments lending themselves to measures having for their object the restriction of the Liberal institutions, to which they are attached, will turn to France for protection; and a strong French party may be created in the heart of Germany which may ultimately produce a material change in the political relations of the country."

Such then are the grounds of the alarm with which Viscount Palmerston views the present state of affairs in Germany. The intention of Your Majesty's Servts is to endeavour to prevent and not to promote revolution. . . .

Viscount Palmerston has only further most humbly to state to Your Majesty that he has again revised the draft of the Despatch and has made some alterations in it, which he hopes Your Majesty may approve.

[1] France in 1823 and Austria in 1821.
[2] From Cartwright, 16 July, 1832: *F.O. Germany*, 38.

(ii)

Foreign Office, 8 *October*, 1832.

Viscount Palmerston presents his humble duty to Your Majesty, and has had the honor of receiving Your Majesty's memorandum of yesterday, containing a succinct review of the prominent points of the latter stages of the negotiation on the affairs of Belgium, together with Your Majesty's just reflections thereupon, and Viscount Palmerston will not fail to lay that paper immediately before his colleagues.

Your Majesty will no doubt read with satisfaction Mr. Jerningham's last dispatch[1] from the Hague of the 5th July giving an Account of the instructions which the Prussian Minister at that Court had *at last* received from his Government, and Viscount Palmerston is not altogether without hopes, that this step, however tardily taken by Prussia, may have some effect upon the Cabinet of The Hague. The resolution of Prussia to take this step may, as Viscount Palmerston most humbly submits be in some measure ascribed to the circumstance, that the three Courts have found themselves baffled in all their endeavours to sow dissension between England and France, and to separate those two Governments; that they are conscious that the united determination of the two, to execute the treaty could only be impeded by the armed resistance of the three, and that they shrink from an unjust and groundless war with England and France, the avowed object of which must be deliberately to violate their plighted faith; that, therefore, when they found that they had pushed forbearance to its utmost limit, and that their schemes for further delay had proved abortive, they have set themselves in earnest to procure from Holland an acquiescence which at an earlier time they might have commanded.

Viscount Palmerston hopes the attempt may not be made too late.

The course of the Belgian negotiation seems to afford an illustration of the policy, which Viscount Palmerston very humbly conceives to be most for the advantage of Great Britain in the present state of Europe—

Your Majesty will remember in the earlier period of the transaction, France was unreasonable and encroaching. She wanted Philippeville and Marienbourg as a beginning of the dismemberment of Belgium; she wanted to put the Duke de Nemours on the Throne; she wanted to continue indefinitely to occupy Belgium after the Dutch had been expelled; and she wanted to demolish almost all the fortresses. Upon the occasion of all these pretensions the British Government brought the three Powers to bear upon France, and France was upon all compelled to yield; latterly the three Powers have in their turn been unreasonable and deficient in good faith, and have endeavoured, under false pretences, to defeat the treaty they had ratified and to mar the arrangement they had guaranteed. The British Government then brought France to bear upon the three Powers, and it is to be hoped with ultimate success. Rivals in military strength, as France and the three Powers are, Your Majesty may be said practically to hold the

[1] *F.O. Holland*, 182.

scales of the balance of Europe. France will not venture to attack the three Powers, if she is also to be opposed by England; and the three Powers will pause long before they attack France, if they think that France could in that case reckon upon the support of England. Thus, then, it appears to Viscount Palmerston, that Your Majesty has peculiarly the power of preserving the general peace and that by throwing the moral influence of Great Britain into one scale or the other, according as the opposite side may manifest a spirit of encroachment or injustice, Your Majesty may from the peculiar circumstances of the times, more than perhaps many of Your Majesty's Royal Precedessors, but certainly with far less exertion of physical strength, become on many occasions the arbiter of events in Europe. For in acting upon this system of practical mediation, it is hardly possible that it should ever become necessary for Your Majesty to send an army to the Continent to take part in operations by land; on most occasions the moral influence of Great Britain would probably be effectual; but if that should at any time fail, a prompt and vigorous employment of the powerful naval resources which Your Majesty can at any time command, would be sure to give adequate effect to just and moderate counsels. It is then by supporting and strengthening, on one hand, that party in France who are for peace abroad and order at home, and by tempering, on the other, the zeal of those in other countries, who think that the whole art of government consists in the application of military force, that the propagandists and the republicans may be kept out of power in France, and pretences for disturbance may be avoided in other parts of the Continent. And, if it should be possible to prevent, for a few years longer, any war between the great nations, and any serious civil commotions in Europe, Viscount Palmerston humbly hopes, that the widespread agitation which has been produced by the unfortunate measures of the illfated Charles 10, may at length subside into a comparative calm.

(iii)

Foreign Office, 29 *September*, 1833.

Viscount Palmerston presents his humble duty to Your Majesty, and has had the honor of receiving Your Majesty's memorandum of yesterday's date, upon Earl Granville's private letter of the 23d instant.[1]

Viscount Palmerston begs to assure Your Majesty, that it never was his intention to submit to Your Majesty, a remonstrance to be made to the Russian Government by Your Majesty's representative, and that of the King of the French *jointly*. Viscount Palmerston would humbly submit, that it would be expedient to follow at Saint Petersburgh the same course which was pursued at Constantinople, where the British and French Ambassadors presented *separately*, though at the same time, the protests which each had been instructed by his own Government to deliver. Each acted with perfect independence of the other, although

---

[1] *B.P.* This contained Broglie's draft of the protest to Russia.

the similarity of wording in the two protests, and the circumstance of
their both being given in, in the course of the same day, added essentially to the effect of each, by proving that Great Britain and France,
though acting each for itself, as independent Powers, yet concurred in
taking the same view of the matters to which the protest related.

Viscount Palmerston begs most humbly to assure Your Majesty, that
neither he, nor any others of Your Majesty's confidential Servants wish
to shackle this country by any unnecessary engagements with the
Government of France, and Viscount Palmerston is fully alive to the
propriety of keeping a watchful eye upon the proceedings of that Power.
National character can not at once be changed, and the spirit of enterprise and military activity, which was so sedulously excited among the
French by Bonaparte, can only die away gradually and slowly.

While Monsieur Lafitte was at the head of the French Government,
many things happened which were calculated to require the vigilance
and the resistance of the British Government; and Viscount Palmerston
humbly trusts, that upon those occasions Your Majesty's Servants were
not found wanting in a proper sense of what was due to the interests of
the country and the honor of Your Majesty's crown.

When Monsieur Casimir Perrier [sic] succeeded to power, the policy
of the French Government underwent a change; it became more
friendly to England, more straightforward, and more pacific. With the
conduct of the French Government, the course, but not the principles
of action, of Your Majesty's confidential Servants changed also; and
it appeared to them to be wise to meet the proffered friendship of France
with corresponding demonstrations; to encourage confidence by confidence; and, by drawing closer to the French Government, to confirm
their inclination for peace, and render it more difficult for them to fall
back to a system of war.

Since the Duc de Broglie has directed the councils of France, the
good understanding between the two Governments has every day
become more intimate. The Duc de Broglie possesses all the good
qualities of Monsieur Casimir Perrier, with some which the latter had
not. In integrity and a desire to do right, there is perhaps no difference
between them; but the Duc de Broglie is a man of more attainment, is
more of a statesman, and, therefore, better able to accomplish his
purposes.

Monsieur Casimir Perier cultivated the friendship of England,
because he saw that the union of England and France was the only
means of preserving that peace which he was so anxious to maintain.
The Duc de Broglie, besides this political motive, feels that personal
goodwill towards this country, which arises from a perfect knowledge
of its language, a complete acquaintance with it's institutions, and an
intimate friendship with many of the most distinguished of Your
Majesty's subjects. As long therefore as the influence of the Duc de
Broglie predominates, Your Majesty will probably find the policy of the
French Government friendly to this country, and pacific; and, while the
policy of France bears that twofold character, Your Majesty will no

doubt be desirous of encouraging that Power, and of confirming it in this system, by a corresponding manifestation of confidence and friendship.

Your Majesty has most wisely determined, to make the preservation of peace, as long as it is possible to preserve it, the chief object of Your Majesty's solicitude in the direction of the foreign relations of this country; and, indeed, every year of peace is most valuable for the future, as well as for the present. For not only does Europe, in the mean while, remain free from the calamities of war, but also on the one hand, the French nation are insensibly led to turn their thoughts and energies to the pursuits of commerce and the other occupations of peace, and will gradually lose that military taste which has heretofore rendered them so restless and encroaching; while on the other hand, the German Powers are saved from all the dangers to which they might be exposed, if a war of political principle were now to break out; and thus the great bulwark of Europe against future aggression either from France or from Russia, is preserved unimpaired. Nor are these advantages purchased by any subserviency to France, derogatory to the dignity of Great Britain. On the contrary, it may safely be affirmed, that there never was a period when England exercised so great an influence over the councils of France, as she does at present, nor when the French Sovereign paid so great a deference to the King of Great Britain.

Viscount Palmerston, therefore, humbly trusts that, if he and his colleagues are anxious under present circumstances to cultivate the best understanding with France, Your Majesty will not suppose that it arises from any blind and unreflecting confidence on their part. But they believe, that at the present moment the French Government are conscious that the friendship of England is of the utmost value to them, and its forbearance and neutrality in the event of war absolutely necessary for their existence. Your Majesty's Servants are therefore desirous of taking advantage of this peculiar posture of affairs, and, without abating any of that circumspection which prudence may dictate, they would wish not to repulse the friendly demonstrations of the French Government by any outward shew of coldness or distrust and they are not without hopes, that by continuing to keep even the balance of power, by a due application of the moral influence of Great Britain, Your Majesty may still be enabled to enjoy the satisfaction of preserving the peace of Europe.

(iv)

Foreign Office, 12 *April*, 1834.

Viscount Palmerston presents his humble duty to your Majesty and has the honor to submit, that he has felt it his duty to bring under the serious consideration of his colleagues in the Cabinet, the note[1] from the Marquis de Miraflores, which he has recently had the honor of

[1] Dated 10 April, 1834.

laying before Your Majesty and the verbal communications which he has received upon the same subject, from the Marquis himself and from M. de Sarmento.

It appears as the result of these verbal and written communications, and this result is further confirmed by various despatches recently received from Mr. Villiers and Lord Howard de Walden, that the Governments of Portugal and Spain are agreed upon the necessity of a joint military operation in Portugal; that the Spanish Government would wish to confine that operation to the expulsion of Don Carlos, and wants to send its troops into Portugal without any formal engagement previously contracted with Portugal; that the Portuguese Government requires a previous convention, as a security for the future retirement of the Spanish troops, and insists that the action of these troops shall be directed to Portuguese as well as to Spanish objects, the expulsion of Don Miguel as well as of Don Carlos. But both the Spanish and the Portuguese Governments concur in one thing; they are both equally anxious that Your Majesty should be a party to the arrangement by which their joint operation is to take effect.

Spain solicits this upon the ground that Your Majesty, by concurring, might impose upon Don Pedro conditions as to amnesty, which Spain alone could not exact, but which are necessary for that future tranquillity of Portugal, which it is so important for Spain to see established. She also fears, that if she were, singly and uncountenanced by any other Power, to undertake operations against Don Miguel, she should draw down upon herself the resentment of Austria, which resentment might be injuriously felt through the agency of the Court of Rome acting upon the priesthood of Spain; while on the other hand, if she were supported by the sanction of Great Britain, she would be indifferent as to the displeasure of other Powers.

Portugal on the other hand, is most anxious for the concurrence of Your Majesty, because she feels jealous of the entrance of Spanish troops into her territory, unless under the controul of engagements to which Your Majesty should be a party; for she looks to Great Britain as her trusty friend and as the Power bound by ancient treaties to watch over and to defend her independence.

It appears, moreover, that if Spanish troops are to enter the territory of Portugal, it is most consistent with the dignity and most fitting the engagements and obligations of Your Majesty's Crown, that their entrance should be preceded by a convention, recording that they enter with the free consent of the Sovereign of Portugal, stipulating what shall be the purpose for which they go in, and declaring beforehand when they shall withdraw, and that this convention should be one to which Your Majesty should be a party.

Your Majesty's Servants having given their most serious attention to all these considerations, convinced that a speedy termination of the civil war in Portugal is the only foundation upon which the tranquillity of the Peninsula can be established, sensible that Great Britain has no right to object to the entrance of Spanish troops into Portugal upon the invitation of the legitimate Sovereign of that country, and has no power to prevent it except by sending thither British troops instead, conscious that the treaties between the British and Portuguese Crowns oblige this country to defend the independence of Portugal, and that therefore Your Majesty might hereafter be called upon inconveniently to interfere, if, after the Spanish troops were in Portugal, any dispute were to arise between the Spanish and Portuguese Governments as to their conduct or their continued stay, upon all these grounds, Your Majesty's Servants have come to the opinion, that it is expedient that a convention should be concluded between Spain and Portugal, and that Your Majesty should be a party thereto.

But it would scarcely be consistent with the power and position of Great Britain, or with the influence which she ought to retain in Portugal, that the operations in that country, which it would be the object of such a convention to regulate, should be exclusively carried on by a Spanish cooperation, and it is therefore the opinion of Your Majesty's Servants, that the convention should stipulate a naval cooperation on Your Majesty's part.

But when Your Majesty affords your countenance and cooperation to measures which can scarcely fail to be effectual for ridding the Portuguese territory of Don Miguel and the civil war which his presence keeps alive, Your Majesty is justly entitled to require from the Portuguese Government a sufficient provision for Don Miguel as a Prince of the House of Braganza, and pardon for those Portuguese subjects who have hitherto followed his banner; and the proposed convention ought to contain on the part of the Portuguese Government stipulations to this effect.

The position of France with respect to Portugal is essentially different from that of Great Britain. France is to Portugal at present a friendly Power, but is bound to her by no special engagements; Great Britain is to Portugal as it were a trustee for her estate. The same reasons, therefore, which render it almost necessary that Great Britain should be a party to this convention, do not apply to France.

Nevertheless it is the opinion which Your Majesty's Servants are most humbly led to entertain, and to submit for Your Majesty's consideration, that it would, for more reasons than one be desireable to connect France in some way or other with this transaction.

In the first place the moral effect of the convention would be greater, if it is signed by the four Powers than if it signed only by the three, and Your Majesty's servants are not without some hope that the moral effect, which will be produced by the promulgation of such a convention as that which is suggested, may in a great degree render unnecessary the employment of the physical force for which it would provide.

In the next place, so much pains have been taken of late by the agents of Russia, Austria and Prussia, to spread reports of disunion between Great Britain and France, and those reports, if credited, are likely to be so prejudicial to the policy of Your Majesty's Government in many matters, but more especially with reference to the affairs of the Levant, that it would be desireable to give those reports some public and practical contradiction. But the association of France with Great Britain, Spain, and Portugal in such a convention as that in question, would be such a contradiction, whereas her exclusion from such a convention would not fail to give much credit to the reports of growing disunion.

But, lastly, it is always advantageous, considering the rapid changes of men in the councils of France, to obtain by the binding engagement of treaty, some controul over the conduct of her Government more permanent and secure than what arises from the personal character of the individual who may at any given time be in office.

For all these reasons it appears to Your Majesty's Servants that it would be desireable to invite the accession of France to any such convention, and to propose to her to stipulate, that she will, *if called upon by the other three contracting parties*, give such aid towards the accomplishment of the objects of the convention, *as may then be agreed upon between her and her three allies.*

Such an accession would strengthen the alliance, while it tied up the hands of France.

Viscount Palmerston has accordingly prepared the draft of a convention for the above mentioned purposes, which, with the concurrence of his colleagues, he now most humbly submits for Your Majesty's gracious approval.... [Details of procedure and request for immediate signature.]

(v)

Foreign Office, 15 *April*, 1834.

Viscount Palmerston presents his humble duty to Your Majesty and has the honor of submitting to Your Majesty the draft of the proposed treaty such as it has been finally agreed to between himself, the French Ambassador, the Spanish and the Portuguese Ministers, subject to Your Majesty's gracious approval.

The substance of the treaty remains precisely the same as when Viscount Palmerston previously submitted it to Your Majesty, with the exception of a stipulation in favor of the Infant Don Carlos, which has been introduced, with the consent of the Marquis de Miraflores, in compliance with Your Majesty's desire.

Some slight changes of form have been made in parts of the treaty which Viscount Palmerston would humbly submit, have in some degree improved it. The accession of France has been introduced into the body of the treaty instead of being made by a subsequent act; this was done at the request of the Prince de Talleyrand and it had the advantage of giving more unity to the transaction.

The Prince de Talleyrand also expressed a strong wish that the treaty should mark distinctly that it was in consequence of the union between England and France rather than in consequence of any particular union between France, Spain and Portugal that France became a party to the treaty; and the wording has been altered so as to express this idea.

Viscount Palmerston would humbly submit that as a Frenchman he might perhaps have felt some hesitation as to a change, which instead of stating France to be spontaneously invited by the three other Powers jointly, represents Spain and Portugal as applying to her to join in the treaty, chiefly on the ground of the good understanding between her and England; but as an Englishman, Viscount Palmerston would submit to Your Majesty, that the proposed wording is, of the two, the most complimentary to this country. If Your Majesty should be pleased to approve of this draft, the treaty will immediately be prepared in conformity with it, and may be ready for signature on Thursday. The Spanish and Portuguese Ministers are delighted with the measure; and the Marquis de Miraflores in particular says he has only one regret upon the subject, and that is that he cannot himself have the pleasure of presenting the treaty with his own hands to his Government.

(vi)

Foreign Office, 20 *April*, 1834.

Viscount Palmerston presents his humble duty to Your Majesty and has the honor of reporting to Your Majesty that some difficulties have still arisen with respect to the Quadruple Treaty.

In consequence of the delay necessarily incident to a careful and as far as possible a literal translation of the original into the Spanish, Portuguese and French languages, the copies for signature had not been prepared yesterday, when at an early hour yesterday morning Viscount Palmerston received from Earl Granville the accompanying Note No. 1, and the altered Draft No. 2.[1]

Viscount Palmerston immediately wrote to the Prince de Talleyrand expressing his extreme regret at the difficulties which had thus unexpectedly sprung up, in a quarter where they were not looked for, pointed out the objections which he felt to the new proposal and requested the Prince to call on him in Stanhope Street.

The Prince came soon after twelve. Viscount Palmerston stated to him that it is the interest as well as the wish of Your Majesty's Government to avoid any thing which should unnecessarily tend to lower the French Government in the eyes of the French nation, and consequently, if as appeared from the Princes explanations, the French Government feared that to be mentioned in the latter part of the treaty would be considered by the public in France as derogatory, and that the national feeling would be gratified by a change of form in introducing the King of the French into the treaty, to such change of form Your Majesty's Government certainly could not object. But Viscount Palmerston said that the alteration proposed, was a change of substance as well as form. That the proposed addition to the Preamble as written in red ink, founded the accession of France upon recent applications made to her by Spain; that your Majesty's Government well knew that the only applications made to France by Spain, were for the assistance of French

---

[1] Not printed.

troops *in Spain*; that the British Government thought it very unwise in Monsieur de Zea to have made that application, and very prudent and proper in the French Government to have declined complying with it; that instead of recording and proclaiming that application in a treaty, it would be better to consign it to oblivion; but that Great Britain who disapproved of the application, and who would still advise Spain not to renew it, and France not to yield to it, never could sanction its principle by recording it in a treaty as the ground of French accession to such treaty. Prince Talleyrand in reply pointed out, that even if such a construction could fairly be put on the proposed Preamble, which he denied, the subsequent article 4 corrected the evil, since by that article France was to do nothing except in concert with her Allies.

Viscount Palmerston, however, said that right or wrong he saw in the proposed Preamble a meaning coupled with French interference in Spain and, if this impression struck his mind, it might very possibly occur also to other persons; that the whole object of the present treaty was a military operation by the Spaniards in Portugal, and no operation by any body in Spain; and that, for the reasons which he had assigned, he should positively refuse to sign the treaty with that passage in it.

After much discussion and some communications between Prince Talleyrand, Viscount Palmerston, and Your Majesty's other confidential Servants, with which it is not necessary to trouble Your Majesty, Prince Talleyrand agreed to such a change in the manner of introducing France into the treaty as appears in the altered copy No. 3.[1] . . .

[Discussion of drafting details].

(vii)

Stanhope St., 12 *June*, 1835.

Viscount Palmerston presents his humble duty to Your Majesty, and has had the honor on his return home tonight from the House of Commons, to receive Your Majesty's communication of today,[2] upon the subject of the selection of Colonel Evans to command the Corps about to be raised in this country for the service of the Queen of Spain, and he begs most humbly to submit to Your Majesty the following considerations on this matter; and in the first place with respect to the political opinions which Colonel Evans may entertain, Viscount Palmerston has no other knowledge of them than that which he has gathered from speeches made at elections, and in Parliament, but he would humbly submit for Your Majesty's consideration, that he is not aware that these opinions, though they may go to considerable lengths on some points, such as a ballot, suffrage and duration of Parliaments, have ever been otherwise than entirely consistent with an attachment and with loyalty to monarchy.

Experience moreover has frequently shewn that the real and settled opinions of men may often fall short of the speeches which they are

---

[1] Substantially as in the Treaty as signed.   [2] *B.P.*

led to make on the hustings, in the excitement of a contested election; or even of the language which they may hold in debates in the House of Commons, when striving to make themselves prominent, as leaders of the popular party.

Viscount Palmerston, therefore, would humbly submit, that (although he is far from agreeing with Colonel Evans on a variety of points) there is nothing, as far as he is aware, in the political tenets of that officer which should justly disqualify him from being employed in any military capacity for which his professional qualities might render him fit.

Viscount Palmerston would beg also to submit that it has been re-marked by all foreign Governments, and even by those who are most jealous of strangers, that British subjects, whatever may be their opinions, are scarcely ever found engaged in intrigues or cabals against the Governments of the countries in which they are residing, and there seems to be no reason to suppose that Colonel Evans would be an excep-tion to this rule.

Viscount Palmerston would further most humbly submit that the Spanish people are of all others the most jealous of strangers; that this jealousy has been shewn lately in a striking manner by the prejudice which has been created in Spain against the mission of Lord Eliot and Colonel Gurwood, that it is, therefore, essential that the officers who may be employed on the present occasion, should be men of Liberal opinions; because if they should be persons at all favourable to the cause of Don Carlos, or even lukewarm in that of the Queen, they would immediately be exposed to every kind of suspicion on the part of the officers of the Queen's army; and distrust and dissension would inevitably lead to failure.

It is also to be borne in mind that if it is desirable, as it undoubtedly is, that the Catholics of the South of Ireland should be induced to volunteer, it is necessary that the expedition should be commanded by persons in whom those Catholics may be disposed to place confidence, and whom they may be inclined to follow.

Viscount Palmerston would also beg humbly to submit that the contest in Portugal affords an instance very much in point. The politi-cal opinions of Admiral Napier are probably not very different from those of Colonel Evans (and in each case it may well be doubted whether those opinions are not as much a means as an end) but during the whole time that Admiral Napier was employed in Portugal, though he had political power, which Colonel Evans never can have in Spain, he never was found to exert his influence with a view to bringing his political opinions to bear upon the internal affairs of Portugal, but invariably confined himself, to his professional duties; or if he ever stepped beyond that line, did so, to assist your Majesty's Minister at Lisbon, and to support the Government of the Queen.

Viscount Palmerston therefore would humbly trust that considering the vast importance to England and to Europe of success in this war on the part of the Queen, considering how the national honor would be affected either by a failure in raising men, or by a miscarriage on the part of the Corps when raised, Your Majesty may be disposed not to disapprove of the choice which General Alava has made of Colonel Evans, and may be induced to sanction such facilities as may be useful towards giving the measure the best chances of success.

(viii)

Stanhope St., 10 *September*, 1836.

. . . Viscount Palmerston would also beg most humbly to submit that the expression "revolutionary proceedings"[1] is one which has of late been so much used by some of the Governments of Europe to describe indefinitely anything whether real or imaginary which is at variance with their own views and policy, that Viscount Palmerston would be reluctant to insert it in a despatch for which he was to become the responsible adviser of Your Majesty, unless it were accompanied by some explanation stating the precise nature of the proceedings to which that phrase was by anticipation applied, and shewing why those proceedings ought to call for a protest on the part of Your Majesty. For Viscount Palmerston would further most humbly submit to your Majesty, that the mere circumstance that proceedings in another country are revolutionary, has not been of itself considered a conclusive reason why your Majesty should protest against them, or even refuse to countenance them.

There could not be a proceeding more purely and strictly revolutionary than that which took place in Paris in July 1830, when by a popular insurrection the Royal troops were defeated, and the King together with his own family expelled from France, and another person was raised to the Throne by the tumultuous decree of the inhabitants of the capital; and yet Your Majesty by the advice of the then Ministers of the Crown, wisely given as Viscount Palmerston humbly ventures to think, was the first Sovereign in Europe to acknowledge the new King of the French; and the British Government by that immediate acknowledgement, and by the uninterrupted continuance of diplomatic relations with France, undoubtedly gave a direct countenance to the results of that revolutionary proceeding.

But, in truth, independently of the great political interests which at that time rendered such a decision urgently and immediately expedient, it would perhaps have been difficult for Your Majestys Servants to have assigned the revolutionary character of the events which had led to a change of dynasty in France, as a reason why that change should not be acknowledged by Your Majesty, seeing that in this country a similar

---

[1] In reply to the King's amendment of a despatch to Villiers, on the situation after the acceptance by the Queen Regent of the Constitution of 1812 at La Granja, as follows: "He never will consent to give his countenance, direct or indirect, to the revolutionary proceedings of any Government which the Queen Regent acting on behalf of her infant daughter may accept or which may be forced upon her, nor become a party to measures against the character of which it is his bounden duty to protest."

change brought about in a similar manner was the foundation of the title of the present Royal Dynasty, and is considered by all political parties as the epoch, from whence they date the real and practical liberties of the nation.

With regard to the dispatch itself Viscount Palmerston had humbly hoped that the passage to which he has already adverted would sufficiently announce to the Spanish Government that Your Majesty will not be a party to any proceedings inconsistent with Your Majesty's engagements, and incompatible with the honor and dignity of Your Majesty's Crown; and to go into further detail would rather weaken and limit than strengthen and amplify that declaration. On other points the draft contains observations which Viscount Palmerston thinks ought to be stated to the Spanish Government through the British Minister at Madrid, and which with a view to his own responsibility he is anxious to place upon record as having been so communicated to the Spanish Cabinet at the present crisis.

(ix)

Foreign Office, 21 *February*, 1837.

Viscount Palmerston presents his humble duty to Your Majesty and has had the honor of receiving Your Majesty's memorandum of the 19th instant,[1] in which Your Majesty observes that the matter to which the accompanying draft to Lord Howard[2] relates, is entirely a Portuguese concern, and therefore not one in which Your Majestys Government ought to interfere.

Viscount Palmerston in explanation begs humbly to submit that it has never been the practice of the Government of England, and more especially in its intercourse with the Government of Portugal, to consider it improper or unbecoming to offer advice and to express opinions upon matters even connected with internal affairs, with regard to which such advice or opinion might be thought to be useful to a friendly Government.

But in the present case Viscount Palmerston would humbly beg to submit that he proposes to do no more than he did some little time ago, with Your Majestys sanction, with regard to Spain.

General Sevane stated to Mr Villiers that in a certain contingency, a system of terror and of legal murder would be established in Spain, and Viscount Palmerston felt that it was due to the character and honor of Your Majestys Government that it should not be in the power of any man to say that so revolting a plan had been communicated to them, and that they had by their silence approved it. In the same manner Viscount Palmerston begs on the present occasion to submit to Your Majesty, that it would not be consistent with the character and honor of

[1] *B.P.*
[2] To Lord Howard de Walden, 18 Feb., 1837: *F.O. Portugal*, 460. The despatch protests against any attempt to suppress the insurgent bands in the Algarves by laying waste the countryside.

your Majesty's Government, that such a scheme as that to which the accompanying draft relates, should have been communicated to Your Majesty's Minister at Lisbon by the Portuguese Government and that Lord Howard should not have been instructed to express thereupon those sentiments of disapprobation which so barbarous and impolitic a plan must inspire in every impartial mind. To be silent would be to approve; and to approve would be in the highest degree reprehensible. Viscount Palmerston begs further to submit, that the tendering of the proposed opinion is not the sort of interference in the internal affairs of Portugal which Austria and Prussia and Russia are in the habit of exercising in the detailed administration, or in the constitutional arrangements of other countries, but that it stands on entirely different grounds. The measure in question is a military operation which the Portugueze Government propose to have recourse to, in furtherance of the objects of a treaty to which Great Britain is a party, and if that measure were executed, it is impossible that some part of the disgrace attending it should not be shared by the allies of Portugal.

(x)

Stanhope St., 2 *June*, 1837.

Viscount Palmerston presents his humble duty to Your Majesty and has had the honor of receiving this evening Your Majesty's communication upon Sir Frederic Lamb's Despatch No. 44 of the 23rd May,[1] and he is much gratified to find that the opinion which Viscount Melbourne and himself had come to in a conversation on this subject and which Viscount Palmerston intended to submit for Your Majesty's consideration in the shape of a draft of a dispatch, has already received the sanction of your Majesty's immediate judgement.

Viscount Palmerston entirely subscribes to Your Majesty's opinion that it would be extremely inexpedient to act upon the suggestion of Prince Metternich, who proposes that the British Government should, through him, recommend to the Court of St. Petersburgh to establish a blockade of the coast of Circassia.

Such a course would, as Your Majesty most truly observes, be an abandonment at once of the whole of the Circassian question, which it is at least expedient to keep open, for this country to act upon as may be deemed advisable. Russia would, as Your Majesty observes, interpret such a recommendation, as a virtual acknowledgement of her claim of sovereignty; and she would take care to let the Circassians know that in attempting their subjugation she was advised and encouraged by England.

Viscount Palmerston in his reserved despatch[2] to the Earl of Durham which he shewed to Count Pozzo di Borgo, in alluding to a blockade as a measure which was more applicable than municipal regulations, to the existing relations between Russia and Circassia, took care to throw in

---

[1] *F.O. Austria*, 265.
[2] To Durham, 19 April, 1837: *F.O. Russia*, 231.

precautionary words, stating that "with such a blockade foreign Powers would deal as they might think proper"; intending thereby to intimate to Russia that it did not follow as a mere matter of course, that such a blockade *would* at once be acknowledged by England. But if the English Government were to advise the blockade, no doubt as to acknowledgement could possibly exist.

Again supposing the right of Russia to establish such a blockade to be clear, still the blockade must be effectual, in order to be legal; but if the English Government had counselled the blockade, it would be difficult to insist too strictly upon degrees of effectiveness.

Viscount Palmerston begs humbly to say, that he entirely concurs in the opinion that Your Majesty has expressed with respect to Prince Metternich. That statesman may or may not be, a wise and prudent Minister for Austria, according to Austrian interests; that is a question between him, and his Sovereign and his country; but it cannot be denied that Prince Metternich is a most frail support and a most dangerous ally for any foreign Power to trust to. His timid and temporizing character, his love of indirect ways of attaining his purpose, his habit of sacrificing future interests for the convenience of the moment, his proneness to side with the party he thinks the strongest, all these combine to render him an object of distrust rather than of confidence; and make it vain to speculate what his conduct would be in any given future contingency. No reasonable man can doubt that a partition of Turkey between Austria and Russia would be highly injurious to the interests of Austria; but he would be a bold prophet who would foresay that Prince Metternich would not consent to, and join in such a partition, rather than make war with Russia, in order to maintain the integrity of the Ottoman Empire.

With regard to the suggestion, which has often been made by others and which has recently been adverted to by Sir Frederic Lamb of sending a British fleet into the Black Sea, Viscount Palmerston would beg most humbly to suggest that there are many important considerations connected with such a proceeding, which would require to be well weighed before it was adopted. In the first place the fleet to be so sent, ought to be clearly stronger than the Russian fleet of 12 or 14 Sail of the Line stationed in the Black Sea; and it would require some land force on board, to be used in case of need, to occupy commanding batteries.

But in the next place such a step would of course be considered by Russia as a threat; she would therefore immediately call upon Turkey to close the Dardanelles under the Treaty of Unkiar Skelessi; and to allow a Russian land force to occupy the batteries on one side at least; and this might lead to a military occupation of Turkey by Russia, before Turkey has sufficiently recovered from her late wars to be able to resist by her own means, and while Austria under the councils of Prince Metternich would not dare to do more than protest against such a proceeding.

But further the entrance of a British Squadron by force into the

Black Sea, as a menace against Russia, would justify the Emperor in sending his 29 or 30 Sail of the Line from the Baltic, upon a similar errand to the coast of England; and the position of this country during the interval that would elapse before an equal force could be got together would not be one in which it would be desirable to place Great Britain.

Viscount Palmerston would, therefore, humbly submit, that the forcible entrance of a strong British fleet into the Black Sea, would be a proper and advisable step, as a first and a preliminary measure of war against Russia, and might in such a case obtain advantages of position for this country; but that such a step would not be expedient unless it were simultaneously accompanied by a very large naval armament at home. And Viscount Palmerston would beg further to submit, that in order to obtain from Parliament the considerable funds which would be necessary for a naval armament on so large a scale, it would be requisite to shew that some very great and important national interest was directly at stake.

APPENDIX B

CORRESPONDENCE BETWEEN PALMERSTON AND GREY, 1831–1833[1]

(a) LETTERS FROM PALMERSTON TO GREY

(i)

Stanhope St., 1 *February*, 1831.

[Talleyrand suggested, "in terms sufficiently plain not to be mistaken that we should agree to Nemours becoming King of Belgium."] To this I at once replied that it was impossible we could agree to any such thing; that we looked upon Nemours on the throne of Belgium as tantamount to the union of Belgium with France and, as we could not agree to the one, so neither could we to the other; that I was quite sure the other Powers of Europe would see the matter in the same point of view and that my personal opinion was that the acceptance of the crown for Nemours would produce a general war in Europe and it was for the Government and King of France to consider whether any possible advantage they could gain by the former would be an equivalent for the almost certain dangers which, to them at least, (let the nation face as it might) the latter would bring with it; that Sebastiani himself had said in his speech the other day, that even in war it is well to have right on ones side, but that in this case France would be violating the spirit, if not the letter, of those treaties, the promise to observe which was the condition upon which Louis Philippe obtained the recognition of Europe, and would be manifestly departing from all the recent pledges upon the very matter itself; that I could hardly think that he, Talleyrand, could press a point so entirely inconsistent with the engagements which he had recently entered into, nor that the King would expose himself to such an imputation as this would cast upon his good-faith; that by a recent Protocol the five Powers had renounced all exclusive influence and separate advantage to be derived from the arrangements to be made for Belgium and that, if the placing a son of the King of the French on the throne of Belgium was not precluded by this renunciation, I was at a loss to see the meaning of those words. I said that if there could be any doubt as to the fair meaning of those words or as to the intentions of the King, which I would not believe, I should propose in the conference about to take place a Protocol, to the same effect as a passage in that of the 22nd March, 1829 about Greece, by which the three Courts, who were engaged in the settlement of

<hr>

[1] From the Broadlands Papers. Palmerston's letters begin "My dear Lord Grey" and end "Yours sincerely"; those of Grey begin "My dear Palmerston" and end "Ever Yours".

Greece, agreed that the Sovereign should not be taken from any of their respective royal families. Talleyrand let drop his proposition, alleging, however, that there would be a wide difference between positive union and the election of Nemours, as it was not to be supposed that the King, who is so attached to his family, would think of dethroning his own son.

He said my proposition was new and he would write this night for instructions about it; he had no doubt he should be authorized to agree to it, but could not do so without specific instructions, but he thought that if he agreed to this, we ought to agree entirely to give up the Prince of Orange whose election would bring civil war to their doors. I said I thought this was the moment for such an engagement while the election was not yet made rather than the time when it should actually have taken place and that, if the King and the Government wanted strength to resist the party which might urge them to accept the offer, I was tendering to them the best argument they could wish for a fresh and incompatible engagement; that as to the P. of Orange we had done nothing but express our wishes for him in concurrence with Talleyrand, founded upon the notion that his was the most numerous party, and that I much doubted whether civil war would not be the certain consequence of any other choice but him.

Talleyrand again wanted to return to the subject of Philippeville and Marienburg, but I declined opening a question already disposed of. He begged me not to make any proposition to the conference as it might produce *dissentiment*; I told him that I could not help doing so, but that it would be for the conference to dispose of it. . . .

(ii)

Stanhope St., 12 *August*, 1831.

Bulow has just told me in confidence that having arrived for our conference early, and found only Talleyrand come, the latter immediately began upon Belgium, told him that Belgium could not go on upon the present footing; that Leopold had proved himself a poor creature unfit for a throne, and that the Belgians have shewn themselves unworthy of independence; that if the French troops were to retire Perrier's [sic] administration would fall, and, if they do not, your Government could not stand. That some new arrangement therefore must be tried, and the only good one is a *partition of the country*. That Holland would be for it, and if Prussia united with France and Holland there could be no effectual resistance, especially if public opinion in England was reconciled by making Antwerp a free port.

Bulow said he supposed France meant to have the lion's share and wished to know what was to fall to the lot of Prussia. Talleyrand said all that could be easily settled—and their conversation was interrupted by the arrival of the other Ministers.

Bulow's notion is, that this move of the Dutch has been planned between Talleyrand and Falck, who have been much together since the latter has removed to Portland Place, and that Russia has not discouraged it, partly wishing to help Holland to a share of Belgium, and partly thinking that war in the West would leave her elbow room in the East.

I send you a note from Melbourne[1] confirming Bulow's statement as to the views of France, and the papers say that the French Government is collecting another corps as a reserve for Gerard.

(iii)

Foreign Office, 27 *December*, 1831.

I saw Goblet yesterday evening and found from him that by the last of a succession of different instructions, he was desired not to exchange ratifications till further orders. I told him what we had settled in Cabinet and said I would write to Granville and to Leopold and see Talleyrand. I send you a draft of a dispatch to Granville, and I have written privately to him and to Leopold. To-day I have seen Talleyrand and told him that the Cabinet felt that they could not agree to any change in the stipulations of the convention. Our conversation was very calm on both sides, excepting a little warmth on his part when, in reply to a regret that his communications appeared to have added to the excitement at Paris, he assured me fervently that he had invariably tried to quiet his friends there upon this question and would continue to omit no efforts to do so. We went over the well known arguments on both sides and he ended by asking me what he should write to his Government. I said I concluded he would report that which I had told him as to the opinion of the Cabinet and that I wished him to add such of my arguments as he might think likely to have any weight with his Government; that I begged him to entreat his Government to consider that this question was important or trifling just as they chose to consider and to make it; that, if they chose to create an excitement about it, they as a Government leading the way on such a matter might undoubtedly succeed in doing so; but that if they chose to treat it as a trifle, which in fact it is, we should probably hear very little about it.

He said that what they dwelt upon most was the notion that this convention is a revival of the Holy Alliance. I pointed out all the absurdity of such an idea and he begged me to write to Granville to tell Sebastiani that he had urged that point, and that I had laughed at him for pressing it.

I then requested him to point out to the attention of his Government how foolish it would be to quarrel with us on such a matter as this, when there are so many important affairs pending in question, upon which cordiality and good understanding between France and England are so important for the attainment of objects which interest both. We parted very good friends after discussing several other subjects and my impression is that this little storm will subside. He did not even mention that he has any communication to make on this subject to the con-

[1] Missing.

ference and if he has received any I have no doubt he will do on this occasion, as he has on similar ones, and abstain from acting up to instructions, which a change of circumstances, or his nearer view of things here, may lead him to think it is better to postpone.

(iv)

Stanhope St., 3 *August*, 1832.

I have just received this[1] from the King. With respect to his first objection, that can very easily be removed by acting upon the suggestion contained in your note[2] of yesterday and making our communication to Austria and Prussia as well as to all the other German Courts with which we have relations.

With regard to his difficulty in doing anything as King of England which is not consistent with what he has done as King of Hanover, the answer is, that if the politics of the two countries are to be thus bound together, England being the most powerful and important is entitled to lead Hanover, and not Hanover to lead England; that if the English Government is to be tied by that which the Hanoverian has done, they ought to be previously consulted, and to have a voice in the deliberation. But neither you nor I could venture to tell Parliament that the European policy of England must be shackled and governed by decisions taken by the Hanoverian Cabinet without our knowledge or concurrence.

Such a doctrine would go further than anything else to shake the root of the Hanoverian family in this country.

With regard to the matter itself the real truth is, that the Resolutions of the Diet to which the constitutional Sovereigns have assented, are nearly as inconsistent with the German constitutions as the proceedings of Charles 10th or James 2nd were with those of France and England, and if carried into full execution may produce in Germany consequences similar to those which followed the errors of those monarchs.

I do not see how the English Government can avoid communicating to its allies its opinions and its fears as to the present menacing state of affairs in Europe.

(v)

Stanhope St., 8 *October*, 1833.

Your demur about presenting our protest at Petersburg disturbs and embarrasses me greatly, for I had so entirely considered that this was part of our original decision as to the presentation of the protest, that I have never imagined that any doubt could arise upon the subject; and the last passage in the despatch to Ponsonby of the 7th Aug.[3] distinctly announces our intention of presenting the protest at Petersburgh.

I can quite understand that Madame de Lieven should wish to persuade us not to do so, because not only as a general principle is it,

[1] From William IV, 3 Aug., 1832: B.P.   [2] *B.P.*
[3] *F.O. Turkey*, 220.

under present circumstances, her great object as Russian Ambassadress to paralize us, and to keep the English Government in a state of inaction and nullity, but as we know from Berlin, the presentation of this protest at Constantinople has much annoyed the Imperial Government and staggered them, and it would be a great coup, if the Lievens could persuade us *not* to present the protest at Petersburgh, and thereby could render entirely vain, or still worse than vain, the step we have taken at Constantinople.

I say worse than vain, because I must say, that if, knowing as we do, that the treaty against which we have protested, was forced by Russia upon Turkey, and it being manifest from the nature of the engagement, that the acts which we wish to prevent (and to prevent which in certain cases we are sending ships to the Mediterranean) are to be committed by Russia, and not by Turkey, I must say that, if under these circumstances we should hold a high tone to Turkey, the weaker Power and the tool, and not dare even to whisper our dissatisfaction to Russia, the stronger Power and the plotter, it would have been far better for our national honor, and not less useful towards the accomplishment of our objects, to have held our tongue to Turkey as well as to Russia. If we were to quail before Russia on the question of protest, and fear to risk with her a contest of words and notes, who would ever believe that we should venture to face her in a contest of a more serious kind? We should lose caste in Europe, and Russia would henceforth treat England as a Power from whom no serious resistance need ever be apprehended. She would be mistaken, but the error into which we should lead her might inspire her with a dangerous presumption; and she might be tempted by her reliance on our acquiescence, to do things, which, when done, we could not submit to; and thus our desire not to give offence to Nicholas, might draw us into a situation in which public opinion would force us to go to war with him.

I confess I cannot see any advantage in waiting for the despatch which Mme de Lieven expects from Nesselrode before he leaves Berlin. That despatch may probably contain nothing about Turkish affairs, but if it does, it *can* contain nothing which ought to make us abstain from presenting our protest; and if our protest *is* to be presented, there would be great advantage and convenience in presenting it *before* Russia has offered us her explanations, rather than delaying it till afterwards. In the one case the explanations are the answer to the protest, in the other the protest is the answer to the explanations; and in the second case, it might become necessary to go into a controversial correspondence, and not to give the same simple protest which we gave at Constantinople; whereas, if we have given in our protest before the explanations arrive, we might answer them more shortly, referring to the protest already given in.

I do not know what I shall say to the King on this subject tomorrow if he asks me about it, nor how I can account to the French Government for our apparent hesitation.

(vi)

Stanhope St., 23 *November*, 1833.

It is a saying of old that trouble is inseparable from power, and certainly the King's correspondence with us verifies the maxim.

The main object of this letter[1] seems to be to show that Governments, not being members of the Confederation, have no right to meddle with the deliberation of the Diet; and to shew that the German Confederation is exactly similar to the Swiss.

As to the first point, we do not contemplate any interference, but reserve ourselves to watch the progress of events. As to the second, the difference between the two Confederations is manifest and great. Swisserland is like the United States of N. America, an aggregation of independent elements, politically known to other Powers only in its united mass, and, however divided in its internal jurisdiction, acting externally upon all occasions but as one body. Its aggregate character was, indeed, by the Treaty of Vienna made the condition of its acknowledged political existence.

The German Confederation on the contrary is a treaty of union for certain purposes, entered into voluntarily by a number of previously existing states, who have all a separate existence among the Powers of Europe, who have each a separate policy of their own, who may take different courses in peace and war, and whose sovereigns hold their crowns independently of the general compact.

I explained indeed all this with some care to Ompteda before he went and pointed out to him, that the Act of Confederation was nothing more than a treaty voluntarily entered into by a number of independent states; that if any one state was unable, by the refusal of its legislature to vote supplies, to fulfil the obligation it has entered into towards the rest, of furnishing a contingent of men and money to the common stock, the other Confederates would undoubtedly have a right of war against the defaulting state, in order to compel it to make good its treaty engagement. But that in such a case the forcible action of the Confederates against the contumacious member would be *war*; war namely between independent states, and not civil war between a sovereign Power and its subjects; and that it is quite untenable to say that such a war having begun, other Governments, not members of the League, have not a perfect right to espouse the quarrel of the single state, if they should think it their interest to do so. This is nearly the case contemplated by the triple declaration launched at France,[2] and it would not be difficult to prove, that if the quarrels between the members of the Confederation should lead to an appeal to arms, France would have as good a right to take part in that war, as in any other.

[1] From Sir H. Taylor, 22 Nov., 1833: *B.P.* A long defence of the King's view of the approaching conference of German states at Vienna.

[2] See page 363.

(b) Letters from Grey to Palmerston

(i)

Downing St., 22 *January*, 1831.

These dispatches strengthen the impression under which I woke this morning; and I come more and more to the opinion that we ought now to take no further part in the election of the sovereign, than that of representing amicably the circumstances which, in any particular case, might render the choice of a sovereign, to whom they might apply, objectionable.

When the representation came from Lord Ponsonby, of the increasing strength of the party of the P. of Orange, and of the means which he thought might be effectual in making it prevail, I consented to the measure of the proclamation, and concurred in passing it; but I did this, meaning to confine myself distinctly to such measures only as might afford the Prince a chance of success by an appeal to the people without any other interference on our part.

Now Lord Ponsonby's dispatches lead to measures of a very different description; to concert with the Orange party, for the overthrow of the present Government, at the risk of a civil war, in which we should be implicated as being parties to the measures which had produced it.

Than this nothing, in my opinion, could be more indefensible or more fatal. I think it therefore very necessary to explain to Lord Ponsonby, without delay, to what extent and on what principle we, in concurrence with the conference, had sanctioned the proclamation of the Prince, with a positive instruction to abstain from any measures, either direct or indirect, which might have the effect of instigating his party, under an assurance of our support, to attack the Government.

I have written hastily and perhaps indistinctly but I think you will be able to understand the sort of alarm which these dispatches have created in me.

A further inducement not to take any further or more active measures in this business of the P. of Orange, is the obstinate determination of his Father to resist to all extremity any proposal for settling the crown of the Netherlands on any head but his own.

(ii)

Downing Street, 21 *May*, 1831.

I have just read the Protocol[1] which has been agreed upon today, and I must say that I am a good deal disturbed by it.

The alternative you had before you was, either to adhere strictly to what you had determined upon by the last Protocol or to afford possibilities for an arrangement with the Belgians, according to the representations of Lord Ponsonby.

---

[1] Protocol No. 24, 21 May, 1831, *B.F.S.P.*, XVII, 798.

You seem to me to have done neither the one or the other.

You show in your preamble a disposition to give up something of what you had insisted upon; but, when you proceeded to state distinctly the propositions that are to be made by Lord Ponsonby, you put forward, in the first place, the necessity of adhering to the bases of the separation between Holland and Belgium in a manner that will provoke immediate opposition, and then state the inducements which are held out to engage them to acquiesce with so little certainty and decision as must necessarily expose them to criticism.

I fear, therefore, that you will not have advanced a step by the present proceeding, more especially if, as I greatly fear, King Leopold cannot be persuaded to authorise Ponsonby to say that he will accept the sovereignty on the terms you now propose.

I had hoped that the terms, as they were shaped in the paper, which Lord Ponsonby brought back from Claremont[1] would have been adopted clearly and explicitly in the Protocol, and I do not understand why they were not.

This is a matter of vital importance, the question of peace or war depends upon it; and I could not take upon myself the responsibility of a measure inviting this dreadful alternative, without the sanction of the Cabinet.

(iii)

East Sheen, 3 *September*, 1831.

That we have a right to insist on the immediate evacuation of Belgium by the French is undeniable. The question is whether it is advisable to rest immediately upon the right, or to wait, without showing timidity, or altering our tone, or doing one thing that would bear the character of fear and hesitation, to see what France will do upon the very clear and distinct intimation which has been given to her, that we cannot consent to any portion of her army remaining in Belgium, before we press its retreat in a peremptory tone, which might offend her national pride, and produce a resistance, which patience and management might prevent. It would give us time too to get Leopold, if it be possible, to assist us by desiring that the French troops should retire; whilst on the contrary, if he persists in requiring their presence as security to his safety, it will give a plausible pretext to the French, which will have the greatest effect here, as be assured the prevalent feeling of an infinite majority of the publick is strongly in favour of peace. If we suffer ourselves to be urged by a partial clamour into measures that may produce a war, we shall soon be convinced to our cost, that we have greatly miscalculated the support we are likely to meet with. I must add that I have a great distrust of the Ministers of the three Powers. I have seen, on more than one occasion, great reason to suspect their good faith. Some of them would not be sorry to see a war break out, from which they may expect advantage; and more than one of them I suspect

[1] The residence of Leopold.

is in communication with the Duke of Wellington and Aberdeen. I hope you will take care to let them know that, if a war takes place, they must be prepared to carry it on with their own resources, that we can act only by sea and that they must expect neither subsidies nor pecuniary assistance of any kind from this Country.

I retain, therefore, the opinion I expressed before, that, having stated in the most unequivocal terms our sense of the engagements into which France has entered with the Allied Powers, and our claim to the faithful performance of them, we should wait a short time, and see the effect of these representations before we take a step, which neither policy nor reason seems to me to require, and which might at once put an end to all amicable negociations.

I think we have the right to take a lead in these discussions, and to require of the other Powers an acquiescence in this course, which I again say is no departure from what either the general interest or our national character requires, which shows no want of firmness and determination, but is merely determined by the prudence, which would not precipitate matters into a hostile disaster, while there is yet room for amicable negociation.

I am to be with the King at three tomorrow, and will be in town by one; at which hour you had better summon the Cabinet.

I have only had time to read your letter being unwilling to detain your messenger, but I shall be prepared, after having carefully read the contents of all the boxes you have sent, to discuss these matters fully with you tomorrow.

(iv)

East Sheen, 29 *September*, 1831.

I see there is a Cabinet announced for to-day, but with a view to what subject, I am not informed.

Upon Belgium I think your opinion and mine certainly agree. An equitable arrangement between the parties, a good frontier of Holland, including Maestricht, and as much security as can be obtained for the new State of Belgium, founded on fair territorial arrangements and the establishment of a state of neutrality, are the principles upon which the settlement of this long depending [sic] question must be effected. With this view I entirely approve of your project. Can you mean when you say that Austria, Prussia, and Russia are becoming the partisans of Holland, that they think such an arrangement would not be sufficiently favourable to that Power? If they do, I think they should be told at once and without circumlocution that we cannot agree with them, and that, if they involve themselves in a dispute with France on such grounds, we cannot support them.

I am very glad that you have proposed an extension of the Armistice to the 10th of November. I hope the conference will support you in this demand, and urge it in a tone that will command obedience. If not, I think they should be told that we will resist any new attack, as an

act of hostility committed against us. Have you seen the Dutch
Ministers separately? They ought to be made to feel that we are disposed and determined to do everything that can be fairly required of us
for the advantage of Holland and for the security of the general peace,
both of which may be endangered by their taking measures, which we
feel ourselves compelled to resist.

[Lord] Holland has of course shown you Palmella's letter. It is ably
written and contains much powerful argument. But I find it difficult
to make up my mind to take a decided measure to overthrow a Government established de facto, and which is submitted to by the people.
It is a most embarrassing question, and at all events one on which I
think it would not be prudent to take any decided step, till we see
whether we are to retain the power of conducting to a conclusion the
measures, which we may think it right to adopt.

(v)

East Sheen, 8 *November*, 1831.

I now return the draft of your dispatch to Lord Heytesbury.[1] I have
not had so much time as I could have wished for the consideration of so
important a matter, but we shall probably have to revert to it, after you
have had Lieven's instructions communicated to you. In the meantime
I have marked such alterations as I think might be advisable in the
draft. They are dictated chiefly by a desire to avoid as much as
possible anything that might be felt to be offensive by Russia, and that
might commit us too much on a question, which, if Russia should
resist, approved as no doubt she would be by Austria and Prussia, we
should not have the power of enforcing.

It seems to me too, that, after having suffered the Poles to be subdued
without any interference, we should not carry publick opinion with us,
if we were to get into a quarrel about the intended modification of the
constitution. Experience has shown that the constitution has not been
much respected, nor is it probable that it would be more so, even if we
could get it formally re-acknowledged and established; nor do I know
that the changes, as described by Lord Heytesbury are much to the
disadvantage of Poland. Perhaps the Provincial Assemblies, which are
working very well in the Russian Provinces, would at present be better
suited than the Diet to the state of the people, and might lead hereafter
to a better system of representation.

What Lord Heytesbury says of the vague provisions of the Treaty of
Vienna is admirable. It would be difficult to make out a clear case
upon them, and, upon the whole, I am persuaded that it would be our best
course to satisfy ourselves with friendly representations made in such a
manner as to prevent an offensive answer.

[P.S.] The dispatch will want a new conclusion.

[1] To Heytesbury, 23 Nov., 1831: *F.O. Russia*, 190.

(vi)

East Sheen, 25 *December*, 1831.

The Hollands lingered here so long after breakfast, that I was prevented sending back your messenger as soon as I wished. The delay, however, can be of no consequence.

The difficulty about the two fortresses,[1] if, confined to that point alone, it had led to a serious dispute, would have been almost ridiculous; and if it had occurred, whilst an alteration was yet practicable, one would have been inclined to do much to prevent it.

The more general objection now taken by Sebastiani is of a very different character, and entirely supersedes this minor question. It is in direct contradiction to the previous proceedings of the conference in the course of these negociations, and I am quite aware, even if we could have temporised upon it, that the other Powers would not have consented to give up a point, on which all right is clearly against France. I quite agree with you, therefore, that to retract is now impossible.

Seeing however, the very embarrassing and even dangerous consequences, which may ensue, I was and am anxious, that this matter, which has never been distinctly brought before the Cabinet, should now be submitted to their consideration; and I do not foresee any additional difficulty from the delaying the exchange of the ratifications, if the Belgian Ministers are still ready to exchange them, till five o'clock to-morrow.

I may, perhaps, regret that the treaty respecting the fortresses had not been postponed, till that of the separation was ratified; but I know the difficulties that were offered to this course.

Be this as it may, we have now only to look forward. I sincerely hope with you that this may prove to have been no more than a bluster on the part of the French Government and that it will blow over, when all hope of success has failed. But the events may disappoint our expectations, and the wolf which has been so often the cause of a false alarm, may at last come in earnest. All the accounts from Paris, and none more than the secret bulletin which I have read this morning, shew the insecurity of the present Government, and it is not at all impossible that Perrier and Sebastiani may, if they remain Ministers, take the desperate course of risking a war on grounds, which they might expect to be popular, or that they may avail themselves of what they might think a favourable opportunity of quitting office, to escape from the difficulties or dangers which surround them.

We should be, in either case, "dans notre droit". But I cannot conceal from myself that, if the negociations should break off and war ensue, we should be exposed to very severe attacks, in which plausible grounds would not be wanting; and that a war for the sake of maintaining the Belgian fortresses, for so it would be represented, would not be likely to have the support of publick opinion.

[1] Philippeville and Marienbourg.

This does not alter my view of the necessity of the case, but it renders it indispensable that we should have the full concurrence of the Cabinet in all the measures we are taking.

(vii)

Downing St., 21 *February*, 1832.

. . . I do not think we have much to fear on the subject of Algiers. To be sure if the French could establish a secure dominion to the extent mentioned, it would not be pleasant. But what chance is there of this? It can only be done, if it can be done, after a period of many years and at an immense expense of blood and money. There seems at present to be no chance of their being able to reconcile the native tribes, and if a war with this country should take place, before their dominion is established, all supplies from France being cut off, their army would probably have to capitulate. We have this hold over them on the one hand, if on the other this enterprise gives them the means of diverting the restless spirits, with which France abounds, to the purpose of acquiring a territory which may eventually be of advantage to them.

If you have no engagement that you can shew, it would be in vain to plead it; and at all events it is not probable that this Government would feel itself bound by what had been done by Polignac, unless it was of the most clear and specifick character. . . .

(viii)

Downing Street, 26 *May*, 1832.

The accounts we had before, confirmed by Lamb's assertion that he knew that such a project had been in contemplation some time ago, certainly gives a great air of probability to the scheme of establishing a single Republick in Switzerland.

Upon an attempt to carry such a scheme into effect, our natural and obvious policy would be to leave it to the people themselves, and not to interfere. This, from the influence it may have on the general system of European policy, cannot be done absolutely. But still we must bear in mind the necessity of keeping ourselves in such a situation as not to become parties in any questions that may arise.

My opinion, therefore, is that we should agree to make the representation to the Swiss States of the danger to which such a change in the present system of Confederation may expose them, as has been desired by the Ministers whom you saw yesterday, but separately, and not in conjunction with them, tho' you would of course communicate to them what you do. I think this the best course. It would be equally effectual for the purpose; and would save us from the danger of getting into a new conference, of which, I confess, I feel something like horror, and which you have reason to dread likewise.

But in whatever way we may determine to act, in the critical state into which things are getting in Switzerland, it is necessary that we should have an active and intelligent Minister there. I need not tell you that Mr Percy is far from being of this character, and it appears to me to be indispensable that he shall be recalled.

Whatever we may think right to say to France on this subject, should also I think be done in the same way, i.e. separately, but communicating to the others what we do. From Apponyi's dispatch moreover, it would appear that the French Government is disposed to do, what the other Courts wish, and has, indeed, given instructions to that effect to its Minister in Switzerland.

Ponsonby may go now at any time, and it seems better that there should be no further delay.

(ix)

Downing Street, 21 *July*, 1832.

Further consideration has confirmed me in the opinion which I expressed to you yesterday on the subject of this dispatch.[1] Whatever representations we may think fit to make respecting the late proceedings in the Diet, I think they should be made separately, as in the case of Switzerland, but with a confidential communication of them to the French Government.

I doubt the expediency however, and perhaps the right of interfering in a matter relating to the internal affairs of Germany in which the representatives of all the Governments at the Diet appear to agree, and the more particularly under the difficulty which would arise from the part taken by the King of Hanover.

But it does not appear to me that this objection would apply to a friendly and confidential exposition of our fears, that the measures may lead to consequences of a very dangerous nature to the peace of Europe, and of our conviction that the removal of the chances of war would be the most efficacious mode of putting a stop to the agitation which prevails in so many countries, and which must continue to prevail whilst hopes are entertained by those, whose object it is to excite discontent, that the renewal of hostilities may open a way to the accomplishment of their views. The most desirable thing of all, therefore, is to put an end to the Belgian dispute.

(x)

East Sheen, 31 *July*, 1832.

I have not been able to give so much time and attention to this dispatch[2] as the peculiar nature of the subject to which it relates, its extreme delicacy, and the dangers to which it may lead, would require: and I should like to see it again, if you are not too much pressed in

---

[1] The draft of the despatch of 7 September, 1832 to Prussia and Austria.
[2] See last note.

point of time, after you have remodelled it, if you think it right to do so, according to my suggestions.

I have used a good deal of freedom in the alterations which I have proposed; principally for the purpose of avoiding details, and confining the dispatch more to general views, which appears to me best in matters of this nature. It seems to me enough to point out generally the evil consequences which may result from the measures in contemplation, without entering into argumentation into the manner in which these consequences may take place, or the course that may be pursued both in producing and conducting the contest, if there should be one, between the Diet and the resisting members of the Confederation, or between individual Sovereigns, separate from the Diet, and their States; considering also the situation of the King, as King of Hanover, and the difficulties he may feel in consequence, it is also desireable to avoid entering into any speculations or discussions which are not absolutely required.

I have, however, some doubts, whether I may altogether have accurately conceived the view which you have taken of this matter; and I think the dispatch wants something to wind it up better at the conclusion.

It has also occurred to me that it may appear to encourage Bavaria, in some degree to resist, and that perhaps a friendly representation of this nature would be more properly made to the Courts of Berlin and Vienna; at all events instructions to this effect, in preparing which great care will be required, should, I think, be sent to our Ministers at these courts.

By the account in Durham's despatch, the interview between him and the Emperor appears to have been upon the whole, very satisfactory.

P.S. The more I think of the affair at Oporto, the less sanguine my hopes are in favour of D. Pedro.

(xi)

East Sheen, 3 *August*, 1832.

This is a very serious matter[1] and leads to very serious consequences; and it is necessary that we should come to a clear understanding with the King on the principles on which we are to act.

In one thing only he appears to be right. I think the instructions to Lord Erskine ought rather to have been addressed to our Minister at the Diet, or to our Ministers at Berlin and Vienna; and you may remember that I, at first, expressed some doubt upon this subject, and urged in my last note[2] the necessity of similar representations to Austria and Prussia.

But this is not much more than a matter of form; the question is as to the policy on which we are to act in regard to the proceedings of the Diet.

[1] See Palmerston's letter of the same date, p. 819.   [2] See No. (x) above.

In this view what you say as to the separate capacities of the King of England and the King of Hanover is quite unanswerable. Our conduct must be regulated by English principles and English interests, and we cannot be diverted from the line prescribed by these, because Hanover has taken a different course.

We expressly disclaim interference in matters which do not immediately concern us. But we are deeply interested in what may eventually affect the peace of Europe: and if we see the chief Powers of Germany engaging in measures which may lead to the most dangerous of all wars, a war of opinions, it surely is our duty as well as our right to offer, in the way of friendly counsel, the reasons which induce us to apprehend that such consequences may result from them.

It is in this view, and in this view only, as I understand them, that your instructions to Lord Erskine are framed, and the propriety of them, whether they are to be addressed to Munich or Vienna, must be maintained.

It is the more necessary that this should be clearly explained and understood, because there appears to reign throughout the King's letter, when he speaks of the [basis] of constitutional as opposed to monarchical Governments (a distinction by the way which it is rather odd that an English King should take), of Liberal principles as always revolutionary, and more especially of his disposition or rather his resolution to adhere to the *conservative* party, a spirit which indicates something more than the application of these feelings to German questions only.

It will be necessary therefore to send a well considered and full answer to this *manifesto*, for, to use the King's word, such it is. Nobody can do this better than you, and I shall be very glad to give you any assistance in my power in its construction, previous to its being laid before the Cabinet, which I think ought to be summoned for this purpose on Tuesday morning, that the answer may go the King with the full concurrence and sanction of the whole Administration.

This letter is evidently not the King's. Indeed he could not have written it: and though Taylor's opinions may be of this sort, I cannot help thinking that some more important person must have been consulted. Be this as it may, the question is brought to a point, that obliges us to come to a clear understanding as to the principles on which we are to act. I write in great haste that you may get this to-night. Pray consult Althorp on this subject.

(xii)

Howick, 26 *August*, 1832.

The packet with your letters, and the draft of your intended dispatch to Sir F. Lamb[1] reached me just as I was leaving Lowther Castle, but not in time for me to send an answer by the return of post.

As any instructions to Sir F. Lamb have been so long delayed it has lately more than once occurred to me that it might be as well perhaps

[1] 7 Sept., 1832: *F.O. Austria* ,233

to suspend them till the proceedings of the Diet had assumed a more decisive form, and appeared to be tending to immediate measures of execution. This idea just arose from the thought that the Resolutions of the 28th of June might after all turn out to be a mere brutum fulmen and that they might not proceed further. Perhaps my wish was father to that thought, but, if, now or hereafter, the Diet should proceed in the course which they have begun under the dictate of Austria and Prussia, my opinion, in which we had agreed, remains unchanged, that we should not stand acquitted to the publick here, if we abstained from making a firm but friendly representation of our opinions; nor to Austria and Prussia themselves, if we did not warn them against the consequence of measures to which, if they should produce war, they are not to expect any support from us.

I have, therefore, devoted the first moment of my arrival here, to as careful a consideration of your draft to Lamb, as frequent interruption would allow. It contains a fair expression of our views, and I do not think you will find in any of the alterations which I have suggested, any differences as to the line you have taken. The chief object has been not to commit ourselves by too confident a prediction of consequences, and in the latter paragraph to add a hint, which perhaps is not sufficiently intelligible, that they must be prepared to act without our assistance, if they get into a war. Not having the Treaty of Vienna here to refer to, I depend on your accuracy which I have never found at fault, as to the statement of its provisions.

(xiii)

Downing St., 17 *February*, 1833.

Stratford Canning's letter,[1] both as shewing the critical state of Spanish affairs, and his own ability, adds to my conviction that his continuing at Madrid would be of the greatest advantage; and raising the character of the mission there, if the Spaniards would agree to send an Ambassador here, would give weight to our Minister. The additional expence which would perhaps be balanced somewhere else, is not of that sort which, I think, would create much difficulty in Parliament.

I certainly feel no disposition to truckle to Russia, tho', I confess, I should be sorry to see the Lievens removed, to be replaced perhaps by Matusewitz [sic], as Russian Minister in an inferior rank. But the state of Spain and Portugal would of itself account for the change of Canning's destination, and leave no ground for its being subject to such an imputation.

I am sorry to hear of Granville's relapse and dread the consequences of his taking so much colchicum. . . .

[1] From Stratford Canning, 8 Feb., 1833: *B.P.* This is a long analysis of the situation which he found on his arrival.

(xiv)

Downing Street, 23 *April*, 1833.

. . . The state of affairs in the East certainly becomes very embarrassing. But I doubt very much whether it would have been less so, if we
had taken a decided part in favour of the Turks when we were first
pressed to do so. At all events it was not in our power, already engaged
in the affairs of Belgium and Portugal, to enter into a third business of
the same nature. We had no available force for such a [passage] and I
am quite sure that Parliament would not have granted us one. The
truth is that the fate of the Turkish Empire has long been sealed. It
was sinking from internal decay, and the Greek affair, which led to the
war with Russia, has produced the present crisis in the dangers of which
we might have involved ourselves more deeply but could not have
prevented them by an earlier interference. My great doubt is whether
we may not now have committed ourselves too far. I believe Metternich's opinion in this matter to be well founded. It is evidently
impossible to support the resurgence of the Turkish Empire without
foreign force; and if this is to be afforded by Russia, it establishes at
once a sort of Protectorate, the result of which cannot be doubtful. I
agree with you and Metternich in thinking this question extremely
difficult to solve, and it leads to another of no less nicety: how are we to
proceed without producing on the one hand or the other dangers which
it would be our desire and our interest to prevent? I will not go further
into the discussion, but I shall be glad to enter upon it with you whenever you may find a convenient opportunity, and it is one which it is
absolutely indispensable should be entered into by the Cabinet before
any further measures are taken. The only good side of the business is
that it may very possibly induce Prussia and Austria to assist us in
settling the Belgian affair, and of this we should make the most, more
especially as I quite agree on the probability, to which you allude, that
similar motives may diminish the anxiety of France to bring that
question to an end. I have written this amidst constant interruptions
which I am afraid will be sufficiently apparent.

(xv)

Howick, 18 *September*, 1833.

Tho' I am awaiting with great impatience and anxiety the result of
the operations before Lisbon, I cannot delay answering the letter[1]
which I received yesterday, together with the very interesting communications from Ponsonby, and Sir Fredk. Lamb.[2]

I must however begin with a few words on the affairs of the Peninsula.
The telegraphic account is good as far as it goes, and, coming from
Spain, cannot be suspected of being too favourable to the cause of the
Queen. But if Miguel's army, tho' repulsed, remained in its former

[1] Not found.
[2] From Ponsonby, 25 July, 1833; From Lamb, 9 Sept., 1833; *B.P.*

position, and was in a condition to renew the attack, there remains much cause for anxiety. But, it is only a waste of time and paper to speculate upon the probability of events, which probably must be known before this can reach you.

In the meantime, however, I cannot help saying that I do not like Granville's account of what has passed upon this subject between him and De Broglie. His expectation, derived probably from measures taken by himself, that Spain would make ouvertures to the French Government rather than to us, the repetition of the interest which France takes in the establishment of the Salick Law, tho' accompanied with an acknowledgement that the immediate interest of Louis Philippe is more connected with the succession of the Infanta, and his desire that French officers should be employed, and more especially that Marshall Clausel should have the command, which affords a striking comment on what passed respecting the Duke de Leuchtenberg, altogether seem to indicate, not only a desire, but a design to establish French influence both in Spain and Portugal. It would not be advisable to show any jealousy with respect to these matters in our conduct, but the indications seem to me sufficiently strong to put us on our guard, and to require an attentive observation of the proceedings of the French Government, and a firm language, which we are entitled to hold by the former admissions of that Government itself, in asserting our right to take the lead in any measures which may become necessary in the course of the present contest.

With a view to the same interests, it is also requisite that we should hold an equally plain language to the three other Powers, reminding them, that they concurred with us in reprobating the usurpation of D. Miguel, and that we certainly will not allow any interference on the part of those, whose interests are comparatively so remote, with the policy which, in accordance with the principles which have governed our connection with Portugal, we may find it expedient to pursue. I have been led to this by what Lamb says of his communications on this subject, which mark the spirit of distrust, if not of hostility, which, at this moment, seems to prevail on their part to us in the counsels of Austria upon all questions.

I am therefore much inclined to address the question suggested by Lamb to the three Courts, after the conference is over.[1] The manner in which this should be done, will however, require some consideration. It should of course be civil in terms, but at the same time such as to show that we are not to be made their dupes, and that we are determined to act upon our own views, without any fear of the consequences with which this union may threaten us.

The state of affairs in Turkey seems to afford an additional argument in favour of a proceeding of this nature and perhaps a separate question might be put to Russia, with respect to the existence of any separate Article, if it can be done without danger to the quarter from which we

[1] Lamb (9 Sept., 1833: *B.P.*) suggested that they should be asked if they had entered into any new engagements.

have derived our knowledge. If this consideration can be got over, it will be highly useful with respect to what may follow. If it is denied, it will place us on the most advantageous ground, if it should be acted upon hereafter. If the question is evasively answered, it will afford a complete justification of the precautionary measures which it may become necessary to adopt. How Metternich must have lied upon this subject! If he had been really kept in ignorance, is it likely that he would have so readily expressed his complete approbation of the treaty?

But Ponsonby distinctly says that the draft of the treaty was sent to Sturmer by Orloff; so much for the King's expectation of a separation between Austria and Russia.

It is, therefore, more than ever necessary, that we should be prepared to support our interests in the East, and that our Squadron should be increased, as soon as it can be done with convenience; and I should hope that the state of affairs in Portugal will soon set at liberty some of the ships, engaged in that service. From Ponsonby's account, it appears most probable that a revolution at Constantinople is at no great distance. There can be no question, that our true interests would engage us to support the new Government, if established, in the name of the Sultan's son, tho' really in the hands of Mahomet Ali, and rather more on that account, as this would afford a prospect of a really efficient Government, capable of resisting the designs of Russia.

But our conduct will require delicate management, and, above all things, that we should take ground to meet the charge, to which we may find ourselves exposed, of having acted upon a secret design of favouring the views of Mahomet Ali. Indeed the whole question is one involving so many important interests, and of so delicate a nature, that we ought to have the concurrence of the Cabinet before we can send to Ponsonby the instructions which he desires. It seems almost necessary that he should have power to call for the assistance of our naval force, if the necessity which he foresees should arise; but this is, in fact, to give him the power of doing what would be tantamount to a declaration of war, against Russia. I should not feel at ease either in sanctioning such a measure, unless we were assured that our naval force was quite adequate to insure its success. The whole matter therefore is, I must repeat, of such vital importance that the decision of the Cabinet seems to be previously indispensible.

I return Ponsonby's and Lamb's letters in the box, in which they came, with the dispatches. Ponsonby's to me, I enclose in this.

I need not say, after what I have written, that I think his views just. Pray send it back when you have read it, unless you should wish previously to send it with your own to the King. He ought I think certainly to be empowered to reward the person, from whom he has got his intelligence.[1]

I see Lamb alludes to a paper which you sent him on the state of Germany. I heard, before I left town, that such a paper had been

[1] The intelligence concerning the Treaty of Unkiar Skelessi was obtained by Vogorides.

drawn up, by Mr. Mellish, of your office and had intended to have asked you to let me see it. Perhaps you can send it to me. . . .

(xvi)

Howick, 23 *September*, 1833.

. . . I was very glad that the King asked Talleyrand to Windsor. The way in which it was brought about is rather curious, and I think was the work of Madame de Dino, who pays great court to the Queen, the Dukes of Gloucester and Wellington, and, I believe, also to Bulow. The result is good, let the motive be what it may, but it is rather extraordinary that in a matter of this nature, which must be considered essential, the King should receive the communications of the Dukes of Wellington and Gloucester through the Queen.

I have read the long paper transmitted by the King to you, on the subject of Turkey.[1] His views appear to me very just, except, perhaps, as to our not interfering to prevent the occupation of the Bosphorus by Russia. You will remember what Ponsonby said on this subject. How difficult it will be if Russia is once in possession to dislodge her, and the advantage it would give her in the contest which may succeed, by the controul she would thus acquire over the Turkish population!

To me who dread war like the plague, the turn that affairs are taking in this quarter, as well as in Portugal, is most disturbing; for I almost despair of our being able to preserve peace much longer. The Duke of Wellington's observation with respect to the necessity of our supporting Donna Maria is generally just. But I see at the same time great difficulties, from the evident indisposition of the people generally to her cause, from the character of Don Pedro's Government, and from the amount of force that might be required. 5000 men would I fear be insufficient to command certain success, and, in the present state of Ireland, I do not see how more could be spared: and time would be required for sending out even the inferior number. It is altogether, to use the French word, a complication which makes me very uneasy.

In the mean time any assistance that the Queen's party can get from other quarters, they should neglect no means or time in procuring: but I think you should be very cautious as to any communications you may have with them on this subject. We must not expose ourselves to a charge, better grounded than such charges have hitherto been, that in a case in which, if we interfered at all, it ought to be openly and effectually, we had confined ourselves to measures of an indirect, doubtful, and under-hand character. . . .

(xvii)

Howick, 29 *September*, 1833.

A fit of unconquerable idleness, during the last two days, has prevented my returning a more immediate answer to your letter of the 25th.[2]

[1] From William IV, 17 Sept., 1833: *B.P.*   [2] Not found.

I think I have nothing material to add to what I have already said in my former letters, as to Turkish affairs. When Mandeville comes we shall know more, and be able to judge better of the course to be taken. In the mean time there appears to be an entire agreement in our opinions. However desirable it may be to prevent a second occupation of the Bosphorus by the Russians, an instruction to oppose it by force cannot be given without the concurrence of the Cabinet; and there can be no question that the attempt should not be made without a force of *our own*, adequate to the object. For this therefore we ought to be prepared, and I hope no time will be lost in sending some of the ships now at Cork and at Lisbon to reinforce Malcolm, as soon as the state of Portuguese affairs will admit of it.

The plan of Lisbon will be very useful to me. I do not think there will be another attack there. I am more afraid of its being masked, and a force, that would be effectual, being marched to Oporto. There can, I think, be no doubt that with no very uncommon exertion of courage and discretion, the game may be won for Donna Maria; and that it should be won by the Portuguese themselves, without any assistance from hence but such as they may get without our departing from the assurances we have given, is on all accounts most to be desired. But we must look to the probability, according to the present course of events, of our being compelled to take a part, after due warning to Spain and her having refused her cooperation, to put an end to the contest. I hope therefore that troops to the largest amount that the present state of Ireland will permit (I agree with the D[uke] of W[ellington] that they should if possible be carried to the amount of 10,000) should be in readiness and placed in quarters convenient for embarkation. I think it would also be well if you and Stanley could consider with some safe and confidential military man what, if they should go, ought to be their plan of operations. My notion is that they should if possible act by themselves. This would avoid all jealousies about command, and all the embarrassments which the union of a force, probably not very well officered or disciplined, might occasion. It would also shew the Portuguese Government that they must do something for themselves, and that they must not hope to throw on us, from the moment of our landing, the whole burthen of the war. . . .

(xviii)

Howick, 14 *October*, 1833.

I return enclosed all the letters you sent me two days ago, respecting Turkey and Spain, together with those which I have received from you this morning.

With respect to the last, tho' there appears too much probability of a severe civil contest, I think there is enough in the accounts received from Madrid of the establishment of the Queen's Government, to justify, or rather render necessary, the immediate transmission of new credentials to Villiers, with a discretion to withhold them, if, in the interim, circumstances should have arisen to make him think it expedient to do so. But the circumstances ought to be very strong to prevent, or delay a recognition, which is of the utmost importance in the effect it may have, in assisting to prevent the success of Don Carlos, which must necessarily prove extremely injurious to English interests, and which would render the preservation of peace almost hopeless.

But I have already written so fully on this, that it is unnecessary for me to do more. But I will only repeat that by an immediate recognition it appears to me that we risk little, for, if, after it, Don Carlos' party should prevail, it does not pledge us to any interference, which a consideration of our own interests, combined with the general state of Europe, might not require.

I hope William Russell is right in his estimate of the disposition of the army and the general feeling of the country. Much, as he says, will depend upon the Governor of Estremadura and if Don Carlos should be detained, a great advantage would be gained for the Queen, one, indeed, which would be, I think, nearly decisive. Another not less material, would be the success of Saldanha's concerted attack, which from the stated composition of the contending forces ought, if well conducted, to be hardly doubtful. Indeed with a Corps behind him at Torresvedras, I think Miguel could hardly risk a battle in his present position.

But I am much afraid of a Coup de Tête on the part of Pedro and his Ministers, which might increase all the difficulties already existing in Spain.

In Turkey our prospects are not attended with less anxiety. Ponsonby in a private letter to me, which only repeats what is contained in the letters you sent me, strongly urges the necessity of being beforehand with Russia in getting possession of the Bosphorus. But in the first place, have we any information, on which we can depend, that would justify our attempting the passage of the Dardanelles? That of [Landon] with respect to the rumoured state of the defences appears to be more than doubtful. It appears hardly credible, with the knowledge we possess of Russian officers having been sent to inspect and repair them, and he admits that an additional force of 3,000 men had arrived there.

But if these considerations render such an enterprise too hazardous to be undertaken, are there no objections to it, even with the probable or with an almost certain prospect of success? What pretext could we set forth for such a movement, without some more hostile demonstration, at least on the part of Russia? The effect of it, if successful, would assuredly be a revolution at Constantinople and the deposition of the Sultan; one consequence of this would certainly be the establishment of the power of Mahomet Ali, and how should we be able to defend ourselves against the imputation of bad faith, in view of all our professions of a wish to maintain the independence of the Sultan. I say nothing of the certainty of a war in consequence with Russia, and with the pretext it would furnish to Metternich for the course, which we know he is determined to pursue.

Upon the whole therefore, I concur in the opinion of De Broglie, that we should endeavour to keep Mahomet Ali quiet, and that he should make representations to him in accordance with these proposals by the French Government.   The same thing should be done at Constantinople and for the present things should, in this manner, if possible be kept quiet.

In the meantime, I have strongly recommended to Graham, that our ships should winter in the harbour of Malta.   They would then save the wear and tear, of cruising in the bad season; they would then be in a better state of readiness for action, and would be in a station where little, or any delay, would take place in their receiving, and proceeding to the execution of any orders, which it may be necessary to send; but, at the same time, that we should shape our course in this matter with respect to our affairs in the Mediterranean.

I give it without hesitation as my opinion, that we should hold a firm and decisive language both with Austria and Russia, in any discussions, which may arise on this subject, and that we should tell them frankly and explicitly, should it become necessary, that we are prepared to resist, by all the means in our power the accomplishment of a system which is evidently intended, and by the same process, to place Turkey in the same situation as Poland and to effect its ultimate subjugation and division.

It is all very well for Metternich to fly into a passion when matters are discussed.   It proves at once how much he feels himself in the wrong, and how unable he is to defend the duplicity and treachery of his conduct.   I confess I think Lamb was rather too forbearing in his conversation with him, and that he still leans too much to the opinion that we should become partners in the course which Metternich recommends.

Nothing can more easily be answered than Metternich's complaint that we did not do this sooner; if we had, we should have been the dupes of the scheme, which I have no doubt, has been long prepared between the Courts of Vienna and Petersburgh, and placed ourselves in a situation in which we should have been disabled from making any effectual opposition to it.

But, even it if had been right then, it would not be so after the Russian treaty, considering the nature of its stipulations and the way in which it was negotiated.

But in recommending a firm and decisive tone I should still have preferred waiting for an occasion, which something on the part of the Russia might have produced, and the expectation, announced by Ponsonby, of an answer to our protest has confirmed the opinion which I before expressed, but which I no longer wish to insist upon, that it would have been better not to send the protest to St Petersburg.

Pray write constantly, as I am getting more and more anxious, and should have been much inclined to return immediately to town, if I did not feel a little longer rest here to be absolutely necessary for my health.

APPENDIX C

CORRESPONDENCE BETWEEN
PALMERSTON AND MELBOURNE, 1835–1840[1]

(a) THE RETURN TO OFFICE IN 1835

(i)

Melbourne to Palmerston

South Street, 14 *April*, 1835.

I wrote to Grey the result of your interview and I send you the reply which I have received.[2] It is in some places rather more strongly expressed than I should expressed it, but upon the whole I agree with it.

(ii)

Palmerston to Melbourne

Stanhope St., 14 *April*, 1835.

I return you the inclosed letter from Lord Grey.

Nothing can be further from my wish than to embarrass you in the execution of the task you have undertaken; and the last thing I should desire to do, would be to render myself liable to the charge of appearing to force you to make in my person an appointment which you thought disadvantageous to the public service.

I have a right, on the other hand, to object to your making in my person an appointment which I think disadvantageous to my own personal honour, and to my public character.

But there is an obvious and simple way of reconciling our conflicting sentiments on this matter, and that is, that you should dispose of the Foreign Office in the manner which you may think most advantageous to the interests of your Government, and that I should be allowed to continue in the state of freedom from official labour in which I at present am; and I wish you to understand that I consider such an arrangement as being the result of our communication of this morning, and of this correspondence.

---

[1] From the Broadlands Papers. Palmerston's letters begin "My dear Melbourne" and end "Yours sincerely"; those of Melbourne begin "My dear Palmerston" and end sometimes "Yours faithfully", sometimes "Yours", and sometimes with only a signature, but the manner seems to bear no relation to the contents of the letter.

[2] See above, p. 420.

I should conclude here, but that I cannot refrain from some remarks suggested by Lord Grey's letter.

I am much gratified by the kind expressions towards myself personally which are contained in that letter; but it is not without some surprize that I find Lord Grey to entertain an opinion that "an objection is generally felt to me" as Foreign Secretary.

That the Tories when out of office objected to my manner of conducting our foreign relations, I know full well; though I also know, that since they have been in office, they have upon almost all the great questions followed the track which I had marked out.

That the Courts of Vienna, Berlin, Petersburgh and the Hague, objected to me as Foreign Secretary, has also been long and perfectly well known. But the course of policy with regard to Belgium, France, Portugal and Spain, which excited against me the ill will of the four Courts first mentioned, was approved of, and concurred in, during four years, by my late colleagues in the Government, and was in all respects consistent with the true interests of Great Britain. I do not think, however, that my conduct as Foreign Secretary is objected to by those parties in Parliament and in the country, by which your Administration was, and will be, supported; and I do not believe that it was objected to by any foreign Government with whom we have any established relations, except the four to which I have alluded. Indeed I have the very best reasons for being convinced of the reverse, not only by the nature of my intercourse while I was in office, but by communications which I have received from some of those Governments since I have been out of office.

It is always disagreeable to speak of oneself, but upon this occasion I must be permitted to say, that I consider myself to have conducted our foreign relations with great success, during four years of excessive labour, and through extreme difficulties arising not only from the complicated nature of the questions to be dealt with, but also from the resistance opposed to me by a combination of domestic with foreign opponents.

All the important questions connected with Greece, Belgium, Portugal, and Spain which essentially affected the interests of England, I left either virtually settled or in a satisfactory train of adjustment.

There was but one important matter which when we went out in November last, remained in an unsatisfactory state; and that was the condition of Turkey, with relation to Russia on the one hand, and to England on the other.

But with respect to that matter, the blame does not lie at my door; for if my advice had been taken by the Cabinet in the Autumn of 1832, and if we had then given to the Sultan our moral support against Mehemet Ali, the subsequent Treaty of Constantinople would never have been signed.

Excuse me for these details and believe me.

(iii)

Melbourne to Palmerston

South St., 15 *April*, 1835.

I only sent to you Grey's letter in order to prove to you that it was not my own notion and entirely from my own impressions that I had made to you the communication, which I did yesterday; but that others also were under similar impressions.

You will readily believe that it was very painful to me to have to intimate the least doubt of the propriety of your resuming the Foreign Office, but I was compelled by circumstances and a sense of duty to do so. All I said was that it appeared to me and to others that it would be of service to the Government, if you could reconcile it to your feelings to accept another office of equal rank and almost of equal importance.

I trust, that I am not to consider your communication of last night as going to this extent, that you would now decline the Foreign Seals if they were offered to you.

(iv)

Palmerston to Melbourne

Stanhope St., 15 *April*, 1835.

I have received your note of this morning. The intention of my letter of last night was to set you perfectly free with respect to myself; but undoubtedly the same feelings which I expressed in that letter, and the natural disinclination which every man must have to separate from his political and personal friends, would determine me to accept the Seals of the Foreign Office, if they were offered to me.

(*b*) LETTERS FROM PALMERSTON TO MELBOURNE

(i)

Stanhope St., 8 *June*, 1835.

I dare say this[1] is a pretty correct summary of Metternichs conversations with Strangeways; but after all what does it amount to? and what foundation does it afford for any system of European policy to be built upon the basis of Austrian alliance?

There are indeed abundant declarations of a desire to be the most intimate ally of England: and of a conviction that an alliance with England is the best and most useful for Austria. But when Metternich comes to explain the nature of the alliance which he contemplates, it turns out to be one, which is impracticable for us; and when we inquire what advantages we should derive from it, we are at a loss to discover any whatever.

[1] From Fox-Strangeways, 25 May, 1835: *F.O. Austria*, 253

He begins by describing France as the natural enemy both of Austria and England; and it is manifest that his notion of an alliance with England presupposes an estrangement of both Austria and England from France. Now it is needless to point out that to come to such a new system we must abandon all the objects we have been striving for during the last five years, undo all we have been doing, and, as we should at once become Tories abroad, we ought to begin by becoming Tories at home; for such a change of system would infallibly lose us the support of that party, by whom we are at present upheld. Metternich, in short, sighs for a return of the state of things which existed during the war against Buonaparte, when all Europe was united against France; and when, by the by, if the fate of Europe had depended upon the vigour of Austrian councils, and the enterprize of Austrian armies, we never should have had a Treaty of *Paris*. But he would wish all Europe to be leagued now against France in diplomatic and moral hostility, as it was at that period in active warfare. But here again he takes for granted, that, which to say no more of it, is in the highest degree doubtful, namely that if England was to abandon France in order to take to Austria, France would find no other ally to take the place of England; and what I should like to know, should we gain, if while we exchanged active, powerful, and neighbouring France for sluggish and temporising and distant Austria, Russia were to make the converse of our exchange and instead of being united with Austria, who, though subservient, acts as a clog, she were to strike up an intimacy with France, and gain a more active ambitious and a *naval* ally? It does not appear to me that such a change of partners would increase our chance of winning the rubber.

For what are the advantages he holds out to us as likely to result from this entire change in our system of policy? First of all, that we are to shape our course by his, and to make temporising not even a means but an end, and with respect to whom? Why, with respect to Russia, whom he admits to be a constantly increasing Power. Now nothing can be clearer than that if you pursue a system of temporising, which in other words means perpetually giving way, while your adversary pursues a system of perpetual encroachment, the only problem to be solved is, *how soon* you will be received. Metternich's principle is to submit to everything that is done, thinking that he has got out of all embarrassment by saying "c'est un fait accompli". This is an excellent doctrine for ones adversary to hold, but a very inconvenient maxim to serve as a rule of conduct for a friend and ally in difficult times.

Then again what flimsy and fallacious assumptions he puts forward, as grounds on which to build a system of measures upon great national interests! The personal character of Nicholas, for instance, is represented by him, as a sufficient guarantee for the *conservative* policy of Russia. Now we happen also to know something of the personal character of Nicholas; and I confess that I am disposed to draw from that personal character conclusions exactly the reverse of those which Metternich seems to have formed. I take Nicholas to be ambitious, bent upon great schemes, determined to make extensive additions to his dominions; and labouring to push his political ascendancy far beyond the range of his Ukases, animated by the same hatred to England which was felt by Napoleon, and for the same reasons, namely that we are the friends of national independence, and the enemies of all conquerors. We are an obstacle in his path; he would cajole us if he could; he would crush us if he were able; not being equal to either, he only hates us.

The conclusion which seems to follow from all this is, that we should not quit or loosen our connection with France, but should encourage the friendly disposition of Austria towards us, as far as we can, without departing from our own course in order to please her; and to express on every favourable occasion a strong wish to see her friendly dispositions evinced by acts as well as expressed in conversations and despatches.

(ii)

Stanhope St., 30 *October*, 1835.

Ellice seems to me to take a very limited and erroneous view of these matters, unless he means that we should abandon the affairs of the East altogether to Russia, sit with our hands before us, and say "it's a great pity but we cannot help it".

If we are to stop Russia and encourage and uphold Turkey we must do so by following the maxim principiis obsta.

We must object betimes to things we dislike and encourage betimes the things we wish for. But what can be so ridiculous and unworthy as for a Government to be holding language of either kind in a remote quarter without any visible means of enforcing its objections or giving aid to those whom it may encourage? But the only force we *can* have and the only one that it can be *necessary* for us to have in the Mediterranean is a fleet; and as long as we have a respectable squadron there, we may express our opinions and wishes with some authority to all parties.

The Russians no doubt would be right glad that we should withdraw our ships, and the Austrians to *please Russia* would wish the same.

The French very likely are not particular glad to see us strong in the Mediterranean; but I am not aware that any of these circumstances are reasons *against*, though they seem to me to be good reasons *for* keeping our fleet there. If Portsmouth was where Toulon is, we might be content to keep our fleet at Portsmouth, as the French do at Toulon. But we well know that the keeping the French fleet at Toulon, and the not sending it to sea was an act of toadyism of Louis Philippe to Nicholas; but, if it was agreeable to Nicholas, it could only be so, because he felt that the absence of the French and a portion of the English fleet would be favourable to his influence in Turkey, and therefore conducive to his views in the East.

As to our having *a* Ship of the Line in the Mediterranean and steamers to go and fetch more when wanted, that is absurd. We want to act by moral effect produced by the presence of our fleet, and the *uncertainty* in the minds of others, what that fleet may do; and thus to prevent the necessity of its having to act by force of arms.

But if we keep a fleet in the Mediterranean it cannot be lying all the summer in the harbour of Malta; it must even for health and exercise go cruizing about; and it may as well visit places where matters of interest are going on as go and buy figs at Smyrna.

I am convinced that you will find that all the complaints of the bad effect produced by the *movements* of our fleet resolve themselves into a Russian wish to get that fleet out of the Mediterranean; once establish that, whenever it leaves Malta, explanations are to be given why it goes to one place more than another, and we may as well withdraw it.

Only remember that I wanted the Cabinet to let me write to stop Mehemet Ali, which if I had done, all these ills would have been avoided. The objection was, we must not hold strong language without the means of enforcing it "*and we have no fleet in the Mediterranean*".

But people like Ellice will always find a peg on which to hang and find fault. If the fleet was at home, it would be said, why incur the expence of keeping ships to rot in harbour or to dawdle about the Channel, why not send them to the East where they might be of some use? Turkey is sinking under the grasp of Russia; you have six Sail of the Line doing nothing at home; why do you not send them to practise their duty in the Mediterranean, and thus obtain at once a naval and a political object?

Ellice says that all which passes between our Dragoman and the Reis Effendi is known to Russia. No doubt it is, each party is convinced that the other will tell, and, therefore, each hastens to have the merit of being first, and our "honest and valuable agent Pisani" and our friend and ally the Reis Effendi no doubt both make their report to the Russian, of every conversation they have together. Pisani's near relation is a Russian Dragoman, so he need not go from home to make his report.

Urquhart's appointment may, and I hope will, alter this state of things.

(iii)

Stanhope St., 7 *January*, 1836.

Those who like Mr Edward Ellice[1] labour under the ποιχιλομανια [sic] which shews itself by being busy in all sorts of matters with which the patient has no concern, and of which he knows nothing whatever, are

---

[1] This is a reply to a short note from Melbourne who passed on a message from Ellice adding, "as we have another Minister beside Granville at Paris to conduct our affairs, we may as well take advantage of his information." Ellice wrote: "Ld. Granville will write to you that the American squabble is settled, or is to be settled. The intriguers thought they saw a means in it of shaking de Broglie; but it will not do, he is safe for the present. If you wish, and it is a great object, to keep him so, advise Palmerston to communicate more with Sebastiani and to be less exclusive in his communications through Ld. G. with de B. here. I see that is a subject of jealousy even in the highest quarters, and others foment and wish to take advantage of it." *B.P.*

frequently led, as Mr. Edward Ellice has been in the present case, not merely to talk nonsense, but to say the thing which is not. To propose as a means of keeping a Foreign Minister in office, that we should make cyphers of him and of our own Ambassador, is stuff; the means have no adaption to the end, and, if employed, must render the end valueless. But Mr Edward Ellice's information as to my mode of doing business in the Foreign Office, is about as correct as his cock and a bull story about revolts and revolutions in Greece and probably comes from some authority as friendly and veracious as Admiral Count Dandalo. It is in fact merely a revival of one of the unfounded grievances which old Talleyrand racked his brains to invent during the last few months of his stay here by way of contributing his mite to the Unholy Alliance, which attempted to crush me, because they found me not a convenient tool for their purposes.

I have been much misinformed if Sebastiani complains of want of communication on my part; I have heard exactly the reverse and that he has expressed himself gratified with the confidence with which I have treated him. I am sure he could not with truth complain, because "*the exclusive dealing*", of which Mr Edward Ellice accuses me, is a mere phantasy of his own distempered brain, an image which has remained upon his intellectual retina after reading an account of the practices of the Cambridge under graduate Pitt Club.

As to doing all ones business twice over, once to our own Ministers abroad, and then again to the Ministers at this Court, unless the sapient Ellice could *prove* that there are 48 Hours in every day (he very likely would *assert* it)—such a course of proceeding would be utterly impossible. Besides our Ministers abroad are our own agents; the Ministers here are the agents of other Governments. This is what Mrs Malaprop would call, one of the many *Ellice*cinations which bewilder the mind of our Right Honorable Friend.

(iv)

Stanhope St., 24 *May*, 1836.

I return you Hummelauer's letter and Metternich's dispatches, which afford a curious but by no means unprecedented specimen of Vienna diplomacy. The system of the Austrian and indeed of the other two courts also, is to endeavour to establish personal distinctions, and to create differences of opinions between members of the same Government, and to appeal to other authorities against the head of the foreign department. They were always trying this system here with Grey, and they pursued it at Paris against de Broglie. Grey gave in to it once in the case of a communication with Zuylen,[1] and his civility was made a bad use of, as you may remember, and he was very angry with Zuylen afterwards for the unfair turn which he gave to Lord Grey's communication. But it is quite true, as you say, that there is great inconvenience in departing from the established modes of communica-

[1] See p. 173.

tion, and those who seek to lead a Minister into such a course always have their own views in doing so. Perhaps the best way of dealing with this attempt on the part of Metternich would be to say to Hummelauer, that you cannot as Prime Minister receive a *personal* communication from a foreign Government upon a public question; that you can only consider such communication as being made to you in your capacity of head of the Government; and that in that capacity you would necessarily think it right to make the communication known to the King and to your colleagues; but that the forms and arrangements of the English Government have marked out the Secretary of State for Foreign Affairs as the channel through which all communications between the British Government and foreign Powers are to pass; and that there always is great practical inconvenience in departing from long established forms of proceeding without any adequate necessity; that in the present case you have a further difficulty in accepting the personal communication which is offered to you, because while on the one hand you could not withold it from the Government as a public and official communication, there are on the other hand expressions in Metternich's dispatch which seem to imply that he did not intend it to be so dealt with; and that consequently you thought the best thing you could do was to replace the despatches in Hummelauer's hands with these observations, leaving it to him to take such further steps with regard to them as he might think most comfortable with the intentions of his Government. . . .

You ask what all this means; I should say it was only this, that Metternich has gone on for so many years carrying his points in Europe, by talking twaddle about "foyers d'intrigues" "et brandons de revolution", that at last the language has become natural to him, and he has persuaded himself of the reality of that, which he has so assiduously laboured to make all the rest of the world believe.

There is as you know a free Press in Greece. Metternich has for the last twelve months being labouring hard to bully Armansperg to suppress it. But Armansperg has stoutly resisted; but if we allow Metternich to talk to us about a free Press at Malta, how could we say anything in support of Greece, if we should be called upon to back up our ally there, against the pressure of Austria and Russia?

Metternich's dispatch in fact goes straight to the great point of principle on which the continental Governments and the Liberal party in England have long been at variance. The despotic Powers contend that they have a right to prescribe to other nations what shall and what shall not be their form of Government. In England on the contrary it has been maintained by all with some exceptions, that every nation has a right to chuse its own form of Government and institutions, provided always that it abstained from attacking its neighbours.

(v)

Stanhope St., 19 *July*, 1836.

Ponsonby has really done us a valuable and important service, and has acted with courage, firmness and ability; he was openly opposed by the united influence of Austria, Prussia and Russia and betrayed by the representative of France. He had nothing to work with but his own energy, and the belief on the part of the Sultan that he enjoyed the confidence of his own Government and would be supported by it. The result has been a signal triumph of British influence, and the good effects will not end with the particular occasion out of which the matter arose. It seems to me that with reference to our own character as a Government, and with a view to the future interests of England, we ought not to accept coldly and timidly the success which has been achieved; by so doing, and by appearing to acquiesce in what Ponsonby has done, rather than to approve it, we should weaken the influence of all our foreign agents; and we should, with regard to Ponsonby, give a sort of tacit sanction to all the calumnies and abuse which the agents and Ministers of unfriendly Courts have so unsparingly heaped upon him.

I would therefore wish you to consider whether it would not be both a just and a wise measure to give Ponsonby a step in the Peerage. Such an act would be a better and more dignified rebuke to Metternich and the rest than any controversial and admonitory despatches to be read to them; and, by shewing the Sultan that we entirely approve Ponsonbys proceedings, would inspire the Sultan with additional confidence in the support of England.

With Ponsonby's fortune it would be better for him to be a Viscount than to have the Earldom he asked for.

P.S. You will find John Russell quite of this way of thinking.

(vi)

Broadlands, 29 *October*, 1837.

Glenelg spoke to me some time ago about the question whether a free Press should be established at Malta, and he has now requested me to write to you that which I said to him upon this subject.[1]

Upon the question itself I have as yet no formed opinion, because I have only hastily read the report of the Commissioners. But I have a very strong opinion upon the inexpediency of our admitting the objections of a foreign Government to be even an element of consideration in making our determination on the matter.

It seems to me that we cannot hold too high both in theory and practise the doctrine that no foreign Government can ever be allowed to talk to us upon matters belonging to the internal legislation and administration of any part of the Dominions of the British Crown.

To permit such interference even in the most mitigated shape would be extremely inconvenient to the Government and excessively dero-

[1] From Glenelg, 27 Oct., 1837: *B.P.*

gatory to the dignity and independence of the country. No Minister of the Crown could venture to acknowledge in his place in Parliament that such interference had been submitted to; and if it was known that a foreign Government had been allowed to remonstrate against a measure which upon other grounds had been abandoned, the Government would be taxed with having given up the measure, in deference to the foreign remonstrance, and would be much discredited thereby both at home and abroad.

But, if the precedent were once established in one case, it would be quoted in others, and there would be numerous repetitions of friendly advice and neighbourly warnings as to the dangerous consequences to other states of the measures which from time to time we might propose to adopt for ourselves.

Glenelg suggests that the Commissioners might prepare a report shewing how unfounded are the apprehensions of Austria and Naples of any danger to them that could result from a free Press at Malta. Nothing would be more easy than to draw up such a report, and to prove such alarms to be groundless; and if we determine to have a free Press, we might, after we have adopted the measure, make some such confidential communications to those Governments: but as to convincing them that a free Press anywhere is not an abomination, that I apprehend would be a task exceeding the powers even of Austin and Cornewall Lewis.

(vii)

Carlton Terrace, 26 *October*, 1840.

I return you these two letters.[1] Lansdowne's is evidently written upon the receipt of one from Broglie, who we know has been entirely won over by Thiers on the Turkish question. I cannot say that I share these great apprehensions as to L. Philippe's being able to hold his ground; I suspect on the contrary that he knows pretty well what he is about; he certainly understands his French subjects and their character, and has shewn that he knows how to manage them.

Guizot assured me the other day that there is far more stability in France than people seem to suppose; that the middle classes who are numerous and well to do in the world, are all for peace and internal order; that the agricultural population is well disposed and easily governed; but that there are in all the towns a certain number of turbulent men, without profession, occupation or principles, idle and thoroughly demoralized, passing their time in reading newspapers and talking politics, and that these people give a fictitious character to public opinion, and furnish in times of excitement individuals capable of the most atrocious crimes; but it would be a mistake to suppose the opinions of these men to be the opinions of the nation.

<hr>

[1] Lansdowne to Melbourne, 25 Oct., 1840: *B.P.* John Russell to Melbourne, 25 Oct., 1840: G. P. Gooch, *Later Corres.*, I, 29 and *B.P.*

Of course we should all be desirous of supporting L. Philippe but, if the clamour of the Press and the Coffee Houses is to be taken as the true expression of public opinion in France, what the French want just now is not alliance with England, but the submission of England to the will of France, and it does not seem very politic to support L. Philippe in that way, nor can it be necessary to do so.

The French have on every occasion since 1830, when they wanted to drive us to make some concession to them, used this same argument; but we have on many occasions disregarded it, and without any realization of the predicted dangers. When they wanted Nemours to be King of the Belgians, when they wanted to alter the territorial arrangement between Belgium and Holland, and on several other occasions they used the same arguments; but we were hard hearted, and yet L. Philippe continued to reign.

It seems quite clear that we shall at no distant time recover for the Sultan the whole of Syria, and it would be exceedingly unwise to throw away so great an advantage. If we can accomplish this, doing it as we shall by our own means in conjunction with the Turks, and without any active assistance from either Austria or Russia, it will give us great additional weight in all the transactions and discussions in which for some years to come we may be engaged with any of the Powers of Europe, while, on the contrary, if we allow ourselves to be persuaded out of a success which we have almost in hand, we shall inevitably be made to suffer for our softness by the future difficulties which we shall in consequence thereof experience in our dealing with other Powers.

(c) LETTERS FROM MELBOURNE TO PALMERSTON

(i)

South St., 14 *December*, 1835.

With reference to the questions which may be asked in Parliament upon the subject of the Emperor of Russia's speech at Warsaw,[1] it appears to me that, whether any notice of that speech is taken or not, it will be easy in answering such questions to express, and that without giving great offence to Russia, such an opinion of that speech as will be satisfactory to the House and the country. I would consider the question therefore upon its own merits solely. Are we justified in taking any diplomatic notice of the speech, and if we are justified, is it prudent to do so? As you state in your letter[2] to Durham, the speech never has been published by authority and the reports of it differ the one from the other. It remains in fact uncertain what was delivered; and your despatch[2] adverts to expressions, which you can only state "to have been said to have been used by the Emperor etc, and which are not contained

---

[1] 16 October, 1835.
[2] Drafts are enclosed but it would seem that they were not sent.

in the published reports". These supposed expressions are the only ones which give you the least right to make any observations. Whatever may be your opinion of the prudence feeling or propriety of the Emperor's reproaches for the past, and menaces for the future, he has a right to employ them towards his subjects, if he pleases, and you have none to remark upon or remonstrate against his conduct in this respect. Is it nice or gracious to try to fix the Emperor with expressions from which he is himself anxious to withdraw and escape? Is it discreet to say to him upon the authority of newspapers, we believe you to have said so and so, and, therefore, we tell you what are our opinions upon that language; he can hardly reply "to assure you I never said so"; that would be beneath his dignity, and you almost, therefore, force, at least you provoke, him to avow and maintain words of which he is clearly desirous to disembarrass himself.

The question is large and difficult, but I own I am not prepared to lay down that "the events which have happened in Poland since the conclusion of the Treaty of Vienna, do not affect the stipulations of that treaty". I cannot think that this is practical sense or reason. One of these provisions, if I mistake not, was that the Polish army should be separate and independent; but can it be said that such a stipulation is to continue to be binding upon a Government against which that army has made a desperate rebellion and the existence of which it has endangered?

Besides it appears to me that if the opinions laid down in this letter are correct, we are doing too little. If the Articles of the Treaty of Vienna are still binding and we are guarantors of them, they have been so decidedly done away with, that we ought to be now at war with Russia, or at least we ought to have called upon those Powers, who are also parties to the treaty, to unite with us in enforcing the observation of it.

(ii)

South St., 8 *January*, 1836.

Adairs letter[1] is not only a proof of the intimate communication between the three Powers, but also of the great jealousy with which an overture made to one of them is viewed by the others. If Austria makes a proposition to us, it is considered as an attempt to detach us from France; if we say a word to Austria, it is interpreted into a design to divide her from Russia and Prussia, and in both cases perhaps truly; for I have never thought that we should effect a cooperation with Austria, but that an honest attempt to do so would put us in a better condition; but I am open to conviction upon the subject.

I feel the thing to be one of great importance.

[1] From Adair, 16 Dec., 1835: *B.P.* He reported Ancillon's suspicions that Britain was trying to detach Austria from Russia and statement that the three Eastern Powers would stick together.

(iii)

South St., 10 *February*, 1836.

... From all I hear of the real temper of the House of Commons, we must be very careful what we do in foreign affairs. They will vote our increased navy estimate with some alarm and reluctance, but they are determined against war, and if any step were proposed in that direction, they would leave us in the lurch. The evil consequences of such an event in encouraging Russia are sufficiently evident. It must upon no account be hazarded.

(iv)

South St., 17 *February*, 1836.

This event is, as you say, worthy of attention. I was pretty well aware of the acquisitions of Russia, of their extent, their direction and the time at which they had been made; a map of England with her acquisitions during the same period would make a very respectable figure and colour no inconsiderable portion of the globe. I quite agree also in the way she has made them and in her disposition to make them still. But the question is what is the best way to deal with her. Her proximity and her great military power give her great advantages. You would not make war to try to restrict her power and her dominion and to drive her back; any inconsiderate, ill-conceived hostilities will certainly have the effect of hastening and assisting her views. This big map shews most clearly the situation of Austria, the advantages of her position and the direct interest she has in the question. It appears to me to be very unwise not to try to carry her along with us and it appears to me that Metternich's own interest would prevent him from communicating any overture made to him to Russia.

Her advanced posts in Asia may be as distant from St. Petersburg as from our Indian Frontier. But how far are they from both? I take it nearly two thousand miles and their remoteness from St. Petersburg, the present seat of her Empire, is amongst others a source of weakness.

(v)

South St., 29 *February*, 1836.

I have not time to read all these papers about Circassia etc this morning, but will soon return them.

I fairly say I would leave the Circassians to themselves. If their own force enables them to make head against Russia they are sufficiently inclined to do so, and, if they have not of themselves sufficient strength for that purpose, you cannot give it them. I am against exciting people to commit themselves in a warfare in which you cannot give them effectual support.

Besides Russia will have great cause of complaint against you. They are either her subjects in rebellion or an independent nation at war with her. In either case it is an act of hostility on your part to assist them.

Of course it is well known at St. Petersburgh who Hudson is and what he has been doing, and of course this knowledge must make a most unfavorable impression.

I see all the danger of Russia obtaining Constantinople etc.

I doubt whether you can keep her out of it, unless you obtain the [support] and cordial cooperation of Austria for that purpose.

There are great difficulties in the way of obtaining this cordial cooperation and none greater than the civil war in Spain, which I have no doubt Austria assists and supports.

It is quite evident that the position of Mehemet Ali forwards the views of Russia in every way whether he intends to come in as an ally or a conqueror.

Upon the whole these countries seem [at present] to be placed in a position and attitude in which they cannot long remain. I own myself to be much afraid of moving, least it should hasten the catastrophe we dread and wish to avert.

(vi)

South St., 2 *March*, 1836.

There is much, very much, in what you have written; but it takes for granted and certain that it is prudent and desirable to conclude this treaty with France. If it were so certainly desirable there is no question but that a great opportunity has been lost. The change in the French Government changes the case much and I suspect that you will find it so practically. Talleyrand will now be looking to his favourite scheme of a General Congress.

(vii)

Downing St., 4 *March*, 1836.

You know I always leaned to the opinion that the only mode of finishing this war in the North of Spain was by the intervention of the French; but Louis Philippe was always so decided against it, that I could not but suppose that he understood his own policy and situation better than I did, especially as I do not believe either that he wishes well to Don Carlos or that he can be indifferent to the result of the present contest in Spain, which must so deeply affect his permanent interests.

The King is deeply impressed with the notion that Louis Philippe has acted falsely, and he is also persuaded that the entry of French troops into Spain would be the immediate signal for war being made upon her by Austria and Prussia. You will, therefore, find it difficult to induce him to concur in making the proposition, you mention, to France, and I should think it would be better to sound the French Government upon the subject before it is formally made.

The state of these Spanish affairs is most serious and alarming. I fear that pecuniary assistance might now come too late; otherwise I think it would not be difficult to collect what would be the opinion of our leading supporters upon giving it; at the same time the House of Lords, [as you observed] the other morning, is a formidable obstacle.

(viii)

Brocket Hall, 1 *April*, 1836.

This despatch of the 28th ult.[1] from Granville upon Spanish affairs is very bad. If the Queen changes her course in the manner there mentioned, it is all over with her and her Daughter too. Her success is identified with the success of the representative form of Government. It is possible that a constitution cannot be established and had [sic] in Spain. It is possible that absolute monarchy may be restored there, but she cannot change her course from constitutional to absolute. It will not be under her that it will take place. I am afraid from Rayneval's eagerness to announce the fall of Mendizabal that he has been contributing to it and also perhaps to the projected change of policy. It has been to be [sic] regretted from the beginning that he has not acted more in concert with Villiers. Whether this be his fault or the fault of his Government it is difficult to conjecture, as well as whether it is to be in any degree to be attributed to Villiers. I am afraid we are approaching a crisis in Spain. Many who know Cordova, have little confidence in him. If the Queen either throws herself upon the army for personal protection or attempts by means of the army to govern the country without a Cortes, it appears to me that it will soon be all over with her.

(ix)

Panshanger, 6 *April*, 1836.

It may be as you suppose and it is well to keep this probability in view; but do not permit pictures in your own mind and set them down for realities nor think that you see into a mill-stone further than the density of its material will permit you. Busybodies and tattlers like Ellice generally get credit for more steady views and deeper designs than they really act upon or entertain. I will however admit that there is a sort of general connection between Durham and Ellice, which is rather strange, but that it is the great object of the life of the latter to promote the views of the former, I cannot quite set down for a certainty.

(x)

Downing St., 6 *February*, 1837.

I had much rather send ships etc. than have anything whatever to do with these proposed money transactions. You know what I think

[1] *F.O. France*, 520.

of all that Villiers says about establishing influence in Spain, or in any other country. It is impracticable, and, if it were practicable, doubtful whether worth while. But with respect to the increased naval assistance I have no objection but of a prudential character—the King and Parliament. We shall certainly excite opposition by it, and if we push the thing too far, we shall hazard our power to give as much assistance as we have already done.

(xi)

South St., 29 *April*, 1837.

You may recollect that I have always felt and expressed the greatest surprise at Metternich's first language about the Vixen, and an entire distrust of it. I cannot now understand it; it was either the habit of deceit, or some scheme, which we do not yet fathom; but I entirely agree that neither in small nor in great affairs is any reliance to be placed upon Austria. She fears all revolutionary Governments and she considers ours as the most revolutionary Government in Europe. She may perhaps not fear us so much as she does France, because danger from us is neither so possible nor so immediate, but depend upon it she hates us more than she does France.

(xii)

Brighton, 18 *October*, 1837.

There is room for you in the Pavilion, and the Queen would wish you to come here. I did not mention it, as if you wished it, but I was aware from what she had said of there being room for two Ministers that she would wish you should come.

I return you Granville's letters.[1] Molé is right enough in his conjecture or rather his certainty that Talleyrand, when here, did everything in his [power] to make him (Molé) disliked and distrusted. I fancy that the French King and Government have had no difficulty in ascertaining the implacable animosity of the Emperor of Russia, which is very foolish in the Emperor, but not a bad thing for us.

I have received your box this morning. Your proposed application to the Continental Powers is a very serious matter. I will write to you in the course of the day what I think about it.

(xiii)

Brighton, 19 *October*, 1837.

... I rather doubt the prudence of stirring the question of Spain with the Northern Powers, unless you have previous reason to think that such a communication will be well received and tend to a good end.

[1] From Granville, 13 Oct., 1837: *B.P.* Molé had described Talleyrand's underhand conduct towards himself in 1830.

I think, unless this be the case, the consequences of your mentioning the subject will be; first they will deny that they have given any assistance or encouragement, and you will not be able to prove that they have; secondly, they will say, if you talk to us about Spain, we also have a right to talk to you and we shall have a long paper of Metternichs condemning the whole of our policy. This will lead to useless altercation. But the great danger of our moving in it appears to me to be this, least they should agree with you that something ought to be done and propose a Congress or some concerted measure for a suspension of arms etc. We should be unwilling to embark with them in such a matter, and yet, if we opened the business, it would be difficult to avoid it.

(xiv)

South St., 30 *March*, 1838.

I have always been against any negotiation or attempt at negotiation with the Northern Powers about Spain for the reason you mention.

The only objection to making an overture to the Basques is that you cannot promise for the Spanish Government, and that, even if you have the consent of that Government to the overture which you made, you cannot be sure of their afterwards observing the terms and thus you will be involved in the odium of their perfidy.

(xv)

South St., 3 *June*, 1838.

Send me back Leopold's letter with your notion of what should be written.

I cannot see the advantages of a treaty in as strong a light as you do. I do not see my way and, therefore, should not like to enter on it. It may be necessary to defend Turkey, but I should not like to be bound to defend her. France whether bound by treaty or not will be attending to her own interests and her own policy; what those interests and that policy may be in her opinion, it is impossible to say.

As to Servia, if Austria will not interfere, depend upon it we never can with any effect. I agree with you that there is every appearance of the coming on of considerable difficulties, but our policy is to have our hands free.

(xvi)

South St., 14 *June*, 1838.

If all this has been passing at Alexandria and the crisis is so imminent, is it not odd that you have heard nothing from Colonel Campbell?

The question itself is very important. I am unable of course at once to form an opinion of it.

Can you support and prop up the Porte? Suppose you deter Mehemet Ali from declaring his independence or force him to retract his declaration, would the Porte derive much strength from such nominal subjection?

The Porte has lost Egypt and Syria. Can the application of external force now restore them to her? What are we trying to preserve for the Porte? The tribute which it receives and the reversion of the dominions upon the deaths of Mehemet and Ibrahim? The tribute is the only thing of any importance. The reversion the Porte always has a good chance of.

For the balance of power I doubt whether this country will go to war, notwithstanding her hatred of Russia. I am sure that we will not long persevere in war, if its object be not attained at once.

(xvii)

South St., 16 *August*, 1838.

I do not like the despatches from Egypt and Constantinople, which I read last. By his own account in his despatch[1] of the 9th of July Campbell does not appear to have spoken half strongly or decisively enough to the Pasha respecting his intention of declaring his independence. I hope he has now instructions which will cause him to assume a firmer tone.

From the tone of Ponsonby's despatch and from his known opinions I very much think he will urge the Sultan to undertake [maritime] hostility on his side. In this point of view, I a little doubt the policy of allowing our fleet to cruise with the Turkish fleet. Its presence may encourage the Turks to act, and we may be engaged in an attempt to reduce Mehemet Ali and embroiled before we are aware and in a manner, which we do not intend.

[P.S.] Considine is at Tunis, I presume against the French. Do you mean him to act against the Turks, if hostilities should take place between them and the Bey?

(xviii)

Windsor Castle, 23 *September*, 1838.

I would give him a passport,[2] but not in a false name. He is a strange young man, and nobody knows what he intends to do, or what he may do. The only use of a Passport is to enable him to leave Switzerland. It is not necessary to empower him to come into England. Now if he should go to France and kick up a row anywhere there, as he did at Strasburgh, it would be an awkward thing, that he should do so under an English Passport, knowingly given by our Minister in a fictitious name.

[1] *F.O. Turkey*, 343.
[2] The note is endorsed: "Application of P. Louis Buonaparte to Morier our Minr at Berne for Passport under an assumed name to come to England."

(xix)

South St., 19 *June*, 1839.

I cannot think that in any case it would be wise or prudent to attempt to force the passage of the Dardanelles, if it is absolutely refused by the Porte.

Such a refusal can only arise in the case of determined hostility on the part both of Russia and Turkey, and in that case the enterprise would be most difficult and the situation of the fleet, even if it succeeded, most hazardous.

I think the Admiral should not be advised to go to Constantinople and the Black Sea, as the enemy of the Porte. He can only do it as her ally and with her good will.

In other respects I think the draft quite right.

I do not know whether the Admiral should not be simply instructed to take the measures necessary to prevent collision, without saying any thing about interfering between the fleets etc. He must take care not to act so as to give the advantage to the Egyptians. We must not have another Navarino.

(xx)

South St., 4 *July*, 1840.

Metternich seems to me to vex himself about very small points in diplomacy and to be very anxious about the exact manner in which his propositions are urged.

The more I think of the matter the more I am convinced that you will not be able to persuade a majority of the Cabinet to concur in measures which may lead to long and difficult operations. Some are, as you know, entirely for Mehemet Ali, others will be apprehensive of the House of Commons and the country, upon neither of which can any reliance be placed for support, and depend upon it that the intelligence from Alexandria and the disposition shewn by Mehemet with respect to the English fleet will, whether it ought or not, have a great effect upon their minds.

(xxi)

South St., 6 *July*, 1840.

I have received your letter. You have of course so entirely considered the general grounds upon which you are acting, that I do not pretend to argue them with you or to shake you in your conviction.

You are also no doubt fully aware of the necessary and immediate consequences of the step which you are taking. It must lead at once to the dissolution of the Government, the consequences of which both at home and abroad and particularly upon this eastern question must be most grave.

But what I wish earnestly to press upon you, is the consideration whether this decided course upon your part is not premature, and whether the opinion of the majority of the Cabinet is sufficiently pronounced to justify you in taking it. Would it not be more fair to have another Cabinet upon the subject, a more deliberate discussion and a formal decision? It will now be said and with some truth that it was deferred to another time for consideration, and that the minds of many were by no means made up and certainly not declared upon it.

Consider also the peculiar position in which our affairs stand at present. Lord Hardwick's motion on Tuesday night may bring on a crisis. If the Calendar Bill were lost I do not think that John Russell would consent to continue in office, and if we are to resign would it not [be] better that we should do so upon that question, than upon an acknowledged difference upon these oriental affairs, which must be themselves so seriously affected by the knowledge and avowal of such a difference?

If we are beat tomorrow night, let us act upon that. If not, have a Cabinet on Wednesday on this question and act upon their decision.

[P.S.] I shall of course not mention the matter at present.

(xxii)

South St., 7 *July*, 1840.

Many thanks for you letter. For Gods sake do not think one thing. I have no notion that your resignation must not dissolve the present Government and how another is to be formed in the present state of parties and opinions I see not. I will call in the course of the morning.

(xxiii)

South St., 8 *July*, 1840.

I have received this from John Russell.[1] Would it not be possible to adopt it? What you propose is a convention between the four Powers upon the subject without specifying actual measures. Might it not be understood that this should be the point; we have proposed to the Sultan to undertake the management of the question for him, might we not now make the same proposition to the other party?

(xxiv)

Windsor Castle, 25 *August*, 1840.

I send you a letter[2] which I have received from John Russell this morning. It is most highly desirable that something should be done to withdraw us from our present state of uncertainty. We are now depen-

[1] Missing.
[2] Lord John Russell to Melbourne, 24 Aug., 1840: *B.P.* It suggested an approach to France through Austria.

dent entirely upon accident upon what may happen in the Levant, upon the caprice of Mehemet Ali, upon the irritation of the French people, upon the tone of the French and of our own Press.

Depend upon it also, you mistake Louis Philippe's character if you suppose that he will act solely according to his interest, and not from passion. He has a great deal of Jemappes left about him still.

I have a letter from Minto upon our naval state. There are two things I do not at all like.

1st To trust to the French not being able to man their ships. It is often found that people *can* do what they attempt with resolution.

2. To trust to Russia for naval assistance and defence.

The last great conflict in Europe brought Russia down into the middle of Europe and gave her a power on the land which she never had before. Take care that the next does not give her the same power upon the sea. This is for France as well as for us to consider.

(xxv)

South St., 29 *September*, 1840.

I am going down to Windsor and shall be back perhaps tomorrow; certainly on Thursday morning. I received a letter yesterday from the Queen in which is the following passage: "The right way would be to forget all irritation and to try to do what is fair by France without appearing to bow to her. We should try, while we have still the chance of success to make overtures to France to give in the principle [sic]. If we fail and then have recourse to France, she will exult exceedingly and we shall be lowered. This is the Queens opinion and she wishes Lord Melbourne would mention this both to Ld. Palmerston and Ld. John."

Now consider whether it is not possible to take a step in this direction. If our measures fail, you must do something of this kind. If they succeed, you have said that you would then be ready to concert with France the further steps to be taken. Things must be by this time in such a state as to shew whether your measures will ultimately succeed or fail. They must, in fact, have virtually done the one or the other; any step you now take will, therefore, have no effect upon the result, and it will have from the time at which it is taken the advantage which the Queen points out. If you fail, it is better to have taken this course, before you know of the failure. If you succeed, there will be no humiliation, but on the contrary all the credit which naturally belongs to moderation in prosperity.

(xxvi)

Windsor Castle, 30 *September*, 1840.

I send you a note which I have this morning received from Lansdowne.[1] He is to be in town to-day and therefore you may probably see him and hear his opinion from himself.

[1] Lansdowne to Melbourne, "Tuesday night": *B.P.*

I send you also a note which I have received this morning from Prince Albert,[1] who is of course very anxious about the matter. He thinks that a proposal to France might be based upon Metternich's proposition, that France should reaccede to and reassert the principle of supporting the Sultan. This is not a bad notion, but it requires France to take the first manifest step, which I fear that it would not suit her present purpose and position to do. It would not settle the affair because, I am afraid, that, France being readmitted into the negotiations, we should still differ about the further steps to be taken, but it might get France out of the present difficulty which is always worth while. I shall be in London by 12 o'clock to-morrow and will see you before the Cabinet.

(xxvii)

South St., 10 *October*, 1840.

I send you a letter which I received yesterday evening from Prince Albert. I have received one still stronger from the Queen.[2] I wish you would think seriously of some mode of reconciling matters. Provided the operations were not arrested, which now they cannot be, it has never appeared to me that it would be either a humiliation or a disadvantage to make an overture to France to the extent of asking her what ultimate arrangement she would agree to. [Health]. . . .

(xxviii)

South St., 12 *October*, 1840.[3]

Guizot wrote to me this morning desiring to see me and he has just been here. He came to state that he was desirous that I should know the actual posture of affairs in France and the importance of the moment, in which we were acting; that the Note [October 8th] which he had presented to you on Saturday, whether good or bad, well-argued or the contrary, he thought it unnecessary to discuss, was the result of a great effort of the party who were for peace in France; that this question, if now neglected, could not be resumed, and that affairs would infallibly fall into the hands of the violent and those who were disposed to war, and that the worst consequences would probably come. I said of course

---

[1] Prince Albert to Melbourne, [undated]: *B.P.*
[2] On 6 October he had written: "The Queen has also repeatedly asked me whether I had news that you had written to Granville, directing him to consult Thiers as to how he would receive a proposition founded upon Metternich's views."
[3] This letter was later endorsed by Palmerston:
"Giving me an account of Guizots (humbugging) conversation to him about the last French Note."
"Anxiety of Cabinet that negotiation should be *entered into with* France."
"That is, that we should yield to French threats and intrigues, which I was fully resolved never should be done by *me*."

little or nothing to him, and he added that he did not expect that I should; that all that he wished was to make me fully acquainted with the real state of things.

You must have observed how strong was the opinion of the Cabinet on Saturday, that this opening should be taken advantage of, and I urge you not to lose any time in proceeding with the negotiation. If you find any difficulty with the Ministers of the other Powers, it will be important instantly to inform the Cabinet of it. [Health] . . . .

(xxix)

South St., 18 *November*, 1840.

I have been very unwell this last two days or I should have written to you before upon the subject of this. I cannot help doubting the policy of this superceding of Sir C. Smith in the circumstances. In the first place it is doubtful into whose hands the command will fall, as it appears that Colonel Mitchell was only about to depart for Madrid on the 29th of October last.

Next from the news lately received from France it is probable that this dismissal will reach the force whilst engaged in active operations. If those operations are in a train of success, it is evident that the removal of the Commander will be prejudicial and may interrupt that success. If they are unsuccessful, it will probably add to the confusion and aggravate disaster.

These reasons make me think the step hazardous, yet, if it is to be taken, it appears to me that it would be best to take it simply and without giving the reasons contained in the draft [marked] circulated.

The opinion that Ibrahim has acted judiciously by withdrawing the [garrisons] of Tripoli and Latikea may be an erroneous opinion, but surely it is no more, and hardly affords a ground for so strong a measure.

It also appears to me to be impossible to pronounce so decided an opinion with respect to Napier without further information. All that you say is true, but what Sir C. Smith says, may be true also. The successes have been very brilliant, but they may have been accompanied by bold expressions of authority, which you cannot expect an officer of the army to approve.

Think again about superceding him and if you supercede him, it seems to me unnecessary to give reasons for it, which must bring on a vindication upon his part and a contest.

APPENDIX D

(i)

Private letter

Londres, 21 *Décembre*, 1839.

Je suis arrivé le 18 du courant après avoir été retenu tout un jour à Calais, où je ne trouvai pas de paquebot allant à Douvres dans la journée du 17.

Mr. le Baron de Brunow[2] étant arrivé quelques heures après moi à Calais dans la nuit du 16 au 17 et obligé de s'arrêter comme moi, je profitai de ce délai pour lui communiquer les instructions dont je suis muni et que Votre Altesse m'a chargé de porter à sa connaissance. Mr. de Brunow les lut avec un grand intérêt ainsique leurs volumineuses annexes dont il n'avait pas connaissance; j'ajoutai verbalement qu'il avait suffi du vœux exprimé par l'Empereur son Maitre de voir sa mission appuyée par nous pour que notre Gouvernement s'empressât à y déférer en envoyant une personne ad hoc, afin de mieux marquer cet appui et l'union de nos deux Cours aux yeux du monde. Mr. de Brunow observa que cette heureuse union avait produit de si grands bienfaits, qu'elle était de nouveau si essentielle pour la réussite de la grande affaire du moment, que sans un accord parfait entre nos deux Cours, il ne croyait pas pouvoir la mener à un résultat satisfaisant; je l'assurai qu'il ne dépendrait pas de nous que ce résultat ne fut atteint, que notre pensée à cet égard était suffisament connue de sa Cour et exprimée dans les expéditions du 19 et 25 Novembre adressées par notre Cabinet à ceux des quatre Puissances, qu'il sortait en outre de ces expéditions, traitant principalement de la pacification entre la Porte et l'Egypte, que nous étions d'accord sur le principe énoncé par l'Empereur Nicolas relativement à la clôture des détroits conduisant à la mer de Marmora, mais que nous devions y ajouter le desir, qui avait été apprécié à St. Petersbourg comme le constatait une dépèche du Comte de Nesselrode à Mr. de Tatischeff en date du 8/20 Novembre que ce fut le Sultan qui se prononçât à ce sujet et en fit la déclaration aux Puissances, en vertu du droit de souveraineté qu'il exerçait sur ces mêmes détroits. Mr. de Brunnow avec une franchise et un abandon de confiance dont je ne saurais assez relever le mérite, voulut bien me développer le plan qu'il comptait suivre et les propositions qu'il ferait

---

[1] Vienna, *Haus Hof und Staatsarchiv, England*, 290 and 295. I have noted the private letters. The others are despatches.

[2] Both the forms, Brunow and Brunnow, are used by Hummelauer and by others writing in French.

au Cabinet Anglais sur ces deux questions distinctes, celles de la pacification et de la clôture des détroits, mais qu'il compte réunir dans un même corps de transaction à formuler.

Cette transaction, dit Mr. de Brunnow, doit être tout au profit du Sultan, tendant à relever sa puissance et à le dégager de l'état de gêne où il se trouve placé vis-à-vis de son vassal ambitieux. Pour atteindre ce but salutaire il serait desirable de rédiger un acte qui ferait partie du droit public Européen; la pacification de l'Empire Ottoman formerait la base de cet acte; pour que cette pacification fut effective et durable, il faudrait rendre au Sultan une grande partie de la force et de l'indépendance qu'il possédait avant le traité de Kutahia, et obliger Mehemed Aly à rentrer dans des limites territoriales raisonables, le replaçant en même tems dans une position de vasselage dont lui ni ses successeurs ne pourraient plus jamais sortir sans s'exposer au ressentiment des Puissances signatoires de cet acte; elles conviendraient de plus entre elles des mesures à prendre pour faire exécuter cet acte dans toute son étendue et dans toute sa rigueur: il serait dit ensuite dans ce document que ces mêmes Puissances en vertu du droit qu'elles reconnaissent au Sultan de tenir clos les détroits, qui conduisent à la Mer de Marmora, aux vaisseaux de guerre étrangers—(principe d'ailleurs formellement établi et reconnu par la législation Ottomane)—prendraient entre elles l'engagement formel, tant pour rendre un hommage éclatant que pour mieux marquer encore le respect qu'elles portent à ce droit souverain du Sultan, de ne jamais l'enfreindre sous aucun prétexte quelconque, de considérer par conséquent la Mer noire et la Mer de Marmara comme des mers closes en tems de paix comme en tems de guerre; que cependant, si malgré tous les soins des cinq Puissances pour mettre le Sultan à l'abri d'une attaque de la part de Mehemed Aly ou de celle de l'un ou de l'autre de ses successeurs, le premier, ou l'un de ceux-ci, se portait à une agression spontanée contre leur Souverain légitime, qui mit celui-ci en danger dans sa capitale, et, qu'en suite de cette agression le Sultan crut dans ce cas devoir réclamer des secours matériels et simultanés des Puissances susdites, les détroits seraient alors ouverts, mais pour ce seul cas exceptionel, aux navires des dites Puissances Alliées, observant toute fois que ces navires prendraient selon leur nationalité, des positions fixes dans l'intérieur de la Mer de Marmara, de manière à empêcher tout contact entre les escadres étrangères.

Ces points convenus, on devrait alors se rendre compte de la nature de l'appui que nous avons promis à la Porte, des limites jusqu'où on croirait pouvoir l'étendre et des moyens à employer pour le rendre efficace, présenter ensuite à la Porte cet arrangement comme résultat de l'appui promis, lui demander s'il est conforme à ses vœux et si elle en accepte l'exécution par les Puissances. Après nous être assurés de son consentement et le consentement obtenu, on présenterait alors cet arrangement à Mehemed Aly pour l'obliger de l'accepter.

Voici, mon Prince, la substance du projet de transaction que Mr. le Baron de Brunnow compte présenter au Cabinet Anglais; s'il l'accepte, avec ou sans modification, et si Mr. de Brunnow parvient à s'entendre avec lui, il l'engagera alors à le présenter à la France; les observations ou les objections qu'elle pourrait y faire, feront foi du degré de sincérité qu'elle professe pour la conservation de l'Empire Ottoman dont elle a ouvertement proclamé le principe; cependant, des objections, telles qu'un refus d'adhérer à la proposition de stations fixes et convenues dans l'intérieur de la Mer de Marmora, ne seraient pas acceptées et prouveraient un obstacle insurmontable pour une entente avec elle, la Russie étant fermement décidée à ne pas transiger sur ce point; dans ce cas les quatre autres Puissances devraient aviser aux moyens d'aller en avant sans la France et de faire exécuter l'acte dont elles seraient convenues entre elles, dès qu'il aurait été accepté par le Sultan.

Mr. de Brunnow me demanda, si une transaction de cette nature rencontrerait les vœux de notre Cabinet?—Je repondis à Mr. de Brunnow que bien que les deux objets dont elle, se composait, celui de la pacification de l'Empire Ottoman, et celui de la clôture des détroits, étaient distincts en eux mêmes et qu'il eut été préférable de ne pas les incorporer dans une même transaction; cependant tout ce qui pouvait contribuer à relever et à rafermir l'autorité du Sultan, relativement au premier point, celui de la pacification, et à constater le respect du à son droit de souveraineté sur les détroits, me semblait d'après mon opinion individuelle devoir rencontrer l'approbation de ma Cour; que pour mieux m'en assurer, je desirerais qu'il me permit de porter à la connaissance de Votre Altesse les confidences qu'il avait eu la bonté de me faire; afin qu'en les jugeant dans leur grand ensemble, Vous puissiez, mon Prince, Vous en former une idée juste, malgré que Mr. de Brunnow n'a pu encore rien faire dans l'objet de sa mission, vue l'absence de Lord Palmerston, il a consenti sans hésitation et avec une complaisance toute particulière à ce que je transmette à Votre Altesse son programme; en général je ne trouve point de termes suffisans pour exprimer à Votre Altesse combien je dois de reconnaissance à Mr. de Brunnow pour l'empressement avec lequel il est venu au devant de tout ce que j'ai pu desirer d'éclaircissement de sa part ainsique pour la confiance sans bornes qu'il me montre.

(ii)

Secret.

Londres, 21 *Décembre*, 1839.

Ma lettre précédente[1] a été écrite non seulement avec le consentement de Mr. le Baron de Brunnow, mais pour être sûr de m'être bien pénétré de ce qu'il m'avait confié sur son plan d'action, je lui ai fait la lecture de ma lettre, à laquelle il a donné sa complette approbation. Il met une grande importance à ce que Votre Altesse soit informée de l'attitude qu'il va prendre ici—"je vois" me dit-il, "que le Prince de Metternich n'a pas reçu de Petersbourg tous les renseignemens qu'il

[1] No. (i)

eut été desirable qu'il obtint sur l'ensemble de ma mission; c'est à moi
à remplir cette lacune, qu'il comprendra lorsqu'il saura que je n'ai
d'autres instructions que celles qu'il a vues et qui ne suffisent pas pour
lui avoir donné une idée claire et exacte de la tâche qui m'est imposée.
Je comprends donc qu'il soit dans le vague sur l'objet de ma mission,
et qu'il ait dans Vos instructions exprimé le désir de connaitre le terrain
sur lequel je me placerai en reprenant la négociation avec le Cabinet
Anglais. Le Chancelier de Cour et d'Etat a l'air aussi de croire que
l'objet le plus important de ma mission et celui qui nous occupe
uniquement est la clôture des détroits et que mes instructions ne
portent que sur cette partie de la question; je conçois qu'il ait pu en
juger ainsi, mais celle de la pacification nous interesse avant tout et
comme je possède à cet égard par mes premières instructions tout ce
dont j'ai besoin pour la discuter et la régler avec le Cabinet Anglais,
on me renvoie à ces instructions; je n'en possède pas d'autres que celles
que Vous connaissez hormi une lettre du Comte de Nesselrode qui
me dit au sujet de ma seconde mission;" "l'Empereur s'en rapporte
entièrement à ce que Vous ferez, Vous connaissez sa pensée et il Vous
laisse la liberté de faire ce que Vous croirez de plus utile pour amener
à une bonne fin l'affaire qui Vous est confiée." "Or" continua Mr. de
Brunnow "j'ai carte blanche et le premier emploi que j'en fais c'est
vis-à-vis de Votre Cabinet, en cherchant les moyens de venir au devant
de ses désirs et de me placer autant qu'il est dans mes facultés sur une
même ligne avec lui; nous le sommes déjà quant à la question de
principe; reste donc celle de forme; le Prince de Metternich met une
grande importance à ce que les droits de souveraineté du Sultan
relativement à la clôture des détroits se trouvent mentionés dans une
déclaration par laquelle le Sultan rappele aux Puissances qu'il entend
que les deux détroits soyent et restent clos aux vaisseaux de guerre de
toutes les nations et dans une contredéclaration des Puissances qui
porterait qu'Elles sauront respecter ce principe."

Mr. de Brunnow croit la manière, dont il compte placer dans le projet
de transaction la reconnaissance de ce droit, plus forte encore, en ce
que les Puissances reconnaissent spontanément le droit *permanent* du
Sultan, sans qu'il ait été obligé de le leur rappeler; cependant il s'est
occupé à chercher un moyen de satisfaire le desir de Votre Altesse à
cet égard et Mr. de Brunnow croit qu'à l'époque ou l'on présenterait
à la Porte la transaction que l'on aurait faite dans son intérêt et comme
preuve et résultat de l'appui qu'on lui a promis, on devrait l'accom-
pagner d'une note, à laquelle la Porte répondrait en forme de déclaration
—(partant de la supposition qu'elle accepte la transaction)—elle s'y
exprimerait satisfaite et reconnaissante du genre d'appui qu'on lui
offrirait contre son vassal, ainsi que de l'hommage rendu par les Puissances à son droit de souveraineté sur la clôture des détroits ainsique
de l'engagement pris entr'elles de le respecter; elle mentionerait en
même tems le cas spécial et exceptionel où ils leur seraient ouverts,
celui d'une demande à ces mêmes Puissances de secours matériels
simultanés contre une attaque spontanée de Mehemed Aly ou de l'un

de ses successeurs. A cette occasion Mr. de Brunnow me répéta ce que j'ai mentioné dans mon rapport N. 1 Litt. B[1] et me dit avec plus de force et de solennité encore, de conjurer Votre Altesse de ne pas reculer devant des objets de forme qui pourraient nuire au fond, et le renverser peut-être. La bienveillance avec laquelle le Prince de Metternich m'a quelquefois écouté, dit-il, la confiance qu'il m'a montrée dans tant d'occasions me donnent le courage de faire ici un appel à sa haute intelligence pour que l'Autriche ne s'efface pas ou ne se tienne trop en arrière dans cette affaire et pour que le cas du traité du 6 Juillet [1827] ne se présente plus, ce qui porterait un coup fatal et irréparable à l'alliance. De son côté, pour l'éviter, Mr. de Brunnow m'a assuré qu'il apporterait dans le projet de transaction, qu'il m'a autorisé à soumettre à Votre Altesse, toutes les modifications qu'Elle lui suggérerait. Pour cela il faudrait qu'elles puissent arriver encore à tems et avant qu'il ne soit tombé d'accord avec le Cabinet Anglais sur l'arrangement qu'il discutera avec lui.

Egalement Mr. de Brunnow n'insistera pas sur l'insertion dans l'acte à conclure de la phrase relative à la clôture des détroits *en tems de paix et de guerre*, il ne la placera qu'en parenthèse pour remplir les ordres de sa Cour, mais il n'ajoute aucune valeur à cette phrase et prendra sur lui de l'écarter, si Lord Palmerston le desire. Quant à la séparation des deux objets distincts, celui de la pacification et celui du droit de souveraineté du Sultan sur les détroits, Mr. de Brunnow ne peut le faire, et le motif principal est à ce qu'il paroit, qu'on ne veut pas laisser à la France la faculté de choisir dans l'un ou l'autre des actes, s'ils étaient séparés, celui qui serait à sa convenance, il faut que la France, me dit Mr. de Brunnow, soit liée par l'ensemble de la transaction et qu'il ne lui soit pas permis de se prévaloir seulement des avantages sans les charges, ce qui lui deviendrait plus facile encore par deux actes séparés.

Relativement à la question de la demande d'un secours matériel par le Sultan en cas d'une attaque de la part de Mehemed Aly ou de l'un de ses successeurs, la refléxion que fait Votre Altesse dans mes instructions sur la nécessité d'une retractation de la déclaration faite par la Russie à cet égard à la Porte, tombe d'elle-même dèsque l'arrangement projetté sera conclu et accepté par elle.

Vous verrez, mon Prince, par ce récit long mais fidèle, tout ce qui occupe l'esprit de Mr. de Brunnow, il espere que Vous viendrez à son secours en lui accordant le bénéfice de vos lumières et de votre appui dans la tâche importante mais difficile qui lui est imposée. La franchise et l'abandon avec lesquels il est entré dans tous ces détails ne sauraient être assez appréciés; il est personellement dévoué à Votre Altesse et dans toutes les occasions s'occupe des moyens de remontrer Vos desirs. La confiance qu'il me témoigne est due au dévouement et au respect qu'il Vous porte, mon Prince.

[1] Of the same date. An ostensible despatch shewn to Brunnow.

(iii)

Londres, 30 *Décembre*, 1839.

Je profite de l'occasion d'un courrier que Lord Palmerston expédie aujourd'hui à Lord Beauvale pour avoir l'honneur de rendre compte à Votre Altesse des entretiens que Mr. le Baron de Brunnow et moi avons eus avec le Principal Secrétaire d'Etat pour le département des affaires étrangères pendant les trois jours que nous avons passés chez lui à Broadlands. Nous nous y rendîmes le 23 dec.; Mr. de Brunnow m'y ayant précédé de quelques heures, entra d'abord en matière avec sa Seigneurie sur l'objet de son second envoi, après lui avoir annoncée que cette nouvelle mission n'était qu'un corollaire de la première, suspendue par un incident qu'il n'avait pas été en son pouvoir de résoudre, mais qui venait de l'être par une détermination généreuse de l'Empereur, Son Auguste Maître, détermination qu'il n'avait pas hésité de prendre dès qu'il avait appris qu'elle pouvait servir à faciliter une entente entre les Puissances pour la solution de cette importante affaire.

Mr. de Brunnow présenta alors le travail qu'il avait fait sur l'ensemble de cette grave complication et qui se trouve consigné dans la lettre qu'il a adressée le 21. de ce mois à Mr. de Tatistscheff;[1] c'est la minute de cette même lettre que Mr. de Brunnow lut au Principal Secrétaire d'Etat qui l'accueillit de la manière la plus favorable. Sa Seigneurie dans l'entretien que j'eus après avec elle me témoigna sa satisfaction sur ce travail et me dit qu'il ne laissait rien à désirer. En le lui présentant, Mr. de Brunnow dit à Lord Palmerston qu'il avait cherché à venir au devant des désirs de tout le monde, que, s'étant aperçu qu'à Vienne on avait été dans le doute sur le véritable objet de sa mission et qu'on y semblait croire qu'elle porterait plus sur l'arrangement de l'affaire des détroits que sur celui de la pacification, il avait cru devoir lever ce doute en présentant et y fesant parvenir sans délai le tableau fidèle de la marche qu'il allait suivre; dans un second entretien qu'eût cet Envoyé avec le Principal Secrétaire d'Etat, il lui déclara, qu'il était un point sur lequel il avait des ordres positifs, celui, de ne point séparer la question des détroits de celle de la pacification, de les renfermer dans une même transaction; Mr. de Brunnow fit cette déclaration à la suite d'une observation faite par le Principal Secrétaire d'Etat, qui avait proposé à côté de la transaction générale un article séparé relativement à la souveraineté du Grand Seigneur sur les détroits, dans le genre de celui convenu entre l'Angleterre et la Porte dans le traité de 1809 (Art. 11) entre ces deux Puissances. Sur cette déclaration de Mr. de Brunnow, sa Seigneurie n'insista plus et demanda le projet de cet Envoyé pour pouvoir le communiquer à Lord Melbourne. Voici, mon Prince, ce qui s'est passé dans le premier entretien qu'ont eu ensemble ces deux Ministres.

Arrivé le 23 une couple d'heures avant le dîner, Lord Palmerston me fit un accueil des plus flatteurs et bienveillans; je lui remis la lettre dont

[1] Russian Ambassador at Vienna.

Votre Altesse m'avait muni pour lui, et sa Seigneurie me dit que nous causerions le lendemain.

Le 24. après le déjeuner le Principal Secrétaire d'Etat me prit dans son Cabinet; je débutai par lui dire que l'Empereur Nicolas ayant manifesté le désir que nous donnions notre appui à la seconde mission de Mr. le Baron de Brunnow auprès du Gouvernement de Sa Majesté Britannique, nous nous étions prêtés avec d'autant plus d'empressement, à ce vœu, que nous avions cru voir dans la résolution que venait de prendre Sa Majesté Impériale un moyen efficace de lever l'obstacle qui avait arrêté jusqu'à présent une entente entre les Puissances tandisque nous pensions que cette résolution devait rencontrer l'entière satisfaction du Cabinet anglais; qu'alors nous avions voulu par en envoi spécial, qui n'aurait pas eu lieu si le Prince Esterhazy avait été à son poste, marquer encore davantage l'union intime de nos trois Cours dans la présente circonstance; que nous étions parfaitement d'accord avec son Cabinet et celui de St. Pétersbourg sur les principes fondamentaux des questions de la pacification et de la fermeture des détroits; que relativement à celle-ci, nous avions énoncé l'opinion qu'il appartenait au Sultan de s'expliquer sur le droit inhérent à sa souveraineté, qu'il possède sur la clôture de ces détroits; en même tems j'exprimai à sa Seigneurie notre désir anxieux de voir une solution prochaine de l'affaire turco-égyptienne; que le moyen d'arriver plus sûrement à un résultat satisfaisant, était de nous montrer unis d'intention et d'action; qu'il était de la plus haute importance que Mr. de Brunnow ne partit pas d'ici sans que ce résultat ne fut obtenu, qu'il fallait ne pas indisposer l'Empereur Nicolas qui venait de fournir une preuve si manifeste de Ses intentions bienveillantes et de Son désir pour le maintien de l'intégrité de l'Empire Ottoman; qu'il avait en Russie bien des personnes qui n'étaient pas de cet avis là; qu'il ne fallait pas renforcer ce parti et refouler peut-être ce Souverain, malgré lui, vers ce parti, si on exigeait de lui, ce que dans son intérêt particulier, il ne lui serait peutêtre pas possible de faire et ce qui alors pourrait compromettre la paix générale; que d'un autre côté, et malgré les difficultés qu'avait suscité la France dans toute cette affaire, il serait cependant plus facile de s'entendre avec un Prince de l'expérience de Louis Philippe, plutôt qu'avec son successeur qui pourrait être entraîné par le parti révolutionnaire et par un mouvement de fausse gloire dont il ne parait que, trop avide; que l'affaire manquée, il serait difficile de la reprendre tandisque nous avions dans ce moment tous les matériaux pour la conduire à une bonne fin.

Le Principal Secrétaire d'Etat voulut bien m'écouter sans m'interrompre et me dit que la résolution que Votre Altesse avait prise d'envoyer une spécialité dans la circonstance du moment répondait à tout ce qu'il pouvait désirer puisqu'elle manifestait l'union de nos deux Cabinets; qu'il y avait entre nos Gouvernemens tant d'intérêts communs qui formaient des points de rapprochement sans qu'il y en ait qui se croissassent; qu'en conséquence toute entente entre nous devenait facile; que le Cabinet anglais apprécie dans toute leur étendue

les services éminens rendus par Votre Altesse et l'intelligente activité
déployée par Elle dans tout le cours de cette importante affaire; qu'en
même tems il rendait une entière justice à la franchise que l'Empereur
Nicolas avait montrée dans cette grave complication et aux facilités
qu'il avait apportées pour aider à la résoudre, en un mot à la position
européenne qu'il avait prise. Sa Seigneurie ajouta, qu'unis comme
nous l'étions, c.à.d. l'Autriche, l'Angleterre, la Russie et la Prusse, il
éspéroit que la France après s'être convaincue de cette union, jugerait
de son intérêt de se joindre à nous, surtout lorsqu'elle aurait acquis la
certitude qu'en dernière analyse on serait décidé à marcher sans elle.
Une coopération de la Prusse nous est surtout nécessaire à cause de sa
position géographique vis-à-vis de la France, ajouta-t-Elle.

Le Principal Secrétaire d'Etat voulut bien entrer en quelques détails
sur les moyens de la pacification: je m'étais, dit-il, d'abord déclaré pour
l'avis de votre Cour qui s'était prononcée pour le Minimum des
concessions à faire à Méhémed Aly; c'était la base la plus correcte,
puisque c'était celle adoptée par la Porte elle même, dans les offres de
réconciliation qu'Elle avait fait faire au Pacha d'Egypte, en le confir-
mant dans ce Pachalik et en lui promettant l'hérédité pour son successeur. La France s'étant opposée à ce plan, je tâchai de la satisfaire en
fesant une part plus large à Méhémed Ali, mais celle-ci ayant également
repoussé cette seconde proposition, j'en suis revenu à ma première
idée, qui est la vôtre et celle du Sultan, le Minimum. A la suite du
refus de Méhémed Aly et dans la crainte de quelqu'entreprise hardie
de sa part contre son Souverain légitime, nous avons promis notre
appui au Sultan, par une Note collective, dûe à la sagacité de votre
Cabinet et présentée par nos représentans à Constantinople; une
promesse faite aussi solennellement ne peut rester infructueuse; la
position usurpée par Méhémed Aly, continua le Principal Secrétaire
d'Etat, est incompatible avec l'existence du Sultan, un Vassal plus
puissant que son Souverain finit par le détruire et l'intégrité de l'Empire
Ottoman sous l'autorité du Sultan est indispensable au maintien de cet
Empire, de la paix générale et de l'équilibre politique des grands
intérêts européens. Pour que cet ambitieux Vassal ne compromette
plus le repos de l'Orient, il faut qu'il rentre dans des limites territoriales d'où lui ni ses successeurs n'ayant plus les moyens de sortir, il
seroit donc à désirer qu'on le restreignit au Pachalick d'Egypte avec la
promesse de la réversion pour son fils Ibrahim; cependant si nous
trouvons de trop grandes difficultés de la part de la France à cet égard,
on pourroit alors étendre un peu la position territoriale de Méhémed
Aly, toutefois de manière à ce qu'il ne puisse jamais plus inquiéter son
souverain légitime; il faudrait placer entre lui et son Vassal, le désert
qui les séparait autrefois, lui enlever le district d'Adana, la Syrie, St.
Jean d'Acre, faire rentrer le Sultan dans la possession des villes saintes,
et de l'île de Candie; par la nouvelle délimitation Jérusalem resterait
probablement au Pacha: en un mot nous devons ôter à celui-ci tous les
moyens de jamais plus chercher à s'affranchir de l'autorité de son
souverain légitime; une plus grande étendue de territoire que celle

qu'il est de mon avis qu'on pourrait lui donner lui ferait toujours nourrir des idées d'indépendance qu'il chercherait à réaliser tôt ou tard si on ne lui en ôtait pas les moyens. Quant à ceux coercitifs pour l'obliger à se soumettre à cet arrangement, il faudrait en établir de différentes gradations selon le plus ou moins de résistance qu'il ferait. Les Puissances après avoir présenté au Sultan le résultat de leurs délibérations sur les moyens de pacification et ce résultat accepté par lui, il serait porté à Mehemed Aly; on lui promettrait une addition de territoire au Pachalick d'Egypte, s'il se soumet immédiatement à la première sommation; sur un refus de sa part, cette offre d'agrandissement de territoire serait retirée et on commencerait par intercepter les communications par mer avec l'armée d'Ibrahim; si cela ne suffisait pas, il faudrait s'emparer de l'île de Candie et la remettre au Sultan; on ne pourrait à la vérité mettre le blocus devant Alexandrie, parceque celui-ci ne se pratique qu'envers un état régulier sous un pouvoir légitime, ce qui n'est pas le cas de Méhémed Aly que nous considérons comme un rebelle, mais cela n'empêche pas que l'on pourrait saisir des vaisseaux de commerce ce qui tarirait bientôt les ressources de son trésor; ceux-ci seraient envoyés à Smyrne pour être placés sous l'autorité du souverain légitime; finalement il faudrait employer la force si toutes ces mesures échouaient. D'après des données que le Principal Secrétaire d'Etat a recueillies d'un officier expérimenté de la compagnie des Indes Orientales, qui connoit l'état intérieur de l'Egypte et de ses points vulnérables, données sur lesquelles il attend encore des renseignemens plus exacts, il semble qu'une expédition de 5000 hommes envoyée de Bombay à Suez, suffirait pour balayer toute l'Egypte dégarnie de troupes.

La Russie pourrait également envoyer un corps de troupes, mais le grand trajet qu'elles auraient à faire au travers de pays stériles et incivilisés, lui ferait mettre un long tems à arriver; ici sa Seigneurie a émis le désir que notre Cour voulût accorder de son côté un secours matériel en soldats qui pourraient à l'aide de bâtimens anglais être débarqués sur un point convenu de l'Egypte ou sur l'île de Candie pour agir simultanément avec des troupes Ottomanes; ce secours qui devrait être tout au plus de quelques mille hommes serait défrayé par la Porte. Si le Pacha laissait venir les choses à une pareille extrémité sa destitution et celle de toute sa famille, en serait la conséquence inévitable. Il est trop rusé pour s'y exposer et risquer le tout pour le tout, en supposant même qu'il tentât de se défendre et qu'il appelât l'armée d'Ibrahim à son secours, à mesure qu'elle avancerait vers Alexandrie, l'armée turque avancerait de son côté et s'emparerait de la Syrie, ce qui lui serait facile vû le mécontentement qui y règne.

Il est à présumer, dit Lord Palmerston, que nous ne serons pas obligés à aller jusque là, si nous fesons comprendre à Méhémed Aly que nous sommes fermement décidés à faire exécuter ce que nous aurons résolu, mais il sera bien d'être préparé à tous les contingens possibles.

Quant à l'affaire des détroits, le Principal Secrétaire d'Etat est

également d'avis, que le droit de souveraineté du Sultan à leur égard ne
saurait assez être relevé; il m'a aussi parlé de la rédaction d'un Article
séparé, semblable à celui de leur traîté de 1809 avec la Porte, mais il n'y
a plus insisté après la déclaration que Mr. de Brunnow lui fit et que
j'ai citée plus haut.

Dans une seconde entrevue que Mr. de Brunnow a eue le 25 avec
Lord Palmerston où j'ai été invité d'assister, celui-ci après avoir
passé avec lui en revue tous les points insérés dans la lettre de cet
Envoyé à Mr. de Tatistscheff formant son projet de transaction, se
montra satisfait de ce projet dans toutes ses parties, et dit qu'il allait
faire la dessus un travail pour ensuite le présenter au Conseil, qu'il ne
sera à même de pouvoir réunir avant 8 à 10 jours. Tous les moyens
graduels de coercition à employer contre Méhémed Aly furent discutés
et convenus en ma présence, je n'y pris aucune part et ne fis qu'écouter;
mais le Principal Secrétaire d'Etat appuya fortement sur la nécessité
d'en venir à un résultat, si non entre les cinq Puissances, du moins entre
les quatre.

L'opinion du Conseil entendue et si elle répond aux vœux des Puissances, il désirerait que leurs Représentans à la Cour de Londres fussent
munis de pouvoirs nécessaires pour conclure et signer l'acte qui ren-
fermera simultanément la question de la pacification de l'Empire Ottoman et de la clôture des détroits, ainsique les mesures d'exécution qui
auront été jugées utiles et mentionnées dans le présent rapport, pour
obtenir les grands résultats qui feront l'objet de cette transaction.
Lord Palmerston nous a dit, à Mr. de Brunnow et à moi, qu'il écrirait à
cet effet à Lord Beauvale et à Sir George Hamilton pour demander de
pareilles autorisations de la part des Cours de Vienne et de Berlin;
Mr. de Brunnow s'est chargé d'écrire à la sienne pour réclamer d'Elle
des pouvoirs spéciaux; il me demanderait la minute de la forme sous laquelle
il les demanderait et voulut bien m'en laisser prendre la copie que j'ai
l'honneur de joindre sous ce pli, observant toutefois qu'il avait formulé
ainsi ce projet de pouvoirs, uniquement pour ce qui le concernait, mais
qu'il n'avait pas la prétention de vouloir rien suggérer à cet égard aux
autres Cabinets qui avaient leurs formes à eux.

Lord Palmerston observa même que Mr. de Brunnow n'aurait pas eu
besoin d'en demander de plus spéciaux, qu'il considérait ceux qu'il
possédait suffisans pour signer avec lui, mais qu'ayant annoncé ne pas
être autorisé pour mon compte à prendre une part plus directe à la
négociation, sa conclusion risquerait d'être retardée si nos Cours
(celle de Vienne et de Berlin) ne levaient pas cet obstacle. Enfin le
Principal Secrétaire d'Etat espère que cette transaction, si elle reçoit
l'assentiment des cinq, ou à défaut de la France, des quatre Puissances,
pourra être terminée et signée d'ici dans un mois, et toute l'affaire, c'est
à dire l'exécution de la transaction dans trois mois. Dès qu'elle aura
obtenu la sanction du Conseil de Sa Majesté Britannique, Lord Palmerston se chargera des démarches à faire auprès de la France, pour
l'engager à se joindre à cette transaction et à marcher de front avec les
quatre autres Puissances; il est trop pénétré de l'importance de gagner

cette Puissance dans nos rangs pour ne pas tout employer afin de l'y amener; lorsque le moment d'agir sera arrivé il ne croit pas qu'elle veuille et qu'elle puisse même s'isoler; il en résulterait pour elle une position de honte à laquelle elle ne peut s'exposer, puisque son impuissance d'empêcher l'action des quatre autres Cours serait démontrée et la placerait dans une attitude humiliante et de faiblesse qu'elle voudra éviter; une forte considération vient à l'appui de la nécessité de ne pas tarder à conclure l'affaire entre nous quatre, celle des embarras que le Gouvernement Français éprouve dans ce moment en Algérie; ils absorbent une grande partie de ses ressources militaires et pécuniaires.

Nous sommes convenus avec lui que lorsque le Conseil aurait prononcé son avis sur l'affaire que nous écririons aux représentans de nos Cours à Paris pour les inviter à seconder les efforts de l'Ambassadeur d'Angleterre auprès du Cabinet Français pour l'engager à se joindre à nous; en attendant nous sommes tombés d'accord de ne leur faire part que du langage qu'avec le Principal Secrétaire d'Etat nous sommes convenus de tenir ici au Général Sébastiani, savoir, que l'Empereur Nicolas ayant levé l'obstacle qui s'était opposé jusqu'à présent à une entente entre les Puissances pour la solution de l'affaire Turco-egyptienne et, cet obstacle ayant été levé non seulement pour une, mais pour toutes les Puissances, nous espérions que son Gouvernement voudra bien concourir avec les autres à l'acte de pacification qui forme l'objet de leurs vœux les plus ardens; le conseil de Sa Majesté Britannique allant délibérer sur les détails de l'arrangement à fixer pour la conclusion de cet acte, nous attendrions comme lui le résultat de ses délibérations, qu'en attendant nous nourissons l'espoir qu'il y aura unanimité entre toutes les Puissances qui doivent toutes désirer une fin prompte de cette crise.

Pour mon compte je me réserve d'ajouter, que l'Empereur Nicolas ayant manifesté le désir que de notre part on appuyât la nouvelle mission de Mr. de Brunnow, et ayant reconnu qu'elle était toute conçue dans un esprit de conciliation, offrant les moyens d'écarter les difficultés qui entravaient la solution de l'affaire et les gages les plus manifestes de la sincérité de l'Empereur Nicolas à cet égard, nous n'avions pas hésité à accorder notre appui pour l'atteinte d'un but qui intéressait également tout le monde; que c'était là une partie de mon envoi, indépendamment de l'injonction que j'avais reçue de fournir au besoin tous les eclaircissemens sur la pensée de notre Cabinet que l'on pourrait désirer obtenir.

(iv)

Private letter

Londres, 30 *Décembre*, 1839.

... L'affaire turco-égyptienne est plus près de sa solution qu'elle ne l'a encore été, tous les obstacles qui l'entravaient sont pour le moment écartés; mais je ne réponds pas pour cela que nous n'échouyons au port; les dispositions du principal Secrétaire d'Etat ne furent jamais meilleures, il est placé sur le terrain le plus correct, il a le premier Ministre et plusieurs membres du conseil pour lui dans cette affaire, mais néanmoins il n'est pas possible de préjuger ce qui pourra arriver. La majorité du conseil, composé d'élémens hétérogènes comme il est à présent, peut suggérer quelque nouvelle difficulté, qu'il ne serait pas possible d'écarter, Mr. de Brunow ayant déclaré qu'il avait dans ses dernières propositions épuisé la latitude de ses instructions; Mr. de Sébastiani travaille cette majorité, et non sans succès, comme il ressort du langage de Lord Holland, qui est identique avec celui de l'Ambassadeur de France.　On peut prévoir de quelle nature sera l'opposition dans le conseil, elle portera sur l'étendue des moyens coercitifs, que l'on voudra peut-être restreindre et rendre par là ineffectifs, et sur l'objection que l'on pourra faire aussi, de marcher sans la France, ce qui prouverait au monde que l'alliance entre les deux Puissances maritimes a cessé; si même la réalité de cette union n'existe, le parti ultra libéral du conseil voudra en conserver l'apparence et surtout empêcher que l'Angleterre s'associe seule à des Gouvernements absolus, tandis qu'avec la France, ce parti dirait que nous nous sommes joints à lui, et non pas lui à nous; enfin Mon Prince je suis loin de voir le procès gagné, malgré que Lord Palmerston était plein d'espoir et de courage; avant de se fixer en ville il passera deux jours à Holland House, c'est ce qui a particulièrement décidé ma visite.　Là il y trouvera les couleurs autrichiennes fortement dessinées, et par les bonnes dispositions de Lord Holland envers nous et par le langage que j'ai tenu à ce chef de parti, s'il ne tient que la moitié de ce qu'il a promis de faire dans nos intérêts, ce sera déjà beaucoup: tous les Ministres plus ou moins absens ne seront réunis ici qu'entre le 3 et le 5; ce ne sera qu'après leur réunion que l'affaire turco-égyptienne leur sera présentée, tout ce qu'il a été possible de faire pour préparer les voies pour une heureuse solution de cette immense affaire a été fait; le moment est grave, attendons en la fin avec courage, et, sans vouloir être trop noir dans notre attente, il faut être préparé à tout.

Il m'en coute de ne pas tenir Mr. le Comte Appony au courant de ce qui s'est passé à Broadlands, mais comme il a été convenu que ce serait Lord Palmerston qui prendrait l'initiative à Paris et que nous ne ferions que appuyer les démarches qu'il fera faire à Lord Granville, nous avons cru lui devoir par procédé ne pas anticiper sur lui; cependant dans l'intérêt de l'affaire, j'informerai notre Ambassadeur de l'attitude et du langage de celui de France ici pour qu'il puisse y opposer un contrepoids. Lord Palmerston compte beaucoup sur le M[aréchal] Soult et se flattait que le Comte Sébastiani serait de son bord; nous avons été tout étonné à notre retour de Broadlands de le trouver dans des dispositions tout à fait contraires.　Mais nous avons fini par nous l'expliquer; plus l'homme du Roi que de son Cabinet, il appuie son Maître, qui a dirigé toute la politique de la France dans cette affaire, et il voudrait pouvoir le tirer d'embarras; Mr. de Sébastiani espère que la majorité du Cabinet ne voudra jamais marcher sans la France; c'est ce qui lui a fait dire "j'attends Lord Palmerston au Conseil", et celle-ci en persévérant dans une attitude passive, en se refusant à l'emploi des mesures coercitives, espère de faire avorter toute l'affaire. Il était de l'intérêt du Principal Secrétaire d'Etat, de connaître le langage de celui sur lequel il avait l'air de compter; Mr. de Brunow et moi avons pensé qu'il serait utile qu'il en fut informé et j'ai requis Mr. de Hummelauer de lui faire parvenir confidentielement des extraits des deux rapports qu'il a l'honneur d'adresser aujourd'hui à Votre Altesse sur ses entretiens avec Mr. de Sebastiani; si je puis voir Lord Palmerston je l'informerai également de ma conversation avec Lord Holland; il est de notre devoir de soutenir les efforts du Principal Secrétaire d'Etat dans la lutte qu'il aura à soutenir dans le Conseil. Outre les objections qu'on pourra y faire et que j'ai signalées plus haut, il n'est pas impossible, que l'on ne trouve pas le rôle et les stations assignés aux deux Puissances maritimes assés brillantes; cependant Mr. de Brunow en les traçant a cherché à concilier tous les amours propres, il laisse Constantinople hors d'action, il croit cette Capitale suffisamment protégée par la place assignée à un chacun, elle ne serait donc pas occupée et je l'ai fortement encouragé à suivre ce plan; dans son projet relatif aux positions des escadres, il n'a pas fait mention de celle qu'il désirerait voir prendre par la nôtre; il croit que notre Gouvernement aimera à la tenir éloignée du pavillon tricolore et voici comment il pense que les escadres pourraient se placer:

Les escadres anglaise et française prendraient leur station depuis Gallipoli jusqu'au Golfe de Mudania, d'après une ligne qui serait tirée à partir de Ganos entre Gallipoli et Rodosto, atteindrait l'île de Marmora, de la l'île de Calokinnus et aboutirait au Golfe de Mudania.

L'escadre autrichienne prendrait une position intermédiaire qui au Sud aurait pour démarcation la ligne ci-dessus tracée et au Nord une ligne tirée à partir de Rodosto et Erekli au Sud des îles des Princes, jusqu'au Golfe de Nicomédie.

La station russe serait celle qu'elle a été en 1833. Il ne serait pas fait mention de Constantinople.

Pour ce qui regarde notre escadre, ce n'est qu'un projet, car la Russie fera à cet égard tout ce qui pourra être de notre convenance, mais Mr. de Brunow croit que cette position intermédiaire est conforme à notre attitude de modération et de médiation entre les parties directement intéressées.

Pour ce qui regarde le secours matériel en troupes nommé par Lord Palmerston, je ne lui ai pas caché que je doutais qu'on s'y prétât chés nous, une coopération avec des troupes ottomanes n'étant pas facile, sous le rapport militaire ni sous le rapport sanitaire; qu'il n'en était pas de même avec une escadre, où l'on tenait son monde reserré et hors de contact avec les turcs.

Le Sous Secrétaire d'Etat Backhouse, que j'ai vu hier, m'a dit que les dépositions d'Avedik coincidaient en grande partie avec celles qu'avait faites le Capitaine Walker à Lord Ponsonby, et qu'il était avéré que l'Amiral Lalande avait mis tout en œuvre pour que le Capudan Pacha ne communiquât pas avec l'escadre anglaise.

Le Baron de Brunow vient de recevoir l'ordre de son gouvernement de faire une communication à celui de S. M. B. sur la résolution qu'a prise l'Empereur Nicolas et la nécessité où il est de faire une expédition contre Khiva, dont les incursions du Khan sur le territoire russe, les déprédations que depuis trois ans il y a commises, outre plusieurs milliers de russes qu'il a enlevés et jetté dans l'esclavage, ne lui permettaient plus de laisser ces actes impunis; l'on a envoyé à Mr. de Brunow la proclamation du Général Peromoski, Gouverneur d'Orenburg, annonçant qu'il allait marcher pour punir ce Khan, délivrer les russes esclaves; la proclamation termine en disant que, l'objet atteint, l'expédition rentrera dans ses foyers. Malgré le bon droit de l'Empereur Nicolas, Mr. de Brunow n'en regrette pas moins le moment inoportun où cet événement se présente; il se flatte que Lord Palmerston comprendra la nécessité où Sa Majesté Impériale a été de ne pouvoir agir autrement, mais il craint que la partie moins raisonnable du Cabinet ne se prévale de cet incident contre la Russie.

Le parlement s'assemblera le 16. Janvier; on y annoncera le mariage de la Reine, dès que la dot du futur époux aura été fixée; on nommera le jour où la Cérémonie aura lieu; on croit que ce pourra être dans la première semaine de Février; elle sera toute religieuse et en famille, le corps diplomatique n'y sera pas invité; la Reine, dit-on, est très anxieuse que cela ait lieu dans le plus court délai possible.

Le Duc de Wellington m'a écrit pour me prier de remercier Votre Altesse de la lettre qu'Elle lui a écrite, il m'a invité d'aller le voir à Strathfieldsaye, mais je n'ai pu encore m'y rendre; peut-être irai-je après demain.

(v)

Private letter

Londres, 31 *Décembre*, 1839.

Le Baron de Brunow sort de chés moi; il a vu Lord Palmerston à qui il a fait la communication relativement à l'expédition de Khiva; le Principal Secrétaire d'Etat l'a fort bien prise et a compris la nécessité où a été l'Empereur Nicolas de la faire; Mr. de Brunow a dit que si Lord Clanricarde avait été à St. Pétersbourg, la communication eut été par lui, mais qu'à son retour on lui donnerait un gage écrit des intentions sincères de l'Empereur, de sa ferme résolution de rappeler ce corps d'expédition dès que l'objet serait atteint: la manière dont Lord Palmerston a pris la chose a mis Mr. de Brunow fort à l'aise. Il est convenu devant moi qu'il se sent soulagé d'un grand poids. Ce dernier lui a parlé de ma visite à Holland House. Le Principal Secrétaire a dit qu'il était enchanté que je l'avais faite et que j'avais parlé comme je l'avais fait à Lord Holland; il est convenu vis-à-vis de Mr. de Brunow que Lord Holland ne pensait rien moins qu'à voir Mehemet Ali à la place du Sultan; c'est une monomanie, dit-il.

Il est fort curieux que dans le courant de ma conversation avec lui, lorsqu'il fut question de l'ambition démesurée de ce Pacha, je lui dis si on lui laisse la démarcation qu'il possède à présent, il ne reposera pas jusqu'à ce qu'il soit à Constantinople, et je ne lui cachai pas que nous ne le souffririons pas plus que la Russie, mais que ce serait la mort de l'Empire ottoman par la lutte qui s'engagerait.

Lord Palmerston est dans ce moment à 18 milles d'ici à Watton chés Lord Tankerville dont la femme est sœur de Madame de Sebastiani, toutes deux Mlles. Grammont; le Général Sebastiani a mis à profit cette circonstance pour aller chés sa belle-sœur sans y être invité; il a attaqué Lord Palmerston sur la mission de Mr. de Brunow et lui a dit: eh bien, Mr. de Brunow a libellé des propositions, dit-on. Lord Palmerston lui a fort sagement répondu que c'était lui qui était occupé à les libeller sur la base du plan qui avait été discuté lors du Ier envoi de Mr. de Brunow, qu'il les présenterait au Conseil d'où nous apprendrions tous l'accueil qu'elles y auraient reçu; dans le fait j'ai oublié de mander dans mon rapport principal A. qu'il a été convenu entre nous à Broadlands que les propositions viendraient de Lord Palmerston qui s'est approprié celles de Mr. de Brunow; cette forme aura plus d'effet sur le Cabinet et sur la France, toute apparence de propositions russes disparaîtra ainsi.

Lord Palmerston m'a fait dire par Mr. de Brunow de ne pas arrêter mon courrier, qu'il ferait ses expéditions à Vienne et à Berlin demain ou après bien surement, dans l'objet de demander pour Mr. de Werther et pour moi des pleins pouvoirs pour conclure, dès que l'affaire aurait obtenu le degré de maturité nécessaire à cet effet.

(vi)

Private letter

Londres, 9 *Mai*, 1840.

J'ai communiqué à Lord Palmerston mon rapport Litt. A. en date d'hier afin de m'assurer que j'avais bien saisi les paroles et les observations de la Seigneurie lorsque je lui communiquai l'expedition de Votre Altesse en date du 25 Avril.[1] Le Principal Secrétaire trouva ma rélation parfaitement exacte et observa au passage où je parle du secours maritime à demander à la Russie pour une action commune contre Alexandrie et la Syrie "Nous n'en aurions probablement pas besoin, dit-il, nous avons dix vaisseaux de ligne dans la Mediterranée, deux que l'on prépare ici et deux à Lisbonne feront quatorze, ajoutant à cela les fregates et autres batimens de guerre, c'est plus qu'il faut pour effectuer le blocus; cependant nous ne pourrions pas nous passer de votre pavillon, c'est un effet moral dont nous avons besoin, deux petits batimens de guerre autrichiens suffiraient *pour constater notre union dans l'affaire que nous donnerions au Sultan.*"[2]

[1] Metternich, *Mémoires*, vi, 454.
[2] Pencil note by Metternich: "Oui, l'union entre l'Autriche et l'Angleterre ; cette démonstration ne constaterait elle pas, par contre, la désunion entre ces deux cours et les 3 autres? Comment pourait-on obvier à ce mal? telle est la question."

Cet appui de notre part parait essentiel, autant vis-à-vis de l'Angleterre que de la France, non seulement pour justifier l'entreprise, mais
pour lui donner un effet plus puissant si elle se trouve placée sans
l'égide d'une alliance qui en Angleterre rencontre toutes les sympathies,
tandis qu'elle impose du respect et de la crainte sur le reste du monde.
C'est pour ce motif que Lord Palmerston a desiré que je parle à Mr.
Guizot vaguement de la possibilité que nous prétions un secours naval
dans le cours de l'affaire; la manière dont je l'ai fait, n'a pas permis à
cet Ambassadeur d'approfondir le *quid* et *le quomodo faciendum*, de
sorte qu'il ignore si notre action navale sera offensive contre la Syrie ou
protectrice pour le Sultan dans le cas où il dut se resigner à se refuser à
toute concession d'hérédité, à défaut d'en venir à la conclusion d'un
arrangement satisfesant pour l'honneur et les interéts de sa Hautesse.

(vii)

Cipher

Londres, 12 *Mai*, 1840.

Malgré la confiance avec laquelle Lord Palmerston envisage sa
position dans l'affaire turco-égyptienne, je suis loin de partager les
illusions qu'il se fait. Ses collègues regardent toujours la coopération
de la France comme indispensable; si donc celle-ci ne souscrit pas aux
moyens de résoudre l'affaire en cinq, la solution en quatre en sera
beaucoup plus difficile; cependant le Principal Secrétaire d'Etat
l'essayera, et comme cette solution ne pourra avoir lieu sans l'emploi
d'une mesure coercitive telle que le blocus d'Alexandrie et des côtes
de la Syrie, envisagé par lui comme facile et suffisant pour atteindre
le but, il nous invite à y prendre part; s'il ne peut se tirer autrement
d'affaire, il se contenterait d'obtenir deux de nos vaisseaux de guerre,
uniquement pour constater par notre union que nous approuvons la
mesure. Il est donc essentiel que Votre Altesse soit préparée à cette
demande. Lord Palmerston paraît décidé à ne pas remettre l'affaire
à un avenir incertain en conseillant au Sultan de refuser l'hérédité sur
la Syrie et l'Egypte, dans le cas où l'on ne parvint pas à conclure un
arrangement favorable ou au moins honorable pour la Porte. Lorsque
ce moment arrivera, les mêmes hommes qui sont au pouvoir à présent,
le seront-ils encore alors, observa-t-il, et nos successeurs partageront-ils
nos vues à cet égard? Ceci est tellement vrai que si Lord Palmerston
devait faire place à un de ses collègues qui lui sont opposés maintenant
dans le Cabinet, tel que p.e. Lord Clarendon ou tout autre de ce bord,
l'affaire prendrait sur-le-champ un aspect tout franco-égyptien, et les
intérêts du Sultan seraient complètement sacrifiés.

(viii)

Cipher

Londres, 22 *Juin*, 1840.

Des nouvelles récemment arrivées de Constantinople à Mr. de Bülow et de Brunow, représentent les choses dans cette Capitale, et surtout dans plusieurs des provinces, sous un jour fort alarmant. Reschid Pacha a dit à Mr. de Buteneff que les délais des délibérations de Londres contribuent à alimenter l'inquiétude qui règne; que Chekib Efendi était autorisé à adhérer sans réserve à tout ce que les Représentans des Cours alliées du Sultan lui proposeraient. Nous convinmes, Mrs. de Bulow et de Brunow et moi, de demander une entrevue à Lord Palmerston pour lui communiquer ces nouvelles, et nous nous concertâmes sur ce que nous lui dirions. Nous tombâmes d'accord de lui représenter que les délais avaient atteint leur terme et qu'il fallait qu'il nous dise quel plan il comptait suivre. Le Principal Secrétaire d'Etat nous reçut hier; nous lui rappelâmes la teneur de nos instructions; je le ramenai à celle que Votre Altesse m'a transmise le 25 Avril[1] et à la dépêche N. 2 faisant mention de l'extrémité des sacrifices auxquels la Porte pourrait souscrire. Mr. le Baron de Brunow observa que l'on devrait tâcher d'obtenir en sus le Pachalik d'Haleb avec Scanderum; le tout dépend d'y faire adhérer la France. Je me suis déclaré pour le Maximum de la part à faire au Sultan, en autant qu'à défaut de ce Maximum, le Minimum ne soit pas perdu; mais je dis, que d'après mes instructions, j'étais autorisé à souscrire à ce Minimum si on ne pouvait gagner autrement la France dans l'arrangement; qu'il fallait lui présenter le plan en cinq, en y joignant le Pachalik d'Alep, se réservant toutefois de revenir au Minimum, si elle ne voulait absolument se rendre à notre proposition; qu'il fallait en même temps lui déclarer que, si nous étions obligés à faire l'affaire à quatre, la position de Méhémed Aly pourrait devenir moins bonne, puisqu'elle serait subordonnée aux événemens qui ressortiraient des moyens coercitifs que l'on serait dans le cas d'employer contre lui. Cette déclaration à la France servira de moyen comminatoire contre elle, pour l'engager à se joindre à nous et à faire l'affaire en cinq. Lord Palmerston a accueilli mon idée, à laquelle se sont joints mes collègues de Prusse et de Russie. Il est convenu, qu'on ne pouvait plus tarder à se mettre à l'œuvre; il nous a promis de s'en occuper dans le courant de cette semaine, de préparer un plan, qu'il présenterait à ses collègues, et il nous a invités à nous réunir dimanche prochain (28) chez lui pour examiner ce plan.

(ix)

Londres, 9 *Juillet*, 1840.

Mes rapports chiffrés du 22, 23, 26, 29 et 30 Juin auront fourni à Votre Altesse la preuve que nous étions allés Messieurs de Bülow, de

[1] Metternich, *Mémoires*, vi, 454.

Brunnow et moi au devant des instructions qu'Elle a daigné m'adresser le 24 et 27 Juin dernier.

Lord Palmerston, pressé par nos instances réitérées et par les nouvelles alarmantes qui venoient de Constantinople, dut enfin céder; il resista pendant quinze jours à l'urgence de nos démarches et ne nous épargna pas quelquefois les effets de sa mauvaise humeur; mais, cet intervalle fut utilement employé par Monsieur de Bülow et par moi pour travailler la partie du Conseil des Ministres la plus opposée aux vues du Principal Secrétaire d'Etat, sans en excepter Lord Melbourne, avec qui j'eus deux entretiens qui eurent le plus heureux succès, en ce que ce Ministre finit par comprendre qu'au milieu de la grande question orientale il y avait des intérêts anglais et autrichiens tellement identiques et d'une si haute portée, qu'ils ne pouvoient être négligés sans se créer pour l'avenir des complications de la nature la plus dangereuse pour le maintien de la paix générale.

Dans le conseil qui fut tenu hier sur cette importante affaire, Lord Palmerston doit avoir développé son plan et ses vues avec une prodigieuse habileté et une grande lucidité. Il prit pour base les démarches réitérées et infructueuses faites auprès de la France pour l'attirer dans nos rangs, cita les conversations que nous avions eues, lui et moi, avec Monsieur Guizot au mois de Mai dernier, sur un plan d'arrangement entre le Sultan et son vassal, plan qui n'étoit pas composé de propositions anglaises ou autrichiennes mais bien celui mis en avant par le Gouvernement français même, l'année dernière; que Monsieur Thiers, sans le nier ou l'avouer, disoit qu'il n'y objecteroit pas si Méhémet Ali y consentoit, ce qui rendoit l'affaire impossible, puisque le Pacha n'accepteroit que ce que la France lui conseilleroit; que même après avoir touché vis-à-vis d'elle le minimum des concessions à faire à Méhémed Ali, elle fesoit déjà entrevoir des doutes sur la restitution d'Adana; qu'en un mot elle cherchoit à s'assurer de la clef de toute la position comme le prouvoit la réponse faite tout dernièrement par Monsieur Guizot de la part de Monsieur Thiers, réponse dont j'ai eu l'honneur de faire mention à Votre Altesse par mon rapport chiffré en date du 29 Juin; que les desseins de la France étoient de fonder une grande Puissance arabe pour en faire une Alliée contre l'Angleterre; que d'un autre côté des événemens pouvoient surgir en Turquie qui obligeroient l'Empereur de Russie d'y intervenir; que l'Autriche y seroit attirée matériellement ou politiquement, et peutêtre de manière à déranger son équilibre; qu'il étoit important à l'Angleterre de conserver égale la balance de notre pouvoir; qu'il y avoit donc un intérêt anglo-autrichien qui tout en se présentant sur des points différens se réunissoit dans un même foyer politique; qu'il étoit de la plus haute importance pour les intérêts anglais de concilier ceux de notre Empire, de ménager une alliance qui avoit toujours été si utile à la Grande Bretagne et rencontroit toutes les sympathies de ce pays-ci, sans vouloir pour cela rompre avec le Gouvernement français; qu'il falloit au contraire, observer envers lui tous les ménagemens et les procédés qu'exigeoit sa position et lui faire comprendre qu'il pouvoit y avoir des circonstances où des intérêts spéciaux imposeroient à l'une des obligations auxquelles l'autre ne pourroit pas s'associer, sans pour cela devoir se séparer; qu'on se retrouveroit plus tard sur un autre terrain d'intérêts communs; que le moment du reste étoit favorable pour marcher sans la France, puisqu'elle étoit trop occupée dans l'Algérie pour intervenir dans l'affaire en instance autrement que par des intrigues; que son action dans la Quadruple Alliance avec la péninsule Ibérienne avoit été plus gênante qu'utile et que l'on seroit plus à l'aise sans elle dans l'objet que les quatre Puissances vouloient atteindre.

Lord Melbourne a franchement soutenu le Principal Secrétaire d'Etat, et ceux qui voyoient avec peine et même avec répugnance le moment arrivé de devoir prendre une décision sur la nécessité de marcher *à cinq* ou *à quatre*, se sont divisés entre eux sur la question de savoir ce qui seroit plus utile, ou de ne pas se séparer de la France ou d'appuyer l'attitude de l'Autriche dans cette grave complication. La dernière considération a été heureusement prépondérante, et Lord Holland même a dit que le "Casting Vote" (le veto) dans cette question appartenoit à l'Autriche, qu'à la suite de plusieurs conversations qu'il avoit eues avec moi, il avoit acquis la certitude que nous ne voulions pas les brouiller avec la France, et qu'au contraire le désir de notre Cabinet avoit été de marcher avec elle, mais qu'il entrevoyoit la difficulté.

Je tiens tous ces détails de Lord Normanby que j'ai rencontré hier soir et qui a assisté au Conseil.

Lord Palmerston a trouvé un grand auxiliaire dans les dernières nouvelles arrivées de Syrie; il s'en est servi pour prouver que tout ce que le Gouvernement français disoit sur l'état intérieur de cette province et sur la position du Pacha étoit des fables et qu'il ne falloit pas donner dans le piège.

La dépêche de Votre Altesse No. 1 du 24 Juin avoit parmi ses annexes la copie d'un rapport de Monsieur le Comte Appony en date du 16 Juin rendant compte d'une conversation avec Monsieur Thiers relative à l'effet qu'avoit produit sur Méhémed Ali, la nouvelle du renvoi de Chosrew Pacha. Monsieur Guizot avoit reçu vendredi passé une soidisant dépêche télégraphique de Marseille annonçant la nouvelle (en date d'Alexandrie le 16 Juin) qui se trouve mot à mot dans le rapport de Monsieur le Comte Appony. Je plaçai celui-ci sous les yeux du Principal Secrétaire d'Etat pour lui montrer que le tout étoit une mystification inventée pour jeter de l'indécision dans le Cabinet; que Monsieur Thiers prévoyoit devoir s'occuper de l'affaire turco-égyptienne après la réponse qu'il avoit chargé Monsieur Guizot de faire. Celle-ci même fut faite deux jours après l'annonce de la dépêche télégraphique que Monsieur Guizot se hâta de communiquer au Gouvernement Britannique avec empressement et en y mettant un grand degré d'importance, comme devant mener à un accommodement à l'amiable entre le Sultan et le Pacha.

Cette démarche de Monsieur Thiers ne servit qu'à décider Lord Palmerston à marcher encore plus vigoureusement en avant surtout lorsqu'il vit qu'elle n'étoit qu'une ruse.

Je dois féliciter Votre Altesse de ce premier résultat; quoique tardif, il n'en sera peut-être que plus effectif. Le Cabinet Britannique, ramené à une saine politique, a fini par entrevoir que la marche sage, indiquée par notre Cabinet, étoit la seule vraie. La résolution, qu'il vient de prendre si Méhémed Ali ne cède pas de bonne grâce, sera exécutée avec force et promptitude pour en rendre le succès plus sûr et éclatant. Le Chef de l'Amirauté, Lord Minto, tout dans l'intérêt de Lord Palmerston, brûle d'impatience de faire agir la marine anglaise pour lui faire reprendre dans la Méditerranée la supériorité que les forces navales de la France cherchent à y usurper. Le Principal Secrétaire d'Etat m'a dit hier qu'il espéroit que dans le cas où Méhémed Ali ne se rendit pas à la sommation du Sultan, nous remplirions la promesse que nous avions faite de joindre notre pavillon au leur, moins pour son utilité matérielle, quoiqu'elle n'étoit pas à mépriser, que pour la force morale qu'il exerceroit en Angleterre et sur les populations de la Syrie. Il est question d'y faire figurer le pavillon ottoman comme partie soidisant principale dans l'action.

(x)

Londres, 16 *Juillet*, 1840.

L'affaire que nous venons de terminer est d'une importance majeure sous le double point de vue de son objet spécial et du bienfait qui en résulte de voir enfin l'Angleterre s'associer à nous dans l'intérêt du soutien de la légitimité et des principes conservatifs; la France révolutionnaire verra enfin que la solidarité avec le Gouvernement de la réforme avait des bornes; celles-ci ont été atteintes lorsqu'elles se sont rapprochées des intérêts matériels et politiques de la Grande Bretagne. Lord Palmerston est le seul qui les ait compris dès leur origine, mais il ne serait jamais parvenu à faire partager ses vues par la majorité de ses collègues, sans l'assistance de l'Autriche et sans le concours de plusieurs circonstances qui sont venues à son aide.

L'attitude sage, droite et honorable qu'a maintenue notre Cabinet dans tout le cours de cette négociation pénible et ardue a été un auxiliaire puissant pour le Principal Secrétaire d'Etat; on a reconnu que nous étions les seuls qui n'avions pas des vues d'intérêts personnels dans l'affaire; que nous nous occupions de celle-ci dans un but vraiment européen; que même vis-à-vis de la France nous avions été justes et franchement désireux de gagner sa coopération, tandisque Lord Palmerston, irrité par la résistance qu'il en avait éprouvée, n'était plus un agent impartial aux yeux de ses collègues qui recevaient ses opinions avec méfiance. Il lui fallait notre appui pour rétablir son équilibre; il l'a trouvé dans ma coopération auprès de Mr. Guizot et cette démarche qui n'a eu que la forme d'une conversation suivie à Paris par Mr. d'Appony avec Mr. Thiers, a été le Wedge (coin) (expression dont s'est servi Lord Palmerston vis-à-vis de moi) qui a rompu la résistance que jusque là on avait opposée au Principal Secrétaire d'Etat, accusé de prévention contre le Gouvernement français.

Une autre considération lui rendait notre soutien indispensable, celle de ne pouvoir se présenter au Conseil de la Reine avec le secours matériel de la Russie seul; il eut été rejetté à l'unanimité; l'alliage de notre pavillon lui était nécessaire pour la combinaison de l'entreprise dont l'Angleterre ne pouvait se charger à elle seule, puisque l'éventualité de l'ouverture des détroits en cas d'un mouvement hostile d'Ibrahim Pacha vers Constantinople devait y figurer en même tems que la conséquence qui devait en résulter de l'apparition de forces navales et militaires russes dans le Bosphore et sur la rive gauche de ce Canal.

La Russie sentait qu'on ne lui permettrait plus, comme en 1833, de se charger à elle seule du protectorat de la Porte et qu'il y aurait pour elle du danger à reparaître dans le Bosphore, si elle ne s'assurait en même tems de la clef des Dardanelles, ce qui devenait une affaire compliquée et grave; elle eut aimé à s'entendre avec le Gouvernement anglais à ce sujet et à marcher seule avec lui, mais celui-ci ne l'eut pu sans être accusée d'avoir renoncé à l'alliance française, et le parti dans le Cabinet Britannique attaché à cette alliance était trop fort pour réaliser un projet que le Cabinet Russe a certainement nourri et qu'il espérait faire réussir à l'aide de notre soutien, qu'il a recherché moins dans un intérêt européen que dans le sien propre. J'ai néanmoins donné à Mr. de Brunnow l'appui auquel j'étais autorisé, aussi longtems qu'il était pratique et raisonnable; il eut cessé d'être l'un et l'autre, si j'avais voulu me mêler de la question de détail dans laquelle cet Envoyé a désiré me faire entrer, savoir celle du plus ou moins de vaisseaux anglais à admettre dans la Mer de Marmora, et des stations qu'ils auraient à y prendre; j'ai fait sentir avec tout le ménagement possible à Mr. de Brunnow, que ceci ne me regardait pas, et que je devais lui rappeler ce que m'avait dit dans le tems le Duc de Wellington, lors de ma première visite chez Sa Grâce à Strathfieldsaye, savoir: qu'il fallait être facile sur les questions de détails, que de vouloir préscrire des conditions sur le nombre et les stations des vaisseaux anglais, était exiger ce qu'aucun Gouvernement, aucun parti dans ce pays ne pouvait accorder, que le Parlement et la Nation s'y refuseraient, qu'il devait se contenter de ce que Lord Palmerston avait exprimé à cet égard dans sa dépêche du 25 Octobre à Lord Clanricarde[1] et rendre confiance pour confiance; que, la France n'étant pas de la partie, les inquiétudes, qui auraient pu naître de la voir figurer dans la mer de Marmora, n'existaient plus; que par conséquent il y avait tous les motifs pour lui de se montrer conciliant, facile et confiant; que la question était de savoir s'il voulait faire l'affaire ou non; qu'en insistant sur une prétention que le Gouvernement anglais ne pouvait admettre, il ferait douter de la sincérité et de la générosité de l'Empereur Nicolas qu'il avait toujours mises en avant; qu'il prenait donc sur lui la double responsabilité de mettre celles-ci en question et de faire manquer l'affaire; que Mr. de Bülow et moi nous ne pourrions le soutenir jusqu'à là auprès de Lord Palmerston, et que s'il reculait après avoir aidé à pousser le Principal Secrétaire d'Etat tandisque celui-ci ne s'en souciait pas, et après lui

[1] *L.P.*, I, No. 352.

avoir dit devant nous que l'Empereur Nicolas ne l'abandonnerait pas
s'il allait en avant, ce serait manquer à sa parole et compromettre Lord
Palmerston devant ses propres collègues, ce qu'il ne lui pardonnerait
jamais. Mr. de Brunnow essaya ensuite de nous ébranler en disant
qu'il ne pourrait pas se décider à signer aucune transaction sans savoir
si elle aurait l'approbation de son Maître et qu'il préferait la Lui
soumettre pour mettre sa responsabilité à couvert. Nous lui prouv-
âmes que c'était également ne pas vouloir l'affaire, puisque les six
semaines, qui s'écouleraient avant d'avoir une réponse, la rendrait
impossible, tout dépendant de la célérité et du secret dans l'exécution;
que la France, une fois informé de ce que nous aurions fait, ce qui
serait impossible de lui tenir caché pendant si longtems, le contrarierait
par toutes sortes d'intrigues, qu'il ne nous serait peut-être pas possible
de déjouer. Enfin Mr. de Brunnow céda non sans peine et sans crainte
et nous dit qu'il préviendrait Lord Palmerston de la nécessité où il
était, pour mettre sa responsabilité à couvert, de lui écrire une lettre
dans laquelle il lui rappelerait la phrase de sa dépêche à Lord Clanricarde, relative à l'ouverture exceptionnelle des détroits. Nous lui
promîmes, Mr. de Bülow et moi, de l'appuyer en ceci auprès du
Principal Secrétaire d'Etat, qui trouva en effet la proposition de Mr. de
Brunnow naturelle et lui promit d'y répondre dans un sens propre à
tranquilliser sa responsabilité auprès de son Souverain. En résumé,
mon Prince, l'affaire était impossible sans le concours moral et matériel
de l'Autriche; ce dernier était nécessaire à Lord Palmerston pour
obtenir de ses collègues l'autorisation de formuler un projet de convention renfermant une éventualité telle que celle d'une répétition de l'action
militaire de la Russie dans le Bosphore. La convention est l'acte de
cinq Puissances, agissant chacune selon la nature de sa position et de ses
moyens vers un même but, c'est à dire dans l'intérêt de la légitimité et
des principes conservatifs. Ce qu'il importait était d'y voir figurer
l'Angleterre en première ligne par son action matérielle; une fois
engagée dans celle-ci, elle ne peut plus reculer, son honneur l'oblige à
mener l'enterprise vers une bonne fin; l'esprit d'insurrection qui vient
de se manifester sur plusieurs points de la Syrie présente des facilités
qui n'existaient pas avant; toutes les nouvelles que le Gouvernement
Anglais vient de recevoir annoncent que cette insurrection est devenue
presque générale en Syrie et qu'elle a pris un caractère formidable.
Les peuples qui cherchent à secouer le joug de Méhémet Aly, appelent
à grands cris la protection des Puissances étrangères; il est urgent qu'on
les aide le plutôt possible, afin qu'ils ne périssent pas par le glaive du
Pacha rébelle.

(xi)

Private letter

Londres, 16 *Juillet*, 1840.

Le quart d'heure de Rablais que Mr. de Bülow et moi avons eu à
passer avec Mr. de Brunow, n'a pas été le plus agréable de l'affaire

devant laquelle il voulait reculer après qu'elle avait été arrêtée entre nous.

Jamais un homme ne s'est montré plus pussillanime et servile que lui; l'Empereur Nicolas lui apparaissait comme un phantôme qui le poursuivait jour et nuit; lorsque je fais une affaire, nous dit-il, je vois toujours devant moi la grande image de mon Empereur ayant l'air de me dire: Brunow prends garde à ce que tu fais. A chaque pas en arrière que nous fesions faire à Mr. de Brunow, il fesait un signe de croix à la russe. La position d'un agent russe s'est montrée dans toute sa misère; celle de Mr. de Brunow est devenue fort sulbalterne dans le moment où il fallait du calme et de la dignité: nous avons vu celui où il allait faillir devant la crainte que lui inspirait l'image de son Empereur auquel il voulait, avant de la signer, soumettre une œuvre qui n'admettai pas un instant de délai dans son exécution.

Lord Palmerston, Mr. de Bülow et moi, avons plus d'une raison de croire que l'objet principal de Mr. de Brunow n'était pas de faire l'affaire, mais celui de la ramener dans les mains de l'Empereur son Maître, engagé maintenant dans une partie à cinq, tandis qu'il eut préféré jouer le jeu seul; plus Mr. de Brunow voyait ce jeu échapper des mains de son Maître et plus il tremblait. Ce n'est qu'après l'éloignement de Chosrew Pacha, entièrement dans les intérêts de la Russie, que Mr. de Brunow reçut les ordres les plus pressans de mener l'affaire à un résultat; il ne nous cacha pas qu'il voulait dégager l'Empereur de l'affaire pour qu'il ait la faculté d'agir selon les circonstances; on craignait à Pétersbourg qu'une autre influence à Constantinople prit la place de celle de la Russie.

Mr. de Bülow s'est loyalement serré à moi, je ne saurais assés louer le zèle et l'appui éclairés qu'il a prêtés dans les derniers momens de la crise.

Le billet ci-joint[1] qu'il m'a adressé en réponse à un rendés-vous que je lui demandais pour conférer avec lui sur la situation dangereuse où se trouvait l'affaire à la suite des tergiversations de Mr. de Brunow, prouve son courage et ses bonnes dispositions; ils sont d'autant plus méritoires que la position de la Prusse limitrophe de la France exige de grands ménagemens et que les instructions de Mr. de Bülow parlaient d'un arrangement à cinq et non à quatre; néanmoins il n'a pas hésité à se joindre aux miennes; il a donc pris beaucoup sur lui, mais il espère que Votre Altesse voudra bien faire exprimer son contentement à Berlin sur la conduite qu'il a tenue.

Madame de Lieven a dans les derniers jours redoublé ses importunités pour tâcher de pénétrer ce que nous ferions, elle a poussé la témérité jusqu'à dire à Mr. de Brunow que Lady Palmerston lui avait avoué que le conseil avait adopté les propositions de son mari—espérant par ce mensonge (car c'en était un) faire tomber Mr. de Brunow dans

---

[1] Dated 11 July: "Je passerai chez Vous après les 11 heures. Certes, le moment est grave,—mais j'ai bon espoir. Nous nous montrerons au niveau des circonstances et dignes de la confiance que nos Cours respectives ont placée en nous. C'est aprésent ou jamais! Calmes, réfléchis et résolus nous atteindrons le but. Tout à Vous"

un piège; il n'y donna pas, mais rendit le propos de Madame de Lieven
à Lady Palmerston; celle-ci, piquée au dernier degré, fit à son amie un
sermon très sec, lui conseilla de s'en aller pour ne pas accréditer
l'opinion, qu'on avait, qu'elle avait, été envoyée par Mr. Thiers pour
aider Mr. Guizot à entraver l'affaire orientale.

Telle est la fin de Madame de Lieven, qui après avoir occupé ici la
première position sociale est déchue au point de n'être plus que la
complaisante et l'entremetteuse d'un folliculaire et d'un professeur
d'histoire, tellement épris des charmes surannés et déséchés de la
Sybille ambulante, qu'il est devenu un objet d'amusement pour les
salons, où l'on épie les regards doux et peu lettrés qu'il lui lance; il ne
se doute pas que nous venons d'accomplir ce que son prédécesseur
avait su empêcher et que celui-ci saura faire valoir.

APPENDIX E

(i)

Paris, 14 *Juin*, 1836.

Mon cher Ami, J'ai reçu votre petit mot du 10 [Juin]. La lettre de congé est prête ainsi qu'une dépêche d'informations générales; elles partiront toutes deux aujourd'hui si le Ministre, qui doit avoir préparé, de son côté, une longue *Private*[2] pour le Général,[3] nous revient de la Chambre assez à temps pour l'heure de l'expédition du Portefeuille.

Je sais que le Ministre se proposait d'écrire au Général sur le caractère de ses rapports avec Lord Granville. Il y a dans celui-ci quelque maladresse et du soupçonneux; c'est chose incontestable, mais je ne crois pas aux mauvaises dispositions pour la personne. De son côté, M. Thiers n'a rien des habitudes anglaises et les comprend peu. Que le Général s'interpose avec ce tact qu'il possède à un si haut degré. On est ombrageux et trop insistant sur toute chose au Faubourg St Honoré.[4] On est susceptible et impressionable à l'hôtel des Capucines;[5] voilà les élémens à combiner et à amalgamer.

Vos observations sur le nez à nez des deux marines sont très justes. Nous veillerons de notre mieux à ce qu'il n'en résulte rien de fâcheux. Je regrette, pour mon compte, que le Commandant Roy, au Passage, n'ait pas obtempéré à l'invitation de son collègue anglais. Mais, en vérité, c'était trop que de nous demander de le blâmer et de le blâmer officiellement. Il ne pouvait quitter sa position qu'en commentant, en mettant de côté ses instructions qui, n'ayant pas prévu la circonstance qui a eu lieu, lui prescrivaient de rester au Passage. Il eut bien fait de commenter; mais nous ne pouvons le blâmer de s'en être tenu à la lettre, surtout lorsque le blâme est demandé du dehors. Ajoutons que, l'opération ayant réussi, la démarche évitée était une véritable querelle d'allemand. Enfin, et sous un point de vue plus général, je crois qu'il faut tenir compte de cette facheuse influence des on-dits, des propos de corps de garde et des relations de la Presse sur les Officiers respectifs. Il n'est pas de sottises qui ne soient dites au quartier général d'Evans et dans la Marine anglaise à propos de la chute de Mendizabal et de la prétendue part que nous y avons eue. Faut-il s'étonner ensuite que nos propres marins en concluent qu'il y aurait duperie à faire constam-

---

[1] From the *Bourqueney Papers, Fonds France*, 1899, in the Archives du Ministère des Affaires étrangères, Paris.

[2] Desages occasionally introduces English words such as this one, sometimes underlined, sometimes not.

[3] Sébastiani, the French Ambassador.

[4] The British Embassy.   [5] The residence of Thiers.

ment acte de condescendance pour ceux qui s'élèvent si fort contre l'ombre même d'une influence française; que Lord Minto avec son bon esprit, corrige ses compatriotes; nous obtiendrons alors sans peine que les nôtres mettent de côté toute susceptibilité d'amour-propre. Adieu, mon cher Ami, tout à vous de cœur.

(ii)

Paris, 16 *Septembre*, 1836.

. . . Revenant à l'Espagne, les nouvelles en sont fort peu rassurantes. Les paroles du Ministère espagnol sont tout ce qu'elles peuvent être; mais sunt verba et voces preterea qui nihil, ou à peu près. Avec une révolution purement politique on peut prévoir où l'on va et s'arranger en conséquence. Avec une dissolution sociale le plus savant calculateur s'y perd. Quoiqu'il en soit, si nous sommes bien renseignés, la chance tourne plus que jamais, en ce moment à don Carlos—sinon pour faire du définitif, du moins pour culbuter ce qui est. Dans cet état de choses, le thème ici est de se renfermer dans la lettre du traité—rien de plus, rien de moins. Il faut que je vous dise que tous les rapports qui nous sont venus d'Espagne, depuis quelque temps, rapports diplomatiques, rapports militaires et autres, sont unanimes à présenter la Légation anglaise comme ayant plus ou moins connivé aux derniers mouvements. Je ne croirai jamais que ce fut dans l'intention de les faire aboutir à ce que nous avons vu. Mais je crois volontiers que Villiers, par faiblesse pour une femme, par sympathie pour Mendizabal, par manie d'influence, a fait plus qu'il ne devait faire; et je crois aussi que les relations constantes de son attaché, Southern, avec les gens des Clubs et des Sociétés Secrétes ont eu, sinon pour but, du moins pour effet, d'encourager ces gens à se persuader et à persuader aux leurs que l'appui de l'Angleterre leur était assuré. En définitive, la différence qui n'est pas nouvelle mais qui se déssinera de plus en plus peut-être entre l'Angleterre et nous, consiste en ceci: Peu doit importer aux Anglais ce qui se passe en Espagne, pourvu que ce ne soit pas au profit de Don Carlos et de la Sainte Alliance; nous, limitrophes de la monarchie espagnole, en contact avec elle de mille manières et sous mille rapports, nous ne jugeons pas qu'il nous soit donné de pouvoir être indifférents à son état intérieur. . . .

[P.S.] Je m'apperçois que je n'ai pas répondu à ce que vous me demandiez de ma situation personelle. Merci d'abord, mon cher Ami, de ce que vous me dites d'aimable et de bon à ce sujet. Mes premiers rapports avec M. Molé sont très satisfaisants pour moi—du reste vous pouvez savoir que, dans mes habitudes, j'attends toujours la confiance et ne la provoque jamais.

(iii)

Paris, 28 *Mai*, 1839.

Mon cher Ami, J'ai retenu hier le Portefeuille, dans la pensée que le Maréchal[1] nous donnerait à temps la substance d'une réponse à votre dernière dépêche; mais il est revenu les mains vides et il en sera de même encore aujourd'hui, la discussion des fonds secrets l'obligeant à passer sa journée à la Chambre.

Je ne puis donc vous parler que de mes impressions et de celles qu'a fait éprouver parmi les initiés la lecture de ladite dépêche. La première chose qui nous a frappé ainsi que le bon Général, c'est la manière dont Lord Palmerston semble accepter la chance du retour des Russes à Constantinople, sous la seule condition que la Russie ne fasse point un nouveau traité d'Unkiar Skelessi ou quelque chose d'équivalent. *Quantum mutatus ab illo!* Cela, rapproché du singulier speech de Lord Melbourne sur le Czar, donne beaucoup à penser ici—(et par parenthèse, j'aurais bien voulu que vous *nous* ou *me* parlassiez de ce speech, de son but, de son effet et de sa portée); pour en revenir au plan de Lord Palmerston, il me semble que la Russie serait fort ingrate de ne pas souscrire à la condition posée. Car, à quoi bon un nouvel acte, quand, après avoir protesté contre en 1833, l'Angleterre accepte à si bon marché, le protectorat Impérial exclusif sur Constantinople? N'est il pas évident que c'est là le plus gros de ses gains possibles dans les circonstances actuelles? Pour moi, mon cher Ami, je suis disposé à croire qu'il vaut mieux subir en se taisant ce qu'on ne peut ou ne veut empêcher que de prévoir officiellement le fait et de négocier à l'avance pour une conclusion qui doit le sanctionner et le faire passer dans le droit commun.

Ce que je remarque ensuite, dans l'opinion émise par Lord Palmerston, c'est cette disposition marquée à frapper exclusivement sur Mehemet Ali. Dans l'état actuel des choses, ce n'est pas seulement une injustice, c'est une faute, à moins d'une arrière-pensée étrangère à la question du moment. Je suis d'avis qu'il faut frapper sur Mehemet Ali *vainqueur* pour l'arrêter, pour le contraindre à rester ou à rentrer en Syrie. Mais lorsque c'est le Sultan qui fausse promesse et qui attaque, s'il a des avantages, il faut aussi prendre immédiatement les moyens dont on dispose pour chercher à l'arrêter. Il faut tenir sa flotte à distance, ne pas lui permettre de paraître sur les côtes de Syrie ou de l'Egypte etc. Lord Palmerston part de la *doctrine de la légitimité*: Cela peut être beau à Vienne, mais cela me parait singulier venant de Londres. N'est-il pas naturel et plus sûr de partir de l'intérêt politique qui veut l'intégrité de l'Empire Ottoman, quellesque puissent être d'ailleurs les modifications de son régime intérieur, qui veut le maintien du trône du Sultan comme expression de cette intégrité, qui, pour ce faire, demande que l'Asie Mineure ne redevienne plus le théâtre d'une lutte entre les armées turques et égyptiennes qui, dans ce même but, conseille de se jeter entre les combattants et de peser sur l'un comme sur l'autre pour les séparer et les arrêter? Une médiation armée pour

---

[1] Soult.

faire cesser le combat, de quelque côté que penche la balance, voilà
notre rôle: il ne faut pas le compliquer inutilement de questions de
légitimité, de souveraineté de vassalité; ces questions ne doivent se
présenter qu'après la cessation des hostilités et lorsqu'il s'agira d'arbitrer
entre les prétentions respectives; jusqu là, tout doit être égal autant
que possible dans le caractère des moyens à employer pour arrêter la
lutte matérielle. Et puis l'opinion publique de France, et j'imagine
aussi d'Angleterre, est-ce à nous de la compter pour zéro?

Couvrir Constantinople est le principal, sans doute, mais laisser
anéantir Mehemet Ali qui n'a point attaqué, c'est un *incident* qui, pour
le public, est presqu'aussi gros que le principal. If faut se gouverner
d'après ces deux grosses considérations. Lord Palmerston, dans sa
théorie ou explication sur l'accord de Kutayeh est à la fois dans le vrai
et dans le faux. Il n'y a point une garantie positive dans le sens diplomatique du mot, mais il y a une garantie morale au profit de Pacha
comme de la Porte, dans les démarches et efforts incessants que toutes
les Cours ont faits à Alexandrie aussi bien qu'à Constantinople depuis
cinq ans pour exiger le respect du statu quo établi par ledit arrangement.
Je vous écris à bâtons rompus, mon cher Ami, et je ne sais trop où je
vais. C'est aujourd'hui notre jour d'expédition pour l'Orient. Nous
écrivons comminatoirement en Egypte, pour le cas où la guerre serait
déjà commencée—et où Ibrahim aura frotté les Turcs, ce qui est le
plus vraisemblable. En cas de lutte, nous écrivons à l'Amiral[1] de faire
les représentations les plus énergiques, en attendant le chapitre des
résolutions définitives. Nos lettres sont portées par deux officers
d'ordonnance du Maréchal. Mais, en fin de compte, mon cher Ami,
faisons des vœux pour que ce gros nuage se soit dissipé, car ni *vous* ni
nous ne me paraissons en état de parer convenablement à toutes les
éventualités extrêmes d'une pareille crise.

Si demain, nous sommes en mesure de vous dire quelque chose
d'officiel, nous vous enverrons un exprès.

Adieu, tout à vous de cœur; la suite de mon bavardage au prochain
Portefeuille.

(iv)

Paris, 30 *Mai*, 1839.

Mon cher Ami, Nous vous écrivons aujourd'hui à cette fin seulement
de vous dire ce que provisoirement nous avons fait pour la question
d'Orient. Le Maréchal, au lieu de débattre chacun des points de
l'opinion personelle et de premier jet que Lord Palmerston vous a
exprimée, a préféré attendre que vous nous fissiez connaître la pensée
arrêtée, sauf concert, du Cabinet de Londres. Nous n'avons rien reçu
d'Orient depuis les premières nouvelles. Dieu veuille, je le repète,
qu'il n'y ait eu qu'une *démonstration* turque sans plus, ni sans durée.
Vous verrez, parce que nous vous écrivons, que nous n'abandonnons
pas de prime abord le terrain de notre protestation contre le traité

[1] Admiral Roussin, the French Ambassador at Constantinople.

d'Unkiar-Skelessi. C'est bien le moins d'ailleurs que la Russie s'explique sur ce *casus foederis* de son œuvre. Je pense de plus que, même son dit traité à la main, on est parfaitement posé pour soutenir que la clôture des Dardanelles n'étant imposée à la Porte que pour le cas où la Russie se trouve attaquée ou menacée de l'être, rien ne doit s'opposer à ce que, pour la protection du Sultan, les grandes Puissances, les deux maritimes surtout, ne combinent les moyens qui leur sont propres avec ceux qui sont plus particulièrement du ressort de la Russie, vû sa situation topographique, afin de couvrir *ensemble* Constantinople. En Morée l'Angleterre et la Russie ont fourni des vaisseaux, nous des vaisseaux et des troupes. Qui empêcherait qu'on ne convint que, dans le but d'arrêter Ibrahim et de sauver la Capitale, la France et l'Angleterre s'y présenteraient avec tel nombre de vaisseaux, tandis que le contingent de la Russie, en vaisseaux et en troupes de débarquement, serait de telle ou telle force? Je sais bien que la Russie faisait une rude grimace à pareille proposition; mais, en vérité, je ne comprendrais pas qu'elle put y opposer les stipulations d'Unkiar-Skelessi; sa seule ressource plausible serait de suggérer et de se placer behind un refus de la Porte. Mais c'est là où l'intervention de l'Autriche pourrait être de mise et fort salutaire. Tout cela d'ailleurs est opinion mienne et je ne vous la donne que pour telle. Au surplus, pour ce plan comme pour tout autre, il faut avoir le temps de négocier: sans quoi, il n'y a qu'à subir l'impulsion du vent qui souffle dans le moment.

Comme vous le croirez aisément, mon cher Ami, je suis fort tiraillé et occupé, depuis l'installation du nouveau cabinet. Je fais un rude métier et mes services sont d'une terrible longueur. Enfin tant que les forces miennes le permettront, je me résignerai. Adieu, tout à vous de cœur.

(v)

Paris, 20 *Juin*, 1839.

A quo novis, mon cher Ami, car je suis très fatigué, très influxionné, et ma tête est faible—nous ne répondrons pas aujourd'hui à votre dernière dépêche; d'abord parce qu'il faut le temps de se reconnaître et, en second lieu, parce que votre dépêche s'étant croisée avec elle où nous vous donnions nos idées en gros, il est bon que nous sachions ce qu'en aura pensé Lord Palmerston.

Comme vous le savez déjà, nous différons, *vous* et *nous*, d'abord en ceci qu'à l'égard du Sultan vous prenez votre règle de conduite dans le droit rigoureux, dans sa *légitimité*, au lieu de la prendre dans les faits, dans la situation, dans l'intérêt qui consiste avant tout à prévenir ou à arrêter une colision entre Egyptiens et Turcs. J'applique surtout cette observation au plan proposé pour l'attitude et la conduite de nos Escadres. Si la mer est libre pour les Turcs sans l'être pour les Egyptiens vous jouez un jeu d'enfants. Les Grecs c'était aussi des rebelles et pourtant vous avez interdit aux vaisseaux ottomans l'accès des ports et côtes de la Grèce et vice versa. Vous avez bien fait alors; vous feriez mal d'agir autrement. Ce n'est pas connaître le terrain de Constantinople que d'y porter ces distinctions et ces délicatesses qui partout ailleurs sont de rigueur. Voulez-vous avoir chance de sauver le Sultan, de l'empêcher de donner de la tête dans le précipice, *intimidez-le*, ne lui parlez pas de ses droits mais de vos intérêts, ou du moins dites-lui très nettement que les uns et les autres peuvent se concilier dans une juste mesure; vous n'aurez égard aux uns qu'au temps qu'il vous donnera, par sa déférence pour vos avis et représentations, sa garantie dont vous avez besoin pour les autres.

En résumé, si vous ne faites pas que le Sultan soit bien convaincu que nous empêcherons sa flotte d'aborder les côtes de Syrie, et de sortir même de l'Archipel, vous faites une sottise des plus compromettantes. Le second point sur lequel nous différons est celui de la part rigoureuse, *absolue* à faire à Mehémet-Ali. Ce que j'ai dit n'est point par sentiment de partialité pour le Pacha. Il nous importait fort peu en 1833 qu'il mit ou ne mit pas le pied en Syrie. Nous voulions qu'il ne s'étendit pas au delà du Pachalik *d'Acre*, s'il était victorieux, et, enfin, qu'en aucun cas il ne franchit le Taurus. Il a gagné cette dernière limite. Il nous importerait fort peu aujourd'hui qu'il y renonçât. Nous concevons même qu'il n'y a de négociation possible qu'à la condition de l'abandon à perte par lui d'une partie de ses possessions actuelles, en échange de la transmissibilité de son pouvoir sur le reste dans sa famille. Mais déclarer *a priori* qu'on ne lui laissera que l'Egypte (pas même *l'Arabie* et il y a peut-être de *l'Anglais* dans cette dernière restriction) c'est prendre l'engagement, coûte que coûte, d'exécuter cette sentence. Or cela nous serait d'autant plus impossible que, si les défilés du Taurus sont, de ce côté, la clef de Constantinople, St Jean d'Acre et Damas peuvent bien être les clefs de l'Egypte: et, dans ce cas, Mehémet-Ali aurait évidemment raison de vouloir d'autre garantie qu'un chiffon de papier signé Mahmoud, pour la sécurité des pays auxquels il se restreindrait. J'admets donc que l'on prenne pour base la seule possession d'Egypte mais non pour base inflexible, invariable. Il faut se réserver de faire pour le mieux suivant les circonstances et ne pas oublier que le *but* est, non pas de faire telle ou telle distribution de territoire, mais de raffermir ou de rétablir la paix, dans les conditions les moins onéreuses possibles, et le plus promptement que faire se pourra, le tout de telle sorte que le nouvel arrangement satisfasse aux diverses exigeances nées de la situation.

Je finis, sauf à continuer un autre jour, mon cher Ami, tout à vous de cœur.

[P.S.] Encore un mot pourtant; je ne sais trop ce qu'on décidera ici pour l'éventualité du retour des Russes à Constantinople. Je tiens déjà pour certain toutefois qu'on reculera devant l'idée de troupes de débarquement. Quoiqu'il en soit, j'insiste pour qu'on se gouverne de manière à ce que tant à Pétersbourg qu'à Constantinople et même à Vienne on donne fermement à croire qu'à Paris et à Londres on ne reculerait devant aucune mesure extrême. Le tout pour avoir meilleure chance d'arriver à un concert.

(vi)

Paris, 11 *Juillet*, 1839.

Mon cher Ami, Nous avons reçu ce matin votre no 61 et ce soir, nous expédions notre courrier pour Vienne et Constantinople. Je n'ai pas trop compris les objections de Lord Palmerston contre le préambule de notre projet de note. Il me semble que le développement, en pareille circonstance, est moins blessant que le laconisme; quoiqu'il en soit, nous transmettons copie de votre dépêche à l'Amiral Roussin et nous l'autorisons à faire à notre projet de note les retranchements qu'il croirait convenables dans la situation. Si j'avais eu sous les yeux la rédaction même de Lord Palmerston j'aurais pu modifier moi-même mon premier travail. Mais, ne pouvant deviner comment *vous* serez entré en matière, je n'ai pu que proposer au Maréchal d'accorder à notre Ambassadeur l'autorisation en question.

Les explications de Lord Palmerston sur Lord Ponsonby m'ont paru fort embarassées et vos réponses ont été excellentes, jugez où nous pouvions aller, si l'on avait donné carte blanche au second pour disposer à sa guise des mouvements et opérations de l'escadre. Quant à Bassora et aux Iles Bahrim, il est bien que les Anglais n'aient point songé à des troupes de débarquement: mais si je conçois *qu'à la demande et pour compte du Sultan* ils fassent une démonstration, je ne comprends pas encore, je l'avoue, qu'ils puissent arguer *d'un droit-propre* pour s'opposer à ce que les Egyptiens s'établissent sur la côte est de l'Arabie, là surtout, où la suzeraineté ou souveraineté de l'Empire Ottoman n'est pas contestée même par eux. Ici l'opinion se réveille et se prend vivement à ces questions d'Orient: vous en avez pu juger par la dernière discussion. Déjà la prise de possession *d'Aden* par les Anglais a ébranlé beaucoup de gens. La disposition de nos voisins à s'établir en dominateurs dans le golfe Persique n'a pas non plus passée inaperçue. On en conclut volontiers que *la politique anglaise par un bout* n'est pas plus honnête et ne nous est pas plus favorable que la politique russe par *l'autre*; que toutes les deux se ressemblent fort et nous pourrions bien faire un métier de dupes en mettant tout notre enjeu sur la question de Constantinople de concert avec l'Angleterre etc. Je sais à merveille mon cher Ami, que nos imaginations vont vite et qu'elles tendent à nous entraîner bien au delà du but; mais il n'en est pas moins vrai que tout cela incite attention et que plus ira et plus nous serons obligés d'être regardants de très près aux faits et gestes de nos alliés, tout comme à ceux de nos adversaires. Déjà les Russes éclairés sont au désespoir de l'obstination aveugle de leur autocrate dans son aversion pour nous. Ils proclament, même assez haut, qu'il en faudra venir à tout faire, pour se lier de nouveau avec nous; que c'est là la politique naturelle de leur pays et du nôtre, la seule où les intérêts respectifs envers et contre tous puissent trouver une satisfaction légitime et assurée. Ici, à la vérité, tout cela n'a encore qu'un bien faible écho. L'aversion du Czar pour nous et son peu d'égard pour nos sympathies populaires envers la Pologne éloignent encore les russes de toute idée de rapprochement avec lui: mais cela peut n'être qu'une affaire de temps et, dans quelques années, la réaction peut arriver. Je ne sais si à Londres on porte des prévisions dans cette voie.

Voilà bien du bavardage, mon cher Ami, mais ma plume demandait à courir et je l'ai laissée aller. Revenons au plus près. Je persiste à croire que Lord Palmerston a tort de vouloir sur des questions de paix ou de guerre, lutter de *douceur* à Constantinople avec les Russes. C'est ne pas connaître les Turcs, et je les ai vus assez longtemps à l'œuvre, pour savoir à quoi nous en tenir. Ce n'est pas que je veuille les brutaliser; ce serait donner dans l'excès contraire: mais avec eux, même pour les servir, il faut être froid et quelque peu austère dans son attitude et son langage, sans quoi ils n'en font qu'à leur tête. Nous attendons now votre réponse à la proposition Metternich sur la légitimité de la dynastie d'Othman. Nous écrivons à Vienne que pour nous, cela va sans dire; mais que quant à la forme d'une déclaration, nous voulons d'abord nous concerter avec *vous*. Si cette déclaration peut avoir une valeur, c'est comme acte plus ou moins explicite mais réel de garantie pour l'intégrité territoriale de l'Empire Ottoman et surtout contre tout démembrement au profit d'une quelconque des 5 Puissances ou plutôt des trois, Russie, Autriche et Angleterre. Nous sommes donc très portés à y donner les mains.

Adieu, mon cher Ami, je suis tellement interrompu que je ne sais plus trop ce que je vous écris. Tout à vous de cœur.

(vii)

Paris, 8 *Août*, 1839.

Mon cher Ami, Nous n'avons à vous envoyer aujourd'hui que ce que nous avons écrit hier à Constantinople et à Alexandrie. En communiquant nos écritures à Lord Palmerston, retranchez en ce qui est reproché à notre animal d'Amiral et ce que vous jugeriez pouvoir, d'autre part, disposer votre interlocuteur à chercher, comme on dit, *Midi à 14 heures*.

Notre dépêche en réponse à la proposition anglaise a été étrangement défigurée dans quelques parties de sa rédaction par nos MM. du Conseil; vous vous en seriez aperçu du reste; mais cela vous aura-t-il conduit à ne donner lecture que de ce qui était réellement lisible. Je le souhaite fort. Si j'avais pu renvoyer au lendemain l'expédition, nous aurions cherché à corriger les corrections pour mettre le tout d'accord; mais on s'était montré si pressé à vous, de recevoir notre réponse, que sans trop savoir ce qu'elle était devenue dans les mains de nos collègues du Ministère nous avons dû en précipiter l'envoi.

La Russie recule de plus en plus sur le chapitre des délibérations communes; bien que nous préférerions, comme vous le voyez, à chercher à entraver le système d'un arrangement *direct* entre la Porte et le Pacha, il est plus que probable que nous échouerons. J'ai prévu cela dès la nouvelle reçue de la mort de Mahmoud; jusque là le mal ne me parait pas très grand, je l'avoue. L'avantage d'un réglement de la question *intérieure* par les Puissances était de rendre plus facile peut-être, comme conclusion de ce réglement et résultat de la médiation européennes, la garantie solennelle de l'Empire Ottoman *au point de vue extérieur.* L'inconvénient était, ou pourrait être, de donner, plus que de raison, *caractère* Européen, à l'établissement de Mehemet Ali tandis qu'il faut le maintenir établissement turc et partie intégrante de l'Empire, à durer ce qu'il plaira au Ciel. Donc, mon cher Ami, pour conclure, je crois que ce à quoi nous devons désormais nous attacher le plus, c'est à fortifier notre entente à trois, France, Angleterre et Autriche, c'est à lui imprimer un caractère de puissance qui nous donne toujours le droit de traiter d'égal à égal avec la Russie sur ce terrain du Levant et particulièrement de Constantinople. Si nous pouvions parvenir à transformer en traité nos trois déclarations récentes, je regarderais ce résultat comme le gage le plus fort de la paix générale et le frein le plus solide à l'ambition russe. Adieu, tout à vous de cœur.

[P.S.] ... Le Général parle de partir vers le 25 de ce mois pour retourner à son poste; ce n'est pas moi qui l'y pousse. Je trouve au contraire qu'il nous serait plus utile de l'avoir ici comme Conseiller.

(viii)

Paris, 19 *Août*, 1839.

Mon cher Ami, Nous recevons aujourd'hui votre no 77; avant-hier le 76 nous était parvenu. Lord Palmerston passe bien subitement d'un découragement extrême à une confiance sans limites. Cela me prouve qu'il connait imparfaitement le terrain d'Orient et qu'il se laisse aller, comme nos gens d'ici d'ailleurs, à toutes les impressions du moment. Il apprend que les Ambassadeurs à Constantinople, y compris l'Envoyé Russe, ont unaniment conseillé à la Porte de s'appuyer sur les Puissances et de suspendre toute négociation directe entre elle et Méhémet-Ali. Dès lors grande satisfaction, comme d'un succès non seulement inespéré, mais décisif; c'était pourtant chose toute simple: l'offre était convenue depuis assez longtemps déjà entre Londres, Paris et Vienne, et remarquez bien que si la Russie s'est adjointe à nous, c'est, *non pas à Vienne*, mais seulement à Constantinople où, dès l'origine, elle a déclaré vouloir concentrer et borner l'accord, parce que là elle échappe au contrôle, aux obligations d'un caractère Européen, et qu'il lui est plus facile d'y jouer un jeu double comme en 1827, à l'occasion du Traité du 6 Juillet. L'acceptation de l'offre par la Porte n'est pas moins simple et il était surtout aisé de la prévoir depuis que le Grand Vizir Kosrew s'est vu personnellement traqué par Méhémet-Ali: car, chez ces bienheureux orientaux les positions et les intérêts personnels sont la clef de tout. Je crois du reste que Méhémet-Ali a fait une faute en exigeant avant tout le renvoi de Kosrew. S'il s'était borné à lui demander des gages, à l'inquiéter sans menace directe, il en eut obtenu de suite tout ce qu'il eut voulu. Quoiqu'il en soit, il faut bien le dire que ce que nous pensons tenir par les dernières nouvelles de Constantinople et de Vienne peut nous échapper d'un instant à l'autre; que si Méhémet-Ali reste militairement inactif, il ne l'est pas politiquement; que son appel à 16 Pachas pour les liguer avec lui contre Kosrew; que son or et le travail de ses partisans à Constantinople; que l'action souterraine des Russes pressés d'en finir et de pouvoir nous opposer un accommodement quelconque entre la Porte et l'Egypte; que tout cela enfin et mille autres circonstances encore, doivent modérer notre confiance. Au surplus, mon cher Ami, nous sommes parfaitement disposés à suivre cette voie des négociations de bon et entier accord avec nos Alliés. Que l'on propose à Vienne ce que l'on voudra, notre Ambassadeur à Constantinople et notre Consul à Alexandrie l'appuyeront, franchement et sans arrière-pensée; mais de mesures coercitives, d'intervention armée, tant que Méhémet-Ali ne bougera point et qu'Ibrahim restera là où il est, nous n'y pouvons recourir, et cela, croyez-le bien, ce n'est pas par faveur pour le Vice-Roi, ni parce qu'il entre dans notre pensée de l'aggrandir au détriment de l'autorité de la Porte; nullement, c'est uniquement parce que ce serait folie que de s'exposer aujourd'hui à pousser à bout des hommes qui sont plus que jamais en position de provoquer la réapparition des Russes dans le Bosphore et de soulever contre la Porte la plupart des Provinces mêmes qui ne relèvent pas directement d'eux.

Je vois que l'incident de la flotte turque donne toujours le cauchemar à Lord Palmerston. Je reconnais du reste qu'il est déjà bien loin de ses premières dispositions à cet égard; mais je ne goute pas non plus, je vous l'avoue, le rapport des Consuls. Doit-on ou ne doit-on pas exiger le renvoi de la flotte, *avant* d'abord la négociation du fonds, c'est-à-dire, celle qui est relative à la distribution des territoires etc...? Si l'incident ne doit point, comme nous le jugeons, passer avant le principal, le rappel des Consuls n'a pas de sens; c'est se faire d'ailleurs, selon moi, une grosse illusion que de supposer que ce rapport puisse avoir une influence efficace sur les résolutions de Méhémet-Ali. Souvenez vous de 1833. Le Consul de Russie rappelé d'Egypte, les Russes dans le Bosphore, les autres Puissances agissant de leur mieux pour modérer les prétentions du Pacha et celui-ci néanmoins emportant tout ce qu'il voulait alors et les Cours elles-mêmes obligées d'engager la Porte à céder ainsi Adana, pour faire cesser au plus vite une situation aussi tendue; pensez-vous qu'aujourd'hui la situation (Mahmoud de moins et le reste de l'Empire plus ébranlé, plus *anarchisé* qu'alors) soit moins de nature à encourager Méhémet-Ali dans sa résistance? Laissons donc nos Consuls à Alexandrie où ils peuvent, d'un moment à l'autre, être utiles à nos vues, où ils peuvent contenir en surveillant et d'où leur départ serait sans influence sérieuse sur les déterminations du Vice-Roi. Attendons du moins que nous soyions mieux renseignés et sur la dernière démarche des Ambassadeurs auprès de lui et sur l'attitude que, par suite, il aura prise ou laissé pénétrer. Je ne parle point ici de l'idée d'entraver les communications entre la Syrie et l'Egypte; votre dépêche 77 n'y revient pas; cette idée du reste, je l'ai plutôt appuyée que combattue; mais, avant tout, il nous faut voir comment on l'aura formulée à Londres dans les instructions pour Stopford, si on y a persisté. Quant au projet de la conversion des déclarations en un seul et même acte, vous savez qu'il est depuis longtemps nôtre, mais est, à Vienne, une question d'opportunité. Il faut, je crois, n'y pousser que quand M. de Metternich n'aura plus à nous dire: "J'ai encore confiance dans les Russes; ils viendront à nous, attendons les." Ce serait alors un coup dans l'eau; au surplus Saint-Aulaire est en mesure.

Notre dépêche de ce jour vous parle de la communication de Medem; elle est, *par le raisonnement*, de la dernière impertinence et repose sur le proverbe qui dit: "Il n'est pire sourd que qui ne veut pas entendre." Adieu; assez pour aujourd'hui. Tout à vous de cœur.

(ix)

Paris, 22 *Août*, 1839.

Mon cher Ami, Quelques mots seulement. Il se fait tard et le temps me manquerait pour étendre mon bavardage. Il me semble que nos rapports avec Londres se rembrunissent un peu; guerre de presse, des deux côtés; ici mille sottises impressées; là bas Morning Chronicle de plus en plus agressif; indiscrétions sorties, je le crains bien, de l'un ou de l'autre de nos Départements Ministériels; boutade étrange de Lord Melbourne. A Vienne, à Berlin, à Pétersbourg, Lord Palmerston écrivant à tort et à travers contre l'Egypte et notre manière d'envisager ce côté de la question, comme s'il voulait exciter contre nous les autres Cabinets etc. . . etc. . . etc., tout cela est déplorable et ne peut mener à rien de bien. On criera bravo dans les trois Cours et puis on rira *sous cape* à Pétersbourg surtout, de ce dissentiment ainsi affiché par un des deux alliés qui s'appellent *intimes*. En vérité, je ne comprends rien à tous ces soubresauts, à toutes ces illusions de Lord Palmerston, à cette façon de ne tenir aucun compte des éléments si variés de la situation. Pour nous, mon cher Ami, nous préférerons, je l'espère, du moins dans les voies que nous vous avons indiquées *par écrit*, des négociations à Vienne, pour que le résultat en soit porté de là à Constantinople et à Alexandrie; mais là rien que les moyens diplomatiques, les propositions, les avis, les représentations. Nous n'abandonnerons pas plus à St Aulaire qu'à Roussin le droit de discuter pour nous et de régler sans nous, l'emploi de mesures coercitives et l'action de nos forces navales. Si Mehémet Ali redevient agresseur, notre escadre qui a, dès l'origine, des instructions *ad hoc*, agira pour protéger la Porte; mais ce cas excepté, point de coup de canon, ni rien qui y conduise. Ce n'est pas par égard pour Mehémet Ali. Nous voudrions, je le répète, qu'il fît des concessions et de larges concessions à la Porte; mais jusqu'au jour où nous seront convaincus et bien convaincus qu'on peut recourir à la contrainte sans s'exposer à pis que ce qui est, jusque là nous persisterons à nous abstenir. Le mal est qu'à Londres on n'ait pas compris que pour avoir meilleure chance de peser avec fruit sur les déterminations du Pacha, il fallait avant tout, puisqu'on nous suppose plus d'influence en Egypte qu'à d'autres, ne pas nous donner malgré nous, couleur d'être plus favorables à Mehémet Ali que nous ne le sommes, en nous traitant, sous ce rapport de pestiférés et en affichant partout qu'on avait une toute autre manière de voir. Je suis convaincu qu'une diplomatie très serrée à cet égard entre nous et Londres, appelant l'Autriche à son aide, aurait eu de meilleures chances à Alexandrie que ce dissentiment rendu public des deux Cabinets qui disposent de la mer.

Notre dépêche de ce jour est une querelle d'amants. Je désire qu'elle éclaire aussi Lord Palmerston; nous ne disons pas encore tout ce que nous savons de ses équipées en écriture; elles font un détestable effet au dehors—à Vienne surtout en ce sens que l'attitude de Lord Beauvale envers St Aulaire va flottant du haut en bas et du bas en haut suivant la couleur de ce que lui apporte chaque courrier expédié de Londres. Avec cela, dites moi un peu comment on parviendra à enlacer M. de Mett[ernich] pour la signature de l'acte qui nous ferait à tous une si bonne position parlementaire et autre. Ajoutez que Tatischeff arrive et que très certainement il arrive, moins pour prendre part à un accord que pour le faire manquer et imposer à M. de Mett[ernich] plus que ne saurait le faire le pauvre diable de Chargé d'Affaires russe qui a jusqu'ici *l'intérim*. Enfin, comme disent les vieux Turcs, Dieu est grand et nous verrons. Adieu, mon cher Ami, tout à vous de cœur.

P.S. Le Général part le 28 passant par Eu où il s'arretera un jour. Le Maréchal craint beaucoup sa disposition à abonder, en toutes choses, dans le sens anglais. J'aurais désiré, entre nous, qu'il ne retournât à Londres que lorsque le terrain aurait été déblayé; mais enfin, tâchez de l'empêcher de s'engager au-delà de ce que nous écrivons; car infailliblement, avec les dispositions d'ici, qui ont aussi leur excès que je combats, il serait désavoué et la brèche alors s'élargirait au lieu de se combler. Le bruit a couru que vous désiriez revenir, dès qu'il serait de retour; ajournez, si cela est, ajournez; car nous vous recevrions très mal, dans un tel moment.

(x)

Paris, 2 *Mars*, 1840.

Mon cher Ami, La crise est passée; souhaitons qu'il ne s'en présente plus de semblable d'ici à longtemps. Voici Thiers procédant à son installation; mais il lui faudra nécessairement quelques jours avant de se reconnaître et de pouvoir s'engager sur le terrain de nos affaires. J'ai lu le billet qu'il écrit à M. Guizot; c'est du private qui ne touche en rien à la grande question qui nous occupe. Donc un peu de patience. En attendant chercher à pénétrer au fond des instructions Brunow. Vous savez que les Russes ont des dépêches *officielles*, des dépêches réservées qu'on montre pour avoir l'air de faire de la confiance et des dépêches *secrètes*. Il me semble bizarre que la Russie, si elle est sincère, ne réponde pas nettement sur la proposition d'appeler un plénipotentiaire turc; elle veut que le refus d'accord vienne de nous; et nous devons faire en sorte qu'il vienne d'elle. Le Général dont j'ai trouvé hier l'esprit remarquablement net et lucide, est d'avis que nous nous bornions, pour le présent, à appeler et à attendre l'envoyé ottoman. C'est deux mois de gagner, dit-il, et c'est déjà beaucoup; de part et d'autre, c'est à dire France et Angleterre, on s'est trop avancé, Lord Palmerston surtout. Il faut aider la disposition de rétrograder qui est dans les nécessités du Cabinet britannique et qui s'accorde avec les nôtres; pour cela point de reproche qui brise tout, et oblige ceux qu'on veut ramener, à prendre un parti tranchant et définitif. Cela me parait juste; vous jugerez jusqu'à quel point cela est pratique. Adieu, mon cher Ami, tout à vous de cœur. . . .

(xi)

Paris, 21 *Septembre*, 1840

Mon cher Ami, En arrivant ici ce matin, j'ai trouvé votre lettre de samedi. Je ne crois pas vous avoir écrit que, dans mon opinion, nous avions *certainement* le dernier mot de Méhémet-Ali. Je n'en sais rien et la correspondance de nos agents, dont j'ai d'ailleurs pour habitude de rabattre toujours beaucoup, n'est pas de nature à prévenir les doutes. Si M. Thiers a été plus affirmatif dans sa lettre à M. Guizot, c'est, 1^0) qu'il croit volontiers ce qu'il désire, et 2^0) qu'en se montrant sceptique, il craindrait que son scepticisme, passant en vous, ne nuise à votre action. Quant au résultat de celle-ci, je n'ai pas attendu votre lettre, mon cher Ami, pour le présumer négatif. Ce n'est pas qu'il n'y ait d'excellentes choses à dire pour appuyer le thème actuel et qu'en réalité il ne serait de saine politique à Londres d'en demeurer là. Je suis également porté à croire que, dans cette occasion, les membres modérés du Cabinet pourraient, avec moins de risque *intérieur* qu'en Juillet dernier, peser beaucoup plus sur Lord Palmerston: car, dans l'état, il serait plus difficile aujourd'hui, ce me semble, à Lord Palmerston de mettre honnêtement son portefeuille sur la table. Mais je ne compte passer cette chance. Lord Palmerston demandera qu'en tout cas on ne se presse point. Il demandera qu'on se donne le temps de voir si les dernières concessions du Pacha sont, ou ne sont pas, de la faiblesse etc. . . .; et ses collègues résisteront difficilement à ses arguments. Il y a réponse à cela sans doute: à des hypothèses, on peut aisément opposer des hypothèses; et puis la saison des opérations s'avance; et puis le Pacha est un barbare qui, s'il ne dit pas son dernier mot, peut-être à ses amis, soit dans un sens soit dans un autre, ne le dit certainement pas plus, dans l'un ni l'autre sens, à ses ennemis. Mais toujours est-il que je tiens pour assez naturel que Lord Palmerston fait comme il l'est, persiste dans sa voie propre et pour assez probable que ses collègues ne le pressent pas autrement de se déclarer pour la Syrie viagère.

Je ne puis pas dire que M. Thiers soit beaucoup plus confiant que moi dans le succès de vos efforts. Non! L'ensemble de ses démarches à Londres, Vienne, Berlin, Alexandrie et Constantinople, au sujet du nouvel incident tend plutôt à se mettre à couvert pour le cas où le Pacha céderait davantage. La question est redevenue beaucoup pour lui une question *intérieure*. Cela a bien aussi son côté dangereux.

En résumé, mon cher Ami, pour un pays comme le nôtre, avec des têtes comme les nôtres, la situation est très grave. Comme ici l'on exagère tout, le succès et la défaite, personne ne peut prévoir ce qui arriverait, la défaite ou ce que l'on regarderait comme telle ayant lieu. Faites ce que vous pourrez: le reste à la garde de Dieu. . . .[1]

(xii)

Paris, 1 *Octobre*, 1840.

Mon cher Ami, Je réponds à votre lettre d'avant hier. Elle ne me surprend pas dans ce qu'elle a de peu rassurant sur ce qui peut sortir du Conseil d'aujourd'hui. Lord Palmerston est conséquent avec son passé et de plus il a pour lui ce qui parait s'être fait à Constantinople. Son dire est correct: comment dire *oui* à Londres, quand le Sultan a déjà dit *non?* et quand ce *non* repose sur un traité signé, en cours d'exécution depuis deux mois, quand on n'a point encore rencontré, dans cette execution, de ces obstacles qui expliquent une retraite et que, tout au contraire, l'adversaire a déjà fléchi considérablement devant sa simple menace? Il faut être juste en ce moment, Lord Palmerston a de forts arguments pour lui et, engagé comme il l'est et avec lui le Cabinet, je conçois très bien que des considérations générales et d'un ordre plus élevées soient d'autant plus mises de côté à Londres qu'on les avait déjà écartées à une époque où l'on n'était pas justifié d'amour propre à les méconnaître. Mais, direz-vous, la guerre ne menaçait pas alors, la guerre? Lord P[almerston] n'y croit pas et moi non plus je n'y crois pas. Il a donc raison dans le *présent* et pour le but qu'il se propose, il a raison de ne pas encore lâcher prise. Vous voyez, mon cher Ami, que j'accepte froidement le jeu et les nécessités de position d'un adversaire; mais nous, que ferons nous et quel jeu sera le nôtre? à cela, je ne sais trop que vous répondre. Si je ne consultais que mon sentiment propre et n'examinerait la question que pour elle-même, je dirais que rester isolés, regarder faire, refuser son concours pour tout ce qui ne serait pas le dernier thème, refuser sa signature à tout acte partiel ou général sur l'Orient, et accepter froidement au besoin le succès du traité du 15 Juillet dans ses limites et avec son caractère, *faire raide*, en un mot, et le marquer; je dirais qu'à mes yeux ce système serait le plus raisonnable, le seul digne, le seul propre à préparer, avant qu'il soit long-temps, notre rentrée sur la scène d'une manière un peu marquante: car le monde ne s'arrête pas plus que le soleil, mais, je le reconnais, je juge, j'apprécie là, en dehors des situations ministérielles, en dehors des situations des partis, en dehors de la question intérieure. Voilà pourquoi, mon cher Ami, je ne sais ce que nous ferons ni même ce

[1] The omissions concern some dresses for a lady to be sent to his own address, and the possibilities of Bourqueney being made a Minister.

que, placés comme nous le sommes, nous avons à faire. La guerre, je vous l'ai dit, je n'y crois pas et surtout je ne la veux pas; ce serait chose insensée et monstrueuse; mais, c'est aussi parce que je n'y crois pas et que, d'autre part, on a trop tendu la corde dans ce sens, que ses difficultés deviennent énormes pour nous. J'aperçois déjà, parmi nous et dans nos propres rangs, des symptômes d'une vive réaction. Si elle gagne du terrain, si, nos chambres assemblées, elle s'étend et, je ne dis pas détruit, mais seulement balance notre influence et notre action, oh! alors, il y aura déroute et déroute complète dans notre attitude et dans notre politique au dehors—voilà ce que je redoute le plus à cette heure. Tout cela, entre nous, comme de raison. Rien de nouveau d'Egypte et de Constantinople, rien de Vienne, non plus. Adieu, mon cher Ami, tout à vous de cœur.

(xiii)

Paris, 4 *Novembre*, 1840.

. . . Je vous ai dit ma répugnance pour un acte général de clôture. Je ne sais ce qu'on en pense autour de moi: mais je crois fermement que, pour avoir chance d'être accepté just now dans l'opinion (je parle de l'opinion des gens sensés de toute couleur), je crois dis-je que pour être acceptable et accepté, il faudrait que cet acte mit tellement en relief le sens que nous avons toujours attaché ici à l'indépendance et à l'intégrité de l'Empire Ottoman, que cela en ferait un Etat *Neutre* depuis l'embouchure du Danube jusqu'au golfe Persique et à l'extrémité méridionale de la Mer Rouge. Il faudrait que cet acte répondit à la fois d'une manière explicite et aux préoccupations anti-russes et aux préoccupations anti-anglaises. Cela vous parait-il possible? On dira, mais en vous associant à un Traité qui consacrera ce qui s'est fait au point de vue de la pacification *intérieure* de l'Empire Ottoman vous avez meilleure chance de couvrir éventuellement l'Egypte, si de nouveaux incidents, de nouveaux tiraillements venaient à se reproduire entre le Pacha et la Porte. L'argument peut être spécieux mais il n'est que cela, à mon sens du moins. En réalité cette chance vous ne l'avez pas plus au dedans qu'au dehors du traité. Dans un cas comme dans l'autre, nous serons toujours un contre quatre, dès qu'il s'agira de parler pour le Pacha contre la Porte: et cela doit être et, c'est parceque cela doit être, que le Traité ne peut rien valoir pour nous à ce point de vue. Ce qui a faussé toute notre Politique et fait des événements de Syrie, de la déchéance, etc., une défaite pour nous, c'est ce sot engouement pour Méhémet Ali, c'est cette absurde opinion qu'il y avait là pour nous un point d'appui solide, durable, quelque chose, enfin, qui valait que nous la protégassions envers et contre tous, fusse même par la guerre générale. Cette opinion, dieu merci, commence à perdre de son empire. Je ne souhaite absolument pas que Méhémet-Ali perde aujourd'hui l'Egypte. Nous ne sommes pas encore assez guéris pour qu'une pareille secousse ne nous exposât pas à voir tout remettre en question ici; mais d'autre part je craindrais que le traité sur lequel je raisonne en ce moment, n'eût aussi pour effet de ranimer cette même opinion qui veut identifier les intérêts présents et à venir de la France, avec ceux de Méhémet-Ali et des siens; et que tôt ou tard on se trouva ramené au point où nous étions il y a six semaines.

Tout bien considéré donc, mon cher Ami, je suis contre tout projet de convention générale de *clôture*, que le Traité du 15 Juillet soit, comme l'ont été celui de 1827 pour la Grèce et celui de 1834 pour le Portugal et l'Espagne, que ce Traité demeure un épisode, un incident dans l'histoire politique de notre temps; nous n'y pouvons plus rien retrancher puisqu'il est accompli, par la même raison n'y ajoutons rien. Maintenant mon sentiment prévaudra-t-il, je l'ignore. Nous avons des gens pressés qu'un peu d'isolement effraie, et qui se figurent qu'on se fait une situation par cela seul, qu'on donne *après*, ce qu'on a refusé *avant* et qu'on se met soi cinquième autour d'un tapis vert pour signer avec quatre autres. Vous savez que l'art des transitions est connu, parmi nous, de bien peu de monde, à coup sûr. Je souhaite plus que personne que le jour vienne où la France et l'Angleterre redeviennent l'une pour l'autre ce qu'elles étaient il y a trois et quatre ans. Mais pour qu'au vrai cela puisse avoir lieu, il faudra qu'une question bien et duement *anglo-française* par dessus tout, surgisse, et fasse oublier, en même temps, que les folies d'ici, le faux pas trop britannique (je parle poliment) de votre Secrétaire d'Etat.

Adieu, mon cher Ami, vous voyez par la longueur de cette lettre, que je redeviens bavard; prenez-vous à vous même, si je rentre dans cette habitude; vous m'avez reproché d'en être sorti. Tout à vous de cœur.

INDEX